Caribbean Women Writers

OTHER BOOKS BY SELWYN R. CUDJOE

Resistance and Caribbean Literature

Movement of the People

A Just and Moral Society

V. S. Naipaul: A Materialist Reading

Caribbean Women Writers

ESSAYS FROM THE FIRST
INTERNATIONAL CONFERENCE

Edited by SELWYN R. CUDJOE

Calaloux Publications *Wellesley, Massachusetts*

DISTRIBUTED BY THE UNIVERSITY OF MASSACHUSETTS PRESS, AMHERST

First published 1990 by Calaloux Publications.

International Standard Book Number (cloth) 0-87023-731-4
International Standard Book Number (paper) 0-87023-732-2
Library of Congress Catalog Card Number 90–80896

Printed in the United States of America

Library of Congress Cataloging-in-Publication Data
Caribbean women writers : essays from the first international
conference / edited by Selwyn R. Cudjoe.
    p. cm.
  Includes bibliographical references.
  ISBN 0-87023-731-4.—ISBN 0-87023-732-2 (pbk.).
    1. Caribbean literature (English)—Women authors—History and
criticism—Congresses.   2. Women and literature—Caribbean Area—
Congresses.   I. Cudjoe, Selwyn Reginald.
  PR9205.A515C37   1990
  820.9′9287′09729—dc20   90–80896

For my daughters, Frances and Kwamena,
and
Nan Keohane,
who made this project possible

Contents

Contents

Women Writers of the Spanish-, French-, and Dutch-Speaking Caribbean: An Overview

Acknowledgments

This work would not have been possible without the generous support and active encouragement of Nan Keohane, president of Wellesley College, who provided the funds for the conference, Dale Marshall, dean of the college, Edward Stettner, dean of the faculty (1988), and Elisa Koff, associate dean of the college (1988). Another important ingredient in the making of this conference was the guidance of Wellington Nyangoni, chairman of the Black Studies Department when the idea first came about, and Tony Martin, whose unstinting devotion to this project made all the difference in the world. A number of students also worked extremely hard to make the conference happen. They should all be commended for taking such an active part in the making of their education. Chief among them are Teri Cotton, Martha Williams, Gina Walcott, Noel Cade, Alison Reder, Tracy Gee, Tiffany Hurst, Colette Blount, Kathy Boyle, Jill Richman, Kim Mallett, Roni Adams, and Tynetta Darden. Not to be forgotten is Alezah Eisenstein, who made sure that all the books were in order and that proper arrangements were made to take care of our guests. The suggestions and support of faculty and staff members also made the occasion a family affair. Chief among them are William Cain, Timothy Peltason, Marilyn Sides, Lorraine Roses, Marjorie Agosin, Jennifer Schirmer, and Jean Stanley. Staff persons who gave of their time and energy were Joan Stockard, Winifred Holmes, Jan Putnam, Sylvia Hiestand, and Nancy Tobin. Most important, I wish to thank the many women and men who participated in the conference and those who came many miles to be with us. Without them this historic event could not have been as successful as it was. To Trudie Calvert, who was so diligent in copy editing this manuscript, and George Whipple, who, in his quiet manner, guided the overall direction of this project, theirs is a devotion that I will always treasure.

I will always be grateful to A. J. Seymour, editor of *Kyk-Over-Al*, who passed away in December 1989, for triggering this idea in my mind. It was because of our conversation in January 1987 that I began to think of the possibility of having this conference. Certainly the publication of these essays represents a continuation of a project he started forty-five years ago and thus can be seen as a fitting tribute to his memory and his work.

Finally, this work could not have been completed without the generous assistance of two Wellesley College Faculty awards, two Ford grants (administered by Kathy Parks), and a summer Pew grant that allowed my students to work on this project.

To Gwendolyn, my wife, who is always so patient, caring, and, above all, understanding, I thank you for your support. To the members of the Wellesley College community, who continue to support these efforts, it certainly demonstrates our determination to keep on keeping on. As Ralph Ellison says, "Diversity is the word. . . . America is woven into many strands; I would recognize them and let it so remain." Therefore, I give thanks to all those persons who made the publication of these essays possible.

Wellesley, February 1990

Caribbean Women Writers

The Sorrows of YAMBA;

Or, The NEGRO WOMAN's Lamentation.

To the Tune of HOSIER'S GHOST.

" IN St. Lucie's diftant Ifle,
   " Still with Afric's love I burn;
" Parted many a thoufand mile,
  " Never, never to return.

" Come kind death ! and give me reft,
  " Yamba has no friend but thee;
" Thou can'ft eafe my throbbing breaft,
  " Thou can'ft fet the prifoner free.

" Down my cheeks the tears are dripping,
  " Broken is my heart with grief,
" Mangl'd my poor flefh with whipping,
  " Come kind death ! and bring relief.

" Born on Afric's golden coaft,
  " Once I was as bleft as you ;
" Parents tender I could boaft,
  " Hufband dear, and children too.

" Whity man he came from far,
  " Sailing o'er the briny flood ;
" Who, with help of Britifh Tar,
  " Buys up human flefh and blood.

" With the baby at my breaft,
  (" Other two were fleeping by,)
" In my hut I fat at reft,
  " With no thought of danger nigh.

" From the bufh at even tide,
  " Rufh'd the fierce man-ftealing crew ;
" Seiz'd the children by my fide,
  " Seiz'd the wretched Yamba too.

" At the favage Captain's beck,
  " Now like brutes they make us prance;
" Smack the cat about the deck,
  " And in fcorn they bid us dance.

" I in groaning pafs'd the night,
  " And did roll my aching head ;
" At the break of morning light,
  " My poor child was cold and dead.

" Happy, happy, there fhe lies!
  " Thou fhalt feel the lafh no more.
" Thus full many a Negro dies,
  " Ere we reach the deftin'd fhore.

" Driven like Cattle to a fair,
  " See they fell us young and old ;
" Child from Mother too they tear,
  " All for love of filthy gold.

" Then for love of filthy gold,
  " Strait they bore me to the fea ;
" Cramm'd me down a flave-fhip's hold,
  " Where were hundreds ftow'd like me.

" Naked on the platform lying,
  " Now we crofs the tumbling wave ;
" Shrieking, fickening, fainting, dying,
  " Dead of fhame for Britons brave.

" I was fold to Maffa hard,
  " Some have Maffas kind and good ;
" And again my back was fcarr'd,
  " Bad and ftinted was my food.

" Poor and wounded, faint and fick,
  " All expos'd to burning fky,
" Maffa bids me grafs to pick,
  " And I now am near to die.

"The Sorrows of Yamba; Or, the Negro Woman's Lament." (London, ca. 1795). One of a group of broadsides printed under the title "Cheap Repository."

"What and if to death he fend me,
  " Savage murder tho' it be,
" Britifh laws fhall ne'er befriend me ;
  " They protect not flaves like me !"
Mourning thus my wretched ftate,
  (Ne'er may I forget the day)
Once in dufk of evening late,
  Far from home I dar'd to ftray ;
Dar'd, alas ! with impious hafte,
  Tow'rds the roaring fea to fly ;
Death itfelf I long'd to tafte,
  Long'd to caft me in and die.

There I met upon the ftrand
  Englifh Miffionary good,
He had Bible book in hand,
  Which poor me no underftood.
Then he led me to his cot,
  Sooth'd and pity'd all my woe,
Told me 'twas the Chriftian's lot
  Much to fuffer here below.

Told me then of God's dear Son,
  (Strange and wond'rous is the ftory ;)
What fad wrong to him was done,
  Tho' he was the Lord of Glory.
Told me too, like one who knew him,
  (Can fuch love as this be true ?)
How he dy'd for them that flew him,
  Dy'd for wretched Yamba too.

Freely he his mercy proffer'd,
  And to finners he was fent,
E'en to Maffa pardon's offer'd,
  O if Maffa would repent.
Wicked deed full many a time
  Sinful Yamba too hath done ;
But fhe wails to God her crime ;
  But fhe trufts his only Son.

O ye Slaves whom Maffas beat,
  Ye are ftain'd with guilt within ;
As ye hope for mercy fweet,
  So forgive your Maffas' fin.
And with grief when finking low,
  Mark the road that Yamba trod,
Think how all her pain and woe
  Brought the captive home to God.

Now let Yamba too adore
  Gracious Heaven's myfterious plan ;
Now I'll count thy mercies o'er,
  Flowing thro' the guilt of man.
Now I'll blefs my cruel capture,
  (Hence I've known a Saviour's name)
'Till my grief is turn'd to rapture,
  And I half forget the blame.

But tho' here a convert rare
  Thanks her God for grace divine,
Let not man the glory fhare,
  Sinner, ftill the guilt is thine.

Duly now baptiz'd am I
  By good Miffionary Man :
Lord my nature purify
  As no outward water can !

All my former thoughts abhorr'd,
  Teach me now to pray and praife ;
Joy and glory in my Lord,
  Truft and ferve him all my days.
But tho' death this hour may find me,
  Still with Afric's love I burn,
(There I've left a fpoufe behind me)
  Still to native land I turn.
And when Yamba finks in death,
  This my lateft prayer fhall be,
While I yield my parting breath,
  O that Afric might be free.

Ceafe, ye Britifh Sons of Murder !
  Ceafe from forging Afric's chain ;
Mock your Saviour's name no further,
  Ceafe your favage luft of gain.
Ye that boaft " *Ye rule the waves,*"
  Bid no Slave Ship foil the fea,
Ye that " *Never will be Slaves,*"
  Bid poor Afric's land be free.

Where ye gave to war its birth,
  Where your traders fix'd their den,
There go publifh " *Peace on Earth,*"
  Go proclaim " *Good-will to Men.*"
Where ye once have carried flaughter,
  Vice, and flavery, and fin ;
Seiz'd on hufband, wife, and daughter,
  Let the Gofpel enter in.

Thus where Yamba's native home,
  Humble hut of rufhes ftood,
Oh ! if there fhould chance to roam
  Some dear Miffionary good,
Thou in Afric's diftant land,
  Still fhalt fee the man I love,
Join him to the Chriftian band,
  Guide his foul to realms above.

There no Fiend again fhall fever
  Thofe whom God hath join'd and bleft :
There they dwell with Him for ever,
  There " *the weary are at reft.*"

[*Entered at Stationers Hall.*]

Caribbean Woman's Prayer

BY GRACE NICHOLS

Wake up Lord
brush de sunflakes from yuh eye
back de sky ah while Lord

an hear dis Mudder-woman
on behalf of her pressure-down people

God de Mudder
God de Fadder
God de Sister
God de Brudder
God de Holy Fire

Ah don't need to tell yuh
how tings stan
cause right now you know dat
old lizard ah walk lick land
and you know how de pickney belly laang
and you know how de fork ah hit stone
an tho it rain you know it really drought

an even now dih man have start to count
aiee
dih wata he make

God de Fadder
God de Mudder

God de Sister
God de Brudder
God de Holy Fire

give me faith
O God you know
we is ah people
of ah proud an generous heart
an how it shame us bad
dat we kyant welcome friend
or strangah when eat time come
around
you know is not we nature
to behave like yardfowl

You know dat is dih politics
an dih times
an dih tricks
dat has reduced we to dis

An taaking bout politics Lord
I hope you give dig politicians dem
de courage to do what dey have to do
an to mek dem see dat tings must grow
from within an not from without
even as you suffer us not
to walk in de rags of doubt
mek dem see dat de people
must be
at de root of dih heart
dat dis
place ain't Uncle Sam backyard
Lord look how de people in Bhopal get gas

God de Mudder
God de Fadder
God de Sister
God de Brudder
God de Holy Fire

To cut ah laang story short

I want to see de children wake up happy
to de sunrise an food in de pot
I want to see dem stretch limb
an watch dem sleep pun good stomach

I want to see de loss of hope
everywhere
replace wid de win of living

I want to see de man an woman
being
in dey being

Yes Lord
Aleluia Lord
all green tings
an hibiscus praises, Lord

"America," an engraving by Jan van de Straet (Stradanus). The new continent was often allegorized as a woman.

Introduction

SELWYN R. CUDJOE

Then I think that after all I've done it. I've given myself
up to something which is greater than I am. I have tried
to be a good instrument. Then I'm not unhappy—I am
even rather happy perhaps.

—JEAN RHYS, *Black Exercise Book*

ORIGINS OF THE CONFERENCE

On April 16, 1988, the Black Studies Department of Wellesley College
brought together more than fifty women writers and their critics, primarily
from the English-speaking Caribbean, to talk about their work. For the
first time since their ancestors came to the New World in the sixteenth
century these women and men were able to come together to talk about
their writings and to let the world know what they seek to achieve when
they set out to write about their experiences. This volume records their
testimonies as they give voice to their experiences and join in the attempt
of women throughout the world, particularly in the African diaspora, to
define their being without the interference of any other agents. This
conference allowed these women to talk with and about themselves and
to explore areas of mutual concern.

This conference was the founding event of Caribbean women's writing,
for though works have been written by Caribbean women writers, these
writers had never come together as a group to talk about their writings
and to articulate concerns that generated their literary production. This
conference brought together writers from Trinidad, Grenada, Jamaica,
Belize, Toronto, Calgary, London, New York, Paris, Vermont, and California; critics from West Germany, Puerto Rico, California, Leeds,
Washington, Barbados, and Guyana. When broached about the idea
of a conference on Caribbean women's writings, Lorna Goodison

retorted: "It's about time that our [male] critics begin to take us seriously. Such a conference would give our writings the respect they deserve." Jamaica Kincaid, a distinguished Caribbean writer, responded: "Are there many of us?"[1] Sylvia Wynter, author of *The Hills of Hebron* (1965), and Beryl Gilroy, author of *Frangipani House* (1986) and many other novels, were delighted to see each other for the first time since they began writing and studying in England in the 1950s. Merle Hodge, author of *Crick Crack Monkey* (1970), overwhelmed by the experience, vowed to continue writing about some of the things she felt she had lost the urge to write about because of her close involvement with the Grenada revolution. Erna Brodber, author of *Jane and Louisa Will Soon Come Home* (1980), who indicated an initial reluctance to attend the conference, noted that she was happy that she had not missed this historic experience. In sum, the conference was as much a joyous happening as it was a traditional academic experience.

The conference also gave exposure to younger writers (such as Opal Palmer Adisa, Sybil Seaforth, Valerie Belgrave, Afua Cooper, Claire Harris, Marlene Nourbese Philip, Elizabeth Nunez-Harrell, Erna Brodber, and Olive Senior) and critics (such as Rhonda Cobham-Sander, Evelyn Hawthorne, Jeremy Poynting, Maria Cristina Rodriguez, and Brenda Flannigan) and a format to established writers (such as Jamaica Kincaid, Beryl Gilroy, Michelle Cliff, Rosa Guy, Zee Edgell, and Marion Patrick Jones) and critics (such as Sylvia Wynter, Daryl Dance, Elaine Fido, Helen Pyne Timothy, Ena Thomas, Marjorie Thorpe, Sue Houchins, Marie-Denise Shelton, and Ineke Phaf). It also allowed us to integrate the experience of our historians and thinkers including Lucille Mair, Rhoda Reddock, Arthur Paris, Makeda Silvera, and Tony Martin.

Bringing these writers and critics together was of immense importance. It was a recognition that the writings of these women are a part of a larger current of writing that is taking place worldwide. As I indicated in my introduction to the conference, "The rise of women's writings in the Caribbean cannot be viewed in isolation. It is a part of a much larger expression of women's realities that is taking place in the postcolonial world and post–civil rights era in the United States. The enormous production of literature from the women of the Caribbean does not only contribute to our literary development but it begins to change the very contours of that literature as well."[2]

I am convinced that the conference did what it set out to do: bring women writers and their critics together to speak about their work in an open and honest manner. The testimonies contained in these pages are

---

1. See conference brochure, *First International Conference on Women Writers of the English-Speaking Caribbean*, Wellesley College, Wellesley, Massachusetts, April 8–10, 1988.
2. Ibid.

proof of its success. We were also fortunate to include the contributions of Clara Rosa de Lima, Janice Shinebourne, and Grace Nichols (who were unable to attend the conference), a previously unpublished short story by Phyllis Allfrey, and critical essays by Laura Niesen de Abruna, Veronica Gregg, Elaine Campbell, and Donna Perry.

Caribbean Women Writers: Essays from the First International Conference is a very important document that records a very significant event in the history of Caribbean literature. It seeks to rescue and give expression to voices that have not always been heard as loudly and as clearly as they should have been. I hope it will help us to view Caribbean literature in a more comprehensive manner in the future.

ABOUT THE SOCIETY

After Africans became the majority population in the Caribbean, black men and women shared equally in the burdens and difficulties of slavery and worked in unison to defeat that evil system, even though for reasons of gender men and women experienced somewhat different conditions.[3] Angela Davis has demonstrated the truth of this situation in the African-American context, and C. L. R. James, Lucille Mathurin, and Bernard Moitt, among others, have identified the same phenomenon in the Caribbean context.[4] In her essay "Towards Emancipation: Slave Women and Resistance to Coercive Labour Regimes in the British West Indian Colonies, 1790–1838," Barbara Bush characterized Caribbean women as the "primary agents in the emancipation of the slave community."[5] Walter Rodney, however, placed the question in a clearer perspective when he discussed the exploitation of the entire family under the slave and plantation systems and described the Caribbean context:

> Every single member of the family was considered an asset to the plantation. Youngsters at the age of eight or nine were put into what were called the "Creole gang." The youngest members of the plantation, as soon as they could totter around, as soon as they could stand up straight, would learn

3. Around 1645, Barbados became the first colony in the New World to have a majority African population, followed by the French and British islands of the Lesser Antilles a few years later. Jamaica attained her majority black population in the 1660s, followed by St. Domingue in the 1690s.

4. See Angela Davis, *Women, Race and Class* (New York: Random House, 1981); Lucille Mathurin, *The Rebel Woman in the British West Indies during Slavery* (Kingston, Jamaica: Institute of Jamaica, 1975); C. L. R. James, *Black Jacobins* (New York: Random House, 1963); and Bernard Moitt, " 'Vivre la mort': Women and Resistance in the French Caribbean during Slavery" (unpublished).

5. Barbara Bush, "Towards Emancipation: Slave Women and Resistance to Coercive Labour Regimes in the British West Indian Colonies, 1790–1838," *Slavery and Abolition* 5 (December 1984): 222.

to carry certain loads on their heads, would learn to carry tools or to carry water, and were integrated into the plantation system. The women were also given specific functions, usually weeding, which was a very common occupation for women on the plantations. Presumably, it was intended to be some sort of distinction based on the extent to which the women could endure the physical hardships of the fields, but then of course, women did perform all functions. Some women were even cane-cutters, which was the hardest task on the sugar plantation, but the majority would have been weeders. What is important in the post-slavery era is that in Guyana, as elsewhere, given the historical conditions of the time, women were discriminated against in terms of the rate of wages, and of course, children were paid still less. Thus, the ability to command family labor was at the same time the ability to incorporate cheap labor, because women and children were paid less.[6]

In such a system, the attempt to identify the growth of slavery as synonymous with the development and well-being of the society (and, by definition, the control of the family unit) is made clear in the Trinidad situation. In 1823, William Hardin Burnley, the major slaveowner in Trinidad, who believed that "absolute power is the foundation of the Slavery, without which it cannot exist with advantage either to the governors or the governed," insisted that any legislative measure that was introduced to forbid the "flogging" of female slaves would be detrimental to the well-being of slavery and the slave family. Arguing for the natural inferiority of women, Burnley noted that "women are as notoriously addicted as men to lying, theft, broils, and every immoral dissipation." He concluded that "if the power of corporal punishment over the female Slave is taken out of the hand of the Master, she will proceed in a career of vice injurious to herself, destructive to her progeny, and to the utter annihilation of the beneficent expectations of the British Legislature."[7] The female slave, it would seem, presented a challenge to the absolute power of the slave master and mistress which could be kept in check only by physical control (and subsequent humiliation) of the female slave. Giving up such control was tantamount to starting a process that would have resulted in the de facto liberation of the slaves. An uncontrollable slave was an unmitigated threat against the system that was sure to lead to its downfall. In their aggressive and uncontrollable behavior toward the slave master and mistress, slave women presented a challenge to the slave system that was as persistent as it was pervasive.

In this social system, women were valued more as labor units than

6. Walter Rodney, *The Birth of the Guyanese Working Class and the First Sugar Strikes, 1840–41 and 1847* (Georgetown, Guyana: Working People's Alliance, 1989), pp. 7–8.

7. William H. Burnley, *Opinions on Slavery and Emancipation* (London: James Ridgway, Piccadilly, 1833), pp. iv, 42–44.

childbearers and so few concessions were made for pregnant women or mothers with families. They were subjected to the same brutality as were men. Indeed, it was only after the abolition of the slave trade in 1807 that the planters were forced to introduce measures to protect pregnant women to ensure the continuation of an adequate labor supply.[8] Yet in spite of their primary identification as labor units in the larger economy, Caribbean women played an important part in developing a local economy and maintaining the culture of the slave group. Bush has claimed:

> Women were in the vanguard of the cultural resistance to slavery which helped individuals survive the slave experience. Their important contribution to the "private" lives of slaves—the reconstitution of the family and the building of a viable black community life—has been analysed elsewhere. It was this cultural strength, however, which helped women to resist the system in their more "public" lives as workers. In the fields cultural defiance was expressed through language and song. . . . Women field hands were experts in the use of the rich creole language which, with its *double entendres* and satire, was frequently employed as subtle abuse of whites. Through such channels women helped to generate and sustain the general spirit of resistance.[9]

According to Barbara Bush, these women were in the forefront of keeping the slave society together, the focal point around which the resistance to the ideology of the dominant planter class took place.

After emancipation was achieved, the first acts of the newly freed workers were attempts to bargain for wages. As a result, the focus of the system shifted from a "natural economy" to a more commoditized form of production in which there arose what Rodney called a "rural proletariat" (rather than a peasantry.)[10] In this struggle, too, women played their part. During the Haitian war of liberation the "women cultivators refused to take part in the sugar and coffee harvest unless they were promised the same pay-out as male cultivators; the original degrees of emancipation had offered them only two-thirds of a male worker's share."[11] Thus in the postemancipation period, the liberation struggle took place around the issues of "wages and working conditions" rather than "the prices of peasant produce" and the ownership of land.[12] Having to face these issues in that period of their history further defined family life and the role of women.

8. See "Towards Emancipation," pp. 224, 238.
9. Ibid., p. 228.
10. Rodney, *Birth of the Guyanese Working Class*, p. 6.
11. Robin Blackburn, *The Overthrow of Colonial Slavery, 1776–1848*, (London: Verso, 1988), p. 236.
12. Rodney, *Birth of the Guyanese Working Class*, p. 6.

In this new period of freedom, the control of family labor became a crucial issue. The planter class saw the welfare of the plantation and the demands of family life as synonymous and tried to do everything possible to control the livelihood of the emancipated slaves and to maintain the same control over them as before emancipation. They sought to define the family in the context of their own historical needs.

As a result, a relatively new division of labor ensued within the former slave family which left the women working primarily in the domestic economy; that is, more women "devoted most of their time to domestic labor, subsistence cultivation and petty trading,"[13] whereas most of the men concerned themselves with the more public aspects of the economy, working on the plantations and at other jobs that began to open up. Leota Lawerence argues that "the Caribbean woman has always been a multifaceted being whose existence has been marked historically by commitment, strength, and bravery. Not only is this true but it becomes obvious to the serious student that . . . the woman in the Caribbean has actually been the primary shaper of Caribbean destiny."[14]

One ought not, however, to exaggerate the role of either men or women in the struggle for liberation or engage in a game of one-upmanship in seeking to analyze the various facets of the liberation struggle. It required the energies of women, men, and children. Though women certainly played an important part in emancipation, during slavery there were fewer female than male slaves, which led to the importation of an enormous number of slaves into the Caribbean during the eighteenth century.[15] Also, cultural resistance cannot be defined too narrowly as the transmission of language and/or songs to succeeding generations. It also involves the everyday activities of work and physical efforts of all the slaves as they struggled to liberate themselves from the oppressor class. Thus, though it may be tempting to posit that women were the "primary shapers" of Caribbean liberation (I prefer to opt for a certain degree of equal, though diverse, forms of "shaping"), it is certainly true that women were instrumental in overthrowing the slave and plantation systems in the Caribbean and, in the process, constructing their own identities.[16]

13. Blackburn, *Overthrow of Colonial Slavery*, p. 463.
14. Leota S. Lawerence, "The Historical Perspective of the Caribbean Woman," *Negro Historical Bulletin* 47, nos. 1 and 2 (1984): 37.
15. In "Towards Emancipation," Bush contests this position and argues that the figures for the male slave population may have been exaggerated by the slave masters for propaganda purposes (p. 223).
16. See Silvia W. de Groot, "Maroon Women as Ancestors, Priests and Mediums in Surinam," *Slavery and Abolition* 7 (September 1986): 160–74, for an indication of that shared act of resistance. See also Merle Hodge's "Challenges of the Struggle for Sovereignty: Changing the World versus Writing Stories," in this volume, for the way culture functions as an act of resistance.

ABOUT THE LITERATURE

The successful Haitian revolution gave additional impetus to the resistance struggles in the Caribbean and the antislavery activities in England. Not only did the revolution show the way forward to Caribbean and Latin American peoples in the struggle for total liberation, but Haiti became the first republic in the Americas to guarantee civil liberties to all its peoples. It also helped give the antislavery movement in England "greater moral radicalism by the new openness to the experiences of the slave."[17] Slaves who managed to escape were encouraged to tell their stories to the larger British public through the *Anti-Slavery Reporter*, which carried regular accounts of the abuses suffered by the slaves in the Caribbean. Such dedicated efforts by the antislavery advocates were meant to ensure that emancipation would be immediate rather than gradual.[18]

One of the most important slave accounts to appear in the *Anti-Slavery Reporter* was *The History of Mary Prince, A West Indian Slave, Related By Herself* (1831). Encouraged by the editor to tell her story, Mary Prince became one of the few eyewitnesses to capture the brutal reality of slavery and perhaps the only author of a slave narrative from the British Caribbean experience. She had accompanied her owners to Britain in 1828 but eventually left them because of the cruel manner in which they treated her. In her narrative, Prince described and reflected upon the contradictions inherent in slavery, the cruelty of the slave master, and the particular shame to which slave women were subjected. The editor's note that reminds the reader that the sentiments were "given as nearly as possible in Mary's precise words" is of utmost importance in our understanding of the cruelty of the slave situation and the enlightened consciousness of this slave woman:

> I am often much vexed, and I feel great sorrow when I hear some people in this country say, that the slaves do not need better usage, and do not want to be free. They believe the foreign people [West Indians], who deceive them, and say slaves are happy. I say, Not so. How can slaves be happy when they have the halter round their neck, and the whip upon their back?

17. Blackburn, *Overthrow of Colonial Slavery*, p. 442.
18. See Elizabeth Heyriche, *Immediate, Not Gradual Emancipation* (London: R. Clay, 1832), a powerful denunciation and well-argued statement against Thomas Clarkson's and James Stephen's (leaders of the abolitionist movement in Britain) arguments for the gradual abolition of slavery. As she said: "The enemies of slavery have hitherto ruined their cause by the senseless cry of *gradual emancipation*. . . . The slaveholder knew very well that his prey would be secure, so long as the abolitionists could be cajoled into a demand for *gradual* instead of *immediate* abolition. He knew very well, that the contemplation of a *gradual* emancipation would beget a *gradual indifference to emancipation itself*. He knew very well, that even the *wise* and the *good* may, by habit and familiarity, be brought to endure and tolerate almost anything" (pp. 7–8).

and are disgraced and thought no more of than beasts?—and are separated from their mothers, and husbands, and children, and sisters, just as cattle are sold and separated? Is it happiness for a driver in the field to take down his wife or sister or child, and strip them, and whip them in such a disgraceful manner?—women that have had children exposed in the open field to shame! There is no modesty or decency shown by the owner to his slaves; men, women, and children are exposed alike. Since I have been here I have often wondered how English people can go out into the West Indies and act in such a beastly manner. But when they go to the West Indies, they forget God and all feeling of shame, I think, since they can see and do such things. They tie up slaves like hogs—moor [tie] them up like cattle, and they lick them, so as hogs, or cattle, or horses never were flogged; and yet they come home and say, and make some good people believe, that slaves don't want to get out of slavery. But they put a cloak about the truth. It is not so. All slaves want to be free—to be free is very sweet. I will say the truth to English people who may read this history that my good friend, Miss S——, is now writing down for me.[19]

It is noteworthy that the first literary work of the English-speaking Caribbean is that of a woman who fought against what Ziggi Alexander called her "physical and psychological degradation."[20] Published before slavery was abolished in the British colonies, Prince's narrative gives us a good idea of the cruelty of slavery as practiced in the Caribbean and represents one of the earliest attempts to give voice to the sufferings of black women. At one level, it reflects Prince's complete identification with her fellow slaves ("In telling my own sorrows, I cannot pass by those of my fellow-slaves—for when I think of my own griefs, I remember theirs");[21] at another level, it reflects the pain that was engendered by the specificity of her condition ("mothers could only weep and mourn over their children, they could not save them from cruel masters—from the whip, the rope, and the cow skin.")[22] Nor, for that matter, could mothers and fathers save their daughters from the wanton lust of the masters, a theme that seems to be encoded in the text but never examined explicitly. Indeed, the physical and spiritual violation of our women and the psychic cruelty that marked their early lives speak of the crucible of suffering out of which they emerged to assert their womanhood.

The next major work by a Caribbean woman writer was that of Gertrudis Gomez de Avellaneda, the Cuban novelist who published *Sab*, a magnificent feminist and antislavery novel, in 1841. As Pedro Barreda noted in *The Black Protagonist in the Cuban Novel*, *Sab* is "the only extensive

19. *The History of Mary Prince, a West Indian Slave, Related by Herself*, ed. with intro. by Moira Furguson (London: Pandora, 1987), pp. 83–84.
20. Ibid., p. vii.
21. Ibid., p. 65.
22. Ibid., p. 60.

narrative she [Avellaneda] wrote with a Cuban theme." Raymond D. Souza says in *Major Cuban Writers* that *Sab* assumed an "antislavery stance."[23] Pursuing her vocation in an oppressive, sexist environment was a very difficult task for Avellaneda. In 1839, at the age of twenty-five, in a letter to a friend, she noted: "Judged by a society which understand me not, weary of a life which mocks me, superior and inferior to my own sex, I find myself a stranger in the world and alone in Nature. I feel the need to die."[24] In spite of such pressures, she persevered and became one of the most celebrated Caribbean writers of the nineteenth century and "the first woman in the world to serve as editor of a Spanish-language journal." As Beth K. Miller writes, Avellaneda "was conscious of being a woman writer and, ever mindful of the adverse circumstances, often viewed her life, and later her works, as exemplary, especially so, sometimes, for other women."[25]

The next work published by a woman from the English-speaking Caribbean was Mary Seacole's *Wonderful Adventures of Mrs. Seacole in Many Lands* (1857). Mary Seacole, a free woman of color, was born into a well-to-do society in Jamaica in the early nineteenth century. Like Avellaneda, who "never became reconciled to the conventional patterns society set up for a woman,"[26] Seacole broke out of the traditional roles assigned to women at the time by traveling alone extensively (she always referred to herself as an "unprotected female"), practicing medicine, and setting up her own business. Indeed, Seacole was so secure in her status that she stated unequivocally: "It was from a confidence in my own powers, and not at all from necessity, that I remained an unprotected female." As Alexander noted in her biography, *Wonderful Adventures of Mrs. Seacole*, "It is doubtful whether there were any white women who could equal her expertise and training since at that time in Great Britain few females of any class had the opportunity of acquiring such extensive practical experience or of seeking higher education. Fewer still were permitted to regard the 'learned professions' as a possible life's work."[27]

Wonderful Adventures of Mrs. Seacole provides a view of a black woman who asserts herself in a colonial and noncolonial world governed and

23. Pedro Barreda, *The Black Protagonist in the Cuban Novel* (Amherst: University of Massachusetts Press, 1979), p. 72; Raymond D. Souza, *Major Cuban Writers* (Columbia: University of Missouri Press, 1976), p. 5.
24. Quoted in Polly F. Harrison, "Images of Exile: The Cuban Woman and Her Poetry," *Revista/Review Interamericana* 4 (Summer 1974): 188.
25. Beth K. Miller, "Avellaneda, Nineteenth-Century Feminist," *Revista/Review Interamericana* 4 (Summer 1974): 182, 177.
26. Barreda, *Black Protagonist*, p. 73.
27. Mary Seacole, *Wonderful Adventures of Mrs. Seacole in Many Lands* (Bristol: Falling Wall Press, 1984), pp. 61, 17. Avellaneda hated marriage with a passion and saw it as a fate worse than death.

controlled by white men. Well written, philosophical in its ruminations, and witty in parts, the book stresses its author's pride in being black and constantly emphasizes her independence.[28] Not only did she assert her autonomy, she played a crucial role in opening up the medical and nursing professions to women. Although she is not as well known as Florence Nightingale, whom she met during the Crimean War, she was as active in making the profession accessible to women as was "the Lady with the Lamp." Her bravery and nursing skills were so well known in Crimea that her name became legendary among the soldiers who fought on that battlefield. Speaking of the "generous hospitality" that Seacole rendered on "the chilly heights of Balaklava," Da Meritis, a Crimean War veteran, called upon Crimeans to support her in her hour of need (she returned to England bankrupt after the Crimean War) and asked: "Have a few months erased from their memories those many acts of comforting kindness which made the name of the old mother venerated throughout the camp? While the benevolent deeds of Florence Nightingale are being handed down to posterity with blessings and imperishable renown, are the humbler actions of Mrs. Seacole to be entirely forgotten, and will none now substantially testify to the worth of those services of the late mistress of Spring-Hill?"[29]

Although Mrs. Seacole's extensive travel and entrepreneurship were not unique, she emerged as a remarkable woman of the nineteenth century, and her autobiography, as Ziggi Alexander and Audrey Dewjee note, "was one of the most important personal histories written by a Caribbean born woman."[30] Her ingenuity, tenacity, and generosity of spirit testify to important dimensions of the personality of the early Caribbean women and add to our understanding of this period of our history. Her bravado and independence serve as a counterdiscourse to the nineteenth-

28. In a spirited response to a Fourth of July speech by an American in Panama who felt that Mrs. Seacole would have been more acceptable if she were white and American, the author responded: "Gentlemen,—I return you my best thanks for your kindness in drinking my health. As for what I have done in Cruces, Providence evidently made me to be useful, and I can't help it. But I must say that I don't altogether appreciate your friend's kind wishes with respect to my complexion. If it had been as dark as any nigger's, I should have been just as happy and as useful, and as much respected by those whose respect I value; and as to his offer of bleaching me, I should, even if it were practicable, decline it without any thanks. As to the society which the process might gain me admission into, all I can say is, that, judging from the specimens I have met with here and elsewhere, I don't think that I shall lose much by being excluded from it. So, gentlemen, I drink to you and the general reformation of American manners" (ibid., p. 98).

29. *Times* (London), 24 November 1856.

30. Seacole, *Wonderful Adventures*, p. 38. See, for example, "A Narrative of the Life and Travels of Mrs. Nancy Prince, Written by Herself," in *Collected Black Women's Narratives* (New York: Oxford University Press, 1988).

century bourgeois ideology of what a woman's place and behavior ought to have been in her society.

Apart from these three impressive works, there appears to be a significant gap in the recorded novelistic writings of Caribbean women after the latter half of the nineteenth and the early part of the twentieth centuries. The colonial and first periods in Cuban literature saw a broadening in the contributions of Cuban women to poetry and the development of an explicit "Cubanization" of their verse. The involvement of Cuban women in the Ten Years' War politicized them and augmented the sense of patriotism that characterized their verse. The abolitionist and feminist movements in the United States further influenced their verse, and within the second decade of the nineteenth century the poems of more than one hundred women appeared in print. No wonder that at the Constitutional Convention of Guaimaro in 1868, in which the abolition of slavery was declared officially, Ana Betacourt de Mora brought the question of women's enslavement forcibly to the attention of the convention when she noted:

> Citizens: The Cuban woman, in the obscure and tranquil corner of her home, has awaited in patient resignation the sublime hour in which a just revolution breaks her yoke and releases her wings. Everything was slavery in Cuba: birth, race, sex. You were willing to fight to the death to destroy the slavery of birth. The slavery of race no longer exists; you have emancipated the slave. When the moment arrives to liberate woman, the Cuban who cast out the slavery of birth and race, will dedicate his generous soul as well to the conquest of the rights of her, his sister of mercy in time of war, who is today denied those rights; tomorrow she will be, as she was yesterday, his exemplary companion.[31]

The works of a number of Cuban women poets appeared from 1850 to 1910. In his three-volume anthology, *Florilegio de escritoras cubanas*, Antonio Gonzalez Curquejo notes the examples of ninety-nine women poets whose works appeared during that period. In the colonial period (1850–79), the work of Luisa Perez de Zambrana, lauded for its "sweet but firm domestic accent," predominated. In the first period (1880–1909) the works of Nieves Xenes, Mercedes Metamoros, and Juana Borrero were well received. Indeed, much of the feminine bonding that we observe in contemporary black women's writing in the United States was present in the works of Xenes, Metamoros, and Borrero. All of these poets saw love as the primary fact of life and used the various concepts of love to convey a symbolic cluster of meanings. It is in these works that we see the further

31. Harrison, "Images of Exile," p. 191.

emergence of a particular feminine sensibility and the place that women writers were carving out for themselves in Caribbean literature.

Although the next significant work by an English-speaking woman writer from the Caribbean did not appear until the twentieth century, the same spirit of independence and defiance that animated Avellaneda continued to characterize the spirit (if not the work) of the women writers of the Anglophone Caribbean. In 1899, W. P. Livingstone, editor of the *Jamaica Gleaner*, noted the independence of the Jamaican women as they defied attempts by the colonizers to "civilize" them: "The women earned their livelihood, and lived their own robust, independent life. There was no wooing and winning, and permanent companionship thereafter; they gave themselves to each other as they pleased. To be married was, to a woman, to become a slave, a stone's throw in the past. She preferred her freedom, and accepted its greater responsibilities with equanimity. It was this unconscious sensuality which proved the greatest obstacle to the development of their character." Even though there seems to be a slight shift in the themes of some of the writings in the twentieth century, a struggle for women's autonomy is still present in most of these works. In her work on Jamaican writers from 1900 to 1950, Rhonda Cobham-Sander notes a shift in the independent manner in which these women were depicted after World War I in which she argues that there was a tendency of middle-class writers to depict working-class women "as being fulfilled in the role of wife and mother, or, if she could not marry, in chastity and good deeds."[32] Additional themes such as loneliness and problems of adolescence are also examined by these writers.

The next significant work by a Caribbean woman was Jean Rhys's *Voyage in the Dark* (1934), based on her first piece of sustained writing, "This is my Diary," that was recorded in one of her unpublished exercise books in 1910. Rhys, however, offers a different dimension of the Caribbean slave experience. A white Creole and great-granddaughter of a slave-owner, Rhys attempts to capture the ambivalence of what it meant to be white and Creole and the diminishing privileges of her people (that is, the colonial master) in a colonial society composed primarily of black people. Teresa O'Connor observed that "Rhys sometimes intimated that she might have 'black blood' " and Rhys noted that she "felt akin to them [black people]."[33] In her contribution to this volume, Laura Niesen de Abruna argues that "many of Rhys's characters identify with other oppressed groups such as the former slaves and the Caribe Indians . . . [and]

32. Quoted in Rhonda C. Cobham-Sander, "The Creative Writer and West Indian Society: Jamaica, 1900–1950" (Ph.D. dissertation, University of St. Andrews, 1981), pp. 195, 210.

33. Teresa O'Connor, *Jean Rhys: The West Indian Novels* (New York: New York University Press, 1986), pp. 34, 35.

do not buy into sexual and emotional involvement with powerful and monied white men."[34]

As a white Creole, Rhys had an ambiguous relationship to black people. In *Voyage in the Dark* and *Wide Sargasso Sea* she locates her heroines in the slave history of the Caribbean and from that vantage point tries to work out their relationship with the black people of the society. In her private life, she feared and envied them. She empathized with their slave past but felt repulsed by their assertive present in the postemancipation era. In an interview with David Plante she described her complicated relationship with black people:

> At the start I hated my nurse. A horrid woman. It was she who told me awful stories of zombies and *sucriants*, the vampires; she frightened me totally. I was a bit wary of the black people. I've tried to write about how I gradually became even a bit envious. They were so strong. They could walk great distances, it seemed to me, without getting tired, and carry those heavy loads on their heads. They went to the dances every night. They wore turbans. They had lovely dresses with a belt to tuck the trains through that were lined with paper and rustled when they moved.

Although parts of this description are stereotypical—for example, the statement "they went to the dances every night" does not seem to be true—it suggests Rhys's fascination for her fellow Dominicans. In her unfinished autobiography, she confesses, "I prayed so ardently to be black, and would run to the looking glass in the morning to see if the miracle had happened? And though it never had, I tried again. Dear God, let me be black."[35] Viewing scenes from carnival on British television and reminiscing about carnival as she remembered it in Dominica, where she was born, she says, "I have watched carnivals on television. They are doubtless very colourful but it seems to me that it is all planned and made up compared to the carnival I remember, when I used to long so fiercely to be black and to dance, too, in the sun, to that music. The carnival I knew has vanished."[36] In her narratives (both fictional and nonfictional)

34. Laura Niesen de Abruna, "Twentieth-Century Women Writers from the English-Speaking Caribbean," this volume.

35. Jean Rhys, *Smile Please* (New York: Harper & Row, 1979), p. 33. Anna Morgan, the heroine of her autobiographical novel *Voyage in the Dark*, utters similar words: "I wanted to be black, I always wanted to be black. . . . Being black is warm and gay, being white is cold and sad" ([New York: Norton, 1982], p. 31). One finds the expression of analogous sentiments in Phyllis Allfrey, *The Orchid House*, upon which Rhys drew for certain parts of *Wide Sargasso Sea*. In the former text, Miss Joan remarks, "I wish we were coloured and could go to the convent with all the coloured children, instead of having lessons from Mamselle Bosquet and Dr. Caron" ([London: Virago Press, 1982], p. 16). As the slave system breaks down, there seems to be a longing to be a part of the other to which social entrance is denied.

36. Rhys, *Smile Please*, p. 43.

she seems to argue that the blacks on the islands hated her and her family. Yet she retained an indissoluble bond with her island, her youthful life, and the people she knew there.

As a Caribbean woman ("I'm a real West Indian, I'm in the fifth generation on my mother's side," says Anna Morgan in *Voyage in the Dark*)[37] Rhys was steeped in the mythology and history of the Caribbean.[38] She knew all about zombies, *soucriants*, and *loups-garous* (werewolves), learned about obeah from Meta, her nurse, enjoyed the Creole foods (good curries, crayfish, and crab) of her youth, and possessed a continuing love for the beauty and warmth of the Caribbean landscape. As early as 1927, writing in *The Left Bank and Other Stories*, Rhys has the English aunt in "Mixing Cocktails" speak of the rapturous beauty of the West Indies:

> The colours.... How exquisite!... Extraordinary that so few people should visit the West Indies....
> The *sea*.... Could anything be more lovely?
> It was a purple sea with a sky to match it. The Caribbean. The deepest, the loveliest in the world.[39]

In *Smile Please* Rhys speaks of the beauty of her homeland:

> It was there [at Morgan's Rest], not in the wild beautiful Bona Vista, that I began to feel I loved the land and to know that I would never forget it. There I would go for long walks alone. It's strange growing up in a very beautiful place and seeing that it is beautiful. It was alive. I was sure of it. Behind the bright colours of the softness, the hills like clouds and the clouds like fantastic hills. There was something austere, sad, lost, all these things. I wanted to identify myself with it, to lose myself in it. (But it turned its head away, indifferent, and that broke my heart.)[40]

Years later, disillusioned by the physical coldness of England and the spiritual alienation she felt, she wrote:

> I would never be part of anything. I would never really belong anywhere, and I knew it, and all my life would be the same, trying to belong, and failing. Always something would go wrong. I am a stranger and I always

37. *Voyage in the Dark*, p. 55.
38. By mythology I refer to the unexamined but deeply held beliefs of a people that encode or reflect significant issues about their lives. In this sense there is much in common in the works of Jean Rhys and Jamaica Kincaid.
39. Jean Rhys, *The Left Bank and Other Stories* (Freeport, N.Y.: Books for Libraries Press, 1970), p. 90. Jamaica Kincaid responds with similar warmth in describing the beauty of the seas around the Caribbean in "Antigua Crossings," her first short story. See "Antigua Crossings: A Deep and Blue Passage on the Caribbean Sea," *Rolling Stone*, June 29, 1978.
40. Rhys, *Smile Please*, p. 43.

will be, and after all I didn't really care. Perhaps it's my fault. I really can't think far enough for that. But I don't like these people, I thought. I don't hate—they hate—but I don't love what they love. I don't want their lights or the presents in gold and silver paper. . . . I don't know what I want. And if I did I couldn't say it, for I don't speak their language and I never will.[41]

In her fictional work Rhys tries to capture her contradictory feelings toward her West Indian home and her hated encounter with Europe. As she noted in her unpublished exercise books, most of her writing (particularly in *Voyage in the Dark* and *Wide Sargasso Sea* [1966]) was an attempt to capture life in the West Indies. It also reflects her sense of exile and marginality as a West Indian woman in a foreign land, trying to come to terms with her West Indianness, her colonial status, and her womanhood. As Teresa O'Connor notes, "Rhys, herself caught between places, cultures, classes and races, never able to identify clearly with one or another, gives the same marginality to her heroines, so that they reflect the unique experience of dislocation of the white Creole woman, even when not identified as such."[42]

It is this sense of ambivalence that Rhys captured in *Voyage in the Dark* and *Wide Sargasso Sea*, the two most West Indian of her novels. In the former, her most autobiographical text, Rhys identifies with the experiences of slavery (or the effects slavery had on blacks), whereas in the latter she describes the way members of white society saw their position being eroded following emancipation as they became the hated other. The colonizer had become (or certainly was made to feel like) the colonized. Thus Anna Morgan journeys into the darkness of London whereas Antoinette Cosway, the heroine of *Wide Sargasso Sea*, tells Rochester, her husband, how she was mocked by a Afro-Dominican: "It was a song about a white cockroach. That's me. That's what they call all of us who were here before their own people in Africa sold them to the slave traders. And I've heard English women call us white niggers. So between you I often wonder who I am and where is my country and where do I belong and why was I ever born at all."[43] Thus the feeling of exile and loneliness that she expresses in her autobiography is present in her fiction, and these feelings seem to have characterized most of her adult life. If there

41. Ibid., p. 100.
42. Teresa O'Connor, "The Meaning of the West Indian Experience for Jean Rhys" (Ph.D. dissertation, New York University, 1985), p. 14. This work provides a useful discussion of the important influence of the West Indian experience on the shaping of Jean Rhys's sensibility and, consequently, her writing. Her unpublished exercise books, which O'Connor calls her Black Exercise Books, are located in the Jean Rhys Collection at the University of Tulsa. All references to these Black Exercise Books are taken from O'Connor's "The Meaning of the West Indian Experience for Jean Rhys."
43. Jean Rhys, *Wide Sargasso Sea* (New York: Norton, 1982), p. 102.

was some degree of peace and quiet at Morgan's Rest, she was unable
to find any such peace or security in Europe, and her entire adult life
became one of escape, destitution, and dissolution, searching for a home
that was never found. Indeed, *Wide Sargasso Sea*, her last novel, tried to
bring these warring worlds together but with devastating consequences
suggested by the eventual madness of Antoinette Cosway.

There are two other aspects of Rhys's work that are of importance to
our analysis of the writings of Caribbean women writers. First is its specific
West Indian quality that Ford Madox Ford describes so well in his preface
to *The Left Bank and Other Stories*:

> Coming from the Antilles, with a terrifying insight and a terrific—an almost
> lurid!—passion for stating the case of the underdog, she has let her pen
> loose on the Left Banks of the Old World—on its gaols, its studios, its
> salons, its cafes, its criminals, its midinettes—with a bias of admiration for
> its midinettes and of sympathy for its lawbreakers. It is a note, a sympathy
> of which we do not have too much in Occidental literature with its perennial
> bias towards satisfaction with things as they are. But it is a note that needs
> sounding—that badly needs sounding, since the real activities of the world
> are seldom carried much forward by the accepted, or even by the Hautes
> Bourgeoisie.[44]

Ford might have been exaggerating somewhat about the uniqueness of
Rhys's achievement in *The Left Bank*, but in this one major aspect, Rhys
was at one with other Caribbean writers: she admired and supported the
"underdog," that is, the oppressed people of the world. Rhys's oppression may have been somewhat different from that of other Caribbean
women writers, but her life and work were surely the embodiment of a
living hell. To be sure, she cannot be considered a survivor in exactly the
same sense as Mary Prince and Mary Seacole, who exerted some control
over their lives. But she was shaped irredeemably by the Caribbean experience of slavery, and her life and work mirrored the other side of the
tragic and cruel phenomenon called slavery.

The second aspect of Rhys's work that is of interest here is her formal
achievements. From her first stories, *The Left Bank and Other Stories*, Rhys
reveled in a sparseness of prose and an economy of language that went
to the heart of the matter without contrivance or reliance on decorative
and descriptive excesses. She has a translucence of language that strips
human feelings of any artifice or pretense. It is a way of exposing the
pain and suffering of exile and isolation without necessarily asking for
the reader's sympathy. She seems to suggest that this is the way things
are and that one has little choice. No sympathy is asked; none is extended.

44. Rhys, *The Left Bank and Other Stories*, p. 24.

This position is revealed most emphatically in her conclusion to *Voyage in the Dark* and the tremendous controversy over the end of novel. It is in this sense that Ford Madox Ford argues that what struck him most about Rhys's prose "was the singular instinct for form possessed by this young lady, an instinct for form being possessed by singularly few writers of English and by almost no English women writers."[45]

Apart from her revealing depictions of the isolation and loneliness of women, Rhys's contribution to the literature was her singular instinct for using the most appropriate language to capture the feelings of her characters with an exactitude and control that were almost clocklike; no wonder she never gave up a manuscript until she felt it was just right. One is impressed by the lucidity and freshness of her prose, the courage and unflinching nature with which she confronts life.

Una Marson, the next significant woman writer of Caribbean literature, was born in Jamaica in 1905. To be sure, other women such as Kathleen Archibald, Olga Yaatoff, Constance Hollar, and Stephanie Ormsby were writing during this early period, but Marson's desire to speak about the problems of women and her association with working-class women and realization of their need for pride in of their cultural heritage distinguished her as "the earliest female poet of significance to emerge in West Indian literature."[46] In a paper entitled "Una Marson: Black Nationalist and Feminist Writer," Honor Ford Smith has argued that Marson attempted to combine her feminist concerns with her nationalist preoccupations.

The death of her parents forced her to leave Hampton School for Girls and begin work at the *Jamaica Gleaner* in the 1920s. In 1929 she edited the *Cosmopolitan*, the official organ of the Jamaica Stenographers' Association and the first women's publication of Jamaica, and wrote *Tropic Reveries* (1930) and *Heights and Depths* (1931). Between 1932 and 1935 she worked as the secretary of the League of Coloured People, an organization of Caribbean people in Britain, and in 1935 she became the secretary to Haile Selassie when he pleaded Ethiopia's cause before the League of Nations. In 1936 she returned to Jamaica, resumed her work as a journalist, and published *The Moth and the Stars* (1937), one of her more important works. In 1938 she returned to England to continue her social welfare work. By that time, she had done her most important literary work.

Some of Marson's poems, published in *Tropic Reveries*, show the problems that middle-class women in Jamaica faced and also the imitative nature of her style. A typical example reads:

> To wed, or not to wed: that is the question:
> Whether 'tis nobler in the mind to suffer
> The fret and loneliness of spinsterhood

45. Ibid., pp. 24–25.
46. Lloyd W. Brown, *West Indian Poetry* (London: Heinemann, 1978), p. 32.

Or to take arms against the single state
And by marrying, end it? To wed; to match,
No more; yet by this match to say we end
The heartache and the thousand natural shocks
That flesh is heir to; 'tis a consummation
Devoutly to be wish'd. To wed, to match;
To match, perchance mismatch: aye there's the rub;
For in that match what dread mishaps may come,
When we have shuffled off this single state
For wedded bliss.[47]

Heights and Depths and *The Moth and the Stars* are perhaps a better measure of Marson's contributions. Although these poems are imitative of nineteenth-century English nature poetry, they reveal bits of West Indianism and allude to some of the problems that beset Caribbean women. In "A Moonlight Reverie" she problematizes the position of women and the peculiar oppression to which they are subjected. Referring to an apparently illicit affair between a man and woman, Marson meditates on the condition of "man, the victor" and "woman, the vanquished":

I thought of all the talk about the sexes
The women with equality complexes—
And then I saw before me plain and clear
Eternal man—eternal woman fair.
But still I sought the lesson to be learned,
And did not find and so once more I turned
To my wise guide, and thus she made reply:—
"For thy heart's good on these wise words rely:—
Woman is born to eat the bread of sorrow
To weep is today, and know no glad tomorrow.
It is her privilege. . . . "

How many women at this very hour
Are filled with anxious thoughts, and deeply pray
That lover, husband, child may mend his way?
Until the earth shall cease shall woman lay
Her all at manhood's feet and seek in vain
Love constant firm and true from him to gain.
It is her lot. Be thou content—love on
And always welcome him. When he is gone
In vanity some conquest fresh to make,
Console thyself, let not thy lone heart break.
Know thou that God, who formed and fashioned thee,
Gave thee a heart to love, a mind to serve
And never from this noble purpose swerve.[48]

47. Quoted in Cobham-Sander, "The Creative Writer and West Indian Society," p. 218.
48. Una Marson, *Heights and Depths* (Kingston: Gleaner, 1931), pp. 22–23; hereafter cited in the text as *H&D*.

Clearly, the message of the poem is equivocal and confusing. At one level the author is troubled by the unfaithfulness of men, yet she feels that because God has so ordained it, women should "love," "serve," and honor their husbands and "never from this noble purpose swerve." Thus she admonishes:

> Woman thou art: rejoice in sorrow's hour
> That God to thee hast given this great power
> To suffer and to love tho' oft unloved;
> To give and seek for naught; to be reproved,
> And tho' not guilty, still for love's dear sake
> Accept the wrong and all the burden take. (*H&D*, p. 23)

Even though Marson understands the wrong that is perpetrated upon women, she counsels patience and appeals to the "higher" calling of women to accept and endure their lot and to remember their special place in life. She concludes:

> Man may be master of the land and sea,
> And even of thy heart may keep the key,
> But unto woman comes alone the joy
> Of shielding in her form a girl or boy.
> A blessing on thy heart: rejoice, be glad,
> Thank God for womanhood and be not sad. (*H&D*, p. 23)

Such acceptance of their "lot in life" would be rejected by the women who tell their stories in *Lionheart Gal.*

In *The Moth and the Star* Marson is more aware of her blackness and the plight of her people than in her earlier work. There is no doubt that the racial awareness in her poems came from her work with the League of Coloured People and her association with Haile Selassie, and her awareness of race pride that was present in the Harlem Renaissance in the United States. Indeed, a copy of *The Moth and the Star* that she sent to James Weldon Johnson in January 1938 is inscribed: "To James Weldon Johnson, one of the giants of our race, in admiration." It is no wonder that her poems question the Eurocentric notions of beauty and the way such notions led African people in the Caribbean to question their self-worth. In "Cinema Eyes," she ridicules the way she has been taught to "worship" "beautiful white faces" that are projected on the cinema screen. Thus, "I saw no beauty in black faces, / . . . they were black / And therefore had no virtue." In speaking to her son she admonishes,

> I know that love
> Laughs at barriers,
> Of race and creed and colour.
> But I know that black folk

Fed on movie lore
Lose pride of race.
I would not have you so.[49]

In "Kinky Hair Blues" Marson goes a bit more deeply into the psychological trauma that attends such racist indoctrination. First, she notes the ambiguity of her condition:

Gwine find a beauty shop
Cause I ain't a belle.
Gwine find a beauty shop
Cause I ain't a lovely belle.
The boys pass me by,
They say I's not so swell. . . .

I hate dat ironed hair
And dat bleaching skin.
Hate dat ironed hair
And dat bleaching skin.
But I'll be all alone
If I don't fall in. (M&S, p. 91)

Through her repetition of the key phrases, the author alerts us to her discomfort in having kinky hair and dark skin. It is very clear the society has determined that such attributes are not considered beautiful. Thus she concludes on a defeatist note, giving in to the very notions that keep her mentally enslaved. The racist concepts of the dominant culture have won out, and the ambivalence she feels at having to succumb to such incongruities is almost too painful to bear:

I like me black face
And me kinky hair.
I like me black face
And me kinky hair.
But nobody loves dem,
I jes don't tink it's fair.

Now I's gwine press me hair
And bleach me skin.
I's gwine press me hair
And bleach me skin.
What won't a gal do
Some kind a man to win. (M&S, p. 91)

"Black Burden" sounds a more optimistic note. Rather than the defeatist tone at the end of "Kinky Hair Blues," there is greater optimism and

49. Una Marson, *The Moth and the Star* (Kingston: Gleaner, 1937), pp. 87–88; herafter cited as *M&S*.

courage in her desire to affirm her blackness. Playing on the age-old response to white domination and control ("I am black / And so must be / More clever than white folk, / More wise than white folk, / More discreet than white folk, / More courageous than white folk"), she urges a courageous and heroic stance on the part of black folks and notes:

> Black girl—what a burden—
> But your shoulders
> Are broad
> Black girl—what a burden—
> But your courage is strong—
> Black girl your burden
> Will fall from your shoulders
> For there is love
> In your soul
> And a song
> In your heart. (*M&S*, p. 93)

In her evaluation of *The Moth and the Star*, Rhoda Cobham-Sander noted that Marson seems "more firmly in control of her art technically and achieves control over her themes."[50] In his evaluation of Marson's career, Lloyd Brown has argued: "She was not merely a woman who happened to write poetry, but a female poet whose works were concerned, to a considerable degree, with the situation and identity of the West Indian woman. . . . She moves from the clichés and stasis of the pastoral tradition to an innovative exploration of her experience; and she undertakes that exploration in terms that are sophisticated enough to integrate political protest into a fairly complex and committed art."[51]

Marson's work was also important in the struggle against racism and sexism. In 1938 she attended the International Alliance conference of women in Turkey and spoke of the conditions of black women in England and the racism they experienced in housing.[52] She played the same vanguard role as Claudia Jones did in articulating the nature of the African-American women's struggle in the United States and Elma François did in Trinidad.[53]

The work of Louise Bennett of Jamaica was also important in establishing a unique Caribbean literature and a distinctive woman's voice within it. The language and speech of Caribbean women had always played an important part in contesting slave and colonial domination and

50. Cobham-Sander, "The Creative Writer and West Indian Society," p. 219.
51. Brown, *West Indian Poetry*, pp. 32–33, 37–38.
52. Honor Ford Smith, "Una Marson: Black Nationalist and Feminist Writer" (unpublished article, 1986), p. 10.
53. See Claudia Jones, "An End to the Neglect of the Problems of Negro Women," *Political Affairs* (June 1949), and Rhoda Reddock, *Elma François* (London: New Beacon Press, 1988).

so was an important tool in the struggle for liberation. As a consequence, the articulation of the Jamaican experience in the exceptionally flexible and pliable medium of the dialect offered enormous possibilities for its use as a literary language. Because "all linguistic communities evolve systems of power relationships enforced by and repeated in language,"[54] it was not inconsistent that a great amount of interest was displayed in the literary possibilities of the dialect during the 1940s, when discontent with colonial rule in Jamaica reached new heights.[55] Bennett's work challenged the privileged status accorded to the poetic tradition of white discourse in Caribbean letters, empowering the voices and expressions of the masses of Caribbean people. Bennett used the power of Jamaican speech to explore the complexity of the Jamaican experience and, in so doing, forced the members of the upper and middle classes to face their own linguistic and class biases. Her use of oral and scribal forms, as she forced the language to accommodate itself to express the poetic sentiments of the people, was an important breakthrough in Caribbean literature.

Born in Jamaica in September 1919, Bennett attended Excelsior College in Jamaica before going to England to study at the Royal Academy of Dramatic Art. She began to publish her verse in the *Jamaica Gleaner* in the 1930s and developed a large following. As Barbara Gloudon noted in *Jamaica Journal*, "Nothing like those poems had been seen before and each Sunday, when they appeared in the *Gleaner*, people in town and country rushed to get that week's reading of what Miss Louise Bennett was saying. And what she was saying was what was occurring each day in the lives of the ordinary people—their capacity to 'tek bad sinting mek laugh', to 'tek kin teet kibber bun heart'; in other words, to laugh at their problems, to see the best in the worst."[56]

Bennett's first published volume, *Dialect Verse*, appeared in 1942, and by 1962, the year of Jamaica's independence, she had published seven more volumes. She performed in the first Jamaican National Pantomime (*Soliday and the Wicked Bird*) in 1943, and her pantomime performances ran continuously until 1971. In the early 1940s, while she was in London, Bennett hosted "West Indian Guest Night" and worked extensively in radio. Yet her work was not included in any of the anthologies of West Indian poetry that appeared before 1960.[57] Indeed, it was not until the

54. Aldon Lynn Nielsen, *Reading Race* (Athens: University of Georgia Press, 1988), p. 3.
55. See Cobham-Sander, "The Creative Writer and West Indian Society," p. 125, for a discussion of this point. Mervyn Morris defines Jamaican dialect as "English creolised by Africans and supplemented by some African words." Although "On Reading Louise Bennett, Seriously," was first published in 1963, I quote from *Jamaica Journal* (1967), hence the apparent discrepancy.
56. Barbara Gloudon, "The Hon. Louise Bennett, O.J.: Fifty Years of Laughter," *Jamaica Journal* 19 (August–October 1986): 2.
57. See *Kykoveral*, no. 22 (1957), and *Caribbean Quarterly* 5, no. 3 (1958).

publication of Mervyn Morris's "On Reading Louise Bennett, Seriously" (1963) that the Jamaican literati noticed her work. In his prize-winning essay, Morris admonished: "I believe Louise Bennett to be a poet. By many people whose taste and judgement on other matters I respect she is regarded more or less as a local joke; a good, high-spirited joke, but, in the end, only a joke. I believe it is time we took Louise Bennett more seriously; and the purpose of this essay is to suggest literary reasons for doing so."[58] *Jamaica Labrish* (1966), designed to give an overview of Bennett's "art and artistry," helped expose her to a wider "literary" audience and resulted in better formal acceptance of her work.

Without attempting an exhaustive examination of Bennett's poems, it is very clear that her work captures the sentiments of Jamaican people. Poems such as "Candy Seller," "Street Boy," "Dry Foot," and "Back to Africa" are good examples of Bennett's early work. One of her earliest poetic efforts, a poem written for her friend Boysie, who literally dictated the poem to her, is a good example of Bennett's literary beginnings:

> Dear Godfather and Godmother
> Cane, socks, Merry Christmas
> Love fe all de gal dem and some
>   plenty book
> Tanks fe how yuh treat me good
> Mi wi send some banana fe dawg
> Cat and dawg and Godfather,
>   howdy-do
> Dem tief any more a Godfather
>   gungoo?
> Tell Mitchell bwoy dem howdy-do
> And tell dem fe come outa
>   Godfather buggy
> Me and Mama have plenty good
>   Christmas
> De whole a oonu fe come have it
>   too.[59]

"Colonisation in Reverse" offers another dimension of Bennett's classic "brand of satire and the biting irony of the situation,"[60] whereas poems such as "Perplex," "Obeah Win de War," "White Pickney," and "Pass Fe White" give a good sense of the everyday concerns that Bennett poeticized. Two poems that captured Bennett's early inventiveness, style, and

58. Morris, "On Reading Louise Bennett, Seriously," p. 69.
59. Quoted in *Jamaica Journal* 19 (August–October 1986): 6.
60. Louise Bennett, *Jamaica Labrish* (Kingston, Jamaica: Sangsters, 1966), p. 15. Subsequent references to this test are cited as *JL*.

home-grown poetical wisdom are "Votin' Lis' " (1944) and "Back to Africa" (1947). The first goes as follows:

> Me sorry day yuh sick Aunt Sal,
> Yuh doan know what yuh miss!
> Me just go meck sure sey dat me
> Name deh pon votin' lis'.

> Me see it wid me own two y'ey,
> Me touch it wid me han,
> Eehee me deh pon i mah, an
> Afta is noh me one!

> Crimp-toe Marry, bruck-jaw Jane, an
> No-teet Mada Chris,
> Wata mout Aunt Sue, long tongue May
> Dem all pon votin' lis'!

> Tom wat married to Sta Gwenie
> Cousin Youngman darta Sis,
> Min an Fatty, Les and Lotty, name
> Sprawl out pon votin' lis'!

> . . . .

> Bans o' man all ovah islan',
> Dis a-blista up dem t'roat,
> Dis a-chat till dem tongue leng out
> An dah-beg me fe me vote.

> Ah gwine meck dem tan deh beg me,
> Ah gwine meck dem tan deh pine,
> Ah gwine rag an haul and pull dem
> So til ah meck up me mine.

> Me doah know who me gwine vote fa,
> For me doan jine no gang,
> But wat me cross out gwan like storm
> An wat me lef kean wrong. (*JL*, pp. 133–34)

In "Back to Africa" Bennett questions the wisdom of those Jamaicans who wish to go back to Africa, a prevalent sentiment of the Rastafarians in the 1940s. According to Bennett, the confusion it would cause would hardly make it worthwhile:

> Back to Africa Miss Matty?
> Yuh noh know wha yuh dah-sey?
> Yuh haffe come from some weh fus,
> Before yuh go back deh?

> Me know sey dat yuh great great great
> Gramma was African,

> But Matty, doan yuh great great great
> Grampa was Englishman?
>
> Den yuh great granmada fada
> By yuh fada side was Jew?
> And youh grampa by yuh mada side
> Was Frenchie parley-vous!
>
> But de balance o' yuh family
> Yuh whole generation
> Oonoo all bawn dung a Bun grung
> Oonoo all is Jamaican!
>
> . . . .
>
> Wat a debil of a bump-an-bore,
> Rig-jig an palam-pam!
> Ef de whole worl' start fe go back
> Weh dem great granpa come from!
>
> Ef a hard time yuh dah-run from
> Teck yuh chance, but Matty, do
> Sure o'weh you come from so yuh got
> Somewhere fe come-back to!
>
> Go a foreign, seek yuh fortune,
> But noh tell nobody sey
> Yuh dah-go fe seek yuh homelan
> For a right deh so yuh deh! (*JL*, pp. 214–15)

Cobham-Sander argues that "Bennett is one of the first creative writers [in Jamaica and perhaps the West Indies] to register the increase of female oppression which was one of the consequences of the male assertion of radical and political power during the nationalist movement of the 1940s and 1950s."[61] Carolyn Cooper notes that Bennett elaborates upon the "Jamaican female sensibility" by drawing on Jamaican folktales.[62] By examining the folk wisdom of her people and the specific conditions of Jamaican women through the folktales, Bennett allows us to understand the women's psychology in a way that was not as clear before. By plunging to the unconscious of the female experience, she allows us better to see the strengths and weaknesses of the Jamaican women at the bottom of the economic ladder of the society.

Whatever else she may have achieved (and her achievements are many), by giving so much attention to the varied uses of the dialect she initiated a tradition of popular verse to which the entire region is indebted. Her

61. Cobham-Sander, "The Creative Writer and West Indian Society," p. 243.
62. Carolyn Cooper, "That Cunny Jamma Oman," *Jamaica Journal* 18 (November 1985–January 1986): 2–9.

courage in sticking to this form and working it through when respectable opinion in the society suggested that it was the wrong approach makes Bennett's achievement all the more remarkable. Her insistence that she is a writer ("From the beginning, nobody ever recognized me as a writer. 'Well, she is "doing" dialect'; it wasn't even writing you know. Up to now a lot of people don't even think I write"[63]) testifies to her strength and her belief in herself under adverse and negative circumstances. No wonder that on the celebration of her fiftieth anniversary (1986) as an artist and a performer she announced her triumphant achievement in her accustomed medium:

> An' me fling back me remembrance
> To ole-time days gwan by
> W'en me teck kin-teet keiba heart-bu'n
> Fe dry cry outa me y'eye.
>
> For Jamaica talk was less-counted,
> Low-rated, poppishow.
> But now, Jamma talk tun "Culture"
> An' Jamma Culture dah flow—
>
> Eena singin', dancin', paintin'
> Eena Church an T'eatre show,
> Jamma Culture enna "Culture"
> Any part a worl' we go!
>
> Mento, Bruckins', Yanga, Shay-shay,
> Bessi-dung dah sweeten Reggeh!
> An' what ole-time samdy use to sey
> Meck young smady feel proud today.
>
> We ole-generation duppy dem
> Jumpin' duppy-jamboree
> Wen dem se how now-a-days time
> Jamma Culture leggo free!
>
> Tengad fe fifty fruitful 'ears,
> Tengad me live fe se
> Me and me Jamma Culture
> Ketch Golden Jubilee![64]

Another Caribbean woman whose ideas were very important for the liberation of Caribbean women was Claudia Jones, a Trinidadian, who immigrated to the United States at the age of nine and later found herself at the center of the struggle for "Negro" and women's rights. In 1934, at

63. Quoted in Carolyn Cooper, "Proverb as Metaphor in the Poetry of Louise Bennett," *Jamaica Journal* 17 (May 1984): 22.

64. "Tengad!" *Jamaica Journal* 19 (August–October 1986): 11.

the age of eighteen, she became a member of the American Communist party and devoted the rest of her life to the liberation of oppressed peoples throughout the world. In "An End to the Neglect of the Problems of Negro Women," one of the most significant essays written on the women's question at the end of the 1940s, Jones argued for the internationalization of the working-class movement, the African-American liberation struggle, and the latter's link with the "Negro woman's struggle." She noted that the outstanding feature of the African-American liberation struggle at that time was "the growth in the militant participation of Negro women in all aspects of the struggle for peace, civil rights, and economic security" and continued:

> Historically, the Negro woman has been the guardian, the protector, of the Negro family. From the days of the slave traders down to the present, the Negro woman had the responsibility of caring for the needs of the family, of militantly shielding it from the blows of Jim Crow insults, of rearing children in an atmosphere of lynch terror, segregation, and police brutality, and of fighting for an education for the children. The intensified oppression of the Negro people, which has been the hallmark of the postwar reactionary offensive, cannot therefore but lead to an acceleration of the militancy of the Negro woman. As mother, as Negro, and as worker, the Negro woman fights against the wiping out of the Negro family, against the Jim Crow ghetto existence which destroys the health, morale and the very life of millions of her sisters, brothers, and children.[65]

She argued further that black women faced a "special oppression... as Negro, as mother and as worker" and, in early 1949, recognized the way the "white chauvinist" media were freezing these women into stereotypical roles:

> In the film, radio and press, the Negro woman is not pictured in her real role as breadwinner, mother, and protector of the family, but as a traditional "mammy" who puts the care of children and families of others above her own. This traditional stereotype of the Negro slave mother, which to this day appears in commercial advertisements, must be combatted and rejected as a device of the imperialist to perpetuate the white chauvinist ideology that Negro women are "backward", "inferior", and the "natural slaves" of others.[66]

In 1956 she noted the growing participation of Caribbean women in the national struggle at home and their solidarity with the international strug-

---

65. Claudia Jones, "An End to the Neglect of the Problems of Negro Women" in Buzz Johnson, *I Think of My Mother* (London: Karia Press, 1985), pp. 103–4.
66. Ibid., p. 107.

gle for "peace, security and the rights of children." She concluded that
"West Indian women represent an indispensable ally in the fight for
colonial freedom, because women are triply exploited in the colonies, as
women, as mothers and as colonials, subjected to the indignities and
great suffering because of the status of their countries."[67]

Jones, then, was a leader in the international struggle against racism,
sexism, and white male chauvinism. More important, her analysis of the
women's question anticipated most of the issues that were taken up by
the women's movement in the 1970s and the Caribbean women's movement in the 1980s. As Angela Davis noted, Claudia Jones "became a leader
and symbol of struggle for Communist women throughout the country
[the United States] . . . and believed that socialism held the only promise
of liberation for Black women, for Black people as a whole and indeed
for the multi-racial working class."[68]

THE RISE OF NATIONALISM

Living as I do a strenuous 6-day working and social
life, I have gravely missed the company of my true and
simple friends—the workers of Dominica. I have missed
the rains and the huge forest trees, the blue high
mountains and the sound of streams dashing through the
ravines. Surrounded by papers, books and kind new
friends, still I long for the familiar scenes of my
birthplace, as indeed many of us do; only we remember
that we are not just small islanders, or big islanders,
poets or politicians, lawyers or teachers, students or
labourers, but West Indian members of a wonderful
family of races—the most remarkable family of islanders,
perhaps in the world.
                    —Phyllis Allfrey, "Address to a Session of the West
                                        Indian Federal Government"

With the rise of nationalist sentiments in the Caribbean in the 1950s the
writing began to reflect the changing nature of social and political relations

67. Claudia Jones, "I Was Deported Because I Fought the Colour Bar," *Caribbean News*,
June 1956, ibid., p. 131.
68. Angela Y. Davis, *Women, Race and Class* (New York: Random House, 1981), pp.
168–69.

in the Caribbean.[69] More works were being written by women, works that seek to come to terms with some of the specific problems of women even though these problems are intertwined with the larger social and political problems of the society.

One of the first books to attack these problems, a feminist classic, was Phyllis Shand Allfrey's *The Orchid House* (1953) in which a number of white women and men try to understand and accept their changing status in the Caribbean or what Elaine Campbell calls "the gradual disappearance of the last of the West Indian colonising fathers." This position is made graphic when Stella, one of the characters in the text, in speaking about the gradually diminishing dominance of the whites, remarks: "What a lot of poor whites we are becoming!" Later she rues: "Nothing changes here, except that the coloured merchants grow richer and the white people poorer."[70]

From our point of view what is of most interest in *The Orchid House* is the courage displayed by the white West Indian women as their lives literally fall apart (their men are either sick or dying) and the way Lally, the black woman narrator, holds the white family together by providing an arm (more correctly, a lap) upon which they can lay their heads during this perilous period. Told through the consciousness of Lally, the story allows us to chronicle the demise of this family (both the men and the women) and the ultimate strength the women display in the face of crisis, which allows Lally to observe: "Women are always stronger, even up to death."[71]

The Orchid House is one of our earliest feminist texts, setting the stage for much that would follow in *Wide Sargasso Sea.*[72] It chronicles the breakdown of the old colonial society and outlines the formation of a new society built by a previously abused people who have gained a new sense of confidence. Allfrey examines the courage of the women (certainly the capacity of the younger white women to survive the present by coming to terms with their past) as they try to carry on with their lives. In Lally,

69. See, for example, Vic Reid, *New Day* (London: Heinemann Educational Books, 1949), George Lamming, *In the Castle of My Skin* (New York: McGraw-Hill, 1953), and Samuel Selvon, *A Brighter Sun* (London: Allan Wingate, 1952).

70. Phyllis Allfrey, *The Orchid House* (London: Virago, 1982), pp. x, 61, 80. All Europeans did not go to the Caribbean as colonizers. The Irish, for example, went as slaves or indentures rather than settlers. As James MacGuire notes: "Estimates of the total number of Irish sent to the West Indies range between 30,000 to 60,000. At one point, the zeal of the Bristol sugar merchants in transporting the Irish against their will grew so great that Parliament took measures to control it. Young women and girls were particularly prized by the planters, many of these in effect being sold into prostitution" ("Irish in the West Indies," *New York Times,* August 16, 1989, p. A24).

71. Allfrey, *The Orchid House,* p. 164.

72. See Elaine Campbell's introduction to *The Orchid House* for a description of some of the similarities between it and *Wide Sargasso Sea.*

Allfrey depicts the strength of black women (Lally is a typical black ma-
triarch) and reveals something of the courage and wisdom (despite her
love and devotion to the white colonial family) that have characterized
Caribbean people and given them the strength to survive.

After *The Orchid House*, the next novel of importance in Caribbean wom-
en's writing in English was Clara Rosa de Lima's *Tomorrow Will Always
Come* (1965), a powerful novel that examines the political situation in Brazil
before the removal of the capital city from Rio de Janeiro to Brasilia, the
vast psychological role that Macumba plays in the life of the Brazilian
people, and the open corruption of the country's political figures. The
novel openly treats sexual desire and the use of women as objects of
sexual gratification. As the author notes, the title is taken from a song:

> Women, you who have suffered,
> you who have lived, don't lie,
> a sad good-bye in your eyes
> I know, you are a woman of thirty.
> Tomorrow will always come, a
> tomorrow will always bring a new someone.

After quoting this song, the narrator comments: "To Neuza this song had
been composed exclusively for women like her. A woman who suffered
with her husband's death, her Italian lover's departure, later to know
hunger while learning to be a masseuse to support herself and her two
children, could only count on a tomorrow bringing a new someone."[73]
De Lima sees the fate of these women always lying in the hands of others,
their poverty a daunting obstacle to their fulfillment as autonomous
beings.

De Lima is also concerned with the poverty of these women and the
debasement to which they are subjected. In commenting on the behavior
of one of the characters, she notes that "a man to be a man had to beat
a woman," and, of another character, "He was macho and a macho meant
not only a man, but also a brave, bold and audacious one; a man who
could handle a gun as well as any of his opponents."[74]

Stereotypical observations about women abound, for example, the narrator's observation that "politics at times was more of a woman's game
than a man's, Amaral thought, women being masters at intrigue."[75] One
does not get the impression that the author disassociates herself from the
attitudes of her female characters. Yet this does not prevent her from

73. Clara Rosa de Lima, *Tomorrow Will Always Come* (New York: Ivan Obolensky, 1965),
p. 51.
74. Ibid., pp. 83, 111.
75. Ibid., p. 163.

attempting to depict sexual desire openly and suggesting that sexual exploitation is part of the political process and a culture of poverty.

Another remarkable aspect of this well-written novel is the author's treatment of the male homosocial bonding between Amaral, the major male protagonist, and Athos, his homosexual secretary.[76] Indeed, the end of the novel is richly suggestive of unconscious sexual desires between Amaral, in spite of his gay-bashing, and Athos, who stubbornly defends his homosexuality (claiming that he is neither abnormal nor unnatural, as Amaral suggests) when Amaral finally leaves Neuza, his last lover. Throughout the text, we are made aware of a tension between Athos and Neuza and the suggestion that Athos is jealous of the amount of time his employer spends with Neuza. One therefore is not surprised at the supreme joy expressed by Athos when finally Amaral casts Neuza out of his affections. What one is not prepared for (perhaps, not even Athos) is Amaral's response to Athos when Neuza leaves:

> Firecrackers were exploding now everywhere, the drums beating madly, the Macumberios chanting more loudly, throwing their offerings of food and flowers into the water. People were kissing and embracing; the New Year had arrived.
>
> Athos extended his hand to Amaral and Amaral pushing it aside embraced him. "Prosperity, your heart's desire is mine, dear fellow."
>
> Athos muttered his wishes incoherently; his emotions were suffocating; his employer was showing genuine affection.
>
> "Let's leave; bedlam addles me, goes against my grain . . . we would do better to drink a toast in the apartment. Besides, I should call Caxais," Amaral added, going toward the boardwalk and the street. . . .
>
> Damiana was about to drop to her knees to kiss his hand but Amaral said quickly, "None of that, woman, we are compadres now." He smiled. "Until Caxias, good night."
>
> "Athos, that I were able to give a worthwhile tomorrow to all the hungry of our country!" he went on as he walked away from Damiana, Joaquin, and the children, "that I could assist all the Damianas and Joaquims of Brazil! . . . Mark me well, one day I shall be president of this country and I shall help all these poor people."
>
> Athos glowed with admiration; he knew the congressman for Caxias could do whatever he put his mind to."[77]

One can conclude that in the spectrum from heterosexuality to homosexuality there are many unresolved tensions and conflicts in men (Sedg-

---

76. See Eve Kosofsky Sedgwick, *Between Men: English Literature and Male Homosocial Desire* (New York: Columbia University Press, 1985) for a discussion of homosocial bonding and David Van Leer, "The Beast of the Closet: Homosociality and the Pathology of Manhood," *Critical Inquiry* 15, No. 3 (Spring 1989) for a response to *Between Men*.

77. De Lima, *Tomorrow Will Always Come*, pp. 275–77.

wick calls it "homosexual panic") that are yet to be resolved and which de Lima seems to suggest are present in Amaral and Athos's relationship. And in the midst of all of these concerns, the corrupt influences and practices that are identified with Third World politics are also very much present in the novel.

Tomorrow Will Always Come is a magnificent achievement. At one level, the text is erotic in its celebration of the enjoyment of sexual love even though there is a tendency at points to degrade this relationship. Indeed, there is every indication that de Lima means to speak positively about sensuality and the role it plays in the cultures she writes about. One might argue that the poverty of the society leaves the women with few alternatives, but de Lima also wants to suggest that the power relationships inherent in sexual relations and the ways the women are used to carry forward the ambitions (or nonambitions) of the men, whether they are rich like Amaral or poor like Joaquin, warrant attention.

Tomorrow Will Always Come is an important breakthrough for Caribbean writing even though it has not been given the attention it deserves by either our male or female critics. Set in a part of the New World that was shaped by the slave culture, it is well written, powerfully presented, suggests many new avenues of literary exploration, and is deserving of attention. It depicts the poverty, the corruption, and the scheming of some Third World politicians in a way that few Caribbean writers have done before.

Not Bad, Just a Little Mad, de Lima's only novel set in the West Indies, is not as technically strong or socially compelling as Tomorrow Will Always Come. Set around the annual carnival celebration that takes place in Trinidad and Tobago, Not Bad, Just a Little Mad examines the love pentagonal of some affluent members of Trinidad society and the intrigue that results from their idleness and attempts at sexual fulfillment. The characters in Not Bad are not as well developed as those in Tomorrow Will Always Come and de Lima's depiction of black women leaves much to be desired. Her treatment of women, however, is most troublesome to the reader. De Lima is not sympathetic to the activities of "liberated women," and the women in her novel seem to function best when they are under the complete control and tutelage of men. For example, when Donald, one of the characters, needs to control his wife, he acknowledges, "You need a proper screwing, put an end to all your nonsense."[78] Perhaps a more telling example of this attitude arises when Anne, a strong and intelligent woman who comes to Trinidad after two disastrous love affairs, becomes friendly with Robert, a local Trinidadian who is having an affair with

78. Clara Rosa de Lima, Not Bad, Just a Little Mad (Devon: Arthur Stockwell, 1975), p. 148.

Sheelah, her sister. As Robert and Anne begin to enjoy each other's company, she seems to luxuriate in being under his control:

> Finally, "I've waited long, my darling." He held her face with both hands and stared at her. "Let me look at you."
> "Same old me, no change since a minute ago, only a little cleaner."
> "It has been long."
> "It couldn't have been before."
> "Knowing I held strain. You are shivering. It's the air conditioning." He handed her his dressing gown. "Get into this, young lady. Please dry your hair. Next, under the covers while I put on the soup. After a shower I'll feed you and then love you."
> "In that sequence?"
> "In that sequence. Your drink is on the dresser."
> "Would you believe I enjoy your bossing." They exchanged smiles. There was to be no hurrying, what was a few minutes after weeks of waiting? As he started for the door she added, "I should call the house so they don't wait dinner."
> "Do that."[79]

This scene is even more poignant because of the narrator's announcement at the beginning of the text that "Anne was fed up with her career, fed up with being a liberated woman. She had lost Bill because of this and she was losing, or had definitely lost, Carlos for the same reasons."[80] This tendency was dimly evident in *Tomorrow Will Always Come*, but in *Not Bad* it seems to have become the predominant motive.

At another level, it is very clear that de Lima does not understand the complexity of life among the black masses of society, particularly those at the bottom, whose lives are reduced to having a good time at carnival and getting as much sex as is humanly possible. Licentious excesses and mindless abandon seem to be the order of the day. Like V. S. Naipaul, she concludes through one of her female characters: "Trinidadians . . . thrive best on drama and confusion."[81] Such perpetual confusion is meant to be contrasted with the peace, quiet, and orderliness of some of the affluent areas in Trinidad. As the narrator notes: "The exuberance of these people attracted confusion and their flair for high drama overwhelmed. At least at the Crescent [Donald's affluent suburban neighborhood] all was quiet, the house was in total darkness but for the light over the entrance."[82] Because of de Lima's negative depictions of the women in her text and her limited vision of black life in Trinidad, *Not Bad* strikes a false and unconvincing note and fails to achieve the psychological com-

79. Ibid., p. 157.
80. Ibid., p. 9.
81. Ibid., p. 191. See V. S. Naipaul, *Guerrillas* (New York: Knopf, 1975).
82. De Lima, *Not Bad*, p. 185.

plexity and the exciting examination of sexuality that characterized *Tomorrow Will Always Come*.

Four years before Toni Morrison's *The Bluest Eyes* (1970), Maya Angelou's *I Know Why a Caged Bird Sings* (1970), and Louise Meriwater's *Daddy Was a Number's Runner* (1970) inaugurated the second renaissance of African-American women's writing, Rosa Guy eloquently captured the trauma of Wade Williams and his family in her first novel, *Bird at My Window* (1966). In her work, Guy explores her dual heritage (West Indian and African-American) in order to examine the lives of West Indian immigrants in New York and the conditions of African-American people in the United States. Shaped by the Garvey movement of the 1930s, the African liberation, and United States civil rights movements of the 1950s and 1960s, most of Guy's work reflects her involvement with the black liberation struggle and her intense desire to become "a full-blooded person" through her writing. As she said in an interview with Jerrie Norris:

> My life in the West Indies, of course, had a profound influence on me. It made me into the type of person I imagine that I am today. The calypso, the carnival, the religion that permeated our life—the Catholic religion—superstitions, voodoo, the zombies, the djuins, all of these frightening aspects of life that combine the lack of reality with the myth coming from Africa, had a genuine effect on me. But it was an effect that I knew nothing about, didn't realize played an important part in my life until much later when I was writing. But they made for an interesting background. . . . Something that I would call back on, something that I could hold onto as I went into a new life, a new environment. Something that gave me a stake, I suppose one would say. So that when I say I am West Indian, I have all of these little things—all of that broad background—that makes up the thinking, the searching of a person when art becomes relevant.[83]

It is no wonder, then, that *Bird at My Window* reflects the pent-up bitterness and frustration characteristic of the inner cities of the United States. In this text, Guy seeks to demonstrate the impact of racism in the United States on blacks and whites alike, the way it distorts the values of the society, and the resultant hopelessness of black life in the United States. *Bird at My Window* recounts the hardships of the Williams family, forced to migrate from the South because Mr. Williams (Wade's father) refused to sleep with a southern white woman, as they seek to find a place in Harlem. As the narrator notes when Wade finds a dead junkie on a tenement stoop: "And who would care? Who would care that one black boy's dream was snuffed out on a stormy night in the bowels of Harlem? Nobody. There would be two more to take his place and it would

83. Quoted in Jerrie Norris, *Presenting Rosa Guy* (Boston: Twayne, 1988), pp. 13, 1.

go on and on until the disease that the gods created became the disease that consumed them all."[84]

Although it is not the most West Indian of Guy's works, *Bird at My Window* is an important statement because it demonstrates Guy's ability to treat racism's crippling effects on the lives on African-American and West Indian peoples.[85] More important, the novel stands out because of its perspicacious examination of a mother-son relationship long before Gloria Naylor treated that subject in her insightful book *The Women of Brewster Place* (1982). Fighting desperately to break the chains that bind him to his mother, Wade Williams realizes, too late, that his devotion to his mother (that is, her cruel manipulation of his love for her) has enslaved him to her and prevented him from realizing any of his dreams. In speaking of the way his mother (and many black mothers) stifled the dreams of their children, Wade compares these women's treatment of their sons to a game of bowling: "They are the pin boys that set us up, then give us the blame when the bowl comes down. They pinpoint our doom, then put us out into the streets to rot in the gutters. Then they cry so that they can be washed in pity, prayed over by a fucking preacher, hoping like hell that their two faces can pass through the gates of heaven as one. And we let them do it. We love them for it. That's why they become scared when they see their handiwork: They know they don't deserve that love."[86]

It seems to be the author's passionate belief that because of the historical experiences of some mothers and their devotion to religion ("Mr. Charlie had forced her to her knees a long time ago and she had made *them* [her children] pay with her prayers"[87]) eventually they will betray their male children and castrate them emotionally.[88] As a result of this crippling psychological disease, the sons become virtual pigmies unable to respond sensitively to their women or to react in a positive and creative manner toward their social and political environment. Wade's deficiency in this regard becomes painfully evident when he must confront his mother so as to break his chains, so to speak. As the narrator recounts: "Then he was walking up the stairs to Mumma's, his heart beating like anything.

---

84. Rosa Guy, *Bird at My Window* (Philadelphia: Lippincott, 1966), p. 254.
85. Guy's trilogy—*The Friends, Ruby,* and *Edith Jackson*—and *My Love, My Love; or The Peasant Girl* are more West Indian in content, tone, and sensibility than *Bird at My Window.*
86. Guy, *Bird at My Window,* pp. 262–63.
87. Ibid., p. 270.
88. This statement is not intended to infer that Guy does not recognize the strength of the African-American woman, who, as she says, "is the strength on which I believe the American society has survived" (Norris, *Presenting Rosa Guy,* p. 67). Rather, it is meant to acknowledge the complexity of the African-American woman's response to her social condition.

Funny, how much like a little boy he felt, even though he was going to her as a man."[89]

As a result of this Oedipal relationship with their mothers, these male children have so passionate a desire to be free of all control—maternal, environmental, and social—that they are often led to disaster. Wade is a perfect example of the severe adult personality disorders that result because this relationship was not sorted out much earlier in his life. The text seems to place the blame on his mother, and, as in most naturalist works, the desire to free and cleanse himself of that maternal tie demands a ritual blood sacrifice. Wade's words to Faith, his sister, just before he commits the act of murder are very pertinent: "I did what I wanted to do, Faith—once in my life. And I know it's that feeling that makes life worth living. . . . It's doing what you have to do and feeling free with the world around and in you. It's when you don't go against instinct. It's when you can feel free—like a bird—when you can sort of spread your wings and take off."[90]

It is important that this novel was written at a time when African-Americans were rising up to protest their cruel treatment in the United States and that it is dedicated to Malcolm X. Guy's involvement with the Harlem Writers Guild (which she started with John O. Killens in 1951), the sudden death of her former husband in 1962, and "an earlier moment of violence in the life of a childhood friend" all led her to write *Bird at My Window*.[91] But it was the violent death of Malcolm X (she saw Malcolm's dead body being taken out of the Auduborn Ball when he was shot in 1965) that propelled her to finish her novel and publish it the following year. And although there are many echoes of the naturalism one finds in Wright's *Native Son* and Ann Petry's *The Street*, *Bird at My Window* operates at a more sophisticated narrative level and displays a greater degree of psychological depth than either *Native Son* or *The Street*.

Bird at My Window is a magnificent achievement that tackles some of the problems later writers would attempt to examine. Guy's West Indian sensibility informs much of her work, and, in a way, the novel provided an impetus for the breakthrough of the second renaissance of African-American women's writing and signaled a new subject in the writing of West Indian women. Thus, even though the first novels of de Lima and Guy are not set in the Caribbean, they are powerful statements of shared American realities in that they address issues that are pertinent to all the peoples of the Americas. In this context, Guy's sentiments after she

89. Guy, *Bird at My Window*, p. 245.
90. Ibid., p. 281.
91. Norris, *Presenting Rosa Guy*, p. 19.

completed *Bird at My Window* and repeated in "The Human Spirit" are noteworthy:

> Tiptoeing my way through the casualties of poverty in the ghettos—an orphan in New York, ostracized for those traits which being West Indian and Catholic had etched into my personality—wasn't easy. I shall never forget the day I walked, cringing, the length of a snowbound street and not one snowball was hurled at my head. I knew I was grown up: I believed myself immune from those influences molding the lives of the Americans among whom I lived.
>
> Rubbish, of course. I realized that when I looked through the galleys of my soon-to-be-published first book. . . . I had internalized all their pain, their resentment—to the snowballs hurled relentlessly at my head, and firecrackers at my feet—as I ducked and dodged my way through adolescence. But I never looked back in hate—but with a kind of sadness, a regret that there had been no books yet written, no guidelines from caring adults who might have made a difference, guiding us over the deep but narrow ravines dividing us.[92]

The last work of importance in the first phase of Caribbean women's writing was Sylvia Wynter's *Hills of Hebron* (1966), which brings to a close a particular kind of public speaking about the Caribbean self and represents the culmination of a discourse that emphasized the collective rather than the personal self. Set in Jamaica, the novel is about the aspirations of a people who sought to overcome "three centuries of placelessness" through a series of misguided activities and with a misguided leader.[93] Seeking to found "a kingdom of the black God" (p. 143), Prophet Moses and his people leave the corrupt world of the past (colonialism) to found a new colony in Hebron, where "the black man could walk proud on his land and not know hungriness or want," where he could realize a new sense of self. Thus the epigraph from Dostoevsky's *The Possessed* with which the fourth part of the book opens ("With every people, at every period of its existence, the end of the whole national movement is only the search for God, of a God for it, in the synthetic personality of a whole people considered from its origins until its end") seems to capture the nature of that search, and their ultimate achievement is manifested in Obadiah's (Prophet Moses's spiritual heir) carving which, the narrator notes, was created out of a deep sense of need and desire for a new way. When Prophet Moses's dream is confronted with a discourse that speaks of the need of the disinherited to rise up and overthrow the strong through

92. Rosa Guy, "All About Caring," *Top of the Times*, 39.
93. Sylvia Wynter, *The Hills of Hebron* (London: Longman, 1984), p. 276.

the unity of their collective labor, however, he is unable to comprehend this new language and so takes his own life by a self-inflicted crucifixion. With *The Hills of Hebron* we enter the era of black power, black pride, and the quest for self-government. The novel heralds a time of radical reorientation, seemingly linking us with our past and taking us back where we began. For if, as Wynter suggests, slavery involved "the cutting off of a memory of the past, the denial of any indigenous history, and a kind of intellectual alienation from the self and society," *The Hills of Hebron* argues for the repossession of that past and the finding of a voice to express that denial and absence.[94] And if, as Wynter insists, Caribbean people were oppressed first as natives, then as blacks, before the question of gender arose, the relative importance of gender has to be considered in that light. And even though Miss Gatha emerges as a powerful voice in the novel, she is powerful not so much because she is a woman but because of her status as a colonial person anxious to articulate this private sense of dispossession. In this context we can begin to understand the way the people of Hebron saw their past and their present:

> Their instinct for survival was as strong in them as in their slave ancestors. Some weight of memory in their blood carried the ghosts of dark millions who had perished, coffined in the holds of ships, so that some could live to breed more slaves; and they, after their freedom had been won, survived the rootless years. They survived the loss of gods and devils that were their own, of familiar trees and hills and huts and spears and cooking pots, of their own land in which to see some image of themselves. And their descendants, the New Believers, survived the exodus from Cockpit Centre, the passage through wilderness and up to the hills of Hebron, where Prophet Moses had promised them those things that had been lost in their trespass across the seas, across the centuries.[95]

In this novel, Wynter captures the vital instinct of Caribbean people to survive and to create. Although the novel may be much too long in parts and somewhat overbearing in its didacticism, it captures the sense of restlessness with the past and the need to break out of discourses and practices that are designed to keep us coffined within an alien ideology and culture. Structured in the anticolonialist struggle of the 1950s and 1960s, *The Hills of Hebron* brings to a closure the story of Mary Prince, coffined on her slave plantation and subjected to the brutality of the slave master, offered in 1831. *The Hills of Hebron* almost seems a response to Prince's plea for the recognition of her humanity. As she asked: "How can slaves be happy when they have the halter round their neck, and the whip upon their back? and are disgraced and thought nothing more of

94. Conversation with Sylvia Wynter, September 11, 1989.
95. Wynter, *Hills of Hebron*, p. 51.

than beasts?—and are separated from their mothers, and husbands, and children, and sisters, just as cattle are sold and separated? Is it happiness for a driver in the field to take down his wife or sister or child, and strip them, and whip them in such a disgraceful manner?—women that have had children exposed in the open field to shame!"

Certainly, *The Hills of Hebron* reflects the movement toward the creation of a new day, a movement from the symbol of "the halter round their neck[s] and the whip upon their back[s]." Here, indeed, the spirits of the ancestors meet and ask that libation be given to soothe the transition from the old to the new, from the past to the present, from the public to the private sphere of discourse. The women writers of the contemporary era would explore new areas of concern, different continents of sensibility and feelings, and varied ways of speaking about their relationships with each other and with their men. Much of their work would be influenced by the black power, Rastafarian, and women's movements.

THE ACHIEVEMENTS OF THE CONFERENCE

The publication of Merle Hodge's *Crick Crack Monkey* (1970) ushered in a new era in the writing of women in the English-speaking Caribbean. The pieces contained in this volume reflect the diversity of interests of the women writing in this period. When we invited the creative writers to the conference, we asked them to respond to three questions: What are your major concerns as a writer? In what way does your work reflect or represent the development of a Caribbean tradition of literature? And to what degree do you feel that your work has been influenced by feminist concerns? Not all of the writers answered these questions directly. Each expressed the concerns that motivate her writing and what she hopes to achieve when she sits down to write. The social and literary critics gave us a context through which we can examine the writings of these women.

In examining the contributions in this volume we will observe that the social and literary critics give us a context through which the writings of these women can be examined. "The Context," the first part of the volume, begins with Lucille Mathurin Mair's contribution, which forces us to examine the problems inherent in unearthing the female condition in Caribbean history, buried, as it is, in the folk memory of a people. Rhoda Reddock explores the manifestation of feminist consciousness in the first half of the twentieth century in Jamaica, Trinidad, Tobago, and Barbados and the way race, class, and sex intersect in the evolution of that consciousness. Arthur Paris speaks of the Antillian influences in the metropoles (New York, London, Paris, Toronto, and Amsterdam) and the way emigrants from the Caribbean try to make sense of and are shaped by their new environment. He also notes the mechanisms at work in the metropolitan centers that facilitate the publishing and dissemination of these women's work. Laura Niesen de Abruna speaks of the need to include the "woman's story" in Caribbean literature, identifies that which is specifically womanist in the literature, and argues that "rational interaction" can be perceived as *the* special strength and distinctiveness of Caribbean women's writing. Jeremy Poynting advances the reason for the slender production of Indo-Caribbean women writers and outlines the direction such writing has taken.

"In Their Own Words," the second part of the volume, contains statements by the women writers and critiques of their work. Veronica Gregg's "Jean Rhys on Herself as a Writer" organizes Jean Rhys's most significant statements about her writing in a coherent whole and then interrogates what the vocation of writing meant to Rhys. Elaine Campbell analyzes and classifies the unpublished short stories of Phyllis Allfrey. Clearly there is a need to have access to Allfrey's unpublished stories and novel ("In a Cabinet") so that the reading public and the scholars of Caribbean literature can make a better assessment of her work. In this context, the publication of "Miss Garthside's Greenhouse" for the first time is an important gesture.

In "The Human Spirit," Rosa Guy reminisces about growing up in Trinidad before she immigrated to the United States, the seeming contradictions of American society, and the reasons why she chose to be a "romancier." As she notes, it was the spirituality that her mother bequeathed to her that allowed her to survive in her new American home. Sybil Seaforth talks about the peculiar difficulties of being a woman writer and the constant search to find a space of her own. Jan Shinebourne talks about the violent political conflicts that attended Guyanese society in the 1950s and 1960s and their impact on her writing. In "She Scrape She Knee," Opal Palmner Adisa celebrates the womanish knee-scrapers (as opposed to the "nice girls"), who, by their audacity, constantly challenge the prescribed places of women in their societies. She acknowledges that they pay a price for their audacity. As a writer, however, a knee-scraper, performs the valuable function of being "a seer, [and] a mouthpiece for the voiceless, the mute, the talker, the braggart, the fool."

Clara Rosa de Lima, "a so-called white woman of Spanish, [Jewish] descent" (de Lima's description of herself) recounts the exciting life she led, her travels, and the way her novels came to be. Because she resides in the "middle upper" strata of the society, she claims that she is in a good position to see and understand the social divide, that is, the activities of the upper and lower classes. Hers is a welcome, though neglected, voice that expands the fictive landscape and reflects the diversity of interests and experiences of Caribbean women writers.

Leah Creque-Harris does a masterful interpretation of Elizabeth Nunez-

Harrell's *When Rocks Dance* and locates its fictive action within the ancestral memory of the people. Her sophisticated reading of the text demonstrates the complexity of many of these works and, as my interview with Jamaica Kincaid and Daryl Cumber Dance's "Go Eena Kumbla" suggest, there is a spiritual presence (that is, a perception of otherness) in the life of Caribbean peoples.

Erna Brodber interprets her creative work as a part of her sociological practice and notes how she incorporates her particular stance—"a culture-in-personality"—into her teaching and activist praxis. Such a blend of sociology and literature, she argues, allows Caribbean and African-American people to look at their reality in quite different ways. Daryl Cumber Dance's "Go Eena Kumbla: A Comparison of Erna Brodber's *Jane and Louisa Will Soon Come Home* and Toni Cade Bambara's *Salt Eaters*" extends the connection that Brodber makes between Caribbean and African-American women and shows certain similarities in their social practices, which demonstrate "a general cultural pattern" in the literature of these two peoples. Against such a background, Glasceta Honeyghan's intensely revealing story, "Father Sleeps with the Mudpies," her first published work, takes us into the folk culture of Jamaica. In this macabre, almost gothic, story, Honeyghan examines the love-hate relationship between a young girl and her grandfather as she recalls his gradual demise. Indeed, Honeyghan's fertile literary imagination allows us to see an unusual dimension of family relations in Jamaica that is seldom revealed in other works.

Beryl Gilroy's "I Write Because . . ." offers an insightful look into the effect of racist values and attitudes on black children in Britain. Her long experience as a teacher in Britain's schools, her attempt to create positive views about black people via her writing, and her lifelong struggle to combat racism give "I Write Beacause . . ." unique historic and psychological importance.

The theme sounded by Gilroy is picked up by Merle Hodge in "Challenge of the Struggle for Sovereignty: Changing the World versus Writing Stories." Combining art with activism, Hodge relies on "the power of the creative word" to change the world and sees Caribbean fiction playing an important part in Caribbean development. Caribbean literature, she says, "can help to strengthen our self-image, our resistance to foreign domination, our sense of the oneness of the Caribbean, and our willingness to put our energies into the building of the Caribbean nation." Ena Thomas notes that *Crick Crack Monkey* is a picaresque work, a product of a society that allows the individual little dignity and self-respect. Such a situation, she argues, is the fate of Tee, the major protagonist of *Crick Crack Monkey*, an outsider struggling for social respectability.

In her interview, Jamaica Kincaid examines the particular sensibility that makes for a Caribbean woman's *bildungsroman*. From her comments it can be inferred that there is a unique New World sensibility that reaches back into an African and Amerindian cultural heritage that has been alluded to by other Caribbean creative writers such as Wilson Harris and Alejo Carpentier. Helen Pyne Timothy examines the mother-daughter relationship in Kincaid's *Annie John* and traces the sociopsychological development of Annie John and the way Kincaid anchored these experiences within the Caribbean context. In her turn, Donna Perry notes the difference between the portrayal of mother-daughter relations in Caribbean and European literature and uses *Annie John* to argue that the fiction of Caribbean women offers "new myths of female development and new definitions of success."

Picking up from Hodge, Jean D'Costa notes the specific manifestations of folkloric figures in the Caribbean and the particular interplay between English and Creole languages as they structure the production of children's fiction. Her comparision of the European fairy tale with the Caribbean folktale is very instructive. Michelle Cliff notes the nature of speechlessness that inheres in the colonized condition. Rather than viewing such a condition as an act of self-erasure, she uses language to make her mark, that is, to inscribe herself into the historic process and locates her work within or, perhaps, in the contradiction between what can be termed the discourses of the "civilized" and the "savage." In her excerpt from "Parang," Marion Patrick Jones reflects on a particular aspect of middle-class life in Trinidad and shows her continuing fascination with that segment of the society. Grace Nichols notes the diversity of Caribbean society and reflects on the continuous battle "to chisel a new language" out of standard English (imposed) and Creole (ingrained/natural) that fashions her sensibility as an artist. Like Guy, Nichols feels that writing is one way to keep the "human spirit" alive in spite of the difficulties one may encounter. In her turn, Lorna Goodison also speaks of "the double language out of which she writes" and her enduring struggle to "write about truth and light." In Marlene Philip's contribution we observe a similar encounter with language and her struggle to bend language in such a way that it becomes a flexible (useful) instrument to speak about her specific colonial experience. Afua Cooper notes how her work has been shaped by African folklore in Jamaica, whereas Claire Harris explores the condition of marginality as an "immigrant writer" in Canada, the boundaries of poetic expression and the manner in which her verse challenges "the Canadadian compact."

The conscious manipulation of language continues in "Miss Flori's Flowers," Olive Senior's ironic description of the manners and mores of a particular segment of Jamaica's society. In a deliberately muted manner,

the narrator of "Miss Flori's Flowers" engages in a delicate feminist probing of the social behavior of a few women by turning the pretensions of
the society upon itself. In a very significant move, the author elides the
presence of men and takes a conscious decision to make the behavior of
women the central concern of the text.

In their turn, Valerie Belgrave and Sharon Chacko talk about the way
they came to use batik as a medium of artistic expression. Belgrave emphasizes the link between her craft and *Ti Marie*, her historical romance,
and Chacko talks about the historic evolution of batik. Moreover, Chacko
emphasizes the creativity and resourcefulness of the Jamaican cultural
landscape that inspires her work, whereas Belgrave explains the way
Trinidad's history of slavery shapes the making of her romance.

The final part of the volume, "Women Writers from the Spanish-,
French-, and Dutch-Speaking Caribbean" gives a broad overview of the
writings of the different language areas of the Caribbean. In her piece,
Maria Cristina Rodriguez examines some of the problems that face women
writers from the Spanish-speaking countries and explores the contributions of some of the more recent Spanish-Caribbean writers. According
to Rodriguez, there still exists a need for the women writers of the Spanish
Caribbean to be taken seriously.

Marie-Denise Shelton examines the specificity of women's writings in
the French-speaking Caribbean and notes that even though the French-
speaking writers may express a different "knowledge," they all operate
within the similar space created by slavery and colonialism. Like their
colleagues in the English-speaking Caribbean, the women of the French-
speaking islands feel an identical pressure to write in two languages—
French and Creole—even as they map out their own literary territory.
Shelton is particularly astute in her observation that "isolating feminine
expression does not imply that it can be detached from the [Caribbean]
conjuncture" of slavery, colonization, and small island insularity.

In her essay, "Dutch Caribbean Women Writers," Ineke Phaf uses
Astrid Roemer's *Life Long Poem* to demonstrate the peculiar difficulties of
Dutch-Caribbean women, who had to write against all of the stereotypes
in her society. Noting that Roemer has to work through severe linguistic
complexities to gain some understanding of her personal and social history, Phaf is convinced that Roemer uses her work to participate in the
contemporary debate about racism, feminism, and gay rights to which
the modern novel is committed. In this latter endeavor, Roemer is at one
with Hodge in that she sees literature as a powerful medium that can
unlock the linguistic prison that Western literary history has imposed
upon Caribbean people and reveal to us "our essential values."

Collectively, the writings in this volume represent the most comprehensive and up-to-date statement by Caribbean women writers and their critics. The diversity and timeliness of these essays represent particular strengths of this volume and provide a basis upon which we can begin to understand the new configuration of Caribbean literature. Probably one of the more imaginative volumes to come out on Caribbean literature, *Caribbean Women Writers* may prove to be as important an intervention in the literature of the Americas as was Alain Locke's *The New Negro*, Addison Gayle's *The Black Aesthetic*, and Kenneth Ramchand's *The West Indian Novel and Its Background*. Just as important, it enlarges the boundaries of Caribbean literary discourse and thus outlines another of the many histories of America's literary imagination.

THE CONTEXT

Negro slave family of the Loango nation depicted as being in a state of "tranquil happiness." From John Stedman, *Narrative of a Five Years' Expedition against the revolted Negroes of Surinam*, 1796.

Recollections of a Journey into a Rebel Past

LUCILLE MATHURIN MAIR

In the early 1960s I started to seek out the women of Jamaica's past during the period of slavery, women of all classes and of all colors, black, brown, white. I had no feminist motivation, or at least none that I recognized. I was motivated mainly by intellectual inquisitiveness, the usual ambition of the doctoral candidate to investigate virgin territory, which it was at that time. There was almost nothing to guide such a search. There was, in fact, nothing in modern historical scholarship about the women who came before me. But this was not surprising, for historiography, which has for centuries been a male academic preserve, has been stunningly devoid of a consciousness of women as significant beings.

So feminist historians have been faced with the methodological challenge of excavating women from layers of distortion and obscurity, of getting beyond and behind the formal roles conventional history has accorded them and in the process, perhaps, even transforming the discipline of history.

Digging into the lives of the small minority of free white women in Jamaican slave society takes one along a relatively straightforward route. There is a substantial body of data to be found in contemporary histories and accounts by residents and travelers: there is even more valuable material in legal documents, in wills, in diaries, and in the volume of transatlantic and inter-American correspondence that has been preserved in the papers of planter families. Letters and diaries of women of this class reveal some of the personal and domestic implications of absentee proprietorship, an alienating phenomenon that has been distinguished

51

throughout most of Jamaica's history by the nostalgia of its white elite for all things English, an intensely female nostalgia that is communicated through the pens of women with perturbing immediacy.

Other approaches are required to recover the feelings of brown and black women and to gain insight into the multidimensional nature of their lives. Until the very recent development of indigenous scholarship, the Caribbean researcher's main reference point was the Eurocentric, ethnocentric historiography of the colonizer and the slaveholder, which is incapable of addressing the humanity of transplanted Africans labeled chattel, identified for the historical record in an entry on a bill of lading or an estate inventory and rendered voiceless. The state of slavery further compounds the methodological challenge in that women and slaves, as oppressed groups, themselves frequently suppress their objective reality. Their words, if we could only hear them, may have been designed not to reveal but to conceal, not to inform but to misinform.

In attempting to decode the mysteries of the black female condition, the Caribbean scholar is at greater risk than her Afro-American counterpart, who can study collections of slave narratives, with opportunities for testing their authenticity. Nothing has surfaced to date in the Jamaican records comparable to the statements of a Sojourner Truth, or a Harriet Tubman, or the remarkable testimony of the slave woman Harriet Jacobs, whose autobiography has only recently come to light.

Only one woman of color has left a strong imprint on the pages of Jamaica's past, leaving literary evidence of her lively existence: this was Mary Seacole. Her autobiography, a classic of its kind, entitled *Wonderful Adventures of Mrs. Seacole in Many Lands*, was first published in England in 1857. It is a vivid, witty account of the life of a spunky mulatto woman who labeled herself a "female Ulysses." Her ambition and wanderlust took her as innkeeper, huckster, and nurse to Haiti, Cuba, the Bahamas, Panama, England, and the battlefield of the Crimea, where she became celebrated as the "brown Florence Nightingale." Her portrait dominated the platform of the Hall at the University of the West Indies in Jamaica, where I lived and worked during the years of my research.

Mary Seacole's "wonderful adventures" occurred during the postemancipation period and therefore fell for the most part outside of my research time frame, but I expected to meet her on my journey. I did, and certainly she came alive through the picture she drew of *herself*. Today's Caribbean women writers will be intrigued to explore the value of her contribution to our literary heritage, for her autobiography is both a historical document and a creative work, a unique expression of the female mulatto syndrome.

Nanny of the Maroons was more enigmatic. For as long as I can remember, she has been somewhere in the Jamaican consciousness but without acquiring solid flesh and blood. Was she actually an Ashanti chieftainess who wielded power over her people in the Portland mountains of eastern Jamaica and kept the establishment at bay for years as she led the war of black liberation, frustrating colonial designs to make the island free for King Sugar? Or was she a creature of legend, summoned up by the Maroons from the spirit world to sustain their struggle for freedom? The supernatural powers attributed to her in popular sayings seemed so bizarre as to produce skepticism about her humanness. I did not know precisely how much I would discover about this heroic but insubstantial figure, and if one rejected the folk memory as a valid base for scholarly theses, was there any certainty of finding incontestable evidence that she had really lived?

The twilight zone Nanny inhabited symbolized the hazy state of our knowledge about our black foremothers. Records existed, most of them the result of the very nature of the slave society and economy. Estate papers and slave registration returns are rich in the demographic data compiled by proprietors and managers to keep account of the size, age, physical condition, occupation, and other attributes of their human property. Colonial Office and parliamentary reports provide prime evidence of the strategic and commercial interests of imperialism, which shaped the island polity and made precise prescriptions for the functioning of each racial group and, above all, of each unit of the work force. There are data in abundance, but there is very little about the inner lives of slaves.

Clearly, one must probe deeply into the conventional sources of Caribbean history to find those missing women, to attempt new interpretations, and imaginatively to bring new insights to the task of opening up the slaves' private world, where black women lived in cultural antithesis to the white plantation. The historical, sociological, and creative writings of Orlando Patterson and Edward Kamau Brathwaite in the 1960s and early 1970s indicated how and where one might find that Afro-Caribbean world. As Brathwaite expressed it, "history becomes anthropology and sociology, psychology and literature and archaeology, and whatever else is needed to make the fragments whole." In the 1960s, however, we were a long distance away from refining multidisciplinary scholarship.

Understandably, I was nervous about embarking on my venture with such undeveloped professional tools. But I was inspired and supported by a friend and teacher, and a great woman, Elsa Goveia. And there could be no more appropriate occasion than this historic gathering of Caribbean women writers at which to pay tribute to her shining spirit and towering intellect: she was a native of Guyana, the first female professor and the first professor of West Indian history at the University of the West Indies.

Sadly, she died too soon, eight years ago, at the age of fifty-five. But what a legacy she has left us! Her first major publication in 1956 was a study of the historiography of the British West Indies. In it she dissected with a cool and devastating critique the racialist and authoritarian ideologies of those historians who, under the guise of academic objectivity and humanist values, previously attempted to record the Caribbean past.

Nine years later, she produced her landmark history, *Slave Society in the British Leeward Islands at the End of the Eighteenth Century*. In his annual lecture in her memory at the University of the West Indies, Professor Franklin Knight aptly described that work as "magisterial."

Professor Goveia's piercing vision and rigorous scholarship brought fresh understanding of the complex historical forces that have shaped our island societies. Brilliantly, meticulously, she analyzed the decisive force of race and color in constructing Leeward Islands society, demonstrating how "the social order of the whole community hung upon the distinctions established between the constituent races." Simultaneously, she identified the propensity of those same constituents to destabilize the social order. Her thesis tempted me with prospects of an exciting dialectical exploration to illuminate the buried lives of women: if the fact that she was black, or white, or brown ascribed to a woman her status, her functions, and her subversive potential, would her being female make a difference? In short, how far would her sexual identity diminish or enhance her capacity to conform or to resist?

It took time, of course, to find answers, and a great deal of patience, like that of the gold prospector, sifting through tons of material in search of the occasional nugget of enlightenment. But fragments of women's lives came to light increasingly out of the shadows of the archives, and the contours of black, brown, and white women's stories took shape.

The combined ideologies of white supremacy and patriarchalism laid down clear guidelines for the status and functioning of white women in a plantation colony. The majority, conditioned to accept such concepts, performed accordingly, but not all did. Some proved capable of flouting convention, of engaging in economic activities that did not fit the white female stereotype, of indulging in unbecoming social conduct, of violating interracial sexual taboos. Women of the plantocracy struck out with even more spirit in some ways than women of lesser classes, making definitive statements of white female distaste for Creole norms. Many came, saw, and fled, leaving behind awkward social and domestic gaps that threatened to undermine the nice designs of the establishment.

Colored women had their allotted place, initially a marginal one. But selective co-option carried some to the status of surrogate whites, who served partially to defuse the racial imbalance, ten blacks to one white, the highest in the transatlantic plantations and a terrifying specter to the white establishment. Numbers of brown women exploited openings in Creole society, carving out for themselves significant roles that had not been previously prescribed, virtually inverting the social order. Such processes, within the context of Jamaica's sexual and racial demography, have important implications for brown women's assertive capacity to influence the shaping of a society. But under the close scrutiny of research, the black slave woman emerged as the most aggressive of women: she took center stage as rebel.

Rebels on the run are usually the first to catch posterity's eye, for as valuable property that had to be recovered when they fled their estates, they made copy in the local press. That liberating act of "pulling foot" gave them names, faces, and identities. They became conspicuous in the fugitive population, confounding customary perceptions of the passive sex, whose physical mobility is constrained by motherhood. The female runaway often made sure her children joined her escape from bondage in what was one of the most threatening forms of protest, for each missing person, man, woman, or child, jolted the system. A family such as that of Margaret, alias Amey, stands out in the rogues' gallery. She was a "slender black woman, with a large eye, prominent forehead and straight nose, and marked CH or MH"; her daughter Eliza Arnold was also "slender, with very large eyes, and a thin visage"; and her son Richard McHead, aged eighteen, accompanied them. Described in the advertisement for their capture as a "plausible trio," they had crossed the length of the island from the northwestern parish of Hanover and were hiding somewhere in the city of Kingston in the southeast. They and others like them moved through a black underground that sustained fugitives for long periods, over long distances, in the countryside or in the busy subculture of the island's growing towns.

Women featured prominently among the "incorrigible" slaves who ran away again and again, risking recapture and punishment, which increased in severity for each repeated offense. When caught and returned to the plantation, they made common cause with an equally "incorrigible" band of rebels, the industrial saboteurs. Women had the power and the will to destabilize the plantation's labor productivity through a variety of single or collective acts, some blatant, some devious, but all ultimately damaging to the economic enterprise. I developed a special feeling for one such subversive activist, a slave woman of Port Royal, whose owner was so misguided as to name her "Industry." She could not resist that challenge: "For refusing to work and setting a bad example to other negroes on the property by her contumacious conduct," Industry was sentenced by the magistrate to two weeks' hard labor.

Women were highly visible in the go-slows and work stoppages that were endemic on the plantations; for example, a "petticoat rebellion" of those who were assigned to carry cane trash halted the operations of the sugar mill at Matthew Lewis's Cornwall Estate in the parish of Westmoreland during the early nineteenth century. Such open sabotage was frequently supplemented by more equivocal strategies such as pretending illness. When admitted to the hospital, the malingerers would settle in for a long stay to the detriment of the estate's output.

Women often used their reproductive power to erode the productive functions demanded of them. The plantation looked to them increasingly after the abolition of the slave trade in 1807 not only to provide massive inputs of labor but also to replenish the labor force. But slave birth rates declined steadily in the later years of slavery until emancipation in 1834, partly because of the arduous tasks and the physical and sexual abuse to which slave women were often subject but partly also because women willed it so. They aborted regularly with the expertise of that formidable figure of the slave community, the midwife, who was knowledgeable in the use of folk medicine and who projected an image of having almost supernatural gifts. When they did give birth, slave women exercised their maternal prerogatives to the maximum: few female acts provoked more frustration and rage in estate managers than women's insistence on nursing their infants for as long as they could and too often for the estate's liking, often for as long as two years. It was an effective strategy because slave laws provided nursing mothers with time off and special allowances, all charged to the estate's accounts.

Women were clearly determined to retain control over their reproductive and maternal rights. During the last years of slavery and the interim period of apprenticeship preparatory to full emancipation, when the fear of labor shortage haunted the plantocracy, women's withdrawal of their labor and that of their children seriously threatened the viability of sugar plantations. One official report gave evidence: "Negro mothers have been known to say, pressing their children to their bosoms, we would rather see them die than become apprentices." During the four years of apprenticeship, from 1834 to 1838, of the thousands of slave children who were eligible, only nine were released by their mothers for recruitment into the estate work force.

The other side of such reluctant and minimal effort for the plantation was the remarkable industry and productivity of women and their families on their provision grounds. There they labored long, hard hours, traveled miles weekly to nearby towns to sell their crops, and made themselves indispensable to the domestic economy. The profits from such enterprise provided them with the means to acquire possessions for home and person, including the colorful clothes in which women took pride. Personal property represented a degree of economic autonomy which slaves jealously guarded and defended in the courts, where they pressed their legal rights to their own time for cultivating their plots. And there another band of determined rebels made their presence felt, the habitual litigants, among whom women were conspicuous. They stormed the courts, claiming their maternal privileges, and they protested excessive physical abuse and punishments, raising their voices loud and clear, displaying black verbal skills to great effect.

Women's voices, clamorous and ceaseless, were a marvelous medium for affirming their identity and for expressing their "magnificent discontent." Words are tools to which everyone has access. They can be explicit or insidiously shrouded in double entendre. Exasperated whites described woman's tongue as a "powerful instrument of attack and defence, exerted in insufferable insult." With malice and artistry their work songs in the field explored Buckra's frailties, which many women had reason to know well. The use or misuse of the master's language developed into sharp and enduring weapons of resistance which received added force from the mystique that surrounded African cultural perceptions of language and the word.

Far more than the written word, the spoken word established Nanny's awesome reality. Close examination of the official records verifies her status as the civic, military, and religious leader of a free community in the mountains of eastern Jamaica during the period of the first Maroon war of the 1730s. The records also show how false was an often-quoted allegation that she died in 1733 at the hand of Cuffee, "a very good party negro." It is not clear whether this was mistake or misinformation, but she certainly lived and continued to defy the colonial establishment until 1740, when she reluctantly accepted a truce. The land patent she received from the British crown in 1741 can be found today in the National Archives in Spanish Town; it granted to her and her people five hundred acres in the parish of Portland land they still inhabit.

Such documents are invaluable for the reconstruction of Jamaica's history. Of equal value are the oral traditions of the Maroons. Like other Afro-Caribbean groups, they carry their past in their heads. Their storytellers are charged with the sacred and professional responsibility of preserving the historical narrative intact. They have done so with such seriousness and consistency from generation to generation that modern scholarship increasingly acknowledges the ability of the folk memory to validate the authority of the printed page. To do justice to the actual and symbolic presence of a Nanny, as Brathwaite has stated, implies "the commitment of the researcher to undertake an investment in the veracity of our oral traditions and enlist those traditions in the reconstruction of a broken legacy." It is a broken but hardy legacy, not easily lost by the millions of young female adults, who for nearly two centuries crossed the Atlantic carrying, if nothing else, their certainty of being African and being women. The majority, before enslavement, had undergone the rites of passage their societies required of them, which ceremonially expressed a civilization's clear perceptions of the truths and joys as well as the mysteries and dangers of existence. Each new and potentially frightening phase of the life cycle was realistically confronted and exorcised, in the process invoking ordeals that tested physical and spiritual resources to the ultimate and challenged the human will to address, survive, and transcend pain, always seeking and drawing strength from a pantheon of deities whose power and wisdom resided with the ancestors, the guarantors of society's integrity.

Female status within such cultures was clearly articulated and structured to ensure respect and self-respect. Motherhood, sisterhood, age, and healing gifts assumed supreme significance in African women's world view. It was a view perpetuated through chant and drum and dance, languages virtually impenetrable to the outsider or slaveholder but full of meaning for generations of the enslaved and increasingly for the musicologists, linguists, and other cultural explorers of today, without whom that world view could not be reconstructed. Among its main references is a history of regal women, not unlike Nanny of the Maroons.

Wonderful things happened on the journey into that rebel past, of which Nanny became the permanent, powerful icon. I can here only briefly indicate the personal process of self-growth it meant. No one could spend so many years in the company of such women and remain the same. The expansion of one's emotional and intellectual resources, the deepened pride in one's inheritance and in one's womanhood were inevitable and are subjects for another article.

More relevant was the great occasion when a personal conviction about Nanny's profound significance for the Jamaican psyche became a public reality. I advanced it as an opinion and a recommendation, and in 1975 the Jamaican government proclaimed her Right Excellency and thereby enshrined her among the galaxy of national heroes, Paul Bogle, George William Gordon, Marcus Garvey, William Bustamante, and Norman Manley.

Somewhere along the way, I noted that Brathwaite's great verse trilogy of the African diaspora, The Arrivants, is inspired by the almost exclusive assumption of a "poor, pathless, harborless spade," who is male. The next epic creation of this historian-poet-visionary, was his Mother Poem, which met the challenge splendidly. Brathwaite also invited me to join him in filling a vacuum in the existing literature by editing a special volume of the journal of the Caribbean Artists Movement, Savacou, on Caribbean women's writing, and for the first time, such a collection appeared in 1977. It contained contributions among others by participants of this conference such as Merle Hodge, Lorna Goodison, and Opal Palmer. It also contained Maureen Lewis's article "The Nkuyu: Spirit Messengers of the

Kumina," an essay of seminal importance in the growing body of Caribbean literature which acknowledges the integrity of the oral tradition and finds a respected place for "groups like Queenie's Kumina bands which today attempt to preserve a sense of historical continuity through spiritual and cultural means." This pioneer publication was dedicated to the memory of the Jamaican poet and playwright Una Marson, another precious and precocious spirit. She would have been at home with her wayward ancestors, those fractious females who ridiculed their masters, downed their tools, harassed the courts, placed themselves between their children and the slave driver, refused to give birth on order, planted their food crops, walked ten miles to market, flaunted their bright finery, and disappeared in the melting pot of towns, where they joined the men in plotting poison, arson, and rebellion.

One might ask, Where on earth did such women, the "subordinate" sex, get this nerve? Perhaps it came from their very subordination—the moral force of the powerless confronting the powerful—and also from their ability to draw strength from that inheritance of ancestral spirits from the other side of the ocean.

The militant acts and words of Afro-Jamaican women were neither isolated nor inadvertent. They constituted a political strategy that took different forms at different times but at all times expressed the conscious resolve of the African enslaved to confront the New World plantation's assault on their person and their culture. "Victimization," as Herbert Aptheker has written, "does not simply make victims: it also produces heroes." We might add, "and heroines too." Women expressed the will to resist with an intensity fueled by their outrage at the sexual violence in their lives. The passion and persistence of their heroic acts of self-affirmation and rebellion rescued them from silence and invisibility and embedded the meaning of those acts in a people's memory.

Many Caribbean women writers today, also engaged in their acts of conscious self-affirmation, explore history, myth, and memory, seeking cultural continuities. Refusing to pursue futility, they seldom lament the absence of ruins. On the contrary, they celebrate their presence, not the presence of fragmented, desolate remnants that signify nothing, but valued monuments, human artifacts, ready to receive vibrant new forms through the genius of those pens which are today busily creating praise songs for Caribbean women. And here, of course, is where the journey has brought me.

Bibliography

Aptheker, Herbert. *American Negro Slave Revolts*. New York: International Publishers, 1969.

Brathwaite, Edward Kamau. *The Arrivants, A New World Trilogy: Rights of Passage, 1967: Masks, 1968: Islands, 1969.* Oxford University Press, 1973.
———. *The Development of Creole Society in Jamaica, 1770–1820.* Oxford: Clarendon Press, 1971.
———. *Mother Poem.* Oxford University Press, 1972.
———. *Wars of Respect: Nanny, Sam Sharpe and the Struggle for People's Liberation.* Kingston: Agency for Public Information, 1977.
Goveia, Elsa. *Slave Society in the British Leeward Islands at the End of the Eighteenth Century.* New Haven: Yale University Press, 1965.
———. *A Study on the Historiography of the British West Indies to the End of the Nineteenth Century.* Washington, D.C.: Howard University Press, 1980.
Jacobs, Harriet. *Incidents in the Life of a Slave Girl, Written by Herself.* Edited by L. Maria Child. Cambridge, Mass.: Harvard University Press, 1965.
Mathurin Mair, Lucille. "The Arrivals of Black Women." *Jamaica Journal: Quarterly of the Institute of Jamaica* (1975).
———. Ed. with Brathwaite, Edward. "Caribbean Woman." *Savacou* (1977).
———. "Creole Authenticity," review article on Edward Brathwaite's *The Development of Creole Society in Jamaica, 1770–1820. Savacou* (June 1971).
———. "Erotic Expediency: the Early Growth of the Mulatto Group in West Africa." *Caribbean Journal of African Studies* (1978).
———. "A Historical Study of Women in Jamaica, 1655–1844." Ph.D. dissertation, University of the West Indies, 1974.
———. *The Rebel Woman in the British West Indies during Slavery.* Kingston: Institute of Jamaica, 1975.
———. "Women Field Workers in Jamaica during Slavery." Elsa Goveia Memorial Lecture, Department of History, University of the West Indies, 1987.
Patterson, Orlando. *Die the Long Day.* New York: Morrow, 1972.
———. *The Sociology of Slavery.* London: MacGibbon and Kee, 1967.
Seacole, Mary. *Wonderful Adventures of Mary Seacole in Many Lands.* London: James Blackwood, 1857.

Feminism, Nationalism, and the Early Women's Movement in the English-Speaking Caribbean (with Special Reference to Jamaica and Trinidad and Tobago)

RHODA REDDOCK

> That's the basic error of the so-called feminist movement, which is really a masculinist movement. The pervasity of this philosophy is the false assumption that men and women are the same kind of being, and that woman has been kept down by man and has lapsed into an inferior position. Hence it urges women to force themselves onto the same level as man, learning to do all the things men do and behaving as men behave. But this is trying to change nature itself.
> —*Port of Spain Gazette*, September 27, 1927

According to one writer, the first recorded use of the term *feminism* in English was in 1894, close to fifty years after what we now know as the first feminist wave was supposed to have emerged. This term, according to the 1933 Supplement to the *Oxford English Dictionary*, was derived from the French *féminisme*, first coined by Utopian socialist Charles Fourier (Rendall, 1985: 1).

For those of us former colonials who write in the English language, the contradiction of defining our cultural autonomy in the language of the colonizers is a problem we face daily and in some ways surmount. But possibly no other word in modern times has been so vilified for its European origins as *feminism* and its derivative *feminist*.

For us Caribbean women, in recent times the struggle to define our womanness as well as our Caribbeanness has, especially in the 1960s and 1970s, been fraught with demands that we deny and reject any feminist consciousness or the need for a feminist struggle. Feminist consciousness and action preceded the actual coining of the word. This was so not only in Europe, but in all parts of the world where women (at rare times with the support of men) have sought to challenge the subordination and exploitation that have to varying degrees been the history of most women.

What is interesting about emergent feminism is its tendency to develop out of the wombs of other social movements. Contradictorily, it is often the attempts by males to reject this natural interrelationship between movements for women's emancipation and other movements for class, national, or ethnic emancipation that provides the impetus for the emergence of the feminist question.

This essay defines feminism very simply as the awareness of the subordination and exploitation of women in society and the conscious action to change that situation. Feminists differ in their understanding of the nature of the problem and therefore on the strategies for its solution. This paper aims to explore the manifestations of feminist consciousness during the first half of the twentieth century in Jamaica and Trinidad and Tobago. Characteristic of the early women's movement in the English-speaking Caribbean was its close association with the nationalist struggle in its peculiarly Caribbean form.

Little theoretical work has so far been done on the national question in the English-speaking Caribbean. In an area consisting primarily of the descendants of migrants, the search for a national identity goes beyond the boundaries of the individual island, or indeed of the Caribbean region as a whole. Within the English-speaking Caribbean, nationalism during the early twentieth century usually implied an identification with Africa or India for the majority of the people, at a time when these two continents were also under the yoke of colonial rule. In spite of this difference a clear link between the movement for women's emancipation and nationalist movements characteristic of many other parts of the colonial world could be discerned. In the words of Kumari Jayawardena,

> The movement for women's emancipation and the feminist struggles which emerged in Asia and Africa must be considered in the context of the resistance that developed in many countries to imperialism and various forms of foreign domination on the one hand, and to movements of opposition to feudal monarchies, exploitive local rulers and traditional patriarchal and religious structures on the other. (Jayawardena, 1982:8)

In common with other countries, two streams can be discerned. The first contained the dominant middle-class or bourgeois nationalists, many of whom were educated in the colonial country and imbibed colonial liberal values of progress and advancement. The second contained the working-class nationalists strongly influenced by socialist and particularly Marxist (Comintern) approaches to the "national question." By far the majority of the early feminists were associated with the first stream. Many of them were middle-class, educated, cultured ladies who sought to improve the lot of their sex and race. Not surprisingly, their demands reflected the strong influence of liberalism—the right to education, citizenship, and political participation.

For most of these middle-class nationalists, in spite of a reidentification with the ancestral culture, the adoption of "modern" (read "Western") values on family, economy, and society were paramount. Education in general, and for women in particular, was to be the key to enlightenment and modernization. In Asia this meant the rejection of "backward" practices against women such as suttee and foot-binding; in the Caribbean it often meant the rejection of the so-called matrifocal family and female economic autonomy (now known to be largely the result of African adaptations in the New World) and a stress on the Euro-Christian Western nuclear family.

Central to this process were the male reformers, men who went out of their way (sometimes paternistically, sometimes not) to champion the women's cause. Some of these men, the modern educated men, needed companions of equal stature who could converse with them and see to the education of their children. Others believed that basic rights for women in the colonies were only reasonable if these women were to be brought in line with those of the mother country. Still others reflected a genuine concern for the denial of humanity to one half of the human race.

I hope to make it clear that whatever the context, feminism has not been a 1960s import into the Caribbean. The modern women's movement in the English-speaking Caribbean is the continuation of a rich struggle for women's emancipation, a struggle fraught with contradictions but one nevertheless firmly based within the sociopolitical and historical context of the region.

THE WOMEN'S MOVEMENT, 1900–1950: THE WOMEN'S SELF-HELP MOVEMENT

One of the earliest manifestations of women organizing in their own interest was the Women's Self-Help Movement. The first such group, the Lady Musgrave Self-Help Society of Jamaica, founded in 1865, stated as its aim the development "of feminine industries such as embroideries, native jams, jellies and drawn thread work to provide employment for poor needlewomen" (French and Fordsmith, 1984: 170). These self-help societies, although ostensibly to assist poor women, were a main means through which upper-class ladies, white and colored, attempted to gain some economic autonomy or even to survive economically in spite of the norms of society.

The Trinidad and Tobago equivalent, the Trinidad Home Industries and Women's Self-Help Society, was established in 1901 following the example of the Jamaica society. This organization, however, was much more explicit in stating its true aim of providing a means through which "all gentlewomen in reduced circumstances should be assisted to add to their incomes" (Trinidad Information Bureau, 1919:35–36).

A similar organization, the Barbados Women's Self-Help, still exists today. In general, all three organizations provided retail outlets for handicraft and preserves produced by women and sought to train young women in "housewifery skills." In 1899, black activist Robert Love criticized the Jamaica society for "pushing the work of poor women to one side to make way for the work of the upper crust" (*Advocate*, June 10, 1899, quoted in French and Fordsmith, 1984: 171).

It is important to note the class of women involved in this "income-generating" activity. Lady Musgrave, founder of the Jamaica society, was the wife of the governor. In 1901, the Trinidad society was inaugurated by Mrs. Maloney, also a governor's wife, and the revitalized society in 1904 had as its first president another governor's wife, Mrs. Hugh Clifford.

Historically, these groups have usually been perceived as charities, largely because of the widely held view that social or religious work was the only acceptable public activity for women of that class. Apparently this was an issue of some debate in Trinidad society. According to one member, in the beginning many "ladies" refused to work in shops. They would surreptitiously have their products delivered but did not want to be seen to be "in reduced circumstances." Others felt that the work should be done "for sweet charity's sake" because for them working for money was beneath their station. Clearly, this latter view was a minority one. Most of the women saw themselves as making a statement for "honest work" and breaking away from "false pride." They even criticized the common practice of hiring "coolies" to carrying parcels and the shame felt by both women and men in carrying parcels. They defended their right to work when they were attacked for being vulgar (Aldric-Perez, 1920:11).

Clearly, even among the colonial elite of the Caribbean at this time, women could not depend economically on their male breadwinners. In addition, as with some women of their class in other countries, they defended their right to earn an income even in ways circumscribed by the bourgeois sexual division of labor.

THE MIDDLE-STRATA WOMEN'S MOVEMENT

Although social work was not the primary concern of the early self-help movement, this would not be true of other early organizations of women. During the late nineteenth and early twentieth centuries, social work was a highly prestigious activity carried out primarily by the white women of the local and colonial ruling classes. Later in the century and up to the 1950s, women activists of the labor and feminist movements incorporated social work into their political activity as a significant component. For most of these groups, social work with women and girls was especially important.

In 1918, the Women's Social Service Club (WSSC) was formed in Jamaica. Like most middle-strata women's organizations of the time, its attempts to uplift womanhood seldom went outside the parameters of domesticity, morality, and class-boundness defined by the colonial ideology. One of the main foci of the group was women's employment—a recurrent theme in the Caribbean women's movement. Others included illegitimacy and political representation (French and Fordsmith, 1984: 177–86). Unlike the self-help movement, however, the middle-strata women's movement's emphasis was on employment for the working classes and not for themselves, employment in areas suitable to their sex and station in life. In 1919, for example, the WSSC established a Girls' Workroom, training unemployed women in handicraft and needlework and seeking markets for their products. This project expanded to other parts of Jamaica by 1921.

In its campaign against moral vice, the WSSC reflected many of the views of early twentieth-century feminists on women's moral responsibility. They collaborated with the Social Purity Association (SPA) of Jamaica, which was formed in 1917 for the purpose of eradicating immorality and venereal disease (French and Fordsmith, 1984:180). The SPA and WSSC attacked prostitution and joined with the Jamaica Baptist Union to ensure the responsibility of fathers. Although sympathetic with the plight of unmarried mothers and their difficulties with the bureaucracy in getting support from fathers, the transition to the recognition of mothers as economic breadwinners was never made.

The main political struggle was for women's representation on the Legislative Council. In making their demands, women used their housewifery management experience to justify their potential contribution to government. Though seeking political equality for themselves, they accepted that such rights need not be extended to the working classes. A pattern of a complex division of labor based on sex, race, and class becomes apparent. Income-earning activity was necessary for the poor (black) working-class women but not for women of the upper class. These women, however, were due the same political rights as their menfolk, rights that could not be extended to working-class women.

For most of these early twentieth-century middle-strata women's organizations, charity and not solidarity characterized their relationships with women of other classes and ethnic groups.

In 1921, the first of the black middle-strata women's organizations was formed in Trinidad and Tobago. It was the Coterie of Social Workers (CSW) founded by Audrey Layne Jeffers, a member of the then small well-to-do black property-owning class. Although Jeffers could be described politically as a feminist and a black nationalist, like others throughout the world the class differential between herself and those she sought to serve was never in question. In addition, like other black nationalists, especially during the early years, the struggle for the dignity of non-European people took place within the context of the British Empire.

The Coterie membership consisted mainly of black and colored women of the educated middle classes. For these women, participation in social work, once the preserve of the European ladies, was a significant means of raising the status of people of African origin in general and of their class in particular. Participation in social work also became increasingly a form of social fulfillment as more and more women were excluded from the labor force during the post-World War I economic depression. In 1934–35, civil service legislation and the education code banned the employment of married women except when no alternative could be found.

The feminist component of the activities of the Coterie was evident in its social work as well as in its political work. In the 1920s, for example, it founded the St. Mary's Home for Blind Girls and the Maud Reeves Hostel for Working Girls. In 1935, the Bishop Anstey House for (Respectable) Women was founded.

A significant aspect of CSW activity lay in alleviating much of the child-care burden of working-class mothers. This was attempted through the establishment of a school meal program popularly known as Breakfast Sheds, which spread throughout the country, including Tobago. Children at primary schools received hot meals daily free of cost or for one penny. In addition, the CSW established the first day-care centers for children initially in John John, a poor working-class urban area.

In addition to the Coterie's focus on women and girls, an emphasis on the plight of nonwhite women and girls was also evident. During her student years in Britain, Jeffers had been one of the founders of the Union of Students of African Descent, later the League of Colored Peoples. During World War I she had served among the West African troops and started a West African Soldiers Fund (Comma-Maynard, 1971:2).

In its nationalist and political activity the Coterie collaborated with the socialist-oriented Trinidad Workingmen's Association (TWA). Although the Coterie was clearly influenced by that association, there is less evidence of its collaboration with the Garvey movement—the United Negro Improvement Association (UNIA)—which was popular at this time. In 1936, four Coterie members attended the Negro Progress Convention held in British Guiana. They were Laura Beard, Mrs. Scott, Budosy Jeffers, and southern social worker Marcelline Archibald. At this convention, which marked the one hundredth year of freedom from slavery, Audrey Jeffers at a special women's section spoke on women and their responsibility to the race. She called on women to take a serious view of life and to come forward and help in the new epoch of reconstruction of the race (Comma-Maynard, 1971:92–93).

During the late 1920s and early 1930s, three significant events took place. These were the struggle of women to be eligible for seats on the Port of Spain City Council, the Divorce Bill Agitation, and the West Indian and British Guiana Conference of Women Social Workers. Examination of these events is crucial to an understanding of the character of the feminist struggle during this period.

In Jamaica, the equivalent of the Coterie of Social Workers appears to have been the Jamaica Women's Liberal Club (LC), formed around 1937. This organization, consisting mainly of black middle-strata women, carried the women's struggle begun by the Women's Social Service Club in new directions. The core of this organization, according to French and Fordsmith (1984), was a small group of women teachers who had begun to agitate within the Jamaica Union of Teachers for jobs for women in the administration of education and in the colonial civil service in general. Leading members of this group included Amy Bailey, Mary Morris Knibb, and Edith Dalton James. In a speech in 1938, Amy Bailey noted:

> The time has come for women teachers from all colleges to get together and demand improvements which are theirs by right. Why is it that there are no women assistant inspectors drawn from the ranks of the elementary school? If the principal is good enough for men, it is surely good enough for us women. (*Gleaner*, April 26, 1938, quoted in French and Fordsmith, 1984)

As did the Coterie, LC members saw themselves as establishing a place for women within the developing national identity of their country. They saw women's place as clearly defined by their class, however, and accepted their natural superiority in relation to women of the laboring classes. The LC was also influenced by the ideas of Jamaican black nationalist leader Marcus Mosiah Garvey. The early aims and objectives of the club included the study of Negro history, native and foreign, and the advance of the status of Jamaican women socially and politically.

Leading member Amy Bailey defined herself as a feminist and took up a personal campaign against the refusal of commercial enterprises to hire black women. This issue had also been taken up by Audrey Jeffers in Trinidad in 1936 because black women were not yet accepted as suitable advertisement for commercial wares.

Acceptance of class differentiation by these early middle-strata feminists was a key factor in determining their social and political action. On the one hand, there was general acceptance of the colonial housewife ideology, which identified the dependent housewife and male breadwinner as the key actors of the bourgeois family. These feminists, however, accepted the right of women to earn an income even though they felt that this should be done in activities suitable to women's sex and station in life. The LC, in recognizing the contribution of women volunteers to the social services, therefore argued that they should be paid by the state for their work.

The emergence of the Domestic Science/Home Economics movement in North America as an influential section of the women's movement affected these Caribbean feminists. Bailey saw training in domestic science as one means through which women's work within the home could be given dignity. This could take place at two levels, first among middle-strata housewives, who could present certificates to their men showing their ability to "cook *his* food, spend *his* money wisely and train *his* children properly" (Bailey, 1938, quoted in French and Fordsmith, 1984:255, emphasis added). At another level, domestic science could be the basis of vocational training to prepare underprivileged girls for jobs as waitresses, cooks, laundresses, upholsterers, domestics, and dressmakers.

As with feminists throughout the world at this time, little challenge was made to the existing sexual division of labor. Indeed, training in domestic work was a major means of bringing black women closer to European levels of housewifery and domesticity. This movement, unfortunately, was perceived as progress and upliftment.

Today, as Caribbean women contemplate the regional character of our struggle, it is important that we examine earlier efforts in this direction. In April of 1936, the Coterie celebrated its fifteenth anniversary with a little-remembered conference of West Indian and British Guianese women social workers in Port of Spain. The conference was attended by delegates from British Guiana, Barbados, Grenada, and St. Lucia, and it ended with the formation of the West Indies and British Guiana Women Social Workers Association. Throughout the conference a speaking ban was placed on all men who attended. It was temporarily lifted for one evening, when Jeffers announced that "men would be permitted to say a few words" but would not be allowed to ask questions. The highlight of the event was the speech by Audrey Jeffers, "The Urgent Needs of Women in Trinidad." She began by stating that:

> The needs of our women to my mind have been seriously neglected in the past. The men made it a transient concern and the women in high places socially and intellectually took a rather lukewarm interest in their own sex. (*Trinidad Guardian*, May 20, 1936, p. 8)

After an analysis of women's condition, especially that of black and colored women, she called for a scholarship for girls, the establishment of a high school for girls, and the establishment of a women's police force.

One of the most radical speeches of the event was given by Gertie Wood of British Guiana in "Political Aspirations and Achievements of Women in British Guiana." This speech reflected many of the contradictions in consciousness inherent in the early women's movement. In the area of employment, Miss Wood noted:

> Women are engaged in the civil service, in commerce, in teaching, farming, in the professions, in trades, in fact in every branch of life of the Colony. I submit, and do so quite soberly, that woman has attained this position not because things were made easy for her by the powers that be. No! Oh no!—but because, ladies and gentlemen, she has proved without a shadow of a doubt that when she chooses her life job and trains for it she does it with her will, sparing not even herself in the execution of her duty. (*Trinidad Guardian*, May 8, 1936, p. 8)

She pointed out that the army of women engaged in domestic service and as homemakers "bear the brunt of their sex" silently without realizing it. In this way they put in far more self-sacrificing work than did men. She added that women had been taught to bow and smile to men for so long that now in the New Era, when conditions had changed, women were still too timid to do otherwise. In spite of the strident tone of most of her talk, she concluded in a conciliatory manner:

> I am an advocate of "Women's Rights," but am not an extremist and have no patience with extremists, for I know and believe that there is much that man alone can do, so we still have need for them . . . But we aspire to a fair and square deal to be meted out to women workers. (*Trinidad Guardian*, May 8, 1936, p. 8)

Not surprisingly, the next conference was planned for British Guiana and did take place. It was the forerunner of subsequent regional organizations of women that developed over the course of this century.

THE STRUGGLE FOR POLITICAL RIGHTS

The role of male reformers was extremely significant in the struggle for women's rights in many colonial countries. In many instances early feminists had to depend on these liberal or progressive men who held positions of power and influence to champion their legal and political causes. Although gains were made in this area at different periods during the century in both Jamaica and Trinidad and Tobago, the significant political battles took place at different times. In Jamaica, for example, the campaign for the extension of the franchise to women began in the aftermath of World War I, when women of the British middle classes had been granted the vote.

The campaign in Jamaica had the support of black members of the Kingston Council, as well as some sections of the emerging commercial bourgeoisie and its organ, the *Gleaner*. A leading champion was H. A. G. de Lisser, secretary of the Jamaica Imperial Association, which supported planter interests. The *Gleaner* argued that women had performed well during the war. They had done work which had previously been done only by men, and therefore deserved representation (*Gleaner*, July 4, 1918). It was clear, however, that the extension was to be limited to the "better class of women." De Lisser warned against "an army of women voters" swamping the votes of men, women who were not intellectually or academically their equals, and to ensure that this would not happen, he proposed a literacy test.

Black Council members such as Garveyite supporter H. A. Simpson proposed an extension of the franchise to include the black and colored middle strata. This, however, was not to be (French and Fordsmith, 1984:187). In spite of this support, a more forceful campaign was needed to make even this limited gain. This campaign was eventually led by the Women's Social Service Club. Arguments against the franchise of women were similar to those in other countries, but some typically Caribbean ones also emerged. For example, one man feared that women would close down all rum shops and force the registration of fathers of illegitimate children (*Gleaner*, September 9, 1918). Another argument suggested that women's lack of political advancement was the result of their own lack of interest.

Women of the WSSC responded to these attacks through letters in the press, a women's petition, and demonstrations at Ward theater and public meetings. In July 1919, the franchise was extended to women over twenty-five years of age who earned an income of £50 or paid taxes of over £2 per year. Men could vote at the age of twenty-one if their annual income was £40 per year. Few men but even fewer women became eligible for the franchise, but no women could become candidates.

In Trinidad and Tobago, the struggle for women to become eligible for seats on the Port of Spain City Council was another milestone in the regional movement for women's political rights. Although initiated by women, it was eventually taken through the council by male reformer Captain Arthur Andrew Cipriani. On September 8, 1924, according to the *Mirror Almanack*, a delegation of women was received by the governor to discuss the issue of votes for women. This even took place within an atmosphere of legislative reform, which was being considered at the time.

In 1924, a new constitution was introduced. Although elected officials (members) were introduced into the Legislative Council, high property qualifications for voting and even higher ones for candidature were instituted. As a result, only six percent of the total population was eligible to vote (Brereton, 1981:166). To vote, men who qualified had to be over the age of twenty-one and women over thirty. Only men literate in English with large amounts of property or considerable income could become candidates.

Although the 1924 delegation may have called for further legislative reform, it was at the municipal level that the struggle was first manifested. In August 1927, Captain A. A. Cipriani, deputy mayor and president of the Trinidad Workingmen's Association (TWA), moved a motion in the Port of Spain Town Council calling for amendment of the Corporation Ordinance to make women eligible for seats on the council.

In supporting this motion, Cipriani noted that such action had already been taken in other parts of the British Empire and that since the war, women were holding their own in jobs in commerce, banks, and business firms, doing jobs previously carried out by men (*Trinidad Guardian*, September 26, 1927, p. 6). The motion was referred to a committee for consideration over one month, but during that period much debate occurred. It was the beginning of a long struggle, which did not end until 1935. The *Port of Spain Gazette* denounced the feminist movement, finding women chauffeurs, air pilots, professionals, and other "blue-stockinged women" to be "out of place" (*Port of Spain Gazette*, September 25, 1927). But numerous other articles in this and other newspapers reflect the various aspects of the debate.

Although the *Port of Spain Gazette* denounced the issue, the *Trinidad Guardian* bemoaned in an editorial that so far women of the city had given no public demonstration of their views:

> Certainly when their case was being put forward for the first time, one would have expected to see the leading feminists of Trinidad (if there are any) present to encourage and applaud their champion. But there were none. The development of political consciousness in the women of Trinidad does not therefore seem yet to have reached the articulate stage. (*Trinidad Guardian*, September 28, 1927, p. 10)

The *Labour Leader*, organ of the TWA, supported Cipriani's notion and pointed out that women had made no public demonstration because they knew they would win sooner or later and were content to wait. The paper threw out the challenge to find five women as qualified and suitable to sit on the council as any five men whom those opposing the motion could find (*Labour Leader*, September 3, 1927, p. 8).

It is interesting that although the leading feminists of the day were of the landowning or at least the upper middle classes, their support came from the socialist-oriented TWA. Cipriani, a Trinidadian of Caucasian origin, was a landowner who had taken over leadership of the TWA in 1923. The TWA was oriented along Fabian socialist lines and followed the line of the British Labour party. Although worker-oriented, Cipriani sought a rapprochement between labor and capital and saw himself as the mediator between the two—the champion of the barefoot man. As mediator, Cipriani often sought to reduce direct confrontation between opposing forces. Diplomacy and discussion, usually by him on behalf of others, was often his solution.

One woman, however, made public her demands for women's political rights. She was Beatrice Greig, a Scotswoman and wife of a planter who supported feminist and worker-oriented causes. On March 13, 1928, Greig gave a public address, "The Position of Women in Public Life," at the Richmond Street Literary and Debating Association (*Mirror Almanack*, 1929). Throughout this struggle she was the main female protagonist in support of Cipriani's motion, arguing that women were ready to serve because they voted and paid taxes. This argument was strongly rejected by the *Port of Spain Gazette* (September 16, 1927) as not being representative of her sex.

On September 29, 1927, the committee of the town council considering the motion rejected any change in the ordinance. Many male radicals, including Dr. Tito Achong and Alfred Richards, voted against the motion. Again, the arguments against any change were similar to those heard in other countries. Achong argued that in this country women were not sufficiently educationally qualified to deal with the issues of taxation, sanitation, and engineering which were often raised in the council. But he went even further, stating that "at a certain stage of a woman's life she was not even fit to give evidence before a court of law" (*Trinidad Guardian*, September 30, 1927, p. 9). Again, the issue of women's apathy was raised. One councillor suggested they had not asked to serve, and another concluded that they preferred to leave such matters to their husbands, brothers, and other men.

The arguments in favor of the motion excelled in literary eloquence. Councillor Archibald accused the council of being like the mad hatter at the tea party in *Alice in Wonderland* who shouted "No! No!"—to which

Alice replied, "There is plenty of room," and seated herself in a large armchair at the head of the table.

In the end, the motion was rejected by the mayor's deciding vote (*Port of Spain Gazette*, September 30, 1927, p. 12; October 7, 1927, p. 9). The motion was rejected again in April of 1929 but was eventually carried on May 29, 1930, with Cipriani's (as mayor) deciding vote. On this occasion fifty women attended the session. It was not until January 1935, however, that this amendment was actually accepted into the corporation ordinance.

One year later, in 1936, two women presented themselves as candidates for the town council. They were Audrey Layne Jeffers and Beatrice Greig, the country's two foremost social workers and feminists. This move was welcomed by the *Trinidad Guardian* which, in an editorial entitled "Challenge by Women," patronizingly noted:

Should either of the two candidates be elected, an important stimulus would be given to the Women's Movement, which appears to be gathering force in the West Indies and which recently produced the first inter-colonial conference of women welfare workers ever convened in this part of the world . . . The appearance of these two women pioneers in the municipal election area is to be welcomed. They deserve the sympathetic consideration of the burgesses of Port of Spain. And, should they win, the men candidates whom they are expected to oppose could feel that they had lost gloriously to women—albeit of the "weaker sex"—entirely worth their steel. (*Trinidad Guardian*, October 1, 1936, p. 6).

The atmosphere during the rest of the campaign was much less accommodating. One early casualty was Beatrice Greig, whose qualification papers were rejected. The qualifications of Audrey Jeffers were later also questioned, and the issue was eventually taken to court. Opposing Jeffers in the Woodbrook seat was A.P.T. Ambard of the *Port of Spain Gazette*, which had consistently campaigned against seats for women on the council. The election campaign for Audrey Jeffers served as a rallying point for middle-strata women. The court action unsuccessfully served against her only added controversy to the event and awakened greater interest. The *Trinidad Guardian* noted:

Municipal elections continue to provide many thrills, particularly in Woodbrook . . . In this centre Trinidad women are very active and getting ready to give the lie to the statement that they do not wish to be interested in local politics, for they are determined to see Miss Jeffers win. (*Trinidad Guardian*, October 21, 1936, p. 1)

Opposing candidate Ambard was accused of being fascist because he had declared himself on the side of the Spanish fascists who supported

Italy and Germany. In the aftermath of the 1935 Italian invasion of Ethiopia by Mussolini, antifascist, antiracist feeling ran high in Trinidad and Tobago. Responding to this issue, Cipriani declared, "Those who vote for Italy vote Ambard. Those who are voting Ethiopia are voting Miss Jeffers." Ironically, in spite of the class contradictions that continued to be reflected in Jeffers's life, the feminist struggle found its natural (although not always accepted) ally in the workers' and anti-fascist movement. On November 3, 1936, Audrey Jeffers won the Woodbrook seat in the municipal elections, defeating her two opponents and becoming the first woman to contest and win an election in Trinidad and Tobago.

In Jamaica, in the aftermath of the 1938 labor disturbances, women became eligible for seats on municipal councils. In 1939, the Jamaica Women's Liberal Club organized a campaign that resulted in the election of Mary Morris Knibb to the Kingston/St. Andrew Parish Council. As in Trinidad and Tobago, her election proved to be an important rallying point for middle-strata women.

AFRO-CARIBBEAN NATIONALISM AND THE WOMEN'S MOVEMENT

By the late nineteenth century, Afro-Caribbean nationalism and the struggle for women's emancipation had become linked. This was evident in one of the earliest organizations, the Pan African Association (PAA) founded by Trinidadian Henry Sylvester Williams, and its Jamaican counterpart, the People's Convention of Robert Love. According to his biographer Owen Mathurin, Williams emphasized women's participation in the political struggle. In his speeches Williams stressed the involvement of women in the PAA as well as the need for education for girls. Not surprisingly, Williams claims to have first been politically influenced by a woman, Mrs. Kinloch, who spoke in London on the situation in southern Africa. In his 1901 Caribbean tour, therefore, the mobilization of women was a key component of his work.

In Jamaica, a branch of the PAA was founded by radical black nationalist Robert Love after Williams's visit in 1901. Love had previously founded another organization, the People's Convention, in 1895 to assist in the election of blacks to the Legislative Council (French and Fordsmith, 1984: 201–4). The PAA in Jamaica maintained Williams's position on the involvement of women, and the secretary of the Kingston branch, Cathryn McKenzie, can be identified as one of the earliest black feminists in the region (Fordsmith, 1987:1–2).

In a paper entitled "The Rights of Women," published on August 10, 1901, in the *Advocate*, the organ of the People's Convention, Cathryn McKenzie put forward her view on women's emancipation. She argued that "the rights of women left much to be desired" and counseled that only by struggle could women ever win their rights. She referred to the struggles of American and British feminists and the efforts to achieve equality and education for women.

Little else is known of McKenzie because she died soon after in a fire. The work in women's emancipation was continued, however, through the PAA and the People's Convention and in the pages of the *Advocate*. Unlike with the middle-strata women's organizations that developed later, Robert Love challenged the existing sexual division of labor and the sexual division within the school curriculum. He opposed the limiting of girls' education to female teachers and the "domestic focus" in women's education.

The People's Convention was particularly concerned with the need for economic independence of poor black women, and championed their right to land as a means of achieving this independence. It supported one female teacher against the loss of her pension. In the words of French and Fordsmith:

> The People's Convention supported unequivocally the admission of black women of the middle class to all professions and to administrative positions. It tentatively put forward the right of working class women to an independent income and sought to break the skewed sexual division of labour of the period. It was one of the few organizations which does not seem to have seen the solution to the problems of working-class women in their training to be domestic servants and handicraft experts. (French and Fordsmith, 1984:213)

In spite of the PAA's relatively progressive position on women, its influence regionally and internationally was limited. A later organization, the United Negro Improvement Association (UNIA), was to be much more influential in scope both in this region and overseas. UNIA was founded in July of 1914 by Marcus Mosiah Garvey and Amy Ashwood, later Garvey. From an organization of two persons it grew to become one of the largest mass movements of all time. At its height in the 1920s, according to Garvey historian Tony Martin, there were over twelve hundred branches in more than forty countries, a large proportion of which were in the Caribbean, the United States, Canada, and Africa (Martin, 1987:11).

The involvement of Amy Ashwood in the early formation of UNIA may have contributed to the significance of the mobilization of women in the Garvey movement. Amy Ashwood was the first secretary of the Ladies Division of UNIA (Martin, 1987:33), which apparently developed into the Black Cross Nurses section of UNIA. Through its organizational structure, UNIA assured the participation of women in several ways. One of these was through the institution of specific leadership positions for women such as lady president and lady vice-president in branches, so that women were always represented at the executive level. There were also two divisions for women only, the Black Cross Nurses and the Universal African Motor Corps, a paramilitary organization that attracted large numbers of women.

In addition to its actual membership, the Garvey movement had a strong influence on middle-strata black and colored women. In addition to fostering racial pride, it provided a place for women in their quest for personal dignity and that of their oppressed race. In Trinidad and Tobago, for example, feminist Audrey Jeffers and women members of the Coterie of Social Workers stressed their aim of raising the status of black and colored women. Similarly, in Jamaica, middle-strata liberal feminists such as Una Marson, Amy Bailey, and others of the Women's Liberal Club challenged the leadership of white upper-class women's organizations (Fordsmith, 1987:16–17).

From within the movement itself there emerged some of the most important women activists. The most well known was, of course, Amy Ashwood Garvey, Pan Africanist and feminist. Until recently very little had been written about the contribution of Amy Ashwood Garvey, first wife of Marcus Garvey, perhaps because unlike his also outstanding second wife Amy Jacques Garvey, she did not easily fit into the mold of loyal and faithful wife, mother, and supporter. In spite of a five-year courtship, the marriage of Amy Ashwood and Marcus Garvey lasted less than three months. The end of the marriage, however, did not mark the end of the political work Amy Ashwood would do until her death in 1969.

In London, Amy Ashwood, an associate of British socialist and feminist Sylvia Pankhurst, helped found the Nigerian Progress Union in 1924, and in 1926 in Harlem she collaborated with her companion Sam Manning of Trinidad in the production of three Afro-American musicals (Martin, 1987: 34). Two events of relevance here reflect clearly the intertwining of Amy Ashwood's nationalism and feminism. These were the Fifth Pan African Congress of 1945 and her Caribbean tour of 1953. As a leading member of the International African Service Bureau, Amy Ashwood Garvey worked with George Padmore, T. R. Makonnen, Kwame Nkrumah, and C. L. R. James in the organization of the important Fifth Pan African Congress. This congress, held October 13–21, 1945, attracted many of the future leaders of Africa and was to have far-reaching consequences. In the booklet commemorating this event, hers is one of the few names omitted from the cover. Her sterling contribution to the cause of Caribbean women, however, is documented within.

Not surprisingly, throughout most of the conference the issue of women was not mentioned. On October 19, however, in opening that day's first session, Amy Ashwood said:

> Very much has been written and spoken of the Negro, but for some reason very little has been said about the black woman. She has been shunted into the social background to be a child-bearer. This has principally been her lot. (Padmore, 1963:52)

In this session Amy Ashwood, together with fellow Jamaican Alma la Badie (the only other woman participant), spoke on the problems of Jamaican women of various classes. In the final resolutions of the conference, those relating to the West Indies were the only ones to include clauses on women. These included demands for equal pay for equal work regardless of nationality, creed, or race; removal of all disabilities affecting the employment of women; modernization of bastardy laws with legal provisions for the registration of fathers; raising the age of consent to sixteen (or eighteen); and others (Padmore, 1963:61). Despite the consistent work of Afro-Caribbean women in the anticolonial and nationalist movement since the late nineteenth century, they remained marginal to that important congress.

In 1953 Amy Ashwood Garvey embarked on her second Caribbean tour. She visited Antigua, Aruba, Barbados, British Guiana, Dominica, Surinam, and Trinidad and Tobago with the aim of stimulating the women's movement. She hoped especially to reach middle-strata women, whom she felt were of the class best poised for enlightened political activity. In Barbados, she presided over the formation of the Barbados Women's Alliance (*Barbados Observer*, March 21, 1953) and lectured widely throughout the region. During her visit to Trinidad she hailed Audrey Jeffers as one of the region's leading feminists and social workers. In the lecture "Women as Leaders of World Thought" she concluded:

> I hope that when the history of the West Indies comes to be written, you will not only write it on West Indian pages in a heroic manner, but that you will join the great women of the world in writing your own history across the pages of world history. (*Port of Spain Gazette*, May 28, 1953, p. 3)

Garveyism undoubtedly provided a significant impetus for the organization of Afro-Caribbean women. In addition, most of the early feminists saw their struggle for women's emancipation as a component of the struggle for racial equality and human dignity. At the same time, the ideology of women and women's place in most cases reflected the colonial thinking on women and the family and its relation to the sexual division of labor and sexuality. The reality of Garveyite women's lives, however, often covered other issues, according to Fordsmith: "It offered black women a concrete experience in organization and leadership which was unrivaled" (Fordsmith, 1987:ii).

INDO-CARIBBEAN NATIONALISM AND THE WOMAN QUESTION

The early twentieth century was a period of heightening nationalist consciousness for Indo-Caribbean people. By 1917, the system of Indian immigration had been ended and an educated and propertied elite was emerging among Indians in Trinidad and Tobago. In addition, contact with the Indian nationalist movement was maintained through periodicals and newspapers as well as through visits of Indian emissaries. Within this movement two tendencies could be identified. The first involved a group of older propertied men who sought communal representation for Indians in the political system, and the second included younger men allied with the TWA who sought a more representative solution.

Throughout most of this period, however, no Indian women emerged as public proponents of their cause. The male writers in the *East Indian Weekly*, organ of the young Indian liberals, made frequent calls for Indian women to come forward to work for the upliftment of their sex. There is little evidence, however, that any did so. Beatrice Greig became the spokesperson on behalf of Indian womanhood in Trinidad and Tobago. Greig, the daughter of Scottish-Canadian missionaries, had lived in Trinidad since the age of sixteen. After a sojourn in India, she returned to Trinidad to marry William Greig, a large landowner. In India, Greig had been influenced by the theosophist movement and had befriended Catherine Mayo, author of the book *Mother India*, which had highlighted the subjugation of women in India.

In many ways Greig can be seen as one of that group of European women—feminists, socialists, and freethinkers—who participated in the anticolonial and women's movements of Third World countries early in this century. Among them were Annie Besant, an English socialist and feminist who became the first president of the Indian National Congress in 1917, and Margaret Cousins, an Irish feminist who was a founder of the All-India Women's Conference in 1927 (Jayawardena, 1986:20–21).

As a contributor to the *East Indian Weekly*, Beatrice Greig consistently raised issues related to Indian women. In January of 1929, for example, during the visit of Indian emissary Pundit Mehta Jaimini, Greig raised the issue of the subjugation of Indian women:

> Mahatmi Jaimini had come from a meeting which he had addressed to women only...He had explained to them that in bygone years, women were free and equal with men, and not to educate them was considered a crime...In reply to my question, "how is it then that Indian women are kept in such darkness and subjugation today?"—he replied that it is due entirely to men's selfishness and ignorance and a desire to have all power in their own hands, and that these evils had gradually been introduced through the ages. (*East Indian Weekly*, February 2, 1929, p. 4)

On her suggestion, Pundit Jaimini gave a public lecture on October 31, 1929, chaired by Beatrice Greig. Using the title "The Ideals of Indian Womanhood," Jaimini put forward clearly the Indian nationalist position on the "upliftment of women." For him, *Sita* was the ideal of Indian womanhood, "with all patience and suffering she is ever chaste"—and he summarized five ideals of Indian womanhood: chastity, devotion to her husband, mistress of the house, production of children as good and useful citizens, and causing peace and happiness in the family and society (*East Indian Weekly*, November 9, 1929, p. 10).

It is not clear whether this talk achieved what Greig hoped it would, but it provides a clear example of the similarity between the Indian nationalist view of uplifted womanhood and the Victorian ideal.

In 1929, Gandhi's assistant C. J. Andrews visited Trinidad and in a meeting of Indian women at Debe denounced child marriage. On his departure, he left the book *Saroj Nalini: A Woman of India*, which was serialized by Greig in the *East Indian Weekly*. Saroj Nalini Dutt was the wife of an Indian nationalist. Her life combined the Indian nationalist ideals of support for Indian nationalism and loyal wifehood. In serializing this book Greig hoped that it would "inspire the Indian woman of Trinidad by her splendid example, enthusiasm and self-sacrifice to follow in her footsteps." This was not to be, and no Mahila Samitis or Ladies Associations were formed (*East Indian Weekly*, January 18, 1929, p. 5).

In addition to the *Weekly*, Greig also wrote the India section in the *Beacon*, literary journal of the 1930s. She founded the Trinidad Association of Girls' Clubs, was a close associate of the Trinidad Workingmen's Association and the early Teachers' Union, and was generally known as a bluestocking. Although the issue of the upliftment of Indian womanhood was a frequent subject in the pages of the *Weekly*, very few Indian women emerged as champions of this cause. The reasons for this cannot be explored here, but later generations of Indian women would make up for the lack. Nevertheless, early in this century women's emancipation and related issues were central to the nationalist debates of both Afro- and Indo-Caribbean people.

CONCLUSION

I have attempted to give a broad and general insight into the early wom-
en's movement in Jamaica and Trinidad and Tobago. One significant
aspect I have omitted is the working-class and socialist women's movement, which will be discussed in another paper. I have tried here to begin
the process of documenting the feminist struggles and movements of the
women of our region. This history is important because it lays a basis
from which we can analyze the processes that have shaped and continue
to influence the situation of women today.

A key issue explored in this paper is the way in which the contradictions
of race, sex, and class played themselves out in the lives and struggles
of these middle-class women. It is interesting that in spite of their charity
toward working-class women, both Amy Bailey and Audrey Jeffers voted
against universal adult suffrage in the 1940s. In addition, like most middle-
strata nationalists of the time, these women fought to attain colonial
European standards rather than to challenge the extension of colonial
values to our countries.

Maybe it is unfair to judge the past according to our understanding of
the present, but the lesson is clear. The solution is not a greater piece of
this exploitive, racist, and patriarchal system, but its fundamental transformation.

Bibliography

Aldric-Perez, J. *A Review of the Trinidad Home Industries Association, 1901–1920.* Port of
    Spain, 1920.
Brereton, Bridget. *A History of Modern Trinidad, 1783–1962.* London: Heinemann, 1981.
Comma-Maynard, Olga. *The Briarend Pattern: The Story of Audrey Jeffers O. B. E. and the
    Coterie of Social Workers.* Port of Spain, 1979.
French, Joan, and Fordsmith, Honor. "Women, Work and Organization in Jamaica,
    1900–1944." Kingston: ISS/DGIS Research Project, 1984.
Fordsmith, Honor. "Women and the Garvey Movement." Mona: University of the
    West Indies, 1987. Paper presented at Marcus Garvey conference.
Garvey, Amy Ashwood. "The Birth of the Universal Negro Improvement Association."
    Introduction by Tony Martin. In Tony Martin, *The Pan-African Connection.* Cam-
    bridge, Mass.: Schenkman, 1983.
Jayawardena, Kumari. *Feminism and Nationalism in the Third World in the Nineteenth and
    Early Twentieth Centuries.* The Hague: ISS, 1982.
———. *Feminism and Nationalism in the Third World.* London: Zed Books, 1986.
Martin, Tony. "Amy Ashwood Garvey: Wife." *Jamaica Journal* 20, no. 3 (August–
    September 1987).
Padmore, George. *History of the Pan African Congress.* 2d ed. London, 1963.

Reddock, Rhoda. "Women, Labour and Struggle in Twentieth Century Trinidad and Tobago, 1898–1900." Ph.D dissertation, University of Amsterdam, 1984.

Rendall, Jane. *The Origins of Modern Feminism*. London: Macmillan, 1985.

Trinidad Information Bureau. *Trinidad: The Riviera of the Caribbean*. Port of Spain, 1919.

The Transatlantic Metropolis
and the Voices of
Caribbean Women

ARTHUR PARIS

I would like to suggest that Afro-Caribbean literary expression and sensibility are rooted not just in the Caribbean, but in the metropoles of the former colonial and (in the case of the United States) neocolonial countries—London, Paris, Amsterdam, New York, and Toronto, for example. The countries of the Atlantic littoral have had a long and close relationship with the Antilles. Over the last century, the direct economic—if not the political—form of that relationship has attenuated, but has nonetheless remained culturally close. France, England, Spain, the Netherlands, and Portugal spread their seed, cultural and otherwise, over these territories. Their offspring, though composed of mixed parentage, are readily recognizable as the descendants of colonial progenitors, despite denials and rejections on both sides. Having exploited these island territories and their populations, the colonial powers sought (or were forced) to dispense with them. But in each instance, as metropolitan preoccupations turned inward rather than outward toward the Caribbean, Antillean influences have made themselves felt within the metropole.

In the United States, the industrial expansion of the late nineteenth and early twentieth centuries was fueled by a wave of first European and then southern black and Caribbean immigration. In Europe, the metropolitan powers initially fed the manpower demands of their industrialization from domestic sources, but after World War II they too brought into their metropolitan centers additional workers skimmed from the European periphery and the overflow of their former colonies. As a result, in case after case the in-migrating population reconstituted the colony in the very marrow of the metropole. Indeed, especially for the smaller territories such as Montserrat and the French Antilles, there may be nearly as large a population in the metropole as in the Antilles.

Migration from these colonies develops unevenly and is tied to the uneven development of industrialization in the metropolitan countries. The United States, for example, brought in labor first from northern Europe, then increasingly from central, eastern, and southern Europe, and most recently from the circum-Caribbean and the American hinterland. One characteristic of this shifting source is that the people brought in at later stages of the process are less "modern" than the northern European workers—except for the Irish—who figured initially. Indeed, some observers characterize these immigrant labor flows as a search for lesser skilled, more traditional peoples whose lack of industrial experience was paralleled by the increasing level of skill and technology embodied in rapidly advancing technology and who could be employed at lower wages than those of the current work force.

In the present century, this progression is not as straightforward. First, the basic industrialization of these economies is complete and the process is no longer driven by the massive need for new labor resources. Labor emigration is still needed but at a much lower level and for "niche" needs.[1] Second, it appears that those who left the Anglophone isles before World War II were more educated and of higher class standing (if not more "modern") than those leaving after midcentury. It also seems that Anglophone emigrants were of higher socioeconomic standing than Latins (Puerto Ricans and Santo Domingans).[2] I make these points because they bear directly on the sociocultural situation of the emigrant communities. The higher the socioeconomic standing of the in-migrating population, the better equipped they are to confront the larger metropolitan culture within which they find themselves and the faster they are able not just to acculturate or assimilate but also to appropriate resources for their own personal and communal needs—as the success of Cubans and Koreans exemplifies. "Folk" immigrants in the first generation are too busy keeping life and limb together to make much headway in becoming "at home" in the new metropolitan culture. They remain necessarily (Russian) Jews, Italians, Slavs, "Jibaros," "strangers in a strange land." For them, it was

---

1. Puerto Ricans, Jamaicans, Barbadians, and others are sought as migrant labor in agriculture; during World War II, Campbell's Soup brought in Puerto Ricans to man its cannery operations in South Jersey. The Puerto Rican influx into New York City after World War II was partially a result of direct importuning by agencies of the city's government.

2. The two Cuban waves, those fleeing Castro in the mid-1960s and the Marielistas in the late 1970s, are exceptions in that they were political émigrés and not part of the larger, more general international flow of labor, even though the ultimate results to which I am alluding may apply to them as well.

not until the second or even the third generation had clambered higher up the socioeconomic ladder that they could confront metropolitan culture and self-consciously take on the process of accommodation and appropriation.[3]

Schooling, the streets, association with other people, and the general metropolitan cultural soup played a counterrefrain to the pull of family and tradition and induced tensions which, for some, could be resolved in cultural expression. Out of this conjuncture arises hyphenated American writing: Irish-American, Italian-American, Jewish-American.[4]

In this regard, a multiple conjuncture occurred. Examples of the personal conjuncture are Paule Marshall and Rosa Guy, who inherited the legacy of Anzia Yezierska from the 1920s, Dorothy West with *The Living is Easy*, and Ann Petry's *The Street* from the 1940s. A more general intellectual and emotional conjuncture is seen in the work of Theodore Dreiser and Stephen Crane, going back to Walt Whitman—all writers seeking to make sense of the new industrial metropolis that emerged as a new form of social life and organization in the late nineteenth century. A specifically female conjuncture occurred in the writings of women. They came to it with a great deal more difficulty than did men. For them, it seemed a much greater moment of self-assertion than it had for men. The last point is the fulcrum on which the earlier ones turn. It is necessary but not sufficient to have potential writers or other high culture creators available. Their muses need both midwives and publics, both of which are part of the metropole equation.

These metropoli are also the loci of cultural hegemony within the particular societies. New York, London, and Paris are well-known cultural hubs: they are the centers of publishing, the theater, and the visual arts in their respective societies. Thus, they are both the site of official culture and the place where its business is conducted. In addition, as metropolitan capitals, they provide venues and substantial audiences for cultural production. The official cultural life of these cities is thus especially rich, if not broadly accessible. This has two effects: the hegemonic cultural milieu ignores and overshadows the dense undergrowth of ethnic and minority subcultures, which is the soil nourishing the minority creators with whom we are concerned, and its apparent accessibility stimulates and broadens the sensibility of potential minority creative persons.[5]

Above and beyond accessibility to the expressions of dominant culture,

---

3. This is a variation on Will Herberg's famous analysis in *Protestant, Catholic and Jew*.
4. This is not an absolutist assertion, and is merely emphatic for the line of argument.
5. These efforts have been extensively chronicled for New York City by Bayard Still in *Mirror for Gotham* (1956) and much earlier for Chicago by Hugh D. Duncan in *The Rise of Chicago as a Literary Center*. Of course, a number of late nineteenth-century European writers (Balzac, Zola, and others) were grappling with the same themes.

the metropole also affords proximity or, even better, access to the cultural arbiters. This is crucial, for it is the arbiters who are the midwives of artistic muses, and through their control of the canons of official taste and their ability to structure and give access to audiences, they encourage and legitimize new—and in this case, minority—voices and enable them to find audiences.

Into the 1970s, such official sanction was mainly the province of black male writers, but the rise of contemporary feminism has given women writers their own cultural arbiters and different access routes to the audience.[6] The addition of these women's publishers and their new definitions of audiences are among the factors enabling minority women writers to sidestep the larger loss of interest in black writing by mainstream publishers. Metropolitan location also means a sizable local audience and market for such work.[7]

Varying combinations of these factors have favored the metropolitan (as opposed to island) emergence of these Caribbean women's voices. Although there has been a well-educated local island elite, even an intellectual one, until recently there has not been a sufficiently educated, nurtured, or affluent mass to constitute a viable audience or market. This would also seem to be one reason for the continued importance of poetry as a medium of literary expression in the English-speaking Caribbean. Mikey Smith and, of late, Sistren, have found in publicly performed *poésie* an effective tool for reaching their audiences.

These patterns seem to replicate themselves around the Atlantic littoral. As the interest in romantic macho militancy has waned, as second- (and later) generation women have matured and begun to grapple with their history and identity, as a specific women's publishing alternative has emerged, and an audience for that work has been shaped, Caribbean women's voices are being heard. And as the advance of mass education, literacy, cultural modification, and more disposable income moves through the islands, literary voices will increasingly be heard there, as opposed to in the metropoli.

6. The establishment of women's publishing operations—the Women's Press and Virago in England, Sister Vision and Women of Color Press in Toronto, Shameless Hussy Press and Kitchen Table in the United States—has been an important spur to the increased numbers of women writers and the number of titles available to the audience of their work. Kitchen Table gives American women of color a publishing outlet of their own.

7. As with Soca and Reggae, the metropolitan market is of nearly equal, if not greater, importance than the island one.

Twentieth-Century Women Writers from the English-Speaking Caribbean

LAURA NIESEN DE ABRUNA

"Alienation within alienation"—political and social—in Kenneth Ramchand's phrase,[1] is the inchoate pain of women writers from the English-speaking Caribbean. That they are writing very fine poetry and fiction is a simple statement but one we do not hear very often. Until the late 1970s, very little was written about these authors because the critics' attention was focused on the male writers Wilson Harris, George Lamming, Edgar Mittelholzer, V. S. Naipaul, and Edward Brathwaite. As late as 1979, the popular critical text *West Indian Literature*, edited by Bruce King, mentions only Jean Rhys among the many women writers from this area. As Judith Fetterley has noted, we must resist rather than assent to this reading of West Indian literature because the story that is missing here is the woman's story, and the omission is so acceptable that it is not even noticed.[2]

Twentieth-century women writers from the English-speaking Caribbean—those who were born or grew up in the former British colonies in the West Indies—live in societies of extreme diversity and grave fragmentation of both European and African cultures. The insecurity in human relationships within tense social and political climates, particularly between woman and woman, man and woman, or mother and daughter—as well as the uneasiness about personal identity—are the most com-

This essay was originally published in *Modern Fiction Studies*, copyright 1988, by Purdue Research Foundation, West Lafayette, Indiana 47907. Reprinted with permission.

1. Kenneth Ramchand, *The West Indian Novel and Its Background*, 2d ed. (London: Heinemann, 1983), p. 231.
2. Arnold E. Davidson, *Jean Rhys* (New York: Ungar, 1985), p. 43.

mon concerns of the prominent women writers: Phyllis Shand Allfrey (Dominica), Zee Edgell (Belize), Merle Hodge (Trinidad), Jamaica Kincaid (Antigua), Paule Marshall (Barbados), Jean Rhys (Dominica), and Sylvia Wynter (Jamaica). Despite significant differences, these writers have in common the imbalance of power between men and women in their societies and the problems of identity and inequality in relation to male dominance.[3] In many of their novels, the women characters survive by forming a bond, a "mirroring" relationship with other women.

Critics Leota Lawerence, Merle Hodge, and Hermione McKenzie have pointed to several features of women's lives in the West Indies that have become part of literary discussion. The preponderance of the matriarchal family is, according to Lawerence, "the result of a synthesis of an African cultural survival with the realities of slavery in the area."[4] In many cases, the women live in a society in which sexual and emotional relationships have been destroyed by demoralizing and alienating economic manipulations in colonial and neocolonial societies.[5] The single female head of household can be "among the most powerless of the society, the absence of a spouse often implying the absence of a stable family income." Lucille Mathurin points out that this economically depressed condition makes the woman as "sexually vulnerable as she was in the darker days of her history."[6]

Countering the myth of the self-sufficient black matriarchal figures, Hodge points out, in a special edition of *Savacou*, that the ultimate vocation of all women in the West Indies is to marry and/or to become mothers.[7] Lawerence goes further: "It is a fact that many a young woman in the Caribbean has deliberately stifled any pretensions to a career, lest in doing so she outshine her male counterpart and thereby end up an 'old maid.' Thus, with very few exceptions there are no women writers; with very few exceptions there are no women calypsonians. The portrait of women that is revealed to the world in the written and oral literature is that given them by men."[8] Despite Lawerence's assertion that there are no women writers, there are many Caribbean women writing, although, as she admits, sometimes with great anxiety because their models are usually male

3. Lloyd W. Brown, *Women Writers in Black Africa* (Westport, Conn.: Greenwood, 1981), p. 12.

4. Leota S. Lawerence, "Women in Caribbean Literature: The African Presence," *Phylon* 44 (1983): 4.

5. Hermione McKenzie, "Introduction: Caribbean Women: Yesterday, Today, and Tomorrow," in Edward Brathwaite, ed., *The Caribbean Woman*, special issue of *Savacou* 13 (1977): ix.

6. Lucille Mathurin, "Reluctant Matriarchs," ibid., pp. 5–6.

7. Merle Hodge, "Young Women and the Development of Stable Family Life in the Caribbean," ibid., p. 41.

8. Lawerence, "Women in Caribbean Literature," pp. 4–5.

writers and their societies emphasize that the vocation of all women should be to nurture their relationships with men and bear and raise children.

Women writers have overcome these obstacles to create characters who are self-supporting and have great strength and endurance. They struggle and survive because of their basic respect for life; they depend on a strong bonding between and among women in their communities in the fight for basic survival. The negative observations described above should be revised to include the positive and empowering connections between women that we find in such writers as Jamaica Kincaid, Simone Schwarz-Bart, Phyllis Shand Allfrey, Paule Marshall, Jean Rhys, and Merle Hodge. Many of these writers investigate the problems women experience growing up in the West Indies. Significantly, the novels focusing on the African-Caribbean woman's passage into maturity are more positive than those that treat white Creole women.

The theoretical ideas most relevant to this fiction are Nancy Chodorow's theories of bonding, set out in *The Reproduction of Mothering: Psychoanalysis and the Sociology of Gender* and the extension of such theories in Carol Gilligan's *In a Different Voice: Psychological Theory and Women's Development*, an investigation of differences in the ways men and women think about separation and individuation. Chodorow explains the primary importance of the preoedipal relationship between mother and daughter to the daughter's later ability to feel that she is a separate person from her mother. The daughter must also separate so she can negotiate relationships with other people. Gilligan establishes differences between the male and female child's attitude toward the mother, a discussion that is extremely important to feminist critics because her insights about human identity go beyond the model espoused by male identity theorists, especially Freud and his followers. Freud admitted his inability to understand the psychology of adult female sexuality. In his *Essays on Lay Analysis* (1926), he referred to this lack of knowledge about female sexuality as the "dark continent" of psychology,[9] thereby grafting racist images of the black's "otherness" onto his ignorance of female sexuality.

Unlike Freud, Chodorow successfully investigates gender differences in identity formation without assuming a male paradigm. She believes that for both males and females the preoedipal state is characterized by attachment to the mother. During the oedipal phase the male child transfers his feelings of identification to the father figure. The so-called "oedipal crisis" is more complicated for female children, who retain an attachment to their mothers

---

9. Quoted in Sander L. Gilman, "Black Bodies, White Bodies: Toward an Iconography of Female Sexuality in Late Nineteenth-Century Art, Medicine, and Literature," in Henry Louis Gates, Jr., ed., *"Race," Writing, and Difference* (Chicago: University of Chicago Press, 1985), p. 257.

for a much longer time. The mother's love of her preoedipal daughter is more prolonged than that for a boy. There is the potential for tremendous closeness between the women but also the danger that prolonged symbiosis and narcissistic overindulgence on the part of the mother may lead to the daughter's confusion about her own identity as separate from her mother's.

In brief, Chodorow argues that independence from the mother and, in a general sense, all independence, is more difficult for women to attain than for men. Unlike the young male self, the young female self is defined through bonding and identification with the mother. The nature of adult female identity arises from the daughter's relationship with her mother, although the steps are more fluid than in the process for men. Female identity, according to Judith Gardiner, is more of a process than the lockstep development that is the currently favored model for human development. When women's development, which tends to be relational, is defined and then devalued in comparison with men's, which tends toward separation and individuation, self-concept becomes a problem area for women and women writers.[10]

Carol Gilligan's *In a Different Voice* extends Chodorow's insights to psychologists' schemata of human development. Gilligan recorded different modes of thinking about relationships by men and women and connected them with male and female voices in psychological and literary texts. From the responses she received to stories representing ethical dilemmas, Gilligan hypothesized that masculinity is defined through separation, individuation, and achievement, whereas femininity is defined through intimacy, relationships with other people, and an ethic of caring.[11]

Yet the theorists of adult psychosexual development, following Erik Erikson, still use a male model that privileges autonomy rather than reciprocity. Involvement with others is seen as a hindrance to identity rather than its realization. This opens up a gap between women's experience of their human development and what is characterized as human development. The cultural reality here is what Fetterley calls "immasculation," the process whereby women are expected to think like and to identify with them, even to the point of misogyny.[12] Immasculation means that women's concern with relationships will appear as a "weakness of women rather than as a human strength."[13]

10. Judith Kegan Gardiner, "On Female Identity and Writing by Women," in Elizabeth Abel, ed., *Writing and Sexual Difference* (Chicago: University of Chicago Press, 1980), pp. 179, 184.
11. Carol Gilligan, *In a Different Voice: Psychological Theory and Women's Development* (Cambridge, Mass.: Harvard University Press, 1982), p. 35.
12. Judith Fetterley, *The Resisting Reader: A Feminist Approach to American Fiction* (Bloomington: Indiana University Press, 1978), p. xxi.
13. Gilligan, *In a Different Voice*, p. 17.

The strength of the Caribbean women writers is their concern with relational interaction. The fictional women who do not react self-destructively to disasters save themselves because of their strong connection with other women in their cultures. The nature of this bonding deserves much more attention than it has received in the past and than I can give it in this essay. A tentative hypothesis, however, is that in West Indian fiction, the bonding between African-Caribbean women is stronger than the bonding between other women, either between Creoles or between Creoles and African-Caribbean characters.

I will consider some examples from each of these groups. Many of these writers investigate the problems women experience in growing up in the West Indies. Phyllis Shand Allfrey's *Orchid House* examines the identity problems that destroy the descendants of white Creole families. They are both disliked by the African-Caribbeans, who view them as related to the former slaveowners, and patronized by the British, who view them as colonials rather than as genuine Europeans.

In *Orchid House* the main character and narrator is the black woman Lally, who analyzes the white family for whom she works and whose powers are waning. The novel gives a sense of the planter class's decline and of the emergence of new economic and ruling forces in a fictional West Indian island.[14] Because the class system is in decay, the family members are confused about their present social roles and their identities. The father is a recluse suffering from shock and drug addiction, and his nephew Andrew is slowly dying of tuberculosis on an estate called Petit Cul-de-Sac. The three daughters, Stella, Joan, and Natalie, return from abroad and attempt to initiate schemes for political improvement, but none succeeds. The major characters do not take us beyond their white minority environment, nor do they interact with one another in any positive way. The planter's wife suffers increasing apathy and decline that becomes more pronounced after her husband's death.

The novels focusing on the African-Caribbean woman's passage into maturity tell a different story. Beka, the adolescent woman in Zee Edgell's *Beka Lamb*, learns from her family how to survive rejection by males, whereas her friend Toycie, now pregnant, disintegrates when Emilio, her Mexican boyfriend, rejects her because she is not light-skinned. Beka's survival, despite women's traditional dependency on men in her community, shows a strength similar to that of Télumée Miracle in Guadeloupean Simone Schwarz-Bart's *Bridge of Beyond*. Télumée survives the madness caused by the desertion of her lover Elie because the Toussine women teach each generation the endurance and self-reliance needed for survival.

14. Ramchand, *West Indian Novel*, p. 225.

Through identification with her grandmother, Reine Sans Nom—
Queen Without a Name—Télumée feels she has a secure place within her
community. Queen Without a Name does not leave her alone until
she is able to endure misfortune. Cia gives Télumée the grandmother's
advice: "Be a fine little Negress, a real drum with two sides. Let life
bang and thump, but keep the underside always intact."[15] The story of
Télumée's identification with her grandmother is important because it
demonstrates the value of female bonding in structuring identity within
the narrative.

Paule Marshall and Jamaica Kincaid, both of whom have lived for long
periods in the United States, have examined the problems generated by
a young woman's adolescence and the tension she experiences between
the U.S. and West Indian cultures. In Paule Marshall's *Brown Girl, Brownstones*, Selina Boyce, who grows up in Brooklyn, rejects the coldness of
the other Barbadian exiles who have embraced the worst of North American materialism. By the novel's conclusion, she has decided to return to
Barbados, her parents' birthplace, to seek the human values they have
lost through their emigration.

Relationships between women become problematic in this novel. In
one intense scene, after Selina has danced with her friends, she accom-
panies one of them back to her apartment. There she is confronted for
the first time by the mother of one of her white friends. Selina's mother
warned her to expect racism even among her white friends and their
families, but Selina does not believe them dangerous until this point:

Suddenly the woman leaned forward and rested her hand on Selina's knee.
"Are they [Selina's parents] from the South, dear?"
  It was not the question which offended her, but the woman's manner—
pleasant, interested, yet charged with exasperation. It was her warm smile,
which was cold at its source—above all, the consoling hand on her knee,
which was indecent. Selina sensed being pitted against her in a contest of
strength. If she answered unwisely the woman would gain the advantage.
  She muttered evasively, "No, they're not."
  The woman bent close, surprised, and the dry sting of her perfume was
another indignity. "No...? Where then?"
  "The West Indies."
  The woman sat back, triumphant. "Ah, I thought so. We once had a girl
who did our cleaning who was from there...." She caught herself and
smiled apologetically. "Oh, she wasn't a girl, of course. We just call them
that. It's a terrible habit."[16]

15. Simone Schwarz-Bart, *The Bridge of Beyond*, trans. Barbara Ray (London: Heinemann,
1982), p. 39.
16. Paule Marshall, *Brown Girl, Brownstones* (Old Westbury, N.Y.: Feminist Press, 1959),
p. 287.

Although Selina might expect the image of her hope and youth to be reflected in the woman's regard, the white woman's pale eyes reflect only one thing—that Selina is black and must be made to feel inferior. "Those eyes were a well-lighted mirror in which, for the first time, Selina truly saw—with a sharp and shattering clarity—the full meaning of her black skin."[17] This racism obviates any reciprocity between Selina and the older woman.

Merle Hodge, author of *Crick Crack Monkey*, explores the tension between the African-Caribbean and metropolitan cultures. Unlike the majority of other novels addressing this question, *Crick Crack Monkey* examines the African-Caribbean woman's cultural identification.[18] In Hodge's novel, Cynthia, or Tee, must choose between Aunt Beatrice's attempts to imitate British upper-class society and language and Tantie's more honest acceptance of Creole manners and dialect.

Living in a society colonized by Europeans, Beatrice has become what O. R. Dathorne calls an "expatriate of the mind,"[19] denying the worth of locally evolved culture to identify with a foreign tradition. Tee, whose mother has died, is the object of a long custody battle between her Aunt Beatrice, who attempts to identify with the metropolitan culture, and Tantie, who accepts the indigenous black culture. Her acceptance of the black Creole cultural tradition is based on the recognition that imported cultural values evolved in a different environment and historical experience.[20]

Although Tee feels more comfortable with Tantie, the young woman's later contact with Beatrice's values makes it impossible for her ever again to identify completely with the black Creole culture. When the potentially positive bonding between Tantie and Tee is disrupted and Beatrice wins custody of Tee, the girl suffers a gradual cultural displacement. At the novel's end, when Tee goes to her father's house in London, she has already internalized the racist values of the white colonials.[21] Although Hodge does not offer a convincing alternative to the ambivalent balancing of two cultures, she does offer in Tantie a positive model of strength and endurance. She and the other women characters survive, physically and psychologically, because they have formed strong ties with other women in their families or communities. The potentially healthy relationship of

17. Ibid., p. 289.
18. Marjorie Thorpe, "The Problem of Cultural Identification in *Crick Crack Monkey*," in Brathwaite, ed., *Caribbean Woman*, p. 31.
19. O. R. Dathorne, "Toward Synthesis in the New World: Caribbean Literature in English," in William Luis, ed., *Voices from Under: Black Narrative in Latin America and the Caribbean* (Westport, Conn.: Greenwood, 1984), p. 104.
20. Thorpe, "Problem of Cultural Identification," pp. 31, 34.
21. Ibid., p. 36.

Tee and Tantie is unfortunately interrupted by Beatrice's intrusion of values from the dominant culture.

Some of the finest fiction from the West Indies has been written by Jamaica Kincaid. Her collection of short stories, *At the Bottom of the River*, makes interesting use of dream visions and metaphor as the imaginative projections of family life and social structure in her West Indian society. In these stories Kincaid explores the strong identification and rupture in the daughter-mother relationship between the narrator and her mother. The process is mediated through metaphor and, when it is threatening, through surrealistic dream visions.

Each of these stories demonstrates tensions in the daughter-narrator resulting from a prolonged period of symbiosis between mother and child, especially because the mother views her daughter as a narcissistic extention of herself. In "Wingless," the narrator dreams the story as a mirror of her own situation and then imagines herself as a wingless pupa waiting for growth. The narrator uses a dream vision to mediate her sense of helplessness as a child dependent on her mother's care and attention.

In this dream, the mother is perceived as powerful, even more potent than the male who attempts to intimidate and humiliate her. Thus an incident of potential sexual violence becomes instead an easy victory for the mother:

> I could see that he wore clothes made of tree bark and sticks in his ears. He said things to her and I couldn't make them out, but he said them so forcefully that drops of water sprang from his mouth. The woman I love put her hands over her ears, shielding herself from the things he said. . . . Then, instead of removing her cutlass from the folds of her big and beautiful skirt and cutting the man in two at the waist, she only smiled—a red, red smile—and like a fly he dropped dead.[22]

The strong mother threatens death to those who confront her. But there is also a wonderful parable here of the integrity of the woman who shields herself from assault by refusing to listen to the tree-satyr who is trying to assert his power over her.

The story that best demonstrates the daughter's ambivalent relationship with her mother is "Girl." The voice is the girl's repeating a series of the mother's admonitions:

> Wash the white clothes on Monday and put them on the stone heap; wash the color clothes on Tuesday and put them on the clothesline to dry . . . on Sundays try to walk like a lady and not like the slut you are so bent on becoming . . . this is how to hem a dress when you see the hem coming

22. Jamaica Kincaid, *At the Bottom of the River* (New York: Vintage, 1978), p. 25.

down and so to prevent yourself from looking like the slut I know you are
so bent on becoming... this is how to behave in the presence of men who
don't know you very well, and this way they won't recognize immediately
the slut I have warned you against becoming.[23]

The first of the mother's many rules concerns housekeeping. Unlike the
girl's father, who can lounge at the circus eating blood sausage and drinking ginger beer, the woman is restricted to household duties. The many
rules are experienced by the narrator as unnecessarily restrictive and
hostile. The mother's aggression is clear in the warnings of the price a
girl will pay for ignoring her mother's advice. The penalty is ostracism—
one must become a slut, a fate for which the mother is ironically preparing
the daughter. The mother's obsessive refrain indicates hostility toward
her adolescent daughter, activated when the girl is no longer an extension
of herself but a young woman who engenders in the older woman feelings
of competition and anger at losing control of her child. Her anger may
also result from the pressures felt by every woman in the community to
fulfill the restrictive roles created for women. Of the ten stories in the
collection, "Girl" is the only one that is told as interior monologue rather
than dream and thus seems to be the least distorted vision. The ambivalence of the mother-daughter relationship is presented here in its most
direct form. The reasons for their mutual distrust are very clearly stated:
resentment, envy, anger, and love.

In Jean Rhys's *Wide Sargasso Sea*, we return to the victimization Charlotte
Brontë inscribes in *Jane Eyre*. Rhys tells the story of "creolized" West
Indian women, a group whose confusion in identity is rarely explored.
The major characters in *Wide Sargasso Sea* and *Voyage in the Dark*, Antoinette Cosway and Anna Morgan respectively, realize that their gender,
poverty, and powerlessness are the sources of their vulnerability. In their
societies, impersonal and unequal power structures make both blackness
and femaleness significant disadvantages.[24] Despite the frequent com-
plaint that Rhys's characters are passive, there is always a defiance in her
women, an unwillingness to fit into a submissive mold. Many of Rhys's
characters identify with other oppressed groups such as the former slaves
and the Caribe Indians. Despite the difficulty or impossibility of any
adequate bonding among such groups, Rhys's characters do not buy into
sexual and emotional involvement with powerful and monied white men.

In reinventing Bertha Antoinette Mason's past, Rhys is interested in
Antoinette's psychological dignity and sets about explaining her descent
into insanity as a result of a personality diffusion caused by her mother's

23. Ibid., p. 3.
24. Judith Moore, "Sanity and Strength in Jean Rhys's West Indian Heroines," *Rocky
Mountain Review of Language and Literature* 41 (1987): 25, 30.

indifference though also partly the result of living in a colonized environment; but she is also interested in the difficulties of creating an identity that is flexible yet secure enough to survive the marriage to Rochester. Rhys investigates the mother-daughter bond between Annette and Antoinette and shows the destruction caused by the mother's refusal to acknowledge the importance of her daughter.

The destructive relationship between Antoinette and her mother, Annette, is the cause of much of Antoinette's precarious sense of herself. Because Annette Cosway is self-absorbed—"pretty like pretty self" Christophine says[25]—and obsessed with her son, Antoinette tries to cling to her friend Tia, whose life she shares until they separate after a fight over money. A group of local residents, infuriated by Mr. Mason's attempt to run the plantation with impoverished workers from India, burns the Coulibri estate. Seeing Tia in the crowd, Antoinette runs to her. Because Tia is the only reminder of her former life, Antoinette tries to find a reflection of her identity in Tia's eyes. But the violence has gone too far and ruins their desires: "As I ran, I thought, I will live with Tia and I will be like her. . . . When I was close I saw the jagged stone in her hand but I did not see her throw it. I did not feel it either, only something wet, running down my face. I looked at her and I saw her face crumple up as she began to cry. We stared at each other, blood on my face, tears on hers. It was as if I saw myself. Like in a looking-glass."[26] In this passage Antoinette loses her childhood at Coulibri and her friendship with Tia in a wrenching moment that is likened to a sexual encounter by the penetration of the jagged rock and the wetness on her skin.

Later, when Rochester marries Antoinette and then rejects her because "her tastes are obnoxious to him," Rhys clarifies the link between the fear of the sexual and the racial "other." Antoinette is called a "dark" beauty whom Rhys intended to be, like the original Bertha, part Spanish or French. Because she is a "dark" West Indian woman, Antoinette is an easy target for Rochester's venom. He regards her "breeding" as suspicious and, shocked by the island's intermingling of races, wonders about Antoinette's heritage: "She never blinks at all it seems to me. Long, sad dark alien eyes. Creole of pure English descent she may be, but they are not English or European either."[27] Noticing Rhys's preference for dark-skinned characters in her novels, Helen Nebeker argues that Antoinette is mulatto: "Antoinette, herself, is, by heritage, creole, though by implication of mixed blood."[28] Either way, Rochester's attitude is racist because

25. Jean Rhys, *Wide Sargasso Sea* (1966; rpt. New York: Norton, 1982), p. 17.
26. Ibid., p. 45.
27. Ibid., p. 67.
28. Helen Nebeker, p. 139.

he is scapegoating a woman whose "darkness" facilitates a rejection of what he perceives as physically different.

Although Rochester will treat Antoinette abominably, part of her is already dead. Her mother found a daughter tiresome and preferred her son Pierre. Ironically, she and Antoinette are related by imagery suggesting physical and emotional similarity. The mother fatefully refuses to admit a connection with the female child. The mother's inability to help a daughter form a sense of worth, as Chodorow has taught us, is a complex doom for Antoinette. When Annette denies attachment and symbiosis, Antoinette's diffusion is assured. In Part Three of the novel, Antoinette tries to remember something she "must do." She dreams of the night their house burned and experiences a reconciliation with Tia which she had been seeking since that night when her life changed and Tia deserted her.

> The wind caught my hair and it streamed out like wings. It might bear me up, I thought, if I jumped to those hard stones. But when I looked over the edge I saw the pool at Coulibri. Tia was there. She beckoned to me and when I hesitated, she laughed. I heard her say, You frightened? And I heard the man's voice, Bertha! Bertha! All this I saw and heard in a fraction of a second. And the sky so red. Someone screamed and I thought, *Why did I scream?* I called "Tia!" and jumped and woke.[29]

Torching Rochester's baronial cage is an act of liberation engendered by her final ability to find connectedness with Tia. Even though it costs her life, Rhys's Antoinette realizes her revenge in a way that surprises her captors and reasserts her presence.

Lest I end on a naively optimistic note, I should point out that there is a political problem in looking to Rhys, a white Creole writer, for a representation of successful syncretism between black and white Caribbean women. As Abdul R. JanMohamed has stated in *Critical Inquiry*, the comprehension of the "otherness" found in the African-Caribbean woman is possible only "if the self can somehow negate or at least severely bracket the values, assumptions, and ideology of his culture." Although Rhys cannot claim fully to understand the "otherness" of most West Indian women, because most are African-Caribbean rather than white Creole, she does seem able to return to the West Indian Bertha Mason the dignity taken away by Charlotte Brontë. Bertha Mason was a victim of the sexism and imperialism of British culture. And in Rhys's fiction, we do see a successful syncretism between the white Creole woman Antoinette and the black Creole woman Tia. JanMohamed would argue that such an attempt is almost impossible: "As Nadine Gordimer's and Isak Dinesen's

29. Rhys, *Wide Sargasso Sea*, pp. 189–90.

writings show, however, this [comprehension of the Other] entails in practice the virtually impossible task of negating one's very being, precisely because one's culture is what formed that being."[30]

JanMohamed's contention is not only a social determinism denying the possibility of attaining a critical perspective on one's own culture, it is not an accurate description of Jean Rhys's fiction. JanMohamed claims that colonialist literature attempting to explore the racial "other" is only another form of ethnocentrism: "Such literature is essentially specular: instead of seeing the native as a bridge toward syncretic possibility, it uses him as a mirror that reflects the colonialist's self-image."[31] Yet in *Wide Sargasso Sea*, Jean Rhys defies this pessimism. When Bertha Mason stands on the roof of Rochester's burning manorhouse, she looks down at the ground and hard stones, trying to decide whether to jump or to turn to Rochester for aid. As she looks down into the pool, a mirror, she sees not herself or a colonialist self-image but the African-Caribbean woman Tia. Antoinette thus reaffirms her identification with Tia. Antoinette does negate the self in sacrificing that self and thus transcends the values, assumptions, and ideology of her culture. She demonstrates that bonding is possible for white Creole women and African-Caribbean women if the women can bracket the sexism, racism, and imperialism that are thrust upon them.

30. Abdul JanMohamed, "The Economy of Manichean Allegory: The Function of Racial Difference in Colonialist Literature," *Critical Inquiry* 12 (1985): 65.
31. Ibid.

"You Want to Be a Coolie Woman?": Gender and Ethnic Identity in Indo-Caribbean Women's Writing

JEREMY POYNTING

There are at least 1 million persons of Indian origin in the Caribbean. The writing of male Indo-Caribbeans has made its mark so the question was asked in the conference, Where are the women writers? It was a multi-layered question, and one of the responses I overheard the question provoke—that "Indian women can't write"—carried equally multiple meanings. It contained a grain of historical truth about the past when the vast majority of rural Indo-Caribbean women were condemned to illiteracy, but it also carried several powerful cultural stereotypes of backwardness, passivity, and silence.

As Ken Parmasad indicates in the foreword to his collection of folk stories, *Salt and Roti*,[1] it was the women who were frequently the passers-down of these narratives. As Rhoda Reddock reminds us, Indian women have from time to time played a prominent role in industrial struggle.[2] We can recall Kowsillia, who was killed resisting attempts to break the Enmore strike in 1948 in Guyana. As Kuntie Ramdat has revealed, there is a rich vein of sexually expressive bawdy humor in the women's gaari songs of wedding ceremonies.[3]

1. Ken Parmasad, *Salt and Roti: Indian Folk Tales in the Caribbean* (Trinidad: Sankh Productions, 1984).
2. Rhoda Reddock, "Feminism, Nationalism, and the Early Women's Movement in the English-Speaking Caribbean," paper presented to the first International Conference on Women Writers of the English-Speaking Caribbean, 1988.
3. Kuntie Ramdat, "Some Aspects of Indic Pejorative Usage among Hindus in Guyana," paper presented at the Third Conference on East Indians in the Caribbean, Trinidad, 1984.

But it is true that little of this has found its way into written Indo-Caribbean women's literature so that this paper is as much about absences as presences, and my comments will almost certainly be made redundant by the writing of the next few years. To date, in published form, there is one novel by a writer whose Indianness might well be disputed, a collection of short stories, and a dozen slim volumes of poetry. In all, about forty individuals have published in various Caribbean magazines. (About six times that number of male Indo-Caribbean writers have been published.) Perhaps of these forty women half a dozen are writers of either persistence or talent.[4] In the light of this situation, the paper has two objectives.

First, very briefly, it summarizes some of the reasons for the belatedness and the narrow social base of Indo-Caribbean women's writing. Second, it outlines the direction that Indo-Caribbean women's writing has taken so far. Here it focuses on one issue in particular: the tension between gender and ethnic identity. There *are* objective reasons why the two should be experienced as a contradiction, but so far, those Indo-Caribbean women who have written have tended to come from backgrounds where the conflict has been felt most acutely.

The reasons for the delayed emergence of Indo-Caribbean women's writing must be sought not only in economic geography, the marginalization of Indo-Caribbean culture, and general gender disadvantage, but, in the past at least, in Indian attitudes to the education of girls. The conversation between Seth and Mr. Biswas in V. S. Naipaul's *A House for Mr. Biswas*, about the educational attainments of Biswas's future bride, can be taken as a fairly accurate record of attitudes:

> "She is a good child. A little bit of reading and writing even."
> "A little bit of reading and writing . . . " Mr. Biswas echoed, trying to gain time.
> Seth, chewing, his right hand working dexterously with roti and beans, made a dismissing gesture with his left hand.
> "Just a little bit. So much. Nothing to worry about. In two or three years she might even forget."[5]

Only in the 1950s, when, in Guyana, the PPP government made secondary education relatively free to scholarship winners (Janice Shinebourne was one of the early beneficiaries of this scheme), and in Trinidad, when the Hindu Maha Sabha started building schools in the rural Indian

---

4. For a more extensive survey see Jeremy Poynting, "East Indian Women in the Caribbean: Experience and Voice," in *India in the Caribbean* (London: Hansib Publications, 1987), pp. 231–63.

5. V. S. Naipaul, *A House For Mr. Biswas* (London: Fontana, 1961), p. 78.

areas, that access to education widened. Even so, the number of young women who have entered higher education has been very small. Correspondingly, the social and cultural base of Indo-Caribbean women's writing has, until recently, been narrow.

Economic geography has intersected with Indian communities' own cultural frameworks. Studies have indicated that where communities have gained access to better-paid work and the consumer economy, women have gained in independence, whereas in rural communities that have remained dependent on the plantation or subsistence agriculture, women have been much less likely to achieve choice in marriage, control over sexuality, and fertility and equality in marital relations.[6]

The consequences of this relationship between economy and culture and the Eurocentric nature of education have meant that, in general, social mobility has tended to involve a movement away from Indianness. This has been true for both men and women, but for women it has been experienced in particular, gendered ways, and it is within this framework that I want to discuss the Indo-Caribbean women's writing that has emerged.

The issue is given a very clear focus in Janice Shinebourne's novel The Last English Plantation,[7] in its portrayal of the bitter conflict between twelve-year-old June Lehall and her mother, Lucille, a Christian and would-be anglicized Indian. Lucille wants June to escape from the estate and from Indianness via education. Though June rejects her mother's European model of womanhood (she is repeatedly criticized as a tomboy) and though June bitterly resents the way her mother tries to cut her off from her Indian friends, and in particular from her Hindu "alter mater," Nani Dharamdai, the issue of gender and Indianness is much more difficult for June to resolve. For instance, one of the adults whose voice June regularly hears is that of Boysie Ramkarran, the local union leader. Although June admires Boysie for his class politics and ethnic militancy, it is not just for the same reasons that Lucille feels "ashamed to be his race" but because, as June's father admits, "he keeps women in their place." At the heart of the fearful quarrel June has with Lucille, this issue of gender oppression is continually thrown at her. When June announces that she will not go back to school, Lucille's confusion of cultural self-loathing and yearning for independence explodes:

6. See Judith Johnston, "The Changing Cultural Context of the Neo-Natal Period in an East Indian Rural Community in South Trinidad," paper presented to the Second Conference on East Indians in the Caribbean, Trinidad, 1979; and S. Sieunarine, "Social and Cultural Change in the East Indian Community of Eldorado in 1960–1980," Caribbean Studies Project, UWI.

7. Jan Shinebourne, The Last English Plantation (Leeds: Peepal Tree Press, 1988).

All right! Stay at home then. Turn coolie! You used to be a coolie and I manage to turn you into a civilised person. . . . You like that coolie boy Ralph Brijlal? You like him? Well, marry him and see if you still like him when he is finished with you! Their wives cook from three o'clock in the morning to late at night! You want to be a coolie woman! Well, be a coolie woman! I don't care! Coolie women have to carry all the burdens for the men . . . and get no thanks for it, only licks! . . . Yes, go to Dharamdai's house. You talk Hindi, learn mantras, do puja, pick up cow dung with your hands, bring up children with lice in their hair and feed the lice with coconut oil.[8]

After this outburst June runs away to her Nani Dharamdai's. In a moving chapter called "Oblation," Nani soothes her grief by massaging her with coconut oil. Yet afterward, June has to return to the school where she will resume the process of losing her Indianness.

That argument seems to me to define the parameters within which most Indo-Caribbean women's writing has functioned, though very little of it has brought those parameters to consciousness. The tendency has been, on one hand, to focus in a naturalistic way on the image of the Indian woman as victim without dealing with the wider cultural and gender issues, or, on the other, to avoid the issue of ethnic and cultural identity by focusing on personal themes. On the first score, one has to say that, to date, few of the stories dealing with arranged marriages or beaten wives extend the treatments found in male writing. Indeed, some of the stories in Seepersad Naipaul's *Gurudeva and Other Indian Tales* (1943) are more feminist in their admiration for women who resist. Only perhaps in Trinidadian Rajnie Ramlakhan's occasional short stories does one find a perspective that extends the typical passive-victim focus. Her story "Flight"[9] is one of the first to dramatize the conflicts experienced by the first generation of Hindu women with higher education. The main character is pressured by her parents to marry a "good Hindu husband" and by her radical Christian Indian boyfriend to abandon her religion, culture, and family pieties. She wants independence and marriage and children and to retain her cultural identity. The boyfriend rejects her, and though she at first contemplates suicide, she comes to see that "from now on her life was to be hers and hers alone." The story is brief and undeveloped, but it points the way toward territory which future writing will undoubtedly explore. Another writer in this protest vein, whom I would like to mention because her work has passion and conviction, though confined by the limitations of Guyanese newspaper space, is Parvati Persaud Edwards. She has also begun writing some perceptive autobiographical pieces.

8. Ibid., p. 127.
9. Rajnie Ramlakhan, "Flight," *Indian Review* 1, no. 4 (1983): 19–23.

The other tendency can be seen in the writing about love and personal relations. Much of it is mediocre and belongs to the genre of popular women's magazine fiction or poet's corner verse, though it is possible to see the emphasis on love and the awakening of romantic feelings as implicitly challenging the maternal and passive images imposed on women in a patriarchal culture. This can best be seen and seen at its best in the work of Shana Yardan. Her cycle of love poems, *This Listening of Eyes*, published in Guyana in 1976, is a most accomplished, tough-minded, and well-crafted collection which dramatizes the tension between a "feminine" experiencing self and a feminist observing consciousness. When Shana Yardan explores her Indian ancestry, "Earth Is Brown" expresses a sense of distance:

> Oh grandfather, my grandfather,
> your dhoti is become a shroud
> your straight hair a curse
> in this land where
> rice no longer fills the belly.[10]

It is really only in the work of the late Rajkumari Singh and Mahadai Das, both writers from Guyana, that one finds an emphasis on both the gender and the ethnic issues, though the recent work of Rosetta Khalideen and Parvati Persaud Edwards in a little anthology called *Shraadanjali* (1986)[11] also touches on these issues. Parvati Persaud Edwards's poem "Vivah Sanskar," describing the ornate ritual of a Hindu wedding, expresses an ambivalence through the mixed Hindi-English of the diction, the former expressing:

> . . . the magic
> of age-old rituals

while unadorned English is used to warn the doolahin of the:

> . . . reality
> of the expected sacrifice of self
> of the true Hindu wife.

The work of Rajkumari Singh from the late 1940s to the mid-1970s contains a pioneering articulation of an Indo-Caribbean woman's perspective. She was a person of great fortitude. She was crippled by polio at birth, had eight children, led an active political life, was surrogate

---

10. Shana Yardan, *New Writing in the Caribbean*, ed. A. J. Seymour (Georgetown: Guyana Lithographic Co., 1972), pp. 113–14.

11. Rosetta Khalideen and Parvati Persaud Edwards, *Shraadanjali* (Guyana: Guyana Lithographic Co., 1986).

artistic mother to many younger writers, and still managed to write an unpublished novel, several plays, and a collection of short stories and uncollected poems and stories that appeared in magazines. Not all of her work bears close scrutiny, but her best work such as her collection of poems, *Days of the Sahib Are Over* (1971),[12] speaks clearly and resolutely of her commitment to restore the invisible Indo-Caribbean woman to the stage of history. Her poem "Per Ajie," for instance, is dedicated to the first immigrant woman:

> Per Ajie
> I can see
> How in stature
> Thou didst grow
> Shoulders up
> Head held high
> The challenge
> In thine eye.

Although she was intensely proud of her Indo-Guyanese heritage, she was also a fierce critic of Indian racial chauvinism and gender oppression. Her play *The Sound of Her Bells* (1974) is an attack on caste intolerance and male chauvinism in the guise of brahminical Hindu piety. In it, Babu, a priggish pundit, won't let Nirmala, a professional dancer, perform in front of a statue of Shiva in his temple until he is shamed into recognizing the validity of her contribution. Some of Singh's work is marred by a "poetic" stiltedness of diction, though some of her unpublished poetry of the mid-1970s is much more forthright and demotic in tone. "No More Kitchree for the Groom," for instance, attacks the custom of dowry, "as though, treasured maiden daughter / was snatched from brothel / to bag a husband."[13] What is important about Singh's position was that she mounted her attack on the male-centeredness of Indian culture from within Indian culture itself.

Mahadai Das, a generation younger, followed Rajkumari Singh in dealing with Indo-Guyanese, feminist, and radical nationalist perspectives in her work, but it is significant that in general these remain distinct strands. In her first collection, *I Want to Be a Poetess of My People* (1976),[14] the few poems that survive the political sloganeering of the period are those dealing with her Indian heritage, but there is little that explores her experiences as an Indo-Guyanese woman. In her second collection, *My Finer Steel Will Grow* (1982)[15] there is both a real growth in control over language,

---

12. Rajkumari Singh, *Days of the Sahib Are Over* (Georgetown: By the author, 1971).

13. Typescript, read at the Messengers Coolie Art Forms Show, 1973.

14. Mahadai Das, *I Want to Be a Poetess of My People* (Guyana: National History and Arts Council, 1976, 1977).

15. Mahadai Das, *My Finer Steel Will Grow*, Samisdat, vol. 31, no. 2, 1982.

the releasing of a metaphorical imagination *and* the beginnings of an exploration of the connections between personal and political experience, in particular the irony that the men and women who are united in their opposition to political oppression may take on the roles of oppressor and oppressed in their personal relationships:

> I am the insurrection
> your strong hand put down

she writes in one of the poems. But what Das does not do in this collection, or in her third collection, *Bones*,[16] is to explore in any depth the experience of having been a girl in a poor peasant family, coming from

> early country darknesses
> the sooty juglamps of childhood ("Blackout," p. 37)

to the experience of being a doctoral student of philosophy in Chicago, a process sadly interrupted by very serious illness. *Bones* continues the personal self-exploration begun in *My Finer Steel Will Grow*, the experiences of disappointed love, illness, and, in a very fine long poem, "For Maria de Borges," an elegy for a brutally murdered Puerto Rican political activist, the transforming experience for a Third World woman of working in the urban capitalist world of the United States. There are a few poems that deal with her sense of a transformed Indian identity—"Beast," for instance—but the two sides of the experience, as an Indo-Caribbean and as a woman, are rarely brought into a common focus. The reasons for this are suggested in one moving poem in *My Finer Steel Will Grow*.

The poem closes a sequence exploring male-female conflict and in its very deliberate and ironic pastoralism touches on the complexities of her Indo-Caribbean woman's experience. The image is ironic because it presents an altogether simpler and uncomplicated state of relationship which her knowledge, her political involvements, and her view of the role of women had made impossible. Yet underlying the irony there is both a traitorous singing of desire and the affirmation, "I am not ashamed to be a coolie woman":

> Let us sling our pails
> upon our arm's strong rods
> and dance to the well.
> Our men will still be sleeping
> while we stoke the fire. The coals

16. Mahadai Das, *Bones* (Leeds: Peepal Tree Press, 1989).

will leap like joy in our hearts,
to flame. Our lords will wake
to hot curries and fresh-baked wheat.
And while it is still dark, they
will make their way to the fields.

THE TEXT: IN THEIR OWN WORDS

A female slave with a weight chained to her ankle which she had to carry around for months, a common form of punishment for female slaves. From Stedman, *Narrative of a Five Years' Expedition against the revolted Negroes of Surinam*, 1796.

Jean Rhys on Herself as a Writer

VERONICA MARIE GREGG

> I know that to write as well as I can is my truth and why
> I was born.
>
> —JEAN RHYS

Writing gave shape and meaning to Jean Rhys's life: "Until I started to write, and concentrated on writing, it was a life in which I didn't quite know what was going to happen" (Cantwell 208). Rhys brought unswerving commitment and a relentless capacity for hard work to her writing. In an interview in her later years, she referred to her reclusive lifestyle: "I don't see how you can write without shutting everything else out" (Staley 17).

In conversations with David Plante, Rhys emphasized the sacrifices demanded of her craft:

> You have to be selfish to be a writer . . . monstrously selfish. (*A Remembrance*, 271)

> Nothing ever justifies what you have to do to write, to go on writing. But you do, you must, go on. (*Difficult Women*, 38)

> Trust only yourself and your writing. You will write something marvellous if you trust yourself and don't give up. . . . People think they can sit down and write novels. Nonsense. It isn't done that way. It is not a part-time occupation, it's your life. (Ibid., 40)

> Only writing is important. Only writing takes you out of yourself. (Ibid., 50)

You should know it all. You should know . . . all the big, big writers. . . . All
of writing is a huge lake. There are great rivers that feed the lake, like
Tolstoy and Dostoevsky. And there are trickles, like Jean Rhys. All that
matters is feeding the lake. I don't matter. The lake matters. You must keep
feeding the lake. It is very important. Nothing else is important. . . . But you
should be taking from the lake before you can think of feeding it. You must
dig your bucket in very deep. . . . What matters is the lake and man's un-
conquerable mind. (*A Remembrance*, 247)

Implicit in this statement is Rhys's recognition of the connections between
reading and writing and the writer's duty to study her precursors, a
responsibility that demands rigorous intellectual application. Yet she also
suggests that she is an amanuensis:

I'm a pen. I'm nothing but a pen.

And do you imagine yourself in someone's hand?

Of course. Of course. It's only then that I know I'm writing well. It's only
then that I know my writing is true. Not really true as fact. But true as
writing. That's why I know the Bible is true . . . the writing is true, it *reads*
true. Oh to be able to write like that! But you can't do it. It's not up to you.
You're picked up like a pen, and when you're used up you're thrown away,
ruthlessly, and someone else is picked up. You can be sure of that: someone
else will be picked up. (*A Remembrance*, 257)

Rhys's persistent preoccupation with this aspect of her work is also revealed in her letters:

I don't believe in the individual Writer so much as in Writing. It uses you
and throws you away when you are not useful any longer. But it does not
do this until you are useless and quite useless too. Meanwhile there is
nothing to do but plod along line by line. (*Letters*, 103)

In responding to criticism that her work was dated, Rhys argued that
such an opinion was invalid, insisting that a work of art must be grounded
in the material and the particular world in which the writer lives:

Books and plays are written some time, some place, by some person affected
by that time, that place, the clothes he sees and wears, other books, the air
and the room and every damned thing. It *must* be so, and how can it be
otherwise except his book is a copy? (*Letters*, 101)

Rhys's observations point to her awareness of the essential dichotomy of
the artistic enterprise—the particular individual rooted in time and place,

her vision informed by a particular reality, and the recognition of the impersonal nature of art. She expresses the nature of art as inspiration or language—impersonal and ecumenical—and its contradictory complement, solitary meditation. The artistic enterprise consists not in suppressing the personality but in opening it up and converting it into what Octavio Paz in *Peras del Olmo* describes as the point of intersection between the subjective and the objective. This conjunction results in the "destruction" of the artist even as she endures within the work of art. What will endure is not the writer but the artistic product and the language. Yet the work of art cannot exist without its creator, who continues to sacrifice herself to the artistic process in trying to achieve the perfect work:

> I usually dislike my books, sometimes, don't want to touch them. But the Next One will be a bit better. I am always excited and forget all failures and all else. (*Letters*, 103)

In a career spanning more than fifty years, Rhys insisted repeatedly upon the connection between simplicity and artistic truth: "I have written upon the wall, 'Great is truth and it shall prevail.' Simplify—simplify—simplify" (ca. 1939). She believed that even artists operating within the conventional framework of English society were often challenged by the need to tell their truth but bowed to the domination of the prevailing ideology. Referring to English society as a kind of ant civilization, she pointed to the connection between art and life and the damaging constraints which convention imposes upon literature:

> I believe that if books were brave enough the repressive education [of the ant civilization] would fail but nearly all English books and writers slavishly serve the ant civilization. Do not blame them too much for the Niagara of repression is also beating on them and breaking their heart. (British Library, Folio 152)

In the 1950s, a period in which Rhys produced little, she continued to read extensively. In a letter to fellow writer Morchard Bishop she reacts fiercely to what she perceives as a dangerous attempt to control and coerce the production and reception of works of art:

> I read a letter in the *Observer* last Sunday from some editor . . . promising to accept a story up to the standard of *Boule de suif* [by Maupassant]. Well I should damned well think he would. And Hemingway's [*The Old Man and the Sea*]. Why not add Prosper Mérimée's *Carmen* for good measure. . . .
>
> Poor *Boule de suif*. They won't let her rest. . . .

The thing is, I very much doubt whether any story seriously glorifying the prostitute and showing up not one but several English housewives, to say nothing of two nuns!—their meanness, cant and spite—would be accepted by the average editor or any editor.

And *La Maison de Tellier* [Maupassant]—well imagine. . . .

Of course I may be quite wrong. . . . But I do read a lot and have a very definite impression that "thought control" is on the way and ought to be resisted. But will it be resisted?

Why say as Mr. Green does, "I demand a positive and creative view of life"? What is that? And why demand a view of life? Not his business, surely.

It's all very well to talk about *The Old Man and the Sea*, but what about *Hills Like White Elephants* or *A Way You'll Never Be.* . . . Would those be up to his "positive and creative" standard? (*Letters*, 99–100)

Rhys's ideological position and working aesthetic is to create "books written in short, simple sentences depending for the effectiveness on the intensity of the feeling of the author" ("The Bible Is Modern," n.p.). A study of the process of her literary composition, emendations of manuscripts, replacements of one stylistic variant with another, suppressions, and elaborations can further elucidate the way she uses form as ideology.

In her letters (often to impatient editors or to Selma Vaz Dias, who "rediscovered" her and adapted some of her work) Rhys repeatedly refers to the labor involved in her artistic creation: "I do toil, you know, and even a short story is written six times or more before I am satisfied. . . . Of course some things have to be done over and over before the words are in the right place" (Letter to Vaz Dias, December 1963).

Rhys discloses that to get the right word in the right place she must search for each word individually; "I [think] very hard of each word in itself" (Plante 53). Rhys's strategy recalls that of her mentor, Ford, who insists that the writer's mind has to choose each word and her ear has to test it until she has it right. The insistence on the *mot juste* extends even to Rhys's finished work. When Vaz Dias adapts *Good Morning, Midnight*, the author advises her that every word must be exact:

This is about the end of *Good Morning, Midnight*. . . . It's fine—except that . . . I don't think "rustle" is the right word for a man's dressing gown. . . . Taffeta rustles and so do stiff silks, I suppose, but wouldn't a man's dressing gown be a heavy silk? Please don't think me pernickety but every word must be exact. (*Letters*, 137)

Before giving permission for the reprinting of her early works after the success of *Wide Sargasso Sea*, Rhys was "very anxious to make a few alterations in *Postures* which they are going to publish as *Quartet*. . . . These alterations are all cuts of words or sentences." Of *Voyage in the Dark* she observes, "the revisions . . . are small but important, making it a better book for now, 1964" (*Letters*, 197).

In her lifetime, Rhys was acutely aware of the attitudes of critics and commentators to her work. She reacted with outrage when she thought that she was denigrated because she was a woman:

> I think that the Anglo-Saxon idea that you can be rude with impunity to any female who has written a book is utterly *damnable*. You come and have a look out of curiosity and then allow the freak to see what you think of her. It's only done to the more or less unsuccessful and only by Anglo-Saxons. Well . . . if it were my last breath I'd say *hell to it* and to the people who do it. (*Letters*, 32)

In her fiction, Rhys's scathing attack on British society's attitude to women is rendered especially in "I Spy Stranger," a short story written during World War II. The piece bears affinities with the works of Virginia Woolf (*Three Guineas* and *A Room of One's Own*), Dorothy Richardson, and Katherine Mansfield.

Despite similarities of techniques, styles, motifs, and thematic concerns, Jean Rhys does not fit easily or completely within the body of modernist writing or women's fiction of her generation. Jean D'Costa points to the difficulties created by Rhys's particular voice:

> A reader new to Rhys usually puzzles over her viewpoint looking both ways across the channel and the Atlantic, she seems for and against both perspectives. Her insider-outsider's treatment of England, France and the Caribbean gnaws at comfortable ethnocentricisms. . . . Looking for some kind of familiar ground, the reader tries to fit Rhys into available models of contemporary fiction, and fails. . . . She belongs to no recognizable school; fits into no ready-made slot.
>
> Rhys's fiction belongs, as she did, to worlds whose mutual understanding has "the feeling . . . of . . . things that . . . couldn't fit together." The dissonances of seemingly different worlds inform the Rhysian novel, finding coherence in her art. . . . All her work is charged with a sense of belonging in many wheres at once. (D'Costa, 391–95)

As a white female West Indian, her cultural heritage would have bequeathed an odd double vision born of the place of the white West Indian in her native land. She was white but not English or European, West Indian but not black. She was taught the language and customs of a land

she had never seen, England, while living in and being shaped by the
reality of the West Indies. Her sense of belonging to the West Indies
would necessarily be charged with an awareness of being part of another
culture. The ambiguity of being an insider/outsider in both the metropolis
and the colony shaped Rhys's apprehension of the world and was further
complicated by the complexity of the West Indian society in which she
lived—the ambivalences inherent in the color-class relationship and the
simultaneous existence of different cultural modes, Creole, black, and
indigenous. The interaction among the groups was regulated by strict
social and political norms, but at a psychosocial level the relationship was
syncretic. In Dominica, the Creole culture consisted of a blend of French
and English, further complicating the social and historical setting. Out of
this reality and as a means of rendering her vision of the world, Rhys
developed an ideology of secular individualism and psychological privacy
combined with a self-image of isolation expressed through "the solitary,
observing, experiencing self" which is present in all her fiction.

The relationship between her personal history and the nature of her
art is mediated by the writing itself. In talking about herself as a writer,
she observes:

> I can't make things up, I can't invent. I have no imagination. I can't invent
> character. I don't think I know what character is. I just write about what
> happened. Not that my books are entirely my life—but almost... *Though I
> guess the invention is in the writing...* But then there are two ways of writing.
> One way is to try to write in an extraordinary way, the other in an ordinary
> way. Do you think it's possible to write both ways?... I think so. I think
> what one should do is write in an ordinary way and make the writing seem
> extraordinary. One should write too about what is ordinary and see the
> extraordinary behind it. (Plante, 52, emphasis added)

If Rhys uses her life as a pretext for art, she insists repeatedly that life
and a book are very different. Among her major strategies are pastiche
and parody. In analyzing the functions of parody and pastiche in contemporary English writers, Robert Burden offers a useful definition, which
applies to my understanding of Rhys's attitude to the literary traditions,
styles, and principles of Europe and to her relationship with them:

> One of the fundamental purposes of parody in literature has long been that
> of literary criticism; that is to say, the literary technique of parody often
> preempts the activity of the would-be literary critic by offering within the
> text degrees of self-interpretation. It focuses on the limitations, personal or
> historical, of past forms; it often does this by suggesting the obsolescence
> of "previous" styles.... Parody is distinguished as a mode of imitation in
> a subversive form. This distinguishes it from pastiche, which implies a non-
> subversive form of imitation, which depends on systems of borrowing: a

patchwork of quotations, images, motifs, mannerisms or even whole fictional episodes which may be borrowed, untransformed, from an original in recognition of the "anxiety of influence." Pastiche may be the result of the conscious recognition of influence and of the fact that the condition of writing is in fact a condition of re-writing. . . . It may be used to stress the ironic awareness that language, literary forms, themes and motifs regularly come to the writer in, so to speak, second-hand form. ("The Novel Interrogates Itself," 134–35)

In the Rhys canon, pastiche and parody represent a built-in discourse with the European literary tradition and the ideological framework that defines, constricts, and to some extent distorts her as woman, artist, and West Indian.

The use of pastiche and parody is combined with the relentless honing of language to "deconstruct" the literature and language to which she is heir and to expose their absences and render her own ideological and critical position. In using and criticizing the literary resources of Europe while aiming for the simplest and clearest form of expression, Rhys creates a space for her work and for the works of later writers who also experience a "nothingness" in terms of the metropolitan canon.

Writing was the imperative of Jean Rhys's life. In her bleakest moments, she drew courage from the role writing played in her life:

I must write. If I stop writing my life will have been an abject failure. It is already that to other people. But it could be an abject failure to myself. I will not have earned death. (*Smile Please*, 163)

Bibliography

Burden, Robert. *The Contemporary English Novel*. London: Edward Arnold, 1979.

D'Costa, Jean, "Jean Rhys, 1890–1979." In Daryl Dance, ed., *Fifty Caribbean Writers*. New York: Greenwood Press, 1986.

Cantwell, Mary. "A Conversation with Jean Rhys, 'the best living English novelist.' " *Mademoisellle* 79 (October 1974): 170–71, 206, 208, 213.

Plante, David. *Difficult Women: A Memoir of Three*. London: Victor, 1982.

———. "Jean Rhys: A Remembrance." *Paris Review* 76 (1979): 238–84.

Rhys, Jean. "The Bible Is Modern." n.d. Unpublished essay in Jean Rhys Collection, University of Tulsa, Tulsa, Oklahoma.

———. *Jean Rhys: Letters, 1931–1966*. 1984. Harmondsworth: Penguin, 1985; Gollancz, 1983.

———. *Smile Please*. Harmondsworth: Penguin, 1976.

Staley, Thomas. *Jean Rhys: A Critical Study*. London: Macmillan, 1979.

Miss Garthside's Greenhouse

PHYLLIS ALLFREY

"But what a marvellous collection!" I cried. "I've never seen anything like it! Wherever did you get them all?"

The Chief Librarian smiled. Was it my fancy, or did he smile somewhat moodily? "We owe them to Miss Garthside. That is, she owed them to her. It's an odd story. . . . "

"This gorgeous plate, for instance!" I exclaimed. The volume was enormous, lavishly gilt-edged, and under gossamer tissue a life-size ruby-breasted hummingbird hung above one of the rarer Cattleya orchids. One whole shelf in the special room was taken up by these magnificent books on the flora and fauna of Venezuela. On that wintry evening the very sight of the pages transported me to a brilliant sizzling continent.

"She was one of our borrowers," said the Chief Librarian. "I cannot call her a subscriber, for as you know this is a free library. Well, we try to keep up a reputation for service and all that. I'm bound to say Miss Garthside made full use of it."

He pursed his lips in melancholy reminiscence.

"Of course she paid her fines—and as far as I remember, she never had a book out which was not eventually overdue. She kept things so long, you see. But most of the books she read were large and expensive. You know we try and obtain for readers the books they especially ask for. Miss Garthside was forever requesting some work that was practically unobtainable. Yet the Committee was very accommodating. They seemed to enjoy indulging her. She never asked for trash, anyhow."

"And I take it she was singularly charming?"—I rather enjoyed pulling

116

the Chief Librarian's leg. But at this he hummed and hawed and looked dubious. "No, I can't say she was. She was a plain old thing, lived quite frugally, and always seemed to wear the same grey tweed costume. Had a certain persuasive manner, of course. But wasn't a *femme fatale*, or anything like that—"

"Was she a botanist, then?"

"No, that wasn't why these books fascinated her. It was simply homesickness. She came from Venezuela, you see. Always said she couldn't stand the winter without her flora and fauna. We used to call this shelf 'Miss Garthside's Greenhouse.' Birds, too. She had orchids and birds in her bonnet, that poor lady."

I opened another volume. There was a beautiful engraving of a stick insect crawling towards a hibiscus flower. The jutting pistil showered miniature blossoms from a stamen like a painted trumpet.

The Chief Librarian said: "*Nostalgie des tropiques.* That's what she used to say. 'Mr. Hartley, I've got a bad attack of *nostalgie des tropiques.*' In her remarkable bad accent. But one day her father died. We were all surprised to hear that Miss Garthside had a father. She seemed so old—ageless, somehow."

"So he left her a fortune—and she repaid you for all the books that the poor ratepayer had provided!"

"Not so fast, my dear boy. No he didn't leave her a fortune. Just a small sum—a few hundred pounds, I believe. It came one February day, and I recall how excited the dear lady was. 'At last!' she kept on exclaiming, right in this very room. 'At last! My winter dream will come true. I can go home. Away from all this greyness—to the bright colours of the warm south!' She'd never been able to get even as far as Cannes, you see. So poor. We were all very happy for her. She insisted on taking the first cargo boat out, after she got her passport. She came here to say goodbye. Dear me, it was most touching. Holding my hand and all that. 'Mr. Hartley, these books have kept me alive, kept me going all these years so that I could go home.' Quite like a young girl—'blissfully happy!' she kept repeating. We felt upset when we saw that her ship had gone through terrific gales. But she arrived all right—I had an airmail letter. I think I replied to it quite promptly, but it was several months before I heard from her again. And before her letter reached me, she had died."

I was silent. What was there to say? To me, Miss Garthside was just another old eccentric; but it was easy to see that the Chief Librarian had thought her positively lovable.

"The letter is tucked away somewhere, I believe . . . But the long and short of it was that Miss Garthside's greenhouse was more agreeable than the real Venezuelan landscape—for her, anyhow. She suffered out there, you see. She had remembered the hummingbirds, but forgotten the mosquitoes and scorpions. She had remembered the kind servants—all of whom had departed—and forgotten the native birds of prey. She had gone from a borough where she got free medical attention to a place where it cost a fortune to be transported to hospital and have an operation. Worst of all, the change of climate and the blinding sunshine affected her eyes. Poor Miss Garthside died in darkness."

"What a sad story!" I said, a little clumsily.

The Chief Librarian looked shocked. "A sad story? Nothing of the kind my boy—a heroic story. You might as well say that Miss Garthside died to leave these books to the Library. She died for her greenhouse, in fact. We discovered afterward through a lawyer that she had sufficient funds to fly to Caracas and have that major operation. She even had a relative there who might have taken her in for the rest of her life. But she was afraid that if she did that, she wouldn't be able to pay for the books, and as she had written to me, 'those books gave me the happiest evenings of my existence.' You see," said the Chief Librarian loyally, "for all the dreaming and fancying she did among the leaves and orchids and birds in our old books, Miss Garthside was practical and consistent—in fact, a perfect lady."

The Unpublished Short Stories of Phyllis Shand Allfrey

ELAINE CAMPBELL

In her paper "Caribbean Women Writers and the Publishing Market" presented at the 1987 Caribbean Studies Association meetings in Belize, Pierrette Frickey presents a systematic tabulation of Francophone and Anglophone Caribbean creative writing by women. Frickey's focus is upon place and type of publication for novels, reprinted novels, poetry, short fiction, drama, fables, and children's literature. In an island-by-island survey, Frickey compares the number of published women writers to the number of published men in twenty-one islands. She found no instance of more women than men publishing either locally or overseas, and in several cases the figures are remarkably inequitable. For example, she has identified 405 published Haitian male writers compared to 15 female; 69 Martinican male writers compared to 12 female; 85 published Trinidadian male writers compared to 15 female. These figures are neither exhaustive nor fixed, but they are indicative of a pattern worth examining.[1]

Frickey attempts to present reasons for the pattern she documents. It does not reflect a lack of productivity on the part of Caribbean women; she offers examples of rejected or unsubmitted manuscripts culled from materials assembled over the past five years. Literary quality is difficult to address, but quantity of output does not seem to be the operative

---

1. My personal observation is that the pattern might be broken had Frickey surveyed the Dutch- and Spanish-speaking Caribbean nations. For example, in the Netherlands Antilles, women appear to be writing and publishing more actively than men. This situation, however, is anomalous.

factor. Genre may be an important influence. Frickey observes, "Proportionally [to men], women prefer to write poetry, short stories, drama, fables, tales, and literature for children in this order" (Frickey, p. 2). These genres, rather than long fiction or novels, tend to be published—if at all— in small local journals or in collections designed for use in schools. Short fiction, in the Caribbean at least, seems to be written more by women than by men. Coincidentally or not, it also appears to be less valued than longer fiction if publication figures are any indication of approval.

It is, therefore, not surprising that the short stories written by Phyllis Shand Allfrey—more than twenty of which I have in typescript form— remain largely unknown and unpublished. Allfrey is not entirely unknown as a West Indian writer. Virago Press's 1982 paperback reprint of her novel *The Orchid House* restored her literary visibility in England, and Three Continents Press's recent acquisition of the Virago plates has made *The Orchid House* available in the United States.[2] Further, Virago included two of Allfrey's poems in its 1984 anthology of World War II poetry, *Chaos of the Night*, although poems from Allfrey's two known poetry collections, *Palm and Oak* (Roseau, 1950 and 1973) and *Circles* (London, 1940), have not been recovered. At least one of Allfrey's speeches made while she held the portfolio of minister of labor and social affairs in the West Indian federal government (1958–62) will appear in Alan McLeod's forthcoming collection of oratory: *Representative West Indian Speeches*.

Curiously, the genre to which Allfrey contributed the greatest amount of published material—journalism—remains unrepresented in republications of her writing. As editor of the *Dominica Herald* and publisher and primary writer of the *Star* (1965–85), she produced an enormous amount of journalism. Should John Lent either update or expand his classic study of West Indian journalism, *A Case for the Commonwealth Caribbean*, he might include Allfrey's material from these two Dominican newspapers. Finally, Phyllis Allfrey's death in January 1986 leaves her unpublished novel, *In the Cabinet*, in a state of literary limbo.

In addition to the two novels, some oratory, a substantial amount of poetry, and a great deal of journalism, Allfrey wrote and occasionally published short stories. According to Donald Herdeck's *Caribbean Writers*, some of Allfrey's short stories were published in the early 1950s. Herdeck states that "numerous short stories [were] published in many newspapers and magazines" (p. 20), and he cites "O Stay and Hear" and "A Real Person" as published in *Argosy*, "A Talk on China" in the *Windmill*, "Breeze" in *Pan-Africa*, "The Untanglers" in *Writer's Guild*, "The Eyrie" in a Heinemann collection, and "Governor Pod" in an uncited publication.

---

2. Librairie Stock in Paris, however, declined to republish its 1955 French edition of *The Orchid House: La maison des orchidées*.

Of the short stories that Herdeck lists, only "The Eyrie" and "Governor Pod" are missing from the collection I have in hand.

These short stories—previously published and not—display a broad range of literary quality and diversity of subject matter. Although judgments of literary quality are subjective, the number of stories available argues in favor of publication as a collection. Such a collection could be either comprehensive—permitting the reader to make personal judgments—or selective—invoking professional critical judgment to winnow out some of the weaker candidates. In any case, in the interest of capturing the history of West Indian literature, the short stories merit publication. In addition, the need to redress the imbalance between published male and female Caribbean writers provides a third reason for publishing Phyllis Shand Allfrey's short stories.

The stories are listed in the first appendix to this essay. I have twenty-four in hand, and Herdeck cites two more. Others may be among Allfrey's papers in Dominica. One of the twenty-four—"The Carib's Revenge"—bears the subtitle "Idea for a half hour play for TV by Phyllis Shand Allfrey" and thus is not strictly a short story although it could easily be edited as such. Two of the stories are closely related to each other: "Lily" is a shorter version of "I Got, Capital." The lengthy anecdote "The Bodyguard" is a romanticized fictionalization of Allfrey's campaign for election to political office in Dominica during the late 1950s. Two of the stories, "The Warner Brothers" and "The Mystery of Ding-a-Dong Nook," are recastings of stories from the history of the early colonizations of Dominica and Antigua.

Before focusing on the half dozen or so of Allfrey's short stories that I would select as the most appropriate for publication, I will survey the settings of the two dozen extant stories to convey a sense of the range of Allfrey's interests. An attempt to classify the stories according to geographic setting yields four groupings which I list according to frequency of occurrence: (1) West Indies, (2) London, (3) United States, (4) both West Indies and London.

In the second appendix to this essay, I have regrouped the stories according to geographic setting. These settings reflect Allfrey's own life experiences but not in the order of their occurrence. Two of the stories set in the United Kingdom occur in the time period of World War II: "Dancing with George" and "Babes in the Wood." The somewhat dated quality of several of the stories is probably a result of the wartime experiences depicted or of the social attitudes expressed from that period. This dated quality, along with Herdeck's citation of short story publication dates in the early 1950s, suggests that Allfrey wrote most of these stories in the 1950s after she had returned to Dominica from London. I do not believe that Allfrey wrote many, if any, of them during the last decade or two of her life. I believe that journalism was her primary form of literary expression during the last decades, combined with an effort to complete her novel, *In the Cabinet*.

Of the twenty-four stories, eleven are in a West Indian setting that is not identified by name, although a reader familiar with both Allfrey's life and her island can identify it as Dominica. In only one story, "Parks" (set in New York City), does Allfrey name her protagonist's homeland. In this instance, Minta Farrar refers to her home island as "Spathodia." This is an early attempt by Allfrey to fictionalize Dominica—an attempt that is more fully realized in her unpublished novel, *In the Cabinet*, in which she names Dominica "Anonica."

Nine of Allfrey's short stories are set in England. She probably wrote most of them shortly after returning to Dominica from England. A few of these stories such as "The Untanglers," "Miss Garthside's Green-house," and "A Talk on China," do not mention World War II, but several relate to the aftermath of that war. Examples are "Babes in the Wood," "Dancing with George," and "Scraps of Paper."

The U.S.-set stories include "Parks," set in Central Park and in Harlem in New York City, and the two variant stories: "I Got, Capital," and "Lily," both set in New York State, as is established definitely by the frame story for "I Got, Capital."

Only one story, "The Carib's Revenge," has a Carib protagonist from "the Carib Reserve in a tropical island" (which can only be the east coast of Dominica) moving back and forth between that island and London. He is last seen in London, but he is preparing to return soon to Dominica, as indicated in the message he dictates to be sent back from England, "Please to inform my wife I coming soon."

Classifying the stories according to geographic setting does not take into account those in which a character located physically in one setting thinks about and refers to events that have taken place in another place in Allfrey's life experience. In this respect, Allfrey's writing is character-ized by the West Indian authorial tendency to have protagonists travel mentally between two widely separated geographic locations, often a West Indian island and London. Stories with this pattern include "A Talk on China," "How We Spend Christmas Here," and "Parks."

Allfrey's collection displays a variant of this pattern drawn from her own life experience. When Allfrey left Dominica for London as a young woman, she and the man she married in England subsequently emigrated to the northeastern United States—specifically to upper New York State— where she, her husband, and her two children lived for several years, before returning permanently to Dominica. As a consequence, the United States (specifically New England and upper New York State) figures in Allfrey's writing. It provides material for some of her poetry, some of

these short stories, and part of her well-known novel *The Orchid House*.
Short stories not set in the United States but that reflect this U.S.-London
relationship are "Babes in the Wood" and "Scraps of Paper," both of
which concern a mother's loss of contact with her child or children. Both
are based on the need to send children away from the dangers of the
London blitz. One of the greatest tragedies of Allfrey's personal life, which
relates to her own son, informs these stories. That tragedy, in my opinion,
invests "Scraps of Paper" with its special poignancy.

There are several reasons for pursuing this classification of Allfrey's
stories. One has been to discover how extensively Allfrey's writing reflects
patterns evidenced in the writing of better-known West Indian writers
such as George Lamming, Jean Rhys, and Claude McKay. The review of
setting—both physical and mental—demonstrates that Allfrey's stories
do indeed reflect the expatriation/exile theme so frequently associated
with West Indian literature. My personal favorite among the stories, "Miss
Garthside's Greenhouse," reflects this yearning for a tropical homeland
by a West Indian expatriated in England. "Miss Garthside's Greenhouse"
is a Jean Rhys-like story, but it was certainly written without reference
to Rhys's work. It does, however, contribute support to Kenneth Ramchand's reference in *The West Indian Novel and Its Background* to "the natural
stance of the white West Indian."[3]

Another reason for classifying the short stories according to geographic
setting is to discover whether any correlation exists between their physical
and mental setting and the quality of individual stories. A selected rather
than comprehensive collection must consider literary quality, and the
making of such judgments is a fascinating topic of inquiry. My initial
decisions about the literary worth of individual stories were made without
reference to the settings, and these decisions were not significantly influenced by the later analysis. My method has been simply to reclassify
the stories from an alphabetical listing into a geographic setting by
frequently listing with the consequent reclassification to be examined in
terms of the distribution of previously determined preferences.

It is appropriate at this point to name the stories to be selected for
publication based on my personal judgment of their literary worth. Listed
alphabetically, my first ranking includes:
  "Lily"
  "Miss Cashamou's Speakeasy"
  "Miss Garthside's Greenhouse"
  "The Objective"
  "A Real Person"

3. Kenneth Ramchand, *The West Indian Novel and Its Background* (London: Faber and Faber,
1970), p. 224.

"Scraps of Paper"

Allfrey had her own special favorites. In deference to her judgment, I would also add

"Little Cog-Burn"

"The Man Who Pitched Bottles"

"O Stay and Hear"

Additionally, stories that merit inclusion in a published collection, in my opinion, include

"Breeze"

"A Talk on China"

"The Untanglers"

I believe that a few of the stories do not merit publication. These include

"The Bodyguard"

"The Carib's Revenge"

"The Mystery of Ding-a-Dong Nook"

"The Warner Brothers"

By process of elimination, the reader can deduce that I am undecided about the following:

"Babes in the Wood"

"Dancing with George"

"How We Spend Christmas Here"

"I Got, Capital"

"Parks"

"Sitting Around in London"

"Time for Loving"

"The Yellow Horse"

Finally, to indicate intersections between setting and quality, let me match one classification against the other, using geographic setting to form the template:

West Indies	London	United States	Mix
*A Real Person	#A Talk on China	I Got, Capital	Carib's Revenge
Time for Loving	Babes in the Wood	*Lily	
#Breeze	Dancing with George	Parks	
*Little Cog-Burn	How We Spend Christmas Here		
*Miss Cashamou's Speakeasy	*Miss Garthside's Greenhouse		
*O Stay and Hear	*Scraps of Paper		
The Bodyguard	Sitting Around in London		

West Indies	London	United States	Mix
*The Man Who Pitched Bottles	#The Untanglers		
The Mystery of Ding-a-Dong Nook	The Yellow Horse		
The Objective			
The Warner Brothers			

Limiting myself to my own first ranking, and including Phyllis Allfrey's personal preference (indicated by an *), a predictable pattern emerges wherein West Indian stories outnumber British-set stories, which in turn outnumber U.S.-set stories in a relationship of 6/11::2/9::1/3. When second-rank stories are added (indicated by a #), West Indian stories gain one candidate while British-set stories gain two, yielding a possible collection of seven stories set in the West Indies, four set in Britain, and one set in North America.

Of the four British stories, two ("A Talk on China" and "Miss Garthside's Greenhouse") have strong West Indian mental settings. Of our hypothetical collection, then, nine out of a total selection of twelve stories might be called West Indian.

A more indulgent editor might produce a collection of more than the 50 percent I have included. In any case, even a selected collection of Allfrey's short stories, particularly if the two missing published stories ("Eyrie" and "Governor Pod") were included and if more materials could be found in Allfrey's papers, merits consideration for publication. Any publisher of Third World, Caribbean, West Indian, or Commonwealth literature who is seriously interested in publishing these specimens from Miss Garthside's Greenhouse can address me or my colleague, Professor Pierrette Frickey, for photocopies of Phyllis Shand Allfrey's short stories.

APPENDIX 1

Phyllis Shand Allfrey's Uncollected Short Stories with Place of Previous Publication

1. Babes in the Wood
2. The Bodyguard
3. Breeze   *Pan-Africa*
4. The Carib's Revenge
5. Dancing with George
6. How We Spend Christmas Here
7. I Got, Capital
8. Lily
9. Little Cog-Burt
10. The Man Who Pitched Bottles

11. Miss Cashamou's Speakeasy
12. Miss Garthside's Greenhouse
13. The Mystery of Ding-a-Dong Nook
14. The Objective   Unknown publication
15. O Stay and Hear   *Argosy*
16. Parks
17. A Real Person   *Argosy*
18. Scraps of Paper
19. Sitting Around in London
20. A Talk on China   *The Windmill*
21. The Untanglers   *Writer's Guild*
22. A Time for Loving
23. The Warner Brothers
24. The Yellow Horse

The following two stories are cited in Herdeck's Caribbean Writers

25. Governor Pod
26. The Eyrie   A Heinemann Collection

APPENDIX 2

Phyllis Shand Allfrey's Uncollected Short Stories

1. The Bodyguard   West Indies
2. Breeze   West Indies
3. Little Cog-Burt   West Indies
4. The Man Who Pitched Bottles   West Indies
5. Miss Cashamou's Speakeasy   West Indies
6. The Mystery of Ding-a-Dong Nook West Indies
7. The Objective   West Indies
8. O Stay and Hear   West Indies
9. A Real Person   West Indies
10. A Talk on China   England
11. A Time for Loving   West Indies
12. The Warner Brothers   West Indies
13. Babes in the Wood   England
14. Dancing with George   England
15. How We Spend Christmas Here   England
16. Miss Garthside's Greenhouse   England
17. Scraps of Paper   England
18. Sitting Around London   England
19. The Untanglers   England
20. The Yellow Horse   England
21. I Got, Capital   United States
22. Lily   United States
23. Parks   United States
24. The Carib's Revenge   West Indies/England

Bibliography

Allfrey, Phyllis Shand. *The Orchid House*. London: Constable, 1953; New York: Dutton, 1953; Paris: Librairie Stock, 1954; London: Virago Press, 1982; Washington, D.C.: Three Continents Press, 1986.

Campbell, Elaine. "From Dominica to Devonshire," *Kunapipi* 1 (1979): 6–22.

——. "In the Cabinet," *Ariel*, October 1986.

——. Introduction to *The Orchid House*. London: Virago Press, 1982.

——. "Report from Dominica, BWI," *World Literature Written in English* 17 (April 1978): 306–16.

Frickey, Pierrette Monique. "Caribbean Women Writers and the Publishing Market." Paper delivered at the 1987 annual conference of the Caribbean Studies Association, Belize City.

Herdeck, Donald E. *Caribbean Writers*. Washington, D.C.: Three Continents Press, 1979.

James, Louis. *The Islands in Between*. London: Oxford University Press, 1960.

Lent, John. *Third World Mass Media: The Case of Commonwealth Caribbean*. Cranbury, N.J.: Bucknell University Press (Associated University Presses), 1978.

McLeod, Alan. *Representative West Indian Speeches*. Forthcoming.

Ramchand, Kenneth. *The West Indian Novel and Its Background*. London: Faber and Faber, 1970.

Reilly, Catherine, ed. *Chaos of the Night: Women's Poetry and Verse of the Second World War*. London: Virago Press, 1984.

The Human Spirit

ROSA GUY

I was born in Trinidad, West Indies, British West Indies back then. I started school in that British colony, dedicated to upholding British tradition. My family was the proud product of that colonial system, churchgoing, lower middle class. We looked down upon our more unfortunate brothers and sisters who lived in the bush. We had names for them: "chiggar in their feet and yampe in their eyes," was one phrase comparable to those used in the United States to designate the inferior status of nonwhites. They were poor, poorly dressed, and never allowed to step over into our charmed circle. Indeed, we guardians of British culture had been well chosen.

Years later (after my first book had been published) I chanced to be in England and riding on the train through the English countryside. On the plush green meadows, I saw sheep grazing. Oh, there are the sheep in the meadow, I said to myself. And there are the cows in the corn. I even saw black sheep. Upon arriving in London, I was delighted to behold that London Bridge had not fallen down, after all. In other words, generations of my family had spent and were still spending their lives learning things that had nothing to do with their lives on our little island in the sun and denigrating those who provided our sustenance.

After my family moved to the United States we were taught European literature in schools. We read American writing only in the comic strips. On Sundays we read a full page of the Katzenjammer kids, two white boys living in Africa, who spent their days making a fool of an African king who was dressed in a top hat and loincloth and smoked a big cigar, stuck between fat lips painted a bright red. On Saturdays we went to the movies and spent the entire day watching Tarzan. How we cheered when this apeman brought entire tribes to their knees and African chiefs bowed to kiss his feet. We saw all the "road" pictures featuring Bob Hope, Bing Crosby, and Dorothy Lamour. We shook in terror along with them when black cannibals prepared pots of oil in which to boil them. We howled with hysterical laughter, holding our stomachs, when American blacks rolled their eyes in fright or when Stephen Fetchet shuffled across the screen too lazy to lift his feet to walk, too lazy to lift his bottom lip to talk, the weird jingo supposed to be black English. And we clapped our hands to numbness as cowboys shot up Indians for daring to protect their lands from invading hordes of whites and shouted our agreement when our white heroes sneered fom the sides of their mouths: "Ain't but one good Indian, a dead Indian."

We laughed and cheered, internalizing our sense of inferiority and concretizing the superiority of whites.

My mother was ill. But her relief at having her children away from the house on Saturdays, leaving her to her illness, quickly vanished when she learned about the movies we enjoyed. Lamenting the absence of black writings, which might at least have given us an overall portrait from which to draw, she forbade us to go to the movies on Saturdays and refused to allow the Sunday *Journal-American* in our home. From then until her death, we stayed home on Saturdays and read instead.

I read my first novel at age seven. My mother had been reading it and had put it aside, possibly intending to hide it. She was impressed that at my young age I had picked up and read a volume. She had a limited library, but she set out to choose my reading material. Together my mother and I read and discussed man's injustice to man. She taught me to look beyond the obvious, beyond mere words, to see into the soul of man.

She died. But the sharing with someone loved and lost carried with it its own drama and nostalgia. We had lived through experiences together, shared pain, and intellectual suffering, if you will, seeing beyond the threshold of each other's minds. That experience gave me a dimension that transcended age. We might not have interpreted the books the same way. I cannot say what she thought of each book. But she left me a legacy: she had sensitized me to the plight of others.

She never played with me. She had no time. We read, walked through the parks, and talked, talked, talked. I have often wondered if the anguish of the characters in the books we read actually affected me or whether their suffering was an extension of my own in my orphaned state, an anguish that magnified as time went by. Certainly the link that bound my mother and me went beyond the average parent-child relationship, beyond the economics of our situation, beyond pain, the suffering of impending death, and death. We had unlocked doors in our minds, opening them wide, allowing the pain and the suffering of others to infringe on us. Such suffering touched beyond the periphery of our minds, forcing us to plow beneath the surface of eyes, to stretch our imaginations beyond our limits in gauging the plight of others.

Wandering the streets of New York, I have been envious of children with parents, children in homes with the customary three-piece living room sets, where families sat and talked or listened to the radio or looked at television. And I have never seen cubs or kittens or puppies or yearlings or babies that I haven't choked back tears at the care given them. Every species guides its young toward independence, preparing them for their world. But terrifyingly, environmental changes put stress on animals. I have seen cats and dogs eat their young and humans kill their babies.

Tiptoeing through the casualties of poverty in the ghettoes—we called them ghettoes back then—I felt ostracized for those traits which being West Indian had etched into my personality. I was constantly aware of pain. Sensitized to it, I saw things that I alone could see and suffered as a result. I shall never forget the day I walked cringing the length of a snowbound street and not one snowball was hurled at my head. That was a happy day. I knew I was grown.

Although I ducked and dodged my way through adolescence, I never looked back in anger, only in sadness that there had been no books written, no guidelines to carry us over the deep but narrow ravines separating Americans from Americans—Americans from West Indians, from the suffering people of the world.

I have seen changes over generations. I have seen poor black and Hispanic and Indian children, who once upon a time looked on while a white world demeaned them, holding their stomachs in belly-splitting laughter, look back at themselves in anger, hating themselves, hating what they were made to be, and I knew that one day that hatred had to turn outward. And it did. I saw a generation that resented sitting in darkness, watching the occupants of a wall on the other side of the lights, pour champagne, eat caviar, drive in status-symbol cars, and I knew that one day they had to struggle to the death for status. They deserved status. They were Americans. They believed in the American way of life. They believed in democracy—for themselves. They believed in decent education and upward mobility for themselves too. And if barred from getting "things" through a decent education, they had to find a way. After all, they embodied the human spirit.

The United States is a playland. We are a country of exaggerators. We exaggerate everything. Drugs flood our affluent shores at an exaggerated rate. Not too long ago, the black poor were marked for drug abuse. Drugs poured into the ghettoes killed the minds, killed the souls of the poor black youth, and struck terror in the hearts of parents. Poor adults were made into victims by their children.

In a speech I gave in Japan, I spoke of this:

The 1960's, for all its traumas, was one of the most beautiful periods in American history. To those of us who lived through it, it seems like only yesterday. Television sets were in the homes but had not yet taken over parental responsibilities. Drugs on the streets had not yet changed youth gangs fighting over their turf into addicts, robbing everybody's turf.

Young people strong in their belief came out in numbers to follow Martin Luther King, Jr. They marched, sang, professed unity, and dedication to justice and to human dignity. Black and white students understanding the dehumanizing effects of prejudice and poverty shouted the slogans "Black Power," "Black is Beautiful" into black communities to arouse the black youth of their potential. By the mid-1970's that dream had ended with the killing of the Kent State students, the stoning of school children trying to ride buses to integrated northern schools, and the white backlash.

The country could no longer stand the exposure. Indeed, the struggle for human dignity seemed but a fad. Enlightenment had become a disease of the mind threatening to blight the nation.

"Benign neglect" replaced malignant neglect as responsible whites turned away when black youth, in the anguish of betrayal shouted "Burn Baby Burn," putting the torch to the ghettoes and white youth slunk away into some unknown underground to await a time when they were no longer so young; others turned to the cult of noncaring. The years in which it had been criminal to care had given birth to noncaring. Youth had seen the soul of middle America and preferred the forgetfulness, the decadence of drugs.

A generation has grown—is still growing—in those devastated ghettoes now called "inner cities," wastelands upper-class Americans seldom see. Generations are nurtured in the concrete swamps of razed city centers, suckled on mothers' bosoms in the darkness of bombed-out dwellings. Those who toddled with rats as playthings are men and women now. Their hard eyes are the products of dead dreams, descendants of the robbed and betrayed, secure only in their insecurity—their consciences reflecting the concretized dreams of their dead heroes personifying the violence that was done to them in their demands as they move into the surrounding world. Unafraid of dying, unafraid of killing, believing only in the terror that walks with them, they are weakening the fabric of society.

In this culture of exaggeration it had to be. We have gone from where the only good Indian is a dead Indian to every dude being a bad dude. We have the tallest buildings, the brightest lights, while in the dark beneath, the homeless grovel, beg, and starve, and the insane peer at us through eyes that threaten—biding their time, youth that once were poor are getting rich. They are cashing in on the big time, becoming million-aires. A few generations ago, when caught by a policeman, a poor or nonwhite person shook with fear and begged for life. Now a youth stopped for stealing might blow off the policeman's head. The white youths, once thought superior, are deep into drugs, getting their kicks from killing while sexing. Every time is playtime. We play; society crumbles.

The changes wrought by pride and prejudice are everywhere. Young turks from the bush made my little island their island in the sun. The once proud middle and lower middle classes peer through barred windows of their beautiful homes out at the young turks, who walk bravely around the countryside. That human spirit is a remarkable phenomenon: what one man has, another will have. What one can do, another will also do. If not at one time, at another time—when life changes.

I am not a sociologist. I am a novelist. The French call us *romancier*. I like the word. It speaks to the realm of imagination. My becoming a *romancier* might be spiritual, or how can one explain that I, orphaned on the streets of New York, untutored, decided to become a *romancier pour écrire les romans pour les jeunes*—and did. Surely the road between leaving my island in the sun, reading and sharing with my mother, was long, tortured, and twisted, strewn with bitter experiences, tragedies, and disappointments. But I have held on to her spirituality. She instilled in me a deep and abiding love for myself and others which enabled me to overcome clichés imposed by generations. She helped me to grasp the inevitability of change and so dissect the selfishness that makes it easier to hate than to love.

In my life I have experienced deep, dark passions. I have descended into depths of despair, rage, humiliation. But there is always the human will to live, the will to overcome—the human spirit.

In my reading I have lived through the agony of unrequited love with Andersen's Little Mermaid. I wrote about her in *My Love, My Love or the Peasant Girl*. I suffered ostracism with Stephanie in *Well of Loneliness*, the curse of bigotry with Heathcliff in *Wuthering Heights*, despair and confusion with Emma Bovary. The plight of Petit Javais and the injustices visited on Jean Valjean in *Les Miserables* might have been cut from my own childhood. All these authors sounded the warning through their themes that within oppression lies the seeds of liberation. Nothing lasts forever.

This, then, should be the lesson we share. Change is the one constant in life. The human beings populating the planet earth are those with whom we must move from one change to the next. A blending of ideas is important to make change easier. The sharing of cultures—a rare and beautiful concept—is inevitable. We cannot prevent change, but we can guide generational change if we care—only if we care!

To preserve our world we must put tradition where it belongs—in history books—and make current happenings alive with new meanings and new concepts to make a better life for ourselves and the generations to come. It is not easy. It can be exciting. Our society is tottering. Greed, the drug culture, is wreaking havoc on our lives and on the world as we know it. If not drugs there will surely be something else that we have to overcome. But there is after all the human spirit.

Writing about Fiction

SYBIL SEAFORTH

A writer of fiction does not, I believe, write narrative to convert, to disturb, to instruct, to reassure, or to challenge readers, except perhaps to challenge their understanding of themselves. One sets out to write because narrative gives value to experiences that might otherwise vanish, and writing immortalizes things. To write is to learn, to bring knowledge unexpectedly about oneself, and to discover truth as one goes along. But to think seriously about writing is to convince oneself that one's imaginative prompting and experiences will provide an inexhaustible source. But is one ever convinced? Writing line after line, one can never be free of misgivings for there is always a great distance between what is seen in the mind's eye and on the paper. The writer may be pleased with a phrase, a paragraph, or even a page. She may regard her description of a certain scene or character with approval, but self-doubt always lingers in the mind. Having written something, the writer wants to share it with someone and yet is afraid to have it scrutinized by others. She is afraid of baring her innermost thoughts, of exposing her soul. And yet her work has to be seen. For a writer's work appears to be of little value if the public does not approve of it. Approval and praise by others reassure the writer and provide the drive to continue, strengthening her wavering conviction that the source will not dry up.

Writing, like any other human endeavor, needs praise and approval if it is to grow. And yet the writer of fiction, like a poet or a painter, pursues art primarily to satisfy an innate self-yearning. How the writer's work affects the public could be a matter of material rather than spiritual concern. But it is human to be pleased when one's work gives pleasure or when others praise it. But what if approval and praise never come? An artist should find a reward in having satisfied the creative instinct. Yet that reward alone will not be enough, so the writer tries to get her work published.

My inclination to write arose from a strong desire to use words aptly, vividly, to describe people and scenes, to make them real. I have always admired beauty and richness in writing, sentences strung together so eloquently that they fall like muse on a reader's ear. I like phrases and paragraphs that a reader would read and reread, pause and reflect on, unwilling to leave behind: "The moon rises red from out of the still water of the bay. The hanging nets throw a dark shadow on the beach . . . the serried row of nets have come to rest under the trees . . . and only the water is unquiet with the pull of the tide" (Roger Mais, *The Hills Were Joyful Together*).

But what you want to write and how you write are different matters. I had written many stories in my mind before feeling compelled to take up pen. And the ideas I thought originally had led me to begin writing were no longer inspiring. I was unexpectedly learning something about myself. My desire to write, it occurred to me, was an urgent desire to be heard. I wanted to write because in the act of writing I was denying myself the muteness that had been imposed on me as a woman in a patriarchal society. In the act of writing I enjoy a sense of liberation from disappointment and hurts, a feeling of security and freedom.

I discovered that writing was hard work, for it demands time. And for a woman who is also a wife and mother engaged in a full-time career, time for writing is very scarce. Writing takes sustained and uninterrupted stretches of time, and with the division of labor we have been blessed with, "women have been required to produce time for men. Women have different working conditions from men; men have a right to write which women do not." Traditionally, men writers have had only one job; women writers have had two. By producing time for men, women have lost some of their own time, for there is little time left after family needs have been attended to. No wonder Florence Nightingale complained that "women never have half an hour they can call their own." For women with children it is difficult or impossible to find half a minute for themselves. Virginia Woolf's comment that early famous women writers had no children is no coincidence. A woman with family commitments must steal time to write, feel guilty about neglecting duties, and have that guilt reinforced when a thread of thought is suddenly broken as someone asks, What's for lunch? Where is the pen I left on the bed? Is it two cups of sugar or one? Motherhood means being available to be interrupted, responsive, responsible. The first two are qualities not necessarily required of a father.

Men are serviced but women do the servicing. The situation for men who are writers is different. They are shielded from the daily business of living, and women provide that shield. Unlike men writers who have wives, there is no equivalent for women. Men operate from a different context in which servicing remains invisible and unknown. They appear to be severed from day-to-day existence. Marion Glastonbury argues that men "are sincerely ignorant of the processes that supply their comforts, strangers to blisters and backaches." The situation for women writers is very different, for even if some domestic chores are relegated to paid help, the social convenience would be missing as well as the effortless spontaneity of the author's reliance on his wife.

"To be a female human being, trying to fulfill traditional female functions in a traditional way is in direct conflict with the subversive function of the imagination. There must be ways—and we must find out more about them—in which the energy of creation and the energy of relation can be united" (Rich, 1979:43). That women's lives are bounded on all sides by needs, husbands, and children means that women will tend to write differently than men, for their views will be grounded in a very different reality. For women, it is not possible to ignore the servicing or its implications. Marion Glastonbury wrote, "When Mrs. Carlyle told her husband that on a previous occasion she had thought of leaving him, he replied, 'I don't know that I would have missed you. I was busy with Cromwell just then.' He would of course have missed her as soon as he felt hungry or needed a change of clothes. But the master can afford the luxury of forgetting his reliance on his slave, whereas the condition of slavery can never be forgotten. It is permanently present to the mind." But what may be permanently present in the minds of women may be nonexistent in the minds of men. The drudgery of which Glastonbury speaks may be invisible. Women are not required to perform it, but it is unreal if they wish to create it in their writing. And so their muteness is constructed and reinforced.

Of course, both sexes experience problems inherent in writing. Writing takes time and energy. "You have to begin it and stick at it through many long and solitary hours and at the point every writer feels unsure, voiceless and guilty" (Fairbanks, 1978:247).

Fiction has often been regarded as the most successful genre for women writers because the novel makes use of the domestic scene or the life of the feelings or "trivial" observations, all supposedly close to women's experience. If we accept this idea, "it is because that scene is the world of social relations of inter-subjectivity, in which the author can reconcile to some extent her speech and her silence."

My first novel seems to support that suggestion. *Growing Up With Miss Milly* is a narrative rooted in the domestic scene: the life of the feelings and so-called trivial observations abound. I have tried to deal with some aspects of Miss Milly's feelings as a single parent, poor, obscure, a working-class woman with typical working-class problems, with a strong desire to improve her son's economic and social condition through education. She is dedicated to her son's needs, and because she is solely responsible for him, she gives them primacy.

"Working class women, illiterate or literate, play virtually no part in the conversion of raw material into literature," states Glastonbury (1979: 172), "since their preoccupations are not convertible into the accepted currency of truth in the patriarchal order. The prevailing definition of reality necessarily makes working-class women and their lives invisible."

Miss Milly dominates the narrative of my novel in much the same way that she dominates the life of her son Wilby, especially just before the common entrance examination. She is neither muted nor invisible, though at times she chides herself for not "holding her tongue" when she speaks with Wilby's father, a man who only marginally contributes to his son's upbringing. If she could keep a "still tongue," her fear of losing Wilby or even Lenny would not haunt her. Miss Milly's love for her son drives her to stifle him. Wilby is so distressed that he finds ways to rebel. His father's infrequent visits lighten the yoke he feels Miss Milly has placed on his young life.

Wilby cannot understand that his mother's dream is to help him escape the dullness and drudgery of her life. He may make such an escape only by passing the common entrance examination. It is the first step he must take if he is to climb out of the poverty he has inherited and for which Milly feels responsible. The common entrance examination is a source of yearly anxiety to many parents as well as children, regardless of their socioeconomic class. For a poor working-class woman like Milly, the anxiety is heightened because if Wilby fails to secure a place in a prestigious secondary school, in Miss Milly's view he will be able to do no better than be a part-time calypsonian like his father or a professional "standpipe philosopher" like his friend Tallboy. Miss Milly refuses to accept such a future for her son.

Less than three months before the common entrance exam, Miss Milly is deeply disturbed by the nightly beating and tuning of steel pans taking place in the panyards scattered around Chancery Bridge. The sweet, repetitive but now unwelcome sound will pierce the air and Miss Milly's heart for many nights until the Panorama finals. She knows it is difficult for the boy to concentrate on his homework as the music seeps into their small house. Still, she encourages Wilby to work harder. Then, ten days before Carnival Tuesday, the news that calypso singing and mas playing are part of the school curriculum turns Miss Milly's anxiety to rage. For the distractions have multiplied and she is angry, especially against the people in the ministry, who "can't see they trying to keep poor people's children like Wilby from studying hard." The added distractions increase Milly's resolve to ensure that Wilby spend more time with his books. Playing cricket with Tallboy in the savannah will not be tolerated. But Wilby uses his own devices to outwit Miss Milly. When he excels in sports and the calypso competition, his mother is so wounded that she is unable to share his achievements, and Wilby is deeply hurt. But experience has taught Milly that the only way to real success is through "book learning," and she believes that academic success for Wilby will liberate them from the constraints of poverty and improve the quality of their lives.

When I finally came to write the last line of the story, after many interruptions and countless hours, I discovered that writing was much more than putting words on paper, even beautiful words strung together. The narrative appeared to have taken me over. Whatever I was doing, the story was always in my mind, so that it became almost organic. It was a great relief to have finished. The story was no longer a part of me, and I felt a delicious sense of fulfillment. This feeling passed, and I began to hope that the story would be of some value, that it would get published, and yet I felt so tremendously relieved and satisfied in my creative instinct that I postpone worrying about its value. I realize that the reader of a work of fiction or the viewer of a painting is not concerned with the artist's feelings. How well I have communicated with the reader will be a matter for the reader to decide. Artistic creation is an activity that is satisfied by its own exercise in creating the story, the picture, or the poem.

The techniques of any art or craft can only be acquired through arduous labor. Writing, like any other work, has to be pursued vigorously and continuously. Through trial and error and perhaps a period of apprenticeship, I hope I may write well, write much, and make a habit of writing. I would like to be able to develop a writing style that is lucid, simple, euphonic, vivid, sensitive, and harmonious. I would like to achieve success as a writer of fiction so that my character can develop as I continue to discover myself and the many selves that a writer is made up of. To present society as the writer sees it, it is not necessary to copy life. The writer thinks with the narrative and can make an arrangement out of reflections of experiences, strong responses, and imaginative promptings to achieve that purpose. I would like to make some arrangements in the process of writing as a woman to help achieve balance between feelings and intellect to assist in dispelling the commonly held male view that "women may move their readers to sympathy, for this is perfectly consistent with their role in the private sphere, but they cannot stimulate their readers towards an understanding of the 'higher' goals" (Anna Walters, 1977). I would like to make serious matters that appear insignificant or trivial to men. I would like to make arrangements that will not reinforce the tunnel vision of men and to help achieve more recognition and validity for areas of women's experience that have been expressly denied in the male version of literature and truth.

Finally, I would like to have a room of my own in which to write and a reasonable sum of money per year (more than £100). When Virginia Woolf made her famous statement, quoted above, she was claiming for women writers the same material conditions for writing that prevailed for many men. She was claiming time: time when women were not automatically available to men; time when they were not required to assume responsibility for males, caring for and nurturing the young, the old, and the sick; time when they do not have to pay for their economic dependence.

"But perhaps she should also have insisted that men begin to service themselves so that men too would be unable to disregard the contrast between the interminable repetition of work that sustains life and the crystallization of experience that culminates in art" (Glastonbury, 1978). For if men begin to engage in supportive and nurturing tasks so that writers of both sexes share comparable working conditions, in this context the tunnel vision of men may begin to recede; the mutedness of women might begin to be dismantled.

I would like to think that in the course of writing fiction I may be able to make a contribution, however small, toward dismantling the mutedness and invisibility of women.

Bibliography

Fairbanks, Zoe. *Woman as a Writer*. New York: Houghton Mifflin, 1978.
Glastonbury, Marion. *Holding the Pen*. Women's Research and Resources Centre Publication, 1978.
———. "The Best Kept Secrets: How Working-Class Women Live and What They Know." *Women's Studies International Quarterly* 2, no. 2 (1979).
Mais, Roger. *The Hills Were Joyful Together*. London: Jonathan Cape, 1953.
Rich, Adrienne. *On Lives, Secrets and Silence: Selected Prose*. New York: Norton, 1979.
Walters, Anna. *The Value of the Work of Elizabeth Gaskell*. London: University of London, 1977.
Woolf, Virginia. *Women and Fiction: Collected Essays*. Edited by Leonard Woolf. London: Chatto & Windus, 1972.
———. *A Room of One's Own*. London: Penguin, 1974.

Growing Up with Miss Milly by Sybil Seaforth: A Review

IAN ROBERTSON

Growing Up with Miss Milly is perhaps the first West Indian novel that attempts to address the complex forces in the life of a young West Indian boy from the lower socioeconomic bracket in the year he is to try to cross the first major educational hurdle in his life. The problem is typical of the Caribbean, where the belief in education as a source of mobility is almost fanatical. The complex issues involved are examined through the experiences of Wilby, Miss Milly, his mother (though to a West Indian ear, the Miss suggests more of a grandmother), and Lenny, the visiting father.

Miss Milly's primary concerns are the physical welfare of her son and his education as a means to economic independence. She is prepared to forgo anything to achieve these ends. Unfortunately, two powerful forces conspire against her. The first is Wilby's essential boyishness. He feigns illness to avoid going to school; he goes to camp and builds a raft, which he then uses to save the life of a young boy in the village. He is good at pitching marbles. He is the calypso king and champion athlete of his school. But he fails to do as well at his common entrance as Miss Milly wants.

The second force is Lenny, Wilby's father, who, though an irregular visitor, shares a bond with his son which a less understanding mother might envy. Lenny does not share Miss Milly's concern for stability and the future. He is prepared to have his son live life to the full, and Wilby knows this and will exploit it to his advantage.

The novel examines with amazing sensitivity the conflicts of Miss Milly,

140

who, though clearly trying to do her best, does not fully understand the forces pitted against her. Ultimately, Wilby does not live up to her expectations for the common entrance test. Finally, the intervention of the Victoria County Council provides some consolation by awarding Wilby a scholarship, based, ironically, on his "outstanding ability as an athlete and an all-rounder," the very qualities Miss Milly rejected.

The author has the ability to draw clear characters and to present them in a situation that suits their personalities perfectly. Miss Milly is a very strong individual with clear goals in life for her son and, consequently, for herself. If she has one flaw, it is her inability to stand up to Lenny, her child's father, whose carefree lifestyle borders on the irresponsible and often conflicts with Milly's. This flaw contributes to the dilemma of the work because Miss Milly is trying desperately to prove herself an adequate mother in Lenny's eyes. Lenny is the stereotype of the macho West Indian father, though he does show considerable sensitivity to his son's need to have a balanced boyhood.

Wilby is a boy, a prankster, an athlete, a calypsonian, a marble champion. He is conscious of his mother's qualities, they restrain him, and when his boyhood nature gets the better of him, he takes the occasional chance of getting her angry.

The biggest strength of the work is its deceptive simplicity. The matters it treats, single parenting, early adolescence, interparental conflicts, preparing for later life, are all substantial. Yet they are presented at a level that is well within the reach of the average Caribbean reader.

If there are any weaknesses, they are in the use of language and the failure to abstract a clearly defined Caribbean scene. The dialogue attempts to produce levels of Creole which the writer does not actively control. As a consequence, some of the utterances are not genuine in any version of Caribbean Creole even though understanding is seldom affected.

The calypso tradition and the Victoria County Council clearly mark the location as typically Trinidadian, yet the language has more of a Jamaican ring to it, and the fact that these two territories perhaps represent the linguistic poles in the Anglophone Caribbean makes the setting a bit difficult for the Caribbean reader to accept.

The novel provides a very stimulating introduction to West Indian literature on young adults in the Caribbean or any other part of the world and can become the basis of stimulating discussions by sociologists of what it means to grow up in a colonial society. For any adult who has gone through the common entrance experience with his or her Caribbean child the memories of *Growing Up with Miss Milly* remain a haunting reminder of a past and perhaps of a present that cannot easily be forgotten.

Twin Influences: Guyana in the 1960s and Anglophone Caribbean Literature

JANICE SHINEBOURNE

During the 1960s, similar themes were running through Anglophone Caribbean literature and Guyanese political culture. It seemed that both were throwing up issues that everyone was compelled to face. Those issues of national and cultural and racial indentities had been raised at various periods as part of radical activist work, but never before had they come so heavily under education and government patronage.

This was the period when Caribbean literature was being discussed on the university campuses. I was a student at the University of Guyana. A new generation of critics had emerged on the campuses. High on their agenda was making a break with a Eurocentric bias and the attempt to establish a Caribbean critical and literary aesthetic. This was accompanied by a struggle to establish new syllabuses in schools and the universities. University students at that time were all exposed to the polemics. One debate encapsulated all the issues; this was the so-called Brathwaite versus Walcott debate. *Bim*, the *Trinidad and Tobago Review*, *Abeng*, *Moko*, and *Ratoon* participated in this and related debates. The racial politics of the imperial and colonial experience surfaced into national consciousness and put people in touch with their anger and pain, thereby releasing new energies, some of which were channeled into creative work, some of which were squandered in racial chauvinism.

Living in Guyana's political culture, I experienced an extremely rapid transition between revolutionary times and conservative, racial, chauvinistic nationalism. The social and political legacy of Guyanese community, grass-roots political activism was appropriated by a new political elite.

Our political culture degenerated into a quarrel between racially divided parties, the People's Progressive party and the People's National Congress, and into violent clashes between Indo and Afro Guyanese and confrontation between rural and urban Guyana.

The first Caribbean cultural festival was held in Guyana in 1972. This event brought together Guyanese culture and wider Caribbean culture; this was the first Carifesta, plans for which were laid early in the 1960s, and it was the brainchild of Forbes Burnham, the leader of the People's National Congress and the prime minister of Guyana at the time. It brought together Caribbean writers, artists, and performers from a variety of art and folk forms, and it brought them together in a popular context. I met and heard and saw Caribbean writers and performers for the first time. No one in Guyana failed to be excited by Carifesta. Yet, like Eric Williams in a speech to graduating students at the University of the West Indies (called "The University in the Year 2000"), Forbes Burnham had authoritarian views about culture and literature. They both felt very strongly that art and culture should serve nationalism. Carifesta symbolized the strengthening of the bond between art, culture, and nationalism. Andrew Salkey's *Georgetown Journal*, written during his participation in Carifesta, documents the situation of writers and artists functioning within the mold of nationalistic culture. *Georgetown Journal*, although unlike *Havana Journal*, is also written by Andrew Salkey. Both books provide insights into how two different political cultures attempt to appropriate and/or patronize literary and folk culture.

I began to write my first novel, *Timepiece*, during the late 1960s. I had a sense of being influenced by all this and of needing to come to grips with Guyana's political culture. I had a sense that it was a chaotic as well as a creative time. I felt it was important to know the roots of both the chaos and the creativity. In the process of doing that, it was necessary to uncover the contradictions, misguided sentimentality, corruption, psychotic violence, and anger that turned my country upside down, the neglect and betrayals—and also the immense worth, genuine morality, and intense commitment that had come to replace the old complacency about political culture.

In my second novel, *The Last English Plantation*, I still focused on the 1960s though this novel is set in 1956. I wrote this novel to try to get a longer view of the 1960s. Of course, the roots are also much deeper; they go further back into history. But the two novels are an exploration of experiences within my own lifetime, of lived experience in fictional form. The characters in both novels have a sense of their consciousness being dominated by the political culture they are experiencing. I also tried to release into the novel people's awareness that they are not shaped passively by mainstream political culture, that they have a working people's awareness of their tradition of activism, which forced them to evolve new strategies to deal with nationalism. It makes greater demands on their energies and it makes dealing with, for example, 1980s American neo-colonialism of a different order of difficulty, There is still a newsprint struggle going on in Guyana now, as it was when I was a child in the 1950s while in the outside world, in other scenarios, that struggle has become a technological one.

I hope to write one more novel to try to complete my concerns with these issues. I need to write about how the racial psychosis of the 1960s spent itself in the 1970s and brought certain themes to a conclusion. The killing of Walter Rodney in the early 1980s was one of these; it symbolized a culmination of the evil of the times, that relationship between chaos and creativity I mentioned earlier. Those terrible times in Guyana are the times in which I grew up, and I am committed of necessity to write them about.

She Scrape She Knee:
The Theme of My Work

OPAL PALMER ADISA

As a girl I often scraped my knee, not because I had poor balance or tripped over my feet but because I dared to be more or other than what good girls were supposed to be. I was never a good girl, and I passionately disliked those girls who displayed such behavior and loathed their dull expressions. Nice girls never scraped their knees.

As a woman I am often scraping my knee, sometimes without even falling. Perhaps it is because I dare to demand that the way be cleared for me or that I insist on leading the line at times. My choice. Always. Now as I reflect, I see that there is much in common between the little girl who frequently scraped her knee and has scars to prove it and this woman, me, who must often walk stiff-legged in defiance of the scrapes that are inflicted, often by the insensitive, the blind, the upholders of norms, traditions, and antiquated values that I had no part in setting and by which I will not abide. I scrape my knee.

I have found that among my female friends, knee scrapers tip the scale. We are so abundant with our songs, our plays, our poems, our paintings, our research, our cameras, and our children that all of us continuously scrape our knees and will not stop, even though we are not masochistic. But doing what we do, in the society in which we live, demands payment for our disregard of the law—Women, know thy place and thy place is often in the kitchen or horizontally disposed. Let me hasten to add that I find both positions appealing at times, but option is the operative mode in this regard. So we scrape our knees.

To lack scars on one's knees means one has lived safely, followed the rules, not questioned authority, accepted the prescribed rules. Since an energy within does not allow me to believe in blind destiny, I find that I constantly scrape my knees but make marvelous discoveries and have great fun in the process. More important, each time I scrape my knee I learn about my potentials as well as my limitations, and I experience the Mother-God within me. So I celebrate my scraped knees. Now I worry if I go for extended periods unscathed. Fortunately, the nosy child is around in the form of an inquisitive, eavesdropping woman so, alas, pussy scars always grace my knees.

As a writer I try not to scrape anyone's knees, but I must if my work deals with knee scrapers, which it does, even when the gender is male. Yet I do not want to see anyone buckle under and stumble; I do not want to see anyone rub cocoa butter on his or her knees to fade away the dark crust; I do not want to see anyone grit teeth, shrug off the resistance, and walk on stiff legs. But alas, even in my writing I find that both my readers and I scrape knees. Having been born in Jamaica, a very class- and color-conscious society, I watched many women scrape their knees, often without knowing why they were felled, and more often not being allowed a moment to acknowledge the pain or massage the swelling. These were the women who were the most beautiful to me, their beauty more a part of their defiance and independence than such physical whims as nose, mouth, and eye size, length of hair, or color of skin. So I un-knowingly vowed to be a knee scraper and this journey was begun.

To be a writer is to be arrogant, to assume that your "truth" is more valuable, more insightful than that of nonwriters; to write is to commit sin to print, pain to inspection, joy to the communal table. But this is one side; the other side of being a writer is to be humble, to have the desire to share a joy, a pain, a vision not yet realized, sometimes not even formulated. A writer is a person with vision, a seer, a mouthpiece for the voiceless, the mute, the talker, the braggart, the fool. They all scrape their knees.

Although definitions more often limit than elucidate who or what is being addressed, I will join the rank of definers and say I am a Caribbean feminist writer who attempts to highlight the small, to amplify quiet rooms, to thrust the skeleton from the closet, to make noise, to portray more than I see, and to render the ordinary in all its extraordinary sim-plicity. What this means is that I am specifically concerned with women, men, and children and their ability to cohabit and to create a world that is clean, safe, and open to differences; I am interested in planting the idea that equality is an appreciation for all of our talents that combine to make a unit, that equality is an act of love and faith in each other's ability to receive and give love, that to be equal means to agree, understand, and fight for everyone else's opportunity to be heard. This is particularly crucial in the Caribbean context, where neocolonialism wears a perfumed head. We all scrape our knees.

My work is shaped by my childhood experience, and though I have lived in North American for many years, my roots remain buried in the red bauxite soil of Jamaica. I still drink cassava soup and eat breadfruit dough. In my work I attempt to illuminate the myths, to reveal a picture of Caribbean life that is too real for commercials, to reclaim our land and remove us from being simply the property of someone else's dream vacation. I am concerned about neocolonialism and expansionism as exemplified by the invasion of Grenada in 1983; I am concerned with the shortages of schools for our children; I am concerned that my great-grand-aunt Zilla living in rural St. James still does not have running water and must walk two miles to the nearest bus. I am deeply concerned that poor women must bring their own linen to the public hospital and lie two to a single bed after giving birth; I am concerned that within the last five years the increase in brutal rape of women and girls, some as young as ten, has skyrocketed and there has been no outcry from the society; I am deeply concerned that young men are unemployed, left to prowl the streets and hang out at sound systems to try to catch a glimpse of their dreams; I am very concerned that our little piece of the rock, independent as we claim to be, is only so on paper and that we still look to metropolitan countries to set standards of beauty, values, and cultural validation. We crawl, we creep, we walk, we stumble, we scrape our knees.

My writing is an attempt to grapple with what it means to be a woman, black, Caribbean, conscious. These are not different realities; they are integrated. I cannot emphasize the wholeness enough. Too often nothing gets accomplished because we separate into camps and compartmentalize our experiences based on an internalization of our Euro-American education. I am symphonic, and whatever I process is integrated in myself as a woman, a person of African descent, a Caribbean. Like the tree of which I am a branch, I am perennial. I am certain of my continuation even though the form might alter to adapt to a new climate. I/we will be around because we are knee scrapers, survivors of the seas and wind, reapers of cane and banana, makers of history.

I am a delphinium, partly through heritage but mostly by example, and I must admit that my examples were almost women who never showed any diffidence in the face of adversaries. I associate the carnival colors of my girlhood with these women, who were as captivating as the yellow poui blossoms, breathtaking as the flame-red flamboyant, and bittersweet like sugarcane. My short story collection, *Bake-Face and Other Guava Stories*, is a tribute to those women who never have access to microphones, who carry their madness sewed into their skirt hems and tied in their handkerchieves buried in their bosoms. Giving voice to this madness that besieges us, giving voice to the celebration of our lives, giving voice to our quiet fears and invisible tears, giving voice to our struggles, our victories, our determination, I scrape my knee, she scrapes her knee, we all scrape our knees.

Who are these women, Bake-Face, Lilly, Denise, and June-Plum? They are women who are always waiting for some man to enter their lives and change them until they realize that their knees are connected to feet that move, to eyes that show them themselves, to a spirit that guides them. Guava is a fruit that grew in my backyard. Often when it was ripe the exterior skin remained green and rough, unappealing, but when I bit into the pinky meat, I was overwhelmed by the soft-sweet taste. So, too, these women, if simply judged by their physical appearance, seem unflattering, but once you enter them, allow them to tell their stories, the wealth and breadth of their lives assail you like a spider's web. That is why they are presented in my collection, *Bake-Face and Other Guava Stories;* more likely than not you would walk by them without even inquiring if their knees are healed yet. Bake-Face scrapes her knees because she chooses herself over her only love, Mr. Johnson; Lilly scrapes her knee because she cohabits with Richard, who cannot accept himself, so her deceased grandmother has to come and reclaim her by guiding her back to the protection of her mother; Denise scrapes her knee because she loves her nephew Perry to distraction, believing that to be needed completely is the ultimate achievement of womanhood; and June-Plum stumbles and gnashes both knees because she makes another woman, Yemoja, her alter ego, her competitor, rather than recognizing her need simply to be a woman, beautiful and free from the demands and inquiries of children. So they all scrape their knees many times and learn from their injury to walk with themselves. They stumble, but they continue on.

Pina, The Many-Eyed Fruit, my children's book, fascinates and scares young ones; it is intended to warn them about the pain connected with scraping their knees severely. Pina, my little girl, who lives on Tall Trees and Proud Grass Island, who dances with the breeze and always leaves her footprints in the red, dewy soil of her island, turns into a pineapple because she is unkind and very rude to her mother. Sometimes we scrape our knees deliberately and ignore the pus gathering and the pain chanting because, like Pina, we naively believe that we are the center of the world and we need not reciprocate kindness. Then our knee scraping is not merely a lesson learned but an example. That is why Pina remains a pineapple; she learns her lesson too late. As a child, I learned that kindness must be repaid with thanks. I scraped my knees and my sister rubbed them well with a green leaf.

Perhaps I was only seven years old when I first heard Louise Bennett, the Jamaican Queen Mother of verse and humor, recite her poetry. Her voice was resonant and sure, rendering our speech musical, classic, poetic; the rhythm that my prep school was teaching me was the voice of the common uneducated masses. I faltered in my boastful stance that my "proper" speech was enviable, to be admired. Here was Louise Bennett, clearly more proper, more eloquent. I remember my surprise that such a bold knee scraper was allowed to flaunt her sassiness, her tenacity, her affirmation of herself and us. But later I was to learn that knee scrapers are never allowed anything, that we seize the moment, the day. Louise Bennett stole the time, and this created a space for me. And perhaps it was then that I decided to use our rhythm in my poetry, my stories, in the recording of our lives. It gives color and flavor to validate our cultural ethos. Bennett allowed me to be brave and risk the surprised satisfaction of being myself.

To say that I am chronicling our lives would be to limit my role as a historian. Although I believe that all conscientious writers are historians, the good writer is more: sociologist, psychologist, architect, musician, cane cutter, pallbearer, and recorder. My work emerges from the core of my life—my family—from which I weave the memories that we think we no longer know with the memories that we forgot we have with the memories that are lived! As such my writing is encompassing and circuitous, no separation between the past, the future, and this moment.

I am the work, and the work is woman, womanish, leggo, female child of Catherine, Sister of Leonie, aunt of Paul Patrick, mother of Shola Yetunde. I am woman but more, more to my sisters, whose hands, rough from scrubbing clothes and pounding yam, cry out. I am wo/man, womanish. My mother used to declare, threatening/applauding, "Two 'oman can't live in de same house." I, woman, knew I had to comfort the mother who walked away from the drunkard husband and received a slap for daring to be independent and be her own boss when most other women sucked in their lips and mumbled under their breaths; a mother who lived feminism before the word was coined and came to be a label, a badge of honor, disrepute, and struggle. I am female, black, mother, lover, writer, student going against the tides, daring anyone to step in my path, swimming in Yemoja's waves, calling on Oshun, remembering Ida B. Wells, fighting with Mary Nyarijiru, Mau Mau warrior, echoing Sojourner Truth's words, "Ain't I a woman?" Questions! They asked for me. Questions! They sacrificed for me. Nanny, the Maroon warrior, caught bullets in her teeth and made magic from soil. Miss Scott put three husbands in

the grave and was so stern that the most vicious bulldog hid his tail in
her presence and crawled to safety in a corner. Who paints their stories?
Who writes songs in memory of their lives? Who acknowledges their
contributions? Their bravery ensures that fewer knees get scraped.

I am the work, and the work is womanish. The stories are of these
many-varied women, acknowledging that there is not just one kind of
woman; their commonality is their strength, their determination to be
their own bosses, to push their girl-women ahead with education, economic independence, and birth control. My work is of the market women
whose pride is always borne on their heads; of the prostitutes leaning on
the walls of Kingston dying for day to break so they can hurry home to
make porridge for their children and send them off to school with the
money they collected by slaving; for the women who are intimately connected to men and nurture them and are loved and abused by them; for
the girl-women forced by lack of class privilege to grow up too fast; for
the women who have always danced with the sun and felt the wind
caress their hair; for the girls trying to defend themselves against societal
and advertisement constraints that would categorize and limit them with
a reworked package claiming to be for their liberation. My work celebrates
women's need to be loved, to have sex, to be wild and crazy if the occasion
calls for it. These poems are womanish, female, spirited, sponging Winnie
Mandela's feet, rubbing the shoulders of the basket women in Kenya,
raising the backs of Indian women; my writing is an introduction into a
world of womanism. Scrape, scrape, we are scraping knees.

Reflections of a Writer

CLARA ROSA DE LIMA

My father died when I was four years old. I was second to last of six children. There were two boys, a girl, a four-year gap, a boy, me, and a girl. My mother was twenty-six when she was widowed. Three of my mother's sisters lived with us, and there were two girl cousins who came occasionally to visit from Venezuela. Twice an aunt who was half Amerindian came from Barcelona, Venezuela, to care for us while my mother traveled with one of her sisters. My mother's youngest sister was the same age as my oldest brother.

Partly because so much Spanish was spoken at home and also because there was need to communicate with my aunt from Venezuela, who spoke no English, I soon was speaking Spanish, a language in which today I am fluent. I am now sixty-seven years old.

We lived in a large house in which there were many servants. They were mostly women, and the one who was very special to me was our nurse, Ethel. She came to us when she was forty and never left until she died at about a hundred and three. My mother ran the family business so we were left more often than not in the care of the help, the aunts, and our one uncle, who was the same age as my second brother.

When I was eight I pestered my mother to send me away to school, and I was sent to the Ursuline Convent in Barbados. The reverend mother, Angela, and two other women in Barbados took care of me. They were wonderful to me. After two years I was brought back to Trinidad with the excuse that I was starting to speak with a marked Barbadian accent. This was the reason given, and I accepted it. For a year I attended St.

151

Roses Intermediary and for a year Mrs. Lake's private school. Mrs. Lake was an Englishwoman. I studied the normal subjects and French and German.

Once again I persuaded my mother to send me abroad. I was determined to have an education outside of the island. I was sent to Notre Dame of Maryland in Baltimore, chosen because my second brother was studying at Johns Hopkins University.

In those days there were no planes. It was necessary to travel by boat, which took two weeks. The boats on which we traveled were banana boats. I well recall that first trip. I was put in the care of the purser, a friend of the family. One night the purser had the other returning students and me to a gathering in his cabin. A magazine was passed around with an article the contents of which I failed to grasp. I have never forgotten that incident. I told myself then, never again, and, when in doubt, ask, and that has been my approach since.

The three years at Notre Dame of Maryland, a convent, were special. I abided by the rules and benefited from my studies. I was more or less adopted by an extraordinary woman. She was a Cuban named Nena Roca. Her husband was a dentist, and she was a Christian Scientist. I owe her a great deal. She was vital in creating whatever I am today. She introduced me to philosophy. I particularly remember reading Nietzsche. She introduced me to special books and to the theater. I recall that a special touring company came to Baltimore and she sent me to the matinee to see *Julius Caesar*, played by well-known actors of the day. She lived in the heart of downtown Baltimore in a corner apartment. The policeman regularly on the beat was protective, and I was made to feel secure. She taught me to be caring. If I left on the light in the closet, I paid five cents. The same applied to making a phone call or leaving a ring in the bathtub. She impressed upon me that the best clothes last the longest. She proved right. There were always clippings awaiting me on how to behave and what young girls should and should not do. She was supportive of my activities. Although classical music was long a part of my life, for I started taking piano lessons when I was five and attended all the concerts given by important visiting musicians to Trinidad, in Baltimore I attended concerts that were different. Weekends were spent with her as well as Easter and Christmas holidays, with an occasional visit to New York to stay with Italians, friends of the family. The three months of summer vacation made it possible to make the two-week boat journey back and forth. Nena Roca insisted that I take part in all school activities, and she supported me by attending the plays in which I took part. She approved of my going to my first prom, chose my dress, and approved my date, who was none other than the son of the president of Brazil, Gertulio Vargas, who was studying at Johns Hopkins University.

Nena Roca made sure I always met the right people. She was an extraordinary woman. Sadly, she became ill and not long after died. My life might well have been different if she had not.

Because I was doing well at the convent, it was decided that my younger sister should also attend. I was in my third year, and plans were being made for me to attend college. But that was not to be. I was not permitted to return. The excuse given was the possibility of a war. Some years later, my mother's youngest sister, to whom I was very close, told me the real reason. I was hurt to the core. I had been defrauded of the right to graduate. Had I been told the real reason, I would have been able to fight for my rights.

Then came World War II, and I spent most of those years in Caracas with my mother and oldest brother, who was ill and needed special medical attention. I joined the conservatory of music, studied the piano with another special woman, Elena Arratte, and worked half a day in a law firm dealing with patents. There I learned secrecy. I translated the English descriptions into Spanish. Among them were the hardware for the invasion of Normandy.

Two years before the war came to an end, I went back to America again because of my brother's illness. My time was spent between Ann Arbor, Michigan, and New York. I soon learned about traveling on trains with troops. Finally, I enrolled in Long Island University. My reasons for that choice are too complicated to explain. By then Nena Roca had died, and there was no more reason to visit Baltimore, but the knowledge instilled by her was well applied because it was hard going economically living in Manhattan in an apartment shared with two other girls. During those years I started writing short stories. I was dissuaded from sending them to a magazine by one of the many professors with whom we were friends. Perhaps I should have taken a positive stand. I am not a short-story writer, but I am a good storyteller.

Among the girls at the university I made few friends. I was five years older than the average freshman. I was more attuned to the boys; they were closer to my age for having been in the service. Many of the professors were also more my age.

I studied extensively through two summers, and in the third I traveled by myself to Rio de Janeiro, São Paulo, and Buenos Aires. On my return I met a Venezuelan exile and fell in love. I failed to graduate but became involved in those occurrences which appear in my novels.

The Betancourt government was ousted, and the Venezuelan who had been exiled was posted to Washington for two years. He was then appointed chief of national security in the Perez Jimenez regime, and together we went to live in Caracas, Venezuela. There were continuous reports to be written. There was always a constant flow of senators and ministers as well as visiting American journalists to entertain. I was definitely in the know of all that took place.

Then it became necessary for me to make a six-month trip covering every country in South America, and owing to that trip I was asked to report back to Venezuela on the socioeconomic and political situation of the countries I had visited.

During those six months I ran into those very journalists I had met previously, and they not only shared the comments I sent back but were also able to meet many influential people to whom I had been recommended or whom in many cases I knew from before.

Those journalists were Sam Pope Brewer of the *New York Times*, posted to Brazil, where he was domiciled, Ed Morrow, also of the *New York Times* but in Buenos Aires, Bill Forbis of *Time* magazine, who later became senior editor, and Frank Capa of *Life* magazine. Ed Morrow tried to persuade Bill Forbis to take me on as a reporter for *Time* magazine. They were all in Buenos Aires because of a possible overthrow of Juan Perón. These were heady times. I was in my early thirties. We were all lunching when Ed made the suggestion, and my only reply was that I didn't want to make a flying tour of South America. We remained fast friends for many years and often our paths crossed again.

On that trip I met another Venezuelan, who was vice-president of the international department of an American bank. As a result, on my return to Venezuela, I decided to leave for good. After six months in Trinidad with an understanding mother, I went back to New York City.

My friend insisted that I write a diary. Keeping a diary was not new to me. I had kept one when I was in my teens. There are eight or more large loose-leaf books filled with events in my life, and it is because of those diaries that I turned my typewriter, which I have always described affectionately as my talking machine, into a vehicle for writing my novels. I wrote sketches of the personalities I met during trips that I now made with my friend, and with time they, together with past personalities, became characters in my books.

When the regime of Perez Jimenez was ousted, I lived in Caracas for two years. My friend was invited to be ambassador to Brazil to open up trade between the two countries. That led to my living in Rio for three years.

Those trips on propeller planes were an experience. The planes flew low, and the scenery was magnificent, the deserts mauve and pink in color, the snow-covered peaks of the Andes, the lush valleys, the lake Titicaca.

My first real desire to write came when I heard the news that Coronel Albenz had been assassinated. He was president of Guatemala. I thought to myself, it is the only way out, and "The Only Way Out" is the name of my first novel, which is unpublished. It is about Luis, the main character, looking back on a period of his life in exile. He remembers his brother Augusto's impatience about the strong-armed dictatorship. He is convinced that the only way out is assassination. The same applies to Domingo in *Currents of the Yuna* set in Santo Domingo. I have often wondered if these young men had the makings of martyrs or were really heroes. Though I have been much a part of what I have written, I still have not been able to answer this question.

There was also another unpublished novel called "Give Time Time" based on the socioeconomic conditions and way of life in Colombia, Ecuador, and Peru. During my many visits to Peru and Ecuador as well as Colombia and Bolivia, I learned that I should not attempt to write about an Amerindian as if I were one. I could only write as an observer accepting their attitudes as they presented them to me, and even what they presented had to be taken with a grain of salt. The same applies to writing about the Asians in this community, yet I could easily get into the Afro blacks.

In Rio I wrote *Countdown to Carnival* first, but only when back again living in New York did I complete *Tomorrow Will Always Come.*

The closer I looked at Brazilian society, primarily in Rio, the more imperative it became to portray closely the vast differences of the lower lower, the lower middle, the lower upper, the lower middle, the middle middle, the upper middle, the lower upper, the upper middle, and the upper upper. This breakdown is not my invention but that of another author, and I have always kept it in mind when writing how this grouping is affected socioeconomically and politically in the many countries in which I have lived or visited. Another highly political novel that was not published was called "Burdened with Deceit." I am yet to complete the last draft. I wrote it when I was in Venezuela during my two-year stint there with the international banker.

There are similarities and great dissimilarities between Trinidad and Rio. There are many who believe that because of the Afro-European population in both countries there must be some sameness. In Brazil there are no peoples from Asia. The one likeness between the two would be the Carnival, but their Carnival is totally different from ours. In Trinidad rich and poor alike play in the street together. In Rio the rich play in their clubs, and only the tourists and the poor play on the road.

The novel set in Rio is based on observations of life there in the 1950s and 1960s. Life has changed, and the crime rate has risen considerably. Few writers today would dare to visit a favela and take part in Macumba rituals. Yet I am sure the politicians and the so-called do-gooders are still making promises which they will never keep.

Euclides in *Countdown to Carnival* feels defeated by the world into which he is born. There is no way out. When he thinks of ingratiating himself with Lourdes by buying a gift, he realizes he has so little money that he will have to go without lunch for a month if he splurges.

Lourdes, on the other hand, well employed with a reasonable mistress, who makes her living as a seamstress, cannot help but dream of a better life. She loves the movies because they allow her to enter the wonderland of Hollywood stars living in posh homes. Lourdes is not a bad person, she is just desperate for a better life than the drudgery of serving someone else. Lourdes is the perfect example of many of the young maids in Rio and perhaps also in Trinidad in the 1950s and 1960s. I have always felt the need to analyze the relationship between mistresses, and maids in our part of the world because some think that to be a maid is demeaning. Yet Lourdes and Olga live together amicably. They were brought up within a system of mutual respect. For example, foreigners coming to live in those countries ruin the system, and yet some of their concessions improve it. I did not touch on the lives of the very rich living in sumptuous homes or apartments in those novels, but I have in my recently written novel "The Pinnacle."

Let us turn to the *Currents of the Yuna*. In Santo Domingo, where I lived for three or more years, there is what is known as the godfather syndrome. Without the godfather, the peasants or farmers living in those hamlets would not survive. The godfather is the shopkeeper-cum-moneylender. He holds the pursestrings of the hamlet and is intimate with the authorities. He obtains benefits for himself and his own. Hence Rafa is able to enlist in the army, whereas Fernando, Rafa's close friend, is taken to the capital in the hope that his friend Inocente will more or less adopt him. This is another syndrome: many of those living poorly in the provinces give their children to people in a higher bracket to raise. I saw it in Caracas and experienced it personally. One day a shoeshine boy came to the house and stayed. The people of Santo Domingo are docile, perhaps from so many years under a dictatorship. Trujillo had pencils made which had written on them "the first teacher of the republic." There was a picture of himself as well.

Through special circumstances it was possible for me to visit every nook and cranny of that country, visit their hamlets, called parajes, poke my nose into their huts, be given green fried plantain, which they use instead of bread, to taste. The characters are based on those who became close friends. The conversation was highly political, hence political themes were irresistible. There is an enormous distance between the ruling class and the peasants. The students whose eyes have been opened by learning cannot resist perpetrating a revolution against the ruling class, which is very small. What those families don't own is in the hands of foreign companies such as Gulf Western.

Domingo is an abrasive revolutionary. He wants action. How does one fight something so fierce? He asks his teacher, Placido. Placido cannot answer. The dictatorship has gone on too long.

Domingo would have his fellow students imitate those who followed Castro. He is convinced that the peasants will follow. Placido explains that they won't because they are unaware of what is happening in the capital. The radio—there is only one, which is owned by the shopkeeper—says only what the government wishes the people to hear. There are no points of comparison. They have never had access to what those in the capital have. Their diet is different, they go shoeless, there is no electricity or running water, and the campesino is forced to drop his excrement like an animal whenever he feels the need.

Finally, Trujillo is assassinated. A consejo takes over, but under pressure from the Americans there is an election, which brings Juan Bosch into power. He was too lenient. He refused to show strength when he should have against the barrage of attacks against him by a radio commentator. The Americans, having lost a large contract for an oil refinery and feeling that Bosch was too weak, became a part of the conspiracy to oust Bosch. They sent in their troops, and Bosch was forced out of the country. Bosch had been in exile too many years. The rich refused to give an inch, and the little that Bosch was asking for was too much as far as the rich was concerned.

Two graduates of the University of Santo Domingo wrote a thesis on *Currents of the Yuna*. They said the story and the history were authentic and added that I had a right to intervene with an analysis of the happenings and anticipate the behavior of the characters.

My friend was then the representative of the International Agricultural Development Bank and economic adviser to Juan Bosch as president-elect and during his short term in office. He was asked to make a report on the illiterate farmers of the republic, and I wrote the report as a short story. It was published and circulated in his name.

My concern has always been with the poor and their right to dignity and where life will lead them. The older members of the community have grown to accept what life has given them, but not so the young. *Currents of the Yuna* perhaps in a way was born out of that short story. Liniero was the main character in the short story, and he is Fernando's father in the novel. I knew how that novel would begin and how it would end. During our many trips by car to Puerto Plata we would stop at a sort of watering hole and there two little boys always came over to shine our shoes. Then I thought to myself, if I gave them shoes, where would their lives take them. I used the same approach with the masseuse in *Tomorrow Will Always Come*. I made sure she was given a Volkswagen, which proved in the long run to be in her disfavor.

In my opinion, most Caribbean writers relate their tales from the lower lower, the lower middle, and the lower upper, but as a writer in the middle upper, it is easier for me to analyze both sides of spectrum. By standing in the middle, one can see both sides. You will compare their life to your own together with your knowledge as a so-called white woman of Spanish descent also having to cope with living.

It is impossible for me to have the same hurts and resentments as an Afro-Caribbean would when writing about her own experience in her own surroundings.

Their feelings at moments must seem self-pitying, yet I understand those feelings. Nevertheless, I do not think they comprehend totally my sensitivities. Perhaps they do not even wish to understand. But I do know I am well within the Caribbean tradition and relate to the way of life and the way of thinking of the region. I am most definitely another voice of the Caribbean.

When Rocks Dance: An Evaluation

LEAH CREQUE-HARRIS

When Rocks Dance is Elizabeth Nuñez-Harrell's first novel set in her native Trinidad that describes the resistance of three women to their disfranchised condition during the colonialist era of the late nineteenth century. Historically, this postslavery epoch in Trinidadian history was characterized by the economic change from a society dependent upon the production of cocoa and sugar cane to the discovery of oil, the source of the nation's wealth and impetus for multinational exploitation and of the industrialization of the society. Despite the emergence of an international identity of a second-generation population descended from African slaves, Asian indentured servants, and European colonists, there was no place for the black woman in this society. The struggle of these Afro-Caribbean women is intricately linked with the oppression of other ethnic groups, the indigenous Indians whose people have been annihilated and banished to the borders of Venezuela and the indentured class of Asians represented by the East Indian overseer, Ranjit.

The triple dynamics of race, gender, and class greatly affected the lives of the three central characters. Women had no legal rights or access to the traditional measures of wealth without benefit of marriage or inheritance. Emilia's quest for power through land ownership, the predominant conflict of this novel, is a reaction of protest to her experience as the concubine of two European landowners in succession upon whom she is totally dependent for basic survival.

Education also was a privilege denied to women of this era. Virginia, adopted by a childless European couple, attained the coveted ability to read and write, as well as an affinity for Shakespeare through the auspices of her white foster mother, who endeavored to erase Virginia's ethnic origin through acculturation.

Although these two women come from different backgrounds (Emilia is uneducated, uncultured, and amoral, while Virginia is well-bred), their life experiences have taught them how precarious and unstable their status is and how important power and wealth are for their survival. Both women were orphaned in childhood and would have been homeless but for the patronage of whites (Emilia as the concubine of Hrothgar and Virginia as the foster child of the Smiths). Both women were subjected to abuse as the sex objects of men. Emilia becomes a concubine at age twelve to maintain a roof over her head, and Virginia's foster father begins to lust after her in her adolescence, which causes her foster mother to remove her from their home via an arranged marriage to a Portuguese planter. From this experience, Emilia learned the importance of land ownership. Virginia, who already possessed land from her "dowry" and late husband, knew the importance of prestige and status.

The theme of land ownership and prestige as a life's goal is in keeping with the literary tradition of Caribbean women writers as exemplified in Paule Marshall's *Browngirl, Brownstones*. In this tradition, land ownership refers to the ancestral memory of African kinship with the earth and the brutal displacement of African people by slavery. Beyond economic security, property ownership is a legal mode to protest to the violation of one's inherent rights. Nuñez-Harrell keeps this ancestral memory alive throughout the text with accurate accounts of the middle passage experience and the genocide of the native Indians. Secondarily, this quest for land symbolizes the stereotypical feminine trait in nature to seek a nest, a home for the shelter, and security of her offspring.

Emilia endures the pain and humiliation of several unsuccessful pregnancies ending in stillbirths due scientifically to strangulation on the umbilical chord and metaphysically to the Ibo taboo of bearing twins, to reclaim the land for her own security, her progeny, and her people. Hrothgar, in desperate need of an heir, promises that she will inherit his cocoa estate if she bears him a son who lives.

Thus begins her quest for autonomy and power—the ability to control and shape one's environment. In this patriarchal, colonialist setting, power is attained through economic wealth, political might through organized numbers, armed struggle, or spiritual acumen by transcending the oppression of the physical realm to effect change.

Emilia begins to suspect through her continual failure to validate herself as a woman through motherhood that she is indeed cursed according to the Ibo legend. It becomes obvious that she cannot attain her desired economic security without first acknowledging the religion and spiritual powers of her African ancestors as syncretized in the new world in the form of obeah (or in Christian terms, first seeking the kingdom of God). In this call for authenticity and loyalty to one's heritage, Emilia begins to seek salvation through a spiritual journey back to her African homeland. This marks an important juncture in the novel when Nuñez-Harrell presents a reordering of the universe revolving around a theology of liberation where African gods preside alongside Christian rituals to heal the particular sociopolitical condition of colonized people.

The Ibo priest who administered to Emilia's condition warned that her curse could only be lifted through the sacrifice of her soon-to-be-born twin sons. After this ritualistic sacrifice she will bear a child who will be destined for wealth. With the assistance of the Warao Indian whose animistic religion confirmed the obeah prophecy, Emilia sacrifices her first opportunity to be a mother and gives birth to a beautiful mulatta daughter, Marina, who grows up to scorn her mother's plight yet embraces her thirst for land ownership. This sacrifice, though it appears savage, is analogous to the Christian sacrifice of God's "only begotten son so that others may live."

Marina's destiny is linked with Antonio de Balboa, her future husband and the son of Virginia and the Portuguese planter, Vasco de Balboa. As was true for her mother, her birthright of wealth and security from the de Balboa estate is dependent upon her giving birth to a child. She must first, however, break the curse on Antonio, whose first three wives died in childbirth. It is implied that since she embodied the spirits of her eight brothers, she is strong enough to survive this curse without harm.

Although Marina's physicality is female she is, in essence, a male. Is it the author's intent that it would take a masculine identity to possess such power? Or is there strength in the union of genders? This may refer to the obeah or voodoo practice of indiscriminate possession by deities regardless of sex.

Both Antonio and Marina are "children of the damned," of parents who sold their souls rather than live in truth. Here again, when one violates their authenticity, they are condemned. The motif of the sins of the father being visited upon the son is reenacted. Antonio's father was a Roman Catholic priest who defected for academic freedom and became further disillusioned after witnessing the atrocities of slavery. He married and impregnated Virginia only to realize his sin and thereafter ceased to perform as her husband, rendering her a bitter and lonely woman perversely clinging to her relationship with her son. In the telling of this story Nuñez-Harrell introduces the proverbial myth of Oedipus, which the early Greeks created to understand the complexity of their existence and the notion of kinship.

Virginia's demands for Antonio's attention and affection are a frustrated enactment of power over her domicile that cannot be enacted in this patriarchal society. Marina's presence as her daughter-in-law threatens not only her domain but also her European convention. Moreover, Virginia fears Marina's reputed powers and is repelled by the presence of obeah that she discovers in her home. She assumes that Marina, like her mother, is a practitioner of obeah. In reality, what caused Virginia's hysteria at the discovery of obeah in her home was her deep-rooted racial ambivalence as a black female raised by a white woman.

Eventually, Antonio's curse threatens Marina's life when she becomes ill while pregnant with twins. Emilia intervenes with obeah to save her daughter's life. Like her mother in her younger days, Marina is reluctant to use obeah but finally yields to its promise.

Through an eclectic use of spiritual powers which defy science and make a mockery of modern medicine, Marina safely delivers twins, one boy and one girl, and the lives of Emilia and Virginia are restored to order. The trinity archetype as a symbol of divine power is used throughout the unfolding of this drama. The trio of characters alternately represents the three branches of the trinity in this three-tiered examination of women's quest for power in this island whose name is derived from its topological representation of the trinity—one mountain with three peaks. At the moment of greatest danger, when Marina is at the brink of death, these three strong-willed, disparate women are united in their belief and affirmation of African tradition as the source of their salvation. Alternately, each represents the forces of the trinity: Emilia displays the reproductive power of God, the Mother/Father. As God the daughter/son, Marina's life exemplifies the divine aspect of humankind as a way of life. Her destiny as a woman of wealth and power is the fulfillment of divine promise as a devotee of a New World religion. Then there is God the Holy consummate Spirit moving in and through humanity giving knowledge where there is none. Through this spirit, Virginia surrenders to seek obeah after the medical doctor that she summoned, using her white connections, failed to heal Marina.

The obeah ritual that saved Marina's life was achieved through a male medium, who went into a trance to bring the body of Christ to Marina. Antonio had to participate in this ritual by going to a Catholic Mass, receiving communion to bring the unbroken host to Alma, the Diviner, as penance for his father's sin of breaking the vows of chastity and deserting the priesthood. This ritual, which mingles the sacrament of the Catholic church with the obeah ritual, is significant as a mechanism for paying homage to obeah. Again sacrifice is the element of salvation, and Marina's life is saved through the sacrifice of a male. The medium never returns to life from his trancelike state.

At the closing of this story all of the men who are pivotal characters in this story diminish in importance. Antonio is compelled to leave Marina after burning Smith's home to get Marina's property back. Virginia's foster father dies, and the Warao retreats to Venezuela having completed the cycle to wrench the land from the white man's hands. All the men have wielded their limited powers leaving the women as survivors. The Trinidadian expression from which the title is derived, "What right have eggs among rocks when they are dancing?" aptly describes why the fragile and cowardly men in the novel moved out of the way to allow the triumph of strong women. None of the male-female relationships in this book are romantically fulfilling.

The ultimate success of these women in attaining control over their lives can be attributed to the bonding that takes place among them as they become united in their struggle to secure the promise of the future through Marina and her children. It is through these mother-daughter bonds that these women develop their autonomy. In the absence of real mothers, Emilia and Virginia discover their identities through mother Africa. Marina develops the characteristics of self-determination and independence from her mother's transmission of these values, as is often the case with black women worldwide. Although many mothers of the black race would not claim to be feminists, their approach to survival is decidedly feminist.

Elizabeth Nuñez-Harrell has crafted an engaging narrative rich in symbolism and metaphor that is a composite of familiar and traditional themes and of literary devices. As an accomplished scholar in the humanities, she has blended such familiar themes as the tragic mulatto, the noble savage, and the oedipal conflict with the romanticism of the African past contrasted with a critique on the destructiveness of colonialism and capitalism. Although these contrivances along with the superimposed feminist point of view make the telling of the story self-conscious, these devices are appropriately used to handle the complex weaving of issues on race, gender, and class in a multicultural society.

Fiction in the
Scientific Procedure

ERNA BRODBER

To be addressed as a writer, as an artist, still seems strange to me because despite *Jane and Louisa Will Soon Come Home* and *Myal* I still think of myself as a sociologist and my fiction writing as a part of my sociological method. My sociological effort and therefore the fiction that serves it, unlike mainstream sociology, has activist intentions: it is about studying the behavior of and transmitting these findings to the children of the people who were put on ships on the African beaches and woke up from this nightmare to find themselves on the shores of the New World. It is my hope that this information will be a tool with which the blacks and particularly those of the diaspora will forge a closer unity and, thus fused, be able to face the rest of the world more confidently.

The process by which my fiction became part of my scientific strategy helps to explain the connection between the two. I was racially conscious when very young and certainly from age nineteen (1959) felt that my business was to serve my race. At my interview for a scholarship to the University College of the West Indies (London), I asked what course I should take to equip me to do this. I was advised to read honors history. Of the more than twenty papers three years later in my final exam, only one, taught by a slew of lecturers, none with a specialty in it and all admitting that they knew very little about it, dealt with the Caribbean. My special paper, which the English professor tried to dissuade me from choosing, was—mercifully—the Reconstruction period in the southern United States. This, plus the little bit of Caribbean history, was all the university could give me to know and therefore to face my people sensibly.

From this exposure I learned that there was a large gap in information on me and my kind. It pulled me into it. My path was clear: I must fill this gap in a way that the findings could be immediately translated into action. No courses existed at my university to equip me to do this. My postgraduate life was a ghostlike wandering through disciplines—sociology, social psychology, anthropology, psychiatry, social work from my native university to colleges in Canada and the United States in search of a methodology by which information about and action with or on behalf of black people could proceed at the same time.

Boredom with a social science methodology devoted to "objectivity" and therefore distancing the researcher from the people and spurning the affective interaction between the researcher and the researched led me into fiction. To defeat my boredom, I developed the habit of writing down my feeling before entering the field and of writing my speculations concerning the points of my informant's life that questionnaires, observations, and the like could not penetrate. This activity was to me like vomiting and defecating, and I flushed away the effort. It was purely by chance that one of these products did not meet this end. In 1975, nearly ten years after it was written, I found a short story I had written, preserved only because I had wished to keep the questionnaire on the back of the sheet. I consciously kept it. Fiction was to become now not just the outcome of the act of cleansing but something of intrinsic worth.

The new status attributed to this work came from three major impulses. The early 1970s was a very exciting and a very hurting time for blacks everywhere and naturally for me. The women's movement was an object for thought. But my particular pain was settling into my own country after living in areas defined as racist and having here to deal with what I now know to be prejudice against blacks in a country of blacks. The enemy was a ghost that talked through black faces. It was maddening, and to keep my sanity I talked on paper, reviewing from time to time what I had written before. I was now keeping my nonacademic writing for therapeutic purposes.

Another impulse toward assigning new status to my fiction was that I found myself in a circle of writers and would-be writers who valued my comments and made me their reader. I became caught up in this activity, and in my occasionally therapeutic essay into my own writing I saw that my works were no worse than those I was reading. The third and perhaps most important impulse was my need to find data for my students. I had returned from my wanderings to settle in the University of the West Indies at the task of teaching Human Growth and Development II to social work students. This was really a course in abnormal psychology and could not be sensibly taught without case studies, of which there were none. Such were the limitations of the social sciences in the Caribbean.

I had been dragging Roger Mais and Orlando Patterson and any other fiction that dealt with our emotional condition into my classes. They were limited, naturally. In 1975 I felt that I ought to test my sense that my nonacademic writing was no worse than that of my friends. I submitted some poems and the short story I had written on the back of the questionnaire to the National Festival and won prizes. I was now convinced that I could ease myself away from tables and who had said what when and write a case history for my students. *Jane and Louisa Will Soon Come Home* was it. It was not meant to find a public audience. It was cyclostyled, and I had intended that it would get to the classroom in this way. Velma Pollard, my sister, who had a long history of involvement with literature, felt the public ought to share it with my students and undertook to find a publisher.

Anthropology has tried very hard to present people and cultures whole, and the reading public through it has learned about life in a remote village in Martinique, of life in the South Pacific, and of how some American Indian women breastfeed their children. Generally speaking, these works are researched by people outside of the cultures and are directed by concerns not at all those of the researched. I doubt very much whether anybody in Morne Paysan got a chance to see what Michael M. Horowitz said about them. This is not the way of social science. Accountability has not been to the people researched but to fellow academics. It has been my position that the native social scientist cannot operate in this way. She/he is part of the polity examined, and the conceptual framework within which she/he works as well as the way the data are presented have to take this into consideration. Thus although *Jane and Louisa Will Soon Come Home* was intended to provide information such as Erikson, Mead et al. had given to students of culture and personality, I felt that my examination of Jamaican society could not be written from the standpoint of the objective outside observer communicating to disinterested scholars. It had to incorporate my "I" and to be presented in such a way that the social workers I was training saw their own "I" in the work, making this culture-in-personality study a personal and possibly transforming work for the therapists and through them the clients with whom they would work. This study also had to be short enough, sharp enough, and topical enough to make its point quickly because as a poor, half-illiterate people we have neither the time, the skills, nor the paper to deal with long works. It had to have space in which people could do their own dreaming, their own thinking, and their own planning. These considerations account for the format, content, and style of this piece. For whatever reasons, *Jane and Louisa Will Soon Come Home* finds itself on reading lists for Caribbean literature rather than Caribbean sociology. It has failed to inform sociology students.

Writing *Jane and Louisa Will Soon Come Home* had another function for me other than helping me contribute to the sociology of blacks of the diaspora. My exposure to psychiatric anthropology, the last of my journeys in search of a methodology, showed me that my habit of writing through my feelings before entering the field was a valid methodological device. Having through writing out rid oneself of fantasies concerning the field, the researcher is better able to see the field's reality without this particular distortion. This writing helps the worker to see her/his own hang-ups concerning the field and makes them accessible to her/him for evaluating her/his relationship with the persons she/he studies. The fiction writing that I had been doing could, theoretically at any rate, make me a better field tool. There is another way in which this act of writing informed my social science practice. I explain by instancing. Before my entry into published fiction, I had researched and published two pieces in Jamaican sociology: *Abandonment of Children in Jamaica* (ISER, 1974) and *Yards in the City of Kingston* (ISER, 1975). The one rose out of the other, one providing hypotheses which the other investigated. Hypotheses for the more recent work, *Yards in the City of Kingston*, now needed to be examined through a longitudinal study of life in Jamaica. I needed to know if the patterns of behavior I had noticed in the two previous studies were traditional, thus requiring a particular approach to treatment if they could at all be changed and ought to be changed. *Jane and Louisa Will Soon Come Home* was an instrument through which I thought through the cardinal problem implicit here—the relationship between history, tradition, and defense mechanisms, applying the result to the act of producing the research outline for the next academic piece. It was what the theorists call a "heuristic device." All of this mental activity eventuated in a three-year-old field study of Afro-Jamaicans over the age of seventy out of which had come a collection of oral histories, raw data for anyone who cares to use it, a Ph.D. thesis on the history of the second generation of freemen in Jamaica, and several papers in oral history methodology and in Jamaican history and sociology.

My twinning of fiction and science continues. *Myal* (1988) is my tentative exploration of the links between the way of life forged by the people of two points of the black diaspora—the Afro-Americans and the Afro-Jamaicans. It brings to our attention the grounds for cooperation implicit in these links. It was my hope while I wrote that working through this novel would make it easier for me to get my mind to my next major academic piece, which I call the *American Connection*. In it, I continue to express my political concern: black initiative is weakened by the misunderstanding between Caribbean and U.S. blacks and both and Africans. *Myal* and more explicitly the *American Connection* will let us see, I hope, what I do not think has as yet been clearly shown or grasped, that (1) the "shipmates" have made a New World thing of their own; (2) the product in each case has been influenced by happenings in the other's sphere; (3) the process of prior interaction by which each has informed the other, as well as the existence of a newly created product that has meaning for all, are bridges on which to build a strong understanding; (4) the grass-roots building of understandings so far has been mainly done by the unlettered—the domestic servants, stevedores, cane-cutters, minstrels.

It is now time for the intellectuals and political activists to solidify this effort by using their special skills to clarify and describe these connections, thus making dialogue easier and more fruitful and black solidarity and therefore black action more possible.

Now back to where we started. Am I a writer? An artist? I do not know. I know, though, that if tomorrow someone managed to convince me that all is hunky-dory with those who look like me, I would indulge myself in long Fieldingesque works because I love to play with words and to use my imagination, and with that before me and behind me, I would call myself a writer. Right now, I feel the term *intellectual worker*, which I have heard Lloyd Best of the Tapia House Movement in Trinidad use, best describes me.

Go Eena Kumbla: A Comparison of Erna Brodber's *Jane and Louisa Will Soon Come Home* and Toni Cade Bambara's *The Salt Eaters*

DARYL CUMBER DANCE

When I talked with Edward Brathwaite at the University of the West Indies at Mona, Kingston, on November 23, 1978, about the striking similarities in tone, language, subject matter, theme, structure, and symbolism that I noted between his work and that of the contemporary black poets in the United States, he observed, as he heard for the first time many of the comparable pieces I cited, "That's amazing, . . . [but] they're not just coincidental. I think that they are part of a general cultural pattern which we ought to be aware of because I don't think it's an accident, you know, that these similarities are there. I think we have, as you said, the same experiences; it means that you would expect a similar kind of expression." When I returned to Jamaica in July 1982, I took as gifts for friends some recent novels by black American writers, including Toni Cade Bambara's *The Salt Eaters*. Upon my arrival, Erna Brodber gave me a copy of her new book, *Jane and Louisa Will Soon Come Home*. As I read it, I was struck by another instance of how similar experiences (in this case, being black and female in the Americas of the civil rights, black awareness, Rastafarian, and feminist movements) had inspired such strikingly similar

I wish to acknowledge Erna Brodber for kindly allowing me to read the manuscript of *Myal* (which was not published when this essay was being prepared) and sharing with me other helpful materials; Velma Pollard for providing papers and essays that assisted me in this study; Evelyn O'Callaghan for her fine pioneering studies of J&L; and Rhonda Cobham for her critical reading of this paper.

expressions in books published the same year (1980) by an American and a Jamaican born one year apart, who knew nothing of each other.[1]

Erna Brodber did not set out to write a novel but rather to present a case study to teach the dissociative personality to her class in human growth and development. The case study incorporated some of the issues that concerned her and her students such as male-female relations, black liberation, and the women's movement. The decision to publish this material was made by her sister, teacher-poet-critic Velma Pollard.

Toni Cade Bambara's novel began in much the same fortuitous way. Concerned about the alienation between different segments of the black community, Bambara started writing in her journal as a means of clarifying issues for herself: "The novel, then, came out of a problem-solving impulse—what would it take to bridge the gap, to merge those frames of reference, to fuse those camps? I thought I was just making notes for organizing; I thought I was just exploring my feelings, insights. Next thing I knew, the thing took off" (Interview, 16).

Nellie Richmond, the protagonist of *Jane and Louisa Will Soon Come Home*, is born into a virtual Garden of Eden, where "mountains ring us round and cover us, banana leaves shelter us and sustain us."[2] Nellie's world is protected from everything; not even the sun can get in: "Outside infiltrated our nest only as its weave allowed" (*J&L*, 10). But this Edenic existence is short-lived for growth brings with it a series of exposures and revelations that shatter Nellie's sense of herself. She becomes aware of color and class divisions in her family and in her community, recognizes the "shame" and "filth" and precariousness of being a female; has to face "it" (alternately menses, female sexuality, everything associated with being a woman), which sets her apart from everybody, including her favorite neighbor, Mass Stanley, and all the boys who had been her playmates; has to face physical development ("Have you ever seen a new sucker trying to grow out of a rotten banana root? My whole chest was that rotten banana root and there were two suckers"[119]); has to submit to sex (recalled with shame and disgust in images of a "long nasty snail"[28], a "mekke mekke thing"[28]),[3] simply because "you want to be a woman; now you have a man. . . . Vomit and bear it" (28); has to

1. Toni Morrison observes a similar situation in her own case, noting that the fact that she wrote her first two novels before she read the work of Zora Neale Hurston proves the existence of a tradition of black women writers "because it means that the world as perceived by black women at certain times does exist, however they treat it and whatever they select out of it to record" (Naylor and Morrison, p. 590).

2. Erna Brodber, *Jane and Louisa Will Soon Come Home* (London: New Beacon, 1980), 9; hereafter cited in the text as *J&L*.

3. *Mekke* is defined by Carolyn Cooper as a "Jamaica Creole word meaning 'mucous'; decidedly negative connotations; usually used to describe the consistency of unpalatable food" (p. 147, n.8).

accept that as a woman "the world is waiting to drag you down: Woman luck de a dungle heap" (17); and has to acknowledge that "the black womb is . . . an abominable scrap heap thing" (143). Nellie's comment about the frightening, confusing realities of maturity summarizes her dilemma:

> What a weight!
> Slowly it adds up. (24)

It adds up to more than our heroine can bear, and she suffers total psychic collapse. Her condition is sometimes described as a loss or lack of balance. Nellie's Aunt Becca warns her of the precarious position of women in the world, concluding, "Learn that lest you be weighed in the balance and found wanting" (17). Nellie's fear of losing the balance, of being found wanting, is a critical part of her dilemma and is reinforced in the many descriptions of her sensing herself spinning wildly; like Anancy caught in his own trap and convicted by his own words, "spinning around in the woods," she is "twirling madly in a still life" (38). The importance of maintaining the balance is demonstrated in the experience of her neighbors: Mass Stanley's son David had to be cast out of his home because he disrupted the balance when he wanted to be a bull (man) in the same pen with his father (109). Mass Stanley's grandson Baba, on the other hand, "never disturbed their balance" (110).

Nellie's ailment is frequently described as a cold, often icy, lump. This contrasts with the warmth of her original Eden: "Ever see a fowl sitting on eggs in cold December rain. We knew the warmth and security of those eggs in the dark of her bottom" (9). When, because of the onset of puberty, the boys in her neighborhood no longer tussle with her, she laments, "What kind of coldness in this hot sun" (22). After her first sexual experience she speaks of having to live in "an ice cage" and of the "dry ice [that] works my body to a bloodless incision" (29). She learns that displays of anger must be "frozen with a compress of ice" (31); she characterizes her life as having "passed through a seasoning of ice" (63). Often she simply speaks of the lump in her throat.

This coldness contrasts with the warmth or the natural coolness of the kumbla that has been her fortress and protection and now threatens to destroy her. The image of the kumbla derives in this novel from a popular Anancy story in which Anancy dupes Dryhead into believing that he is surrendering all of his sons to him by telling his son Tucuma, "Go eena kumbla," which Dryhead interprets as a bad word uttered by a grief-stricken father as he gives over all of his children; conversely, to Tucuma it means to find himself a camouflage as he poses as first one and then another of his brothers, goes into Dryhead's cellar, and then sneaks out

again.[4] Anancy's whole career has been one of spinning "fine white co-
coons" (124), creating kumblas "designed to protect for generations"
(130). The narrator explains that a kumbla is like a beach ball that never
goes down, like an egg shell that does not crack, like a parachute, like a
spaceship, like a womb, a safe, protective cocoon that protects one from
the outside world.[5] The comfortable, protected world of Nellie's childhood
was her first kumbla. Everybody seeks a kumbla when threatened with
pain or danger: Nellie's great-grandmother Tia Maria "did everything to
annihilate herself" (that is, rejecting everything black, p. 139) and "built
a fine and effective kumbla out of [her white mate] William's skin" (142).
Prayer was apparently her Granny Tucker's kumbla. Nellie's "hoity-toity"
fair-skinned Aunt Becca built a kumbla of respectability and "showed
[Nellie] where to find and how to wear [her] kumbla" (142). Indeed, it
was a given that "black tinged women" had to build a kumbla to protect
themselves as they waited for that unlikely miracle of finding the right
man (142–43).

As comforting and important as kumblas are, however, one cannot
remain indefinitely in one. Nellie observes, "But the trouble with the
kumbla is the getting out of the kumbla. It is a protective device. If you
dwell too long in it, it makes you delicate" (130). Aunt Becca's kumbla
had separated her head from her heart (133) and left her trying to put
the parts together "without risking complete annihilation" (144). Nellie,
who tells us she has been in a kumbla for nearly one-quarter of a century,
knows that she is choking, recognizes her need "to know myself in my
world," but procrastinates, believing "someone had to help me test my
feet outside the kumbla" (70).

When we meet Velma Henry of Toni Cade Bambara's Salt Eaters, she
is in a condition similar to Nellie's: "Everything was off, out of whack,"[6]
"uncentered." Like Nellie, she is often pictured as spinning; at one point,
the statement "Velma was spinning in the music" introduces a refrain
that describes her "spinning" and losing her balance scores of times (Salt,
114–18). The word spinning is repeated over and over, sometimes as a
complete sentence. The quest for balance in Jane and Louisa is repeated in
Salt: "The hunt for balance and kinship was the thing" (267). More frequently in this novel Bambara uses the term centering. In several instances
various other characters seek to find or restore their center, but the focus
is for the most part on the numerous efforts by many people, most notably

4. Four variants of this tale appear in Dance, Folklore, 14–18.
5. F. G. Cassidy and R. B. LePage note that coobla is used to mean a "small calabasha"
(dialect for calabash) (Dictionary, 89).
6. Toni Cade Bambara, The Salt Eaters (New York: Random House, 1980), 5, hereafter
cited in the text as Salt.

the faith healer Minnie Ransom, to try to center Velma, or on Velma's attempts to center herself. Recognizing, even before her breakdown, that "the truth was in one's own people," Velma knew that "the key was to be centered in the best of one's own traditions" (169). She had "thought she knew how to . . . stay poised and centered in the work and not fly off, stay centered in the best of her people's traditions and not be available to madness" (258), but she was wrong.

The novel opens with Velma in a catatonic state, seated on a round stool in the Southwest Community Infirmary, where she has been brought following an attempt to commit suicide by slitting her wrists and putting her head in the gas oven (having, like Sethe of Toni Morrison's *Beloved*, realized that living is harder than dying: "Being alive was the hard part"[*Beloved*, 7]). Like Nellie, Velma has found it necessary (to borrow Brodber's phraseology) to "go eena kumbla," to shield her black female self against problems similar to those faced by Nellie: "She tried to withdraw the self to a safe place where . . . no one could follow, probe" (5). An hourglass seems the perfect kumbla to her: "To be that sealed—sound, taste, air, nothing seeping in. To be that unavailable at last, sealed in and the noise of the world, the garbage, locked out" (19).

Though puberty is not presented as so traumatic an event for Velma as for Nellie, the menses recur time after time as a symbol of something if not shameful and filthy, at least disgustingly inconvenient. There are frequent instances when she is without sanitary products. She tries to sit through a meeting protected only by rally flyers that she has stuffed into her panties because she was unable to find any napkins or tampons. During a civil rights march in a nasty bathroom with no stall doors, she inserted a ragged tampon that was unraveling: "She'd been reeking of wasted blood and rage" (34). Recollections of discomfort and fear of bloody spots occur time after time. But it is not just the problem of stemming the menstrual flow but also the blood that streams from her body because of injuries that sometimes threaten to kill her. In a dream she is clitoridectomized and unable to stop the "bleeding from everywhere" (276). There is a flashback to the time when her head had been slammed against the concrete floor of the jail in which she was imprisoned for participating in civil rights demonstrations and she was refused admission to a white hospital even though she was "trailing blood through the ambulance yard" (272). There is also the time when "the womb had bled, when the walls had dropped away and the baby was flushed out" (94). Vivid images and sometimes detailed accounts of Velma's swollen, bruised, and bleeding feet after long marches occur several times, both in her recollections and those of a friend who bathed her feet. Similar references to other women appear throughout the novel. Her sister Palma experiences a sudden stopping and an early arrival of her period. There is a poignant account of a rape victim scrubbing her own blood up from the floor.

Velma recalls early sexual overtures with "nothing romantic and nice" about them (263). Although relations with her husband are sometimes gratifying, some of her recollections suggest her need to escape from him, "to get out and away from the sour-sweet taste of sex coating her tongue" (102), a response reminiscent of Nellie's repugnance at the recollection of cunnilingus ("one long nasty snail, curling up, straightening out. . . . Popped it out of its roots, stripped off its clothes and jammed my teeth into it sucking. . . . It feels good but it doesn't taste good. Premature but this is your effort so you eat it like it is sweet. . . . Vomit and bear it" (28). Velma is repulsed by and anxious for sex to be over with the strange (and threatening) man who during cunnilingus lifts his head occasionally to sicken her with his reeking breath (271).

Nellie often attributes her breakdown to the death of her sweetheart: "The night my young man got caught up in the spirit and burnt to grease like beef suet caught in a dutchie pot, I wept so hard, my tears no longer held salt" (52). But the tone of this account of his death, her earlier sarcastic description of his radicalism (46), the impact of his life ("he had become a dried up bird and could only crumble into dust"[53]), and her frequent uses of his death to rationalize her problems suggest that perhaps Robin is a figment of her imagination. He clearly serves the same function for her that Mr. D serves for Miss D, the cold-hearted toll collector who explains that she cannot allow anyone to pass without the full fee because Mr D will kill her (50). Nellie notes, "We suspect that she is also Mr D" (50); we may suspect that Nellie is also Cock Robin, for Robin clearly represents the dead part of herself. Images of her "death" (disintegrating into dust and being put in an urn) are consistent with the descriptions of his presumed death by fire. The only reason given for the fire that caused his death is his enthusiasm for his cause—and it is precisely this mockery of a cause that is, she will soon learn, burning her out. Even though others presumably respond to Robin's death, even their "responses" may be creations of Nellie's imagination. For example, Errol's efforts to "pretend that nothing had happened" (52) may result from the fact that indeed, to him, nothing perceivable *has* happened. Finally, Nellie tells us that if *she* is resurrected, "Cock Robin could stand up and sing again" (147). It would appear then that one must look elsewhere for the real causes of her breakdown: "How did it begin?" (21).

With this question that begins Part 2 of "The Tale of the Snail in the Kumbla" and takes us back again to that Eden presented in Part 2 of "Voices," we recognize that a lengthy series of events in her life and the life of her family and community created the malaise that affects her. We trace a series of efforts to define herself, escape herself, and give meaning to her life through sexual repression and sexual capitulation, through education (she is a doctor), through involvement in idealistic programs designed to uplift the people. Nellie might be described as a new black woman—educated, sophisticated, worldly, politically active, career-oriented, but the truth is that she is vulnerable in her relationships with men and in her work in "the Brotherhood," where she is relegated to taking the minutes, performing the thankless labor, and supporting the men, who make the decisions and enjoy the spotlight.

As with Nellie, no single incident seems to have provoked Velma's breakdown. Like Nellie, she is educated, sophisticated, worldly, politically active, and career-oriented. In addition, she has a husband and an adopted son. Her husband, James Lee Henry (variously called Obie, Obeah, and Obo), thinks her problem may have begun when she lost her baby. After that Velma started complaining that her husband and son were driving her nuts, about sexual harassment on the job, and about the problems of balancing working and running a home. Her husband's infidelity and her own vengeful adultery are also contributing factors. She is active in a number of uplift organizations, similar to Nellie's "Brotherhood." She works so hard at the Academy of the Seven Arts (founded by Obie) that it takes seven people to replace her. In working in the academy, the civil rights movement, and similar ventures, she and the women typed, filed, printed posters, catered receptions, fried chickens, solicited contributions, raffled, and did many other tasks while the men "smoked and drummed their fingers on the tabletop" (27). During civil rights marches, she trudged for miles, arriving with swollen, bruised feet and dusty, split shoes, to see the male leader get out of his air-conditioned limousine in shiny boots. Clearly "break[ing] her hump pulling off what the men had decided was crucial for the community good" (25) made her frustrated and angry.

Nellie's journey toward health begins with Baba, a childhood friend, who appears, unseen and unrecognized, when a thirty-six-year-old Nellie is at the point of collapse, crying uncontrollably about everything (herself and others—the world). He mysteriously approaches from behind and kisses her, leaving with her the unforgettable smell of sweet lime[7] and the possibility that she may be able to carry on. He materializes again, presumably unrecognized either by Nellie or by the other neighborhood boys with whom he had played as a child, at a "think in" of their pseudo-intellectual organization that plays at uplifting the community. At a series of meetings for which Nellie records the minutes, he observes and carves

---

7. Carolyn Cooper notes lime's "capacity to 'run duppy,' and its folkloristic associations with asceticism" (146).

a pear seed baby doll that he ultimately presents to her. Predictably, it crumbles in her lap (reminding us of Robin, who had become a dried-up bird crumbling into dust). Baba is clearly warning her that she is a vulnerable, cracked-up doll, being shaped by others, hiding from herself in meaningless activities, being, as she had recognized, "ticked . . . into urns" (53). Angry at his audacity, she later goes to his room to confront him—and he begins the process of leading her on the journey to save herself.

"Straight and tall in a long white gown [and] wearing Jesus sandals," (63) holding his hand out to her "shepherd-like" (63) as she enters his room, Baba is clearly a Christ figure. The Christian imagery is reinforced by his uncertain birth origins and the revelation that he was "sent here for a purpose" (143) and that he has "saving power" (115). From early childhood he has been a self-confident leader. He knows what she is thinking before she speaks. He is always calm, peaceful, at ease, self-assured. His room is "sanctified" and "immaculate," his life absolutely clean and uncluttered. He can effect cures through a laying on of hands: "With just his index finger he had probed the base of my skull that day, had made me sweat and broken my fever. He could draw water from the brain" (68). The imagery associating this Rasta man with divinity is not merely Christian: he is described as "an obeah man of an anancy" (69) and as a "Haitian obeah man" (60); he disappears into an electric bulb, offering "a fleeting glimpse of Nancy's transfiguration" (76). But most important, he performs the miracles that lead to Nellie's resurrection, assuring her "you *too* know what the resurrection is like. You have a clean slate, you can start all over again" (67; italics added).

It is important to note that Baba, like some other men in the novel, is associated with a snail, but he is no "mekke mekke" snail. Nellie notes, "And like a snail, he would curl up into himself. A little bit of sweat but no tears" (69), suggesting his water (sweat and tears) that was necessary to restore life to her dry crumbling self. This is clearly not the appalling snail imagery recalled in her first sexual experience ("long nasty snail"[28]) or even that of the "Mr Anancy," who slips crushed snail in her milk, "the straw dripping slime" (34), or the comparable scene when to appease her father she pretends she is a baby being fed by him as "he lifts the spoon dripping slime to my mouth" (36). This different snail imagery may be seen as evidence of the possibility of a transformation of the heroine's perception of men and sex, comparable to Celie's changing attitude toward men as frogs in *The Color Purple*.[8]

---

8. Celie notes disdainfully that naked men remind her of frogs. Later the possibility of her acceptance of her estranged husband (and sex) is suggested when she puts a frog that he carved for her on the mantelpiece in her bedroom.

Baba begins his task by refusing to allow Nellie to find the easy comfort of tears and insisting that she find herself. He refuses her offer of sex: "That will come later. After I have met you" (69); "I fear you offer yourself because you don't want you. That's no gift love. . . . That's something you throw on a scrap-heap" (71). With his guidance, she renounces the "Brotherhood" and seeks to discover the folk among whom she had been living. It is clear that up to this point Nellie had internalized Aunt Becca's teachings about those "others" who were "different from us," those "others" who "will drag you down" (16), and she had thus, even while living in the government yard with "the folk," believed that "we have unfortunately to make a distinction between them and us" (51). It is clear also that she had felt herself an appointed leader to instruct and save those "others." But with Baba's guidance, she realizes, "My path lay now through the aliens who surrounded me. It is one thing to wander into their quarters, to put on a show for them and quite another to live from day to day with them" (70). Baba also teaches her that she is more than a cracked-up doll; he encourages her to find her own way, to find her own language; he prepares her to move into the spirit world of her ancestors (for after all, he is a "man [who] was dabbling in a higher science"[67]).

Velma's journey toward wholeness begins in the Southwest Community Infirmary, which combines scientific and spiritual modes of healing. Thus, after the doctors have tended her body, twelve spiritual healers (soon reduced to eleven with the departure of Velma's godmother Sophie) called "The Master's Mind" sit in a circle around Velma and Minnie Ransom, "the fabled healer of the district" (3), who tries to coax her back into life's flow, to "ransom" her. Minnie Ransom may not be as much a deity as Baba, but she has a "gift" and a "spirit guide" (63) that have allowed her to "build the chapel in The Mind" (53). She has the power to enter the minds of others, to heal, and to commune with the dead. But Velma resists Minnie, continually wrapping herself in a shawl and retreating into it, insisting, in effect, upon staying eena kumbla.

Like Nellie, Velma waits to be assisted out of her kumbla: "The divinely healthy whole Velma waited to be called out of its chamber, embraced and directed down the hall to claim her life from the split imposter" (148). But as Minnie insists, Velma must seek her own healing. The novel begins with Minnie asking her, "Are you sure, sweetheart, that you want to be well?" (3) And just as Baba realizes that Nellie is not yet ready to take the steps that will lead to her resurrection, Minnie tells Velma, "I can feel, sweetheart, that you're not quite ready to dump the shit" (16). Nonetheless, like Baba, Minnie is patient with her charge: "I can wait" (16). She is so attuned to Velma that she knows what is going on in her subconscious and unconscious mind. She too has the power of curing through a laying on of hands: "She simply placed her left hand on the patient's spine and her right on the navel, then clearing the channels, putting herself aside, she became available to a healing force no one had yet... captured in a name" (47). Velma's healing began with the laying on of hands: "Velma would remember it as the moment she started back toward life, the moment when the healer's hand had touched some vital spot" (278).

Velma's need for self-knowledge is comparable to Nellie's. She recognizes that "the thing to do was invite the self by for coffee and a chat" (259). Again she thinks, "The hunt for balance and kinship was the thing. A mutual courtesy. She would run to the park and hunt for self" (267).

Like Nellie, Velma feels superior to certain of those "others" with whom she came in contact in her efforts to "lift" them, people like that "ole swamphag" Minnie Ransom (4). The organizations in which Velma has been involved are like the "Brotherhood" in *J&L*, uplift groups in which people spend time in abstract theorizing and intellectualizing, activities that may, Velma realizes, "neutralize the venom" but don't "neutralize the serpent" (258). She thus seeks other answers: "The answer had almost come tumbling out of the mirror naked and tattooed with serrated teeth and hair alive, birds and insects peeping out at her from the mud-heavy hanks of the ancient mothers' hair. And she had fled feverish and agitated from the room" (259), not yet ready for the ancient wisdom born into her unconscious mind from the experiences of her foremothers, those mud mothers whose many earlier calls to her she had never heeded.[9] It was only later, after the "ole swamphag" Minnie "opened her up," that "Velma would begin to see what she'd been blind to" (294), that gift that her godmother had always known she had and feared/rejected. Then at last, she would be ready for training—though she might still resist "what could not be explained in terms of words, notes, numbers or those other systems whose roots had been driven far underground" (294), thus implying that she might still need the help of the ancient mothers.

Baba, with all of his spiritual powers, can lead Nellie only to a certain point. One night, she lets herself into a new world, where she travels with her dead Aunt Alice. Through her dead ancestor she is introduced to her people, but she acknowledges that it was "Baba [who] had settled me in with my people" (77). In this new realm she is at first confused: "I wasn't in touch. I couldn't see well enough yet" (79).

9. The use of the mud here to suggest entrapment which one must evade as well as salvation that offers the means to escape and the site of metamorphosis reminds us of the symbolic use of mud in the Anancy tale in *J&L*. In both novels there are other images with such paradoxically symbolic significance: salt as a representation of salvation and destruction (the story of Lot's wife is alluded to in both novels); the circle suggesting entrapment which one must escape as well as community where one finds place and identity.

Significantly, music, especially drums, begins to bring it all together for her; then "it all fitted in" (80). She recognizes the truth that "if I knew all my kin . . . I could no longer roam as a stranger; that I had to know them to know what I was about" (80).

Nellie's Aunt Alice, in contrast to her Aunt Becca, had never been burdened by "it," nor had she been concerned about class and color distinctions. She "never could settle down to housewifing but spent her earthly days visiting with and washing for the fading ones" (75–76); she believed in the curative power of roots (76). Thus she had been regarded as "not quite right in the head" (140). Now even as the spirit/ancestor, she is not regarded by Nellie as a divine or omnipotent being whose words are to be heeded with reverence. Rather, she is an individual with whom Nellie matter-of-factly converses and even challenges. Nellie warns Aunt Alice, "Remember I too can see clearly now," and when Aunt Alice questions her, she retorts, "So what? Who's asking the questions around here?" (131) Aunt Alice reprimands Nellie, "Nellie, I can't stand tears. Self pity wastes time especially when it parades as feelings for others" (132). Her job over, she leaves with the command, "Wake up Nellie. . . . Its [sic] your time now and I can take you no further" (133).

Possessing now the knowledge of her ancestors that will free her from the kumbla and restore her to balance, Nellie is prepared for her resurrection, sure that soon she will exit the kumbla and "be able to sit too, to hold up my head high and to use my two hands" (146). She realizes that "no paths lay before us. We would have to make them." (146) We flash back to all the womblike kumblas that her unresurrected self has dwelt in or known—the mossy covert of her youth, the eggs under the bottom of the fowl.[10] We now see her fetuslike, without developed feet on which to stand, though she does have a belly; here not the scrap heap "that sucks grief and anger" (143) (and thus represents the greatest vulnerability of the female—the fear of unwanted pregnancy), but "that organ which sheaths and protects but gives forth fruit" (147). Then she dreams she is carrying a fish in her belly, but though the nurse has prepared her, she cannot give birth to the fish. The novel ends:

> It will come.
> Goodbye great grandfather Will, Tia, Granny
> Tucker, Corpie, aunts and uncles and cousins.
> Goodbye Aunt Becca.
> We are getting ready. (147)

10. "We knew the warmth and security of those eggs in the dark of her bottom" (9 and 146).

Thus the possibility of birth, rebirth, and resurrection is the optimistic note on which we take our leave of Nellie, a birth made possible by that journey with her ancestor to her ancestors and thus to herself.

Minnie, like Baba, is unable to save her subject without the help of the spirit world. It is Old Wife who comes to assist Minnie, arguing with her and guiding her:

> "Seems to me, Old Wife, that by now you should so well know all these things. . . . You been dead long enough?"
> "There is no age nor death in spirit, Min. Besides, I do tell you things soon's they come to me."
> "Where from? I've been asking you that for years. You don't explain things clearly, Old Wife."
> "You don't listen good, Min. Or maybe it's me. I never was too bright."
> "When I was a young girl I thought you were the wisest."
> "You thought I was crazy as a loon." (56)

Like Aunt Alice, Old Wife was regarded during her lifetime as peculiar, wearing men's shoes, talking to snakes, smelling of dirt and salves and wintergreen, talking of the old days.

Music is important in Velma's cure as well as in Nellie's. At one point the music produced by Pan Man, who has been seven years in the United States trying to teach people the meaning and the wisdom of the pan, and who now "played like a man possessed" (168), drifts toward the infirmary and breaks through Velma's kumbla: "The music pressing against the shawl draped round Velma, pressing through it against her skin, and Velma trying to break free of her skin to flow with it, trying to lift, to sing with it" (168). It is not unusual that Velma would respond to this stimulus when she has been unaware of all else around her, for she had always loved drums and would go to them whenever she heard them: "No matter where Velma was, she'd hear the drums and come to the park" (284). Indeed, "eventually everyone came to the drums" (284).

As she senses Velma starting "to come through," Minnie decides to play some music. The effect is instantaneous: "Y'Bird so bold and urgent and the Hawk doing something to the soles of her feet, she all but pushed off from the floor to fling herself out of the window, out of the window and into the dark socket of the tree knocking on the inside as if eager to be a drum or join the chorus of voices speaking to her" (263). The music takes her so far into her collective unconscious that she calls Min's bowl and jug by their correct names, "govi and zin," names she did not know (263), and she is ready to dance on through the streets "in the direction of resurrection" (264). Old Wife advises, "Let her go, Min. Dancing is her way to learn now. Let her go" (264). But like Nellie's, Velma's legs are not yet strong enough to support her entrance into the world. Min tells Old wife to give her legs, and Velma feels her legs falling away, and, as with Nellie, we flash back to a womblike kumbla that her unresurrected self has dwelt in—"under the quilts in M'Dear's bed" (265). She relives all the times she nearly died but was nudged back to life and ends again in the reality of the situation, pushed "back into the cocoon of the shawl where she died again" (273).

Then in an apocalyptic scene in which the earth echoes with thunder, the ground moves, and rain pours from the heavens as if the world is being destroyed, Velma responds to "the healer's hand," hears the thunderbolt ("the kind . . . that knocked Saul off his steed and turned him into Paul" [278]), and "start[s] back toward life" (278). Bambara writes, "The Lady in the Chair is rising damp but replenished like the Lady Rising from the Sea" (292), and asks, "Would Velma find an old snakeskin on the stool?" (293) Like Nellie, Velma bursts forth from the womb/kumbla/ cocoon with the promise of the power to walk in the world: "The patient turned smoothly on the stool, head thrown back about to shout, to laugh, to sing. No need of Minnie's hands now. . . . Velma's . . . eyes . . . examining her own hands, fingers stretched out and radiant. No need of Minnie's hands now so the healer withdraws them, drops them in her lap just as Velma, rising on steady legs, throws off the shawl that drops down on the stool a burst cocoon" (295).

Brodber and Bambara present their heroines' journeys from madness to sanity, from fragmentation to wholeness, from death to life in novels that are remarkably similar in structure, both of them built around a series of flashbacks into the lives of their respective heroines and concurrently into the lives of those directly and indirectly connected with them in their individual communities. (In the case of Bambara there are also flashforwards.) The two novelists categorically reject any linear development. Time is fluid in both works. Their novels are complex, convoluted structures, making use of constant switchings of time, place, and narrative voices with subtle and easily missed transitions. Seemingly widely divergent scenes may be evoked and tied together by a word, a tone, a mood, an individual, or the coincidence of time, as in the dramatic conclusion of *Salt* when most of the principals respond to the thunder. In both works, words, phrases, snippets of conversations, bits of scenes are introduced and dropped, only to be echoed and expanded at varied subsequent points throughout the novels; repetitions of certain phrases that begin paragraphs and sections build and build and build to a resounding crescendo.[11] Indeed, the

11. A few examples from each novel include Brodber's incremental repetition of "Granny Tucker prays" and variations of that to introduce each new idea in the passage on pp. 86–90; "I came home" to introduce each of the first four sections of the "Miniatures" section (140–44); Anancy's order, "go eena kumbla" (128–30); Bambara's having her dance instructor

works are so rhythmical, lyrical, and eloquent that it seems imperative to characterize them as musical.[12] The novelists move us at will through the worlds of the living, the dead, the actual, and the dream/ fantasy/rumor. Indeed, both reject the divisions between these worlds. The dead walk among and commune with the living, for "there is no death in the spirit" (*Salt* 62); "our dead and living are shrouded together" (*J&L* 12). The ultimate effect is works (to appropriate Gloria T. Hull's characterization of *Salt*) "of extraordinary brilliance and density which [swirl] the reader through multiple layers of sound and sense" (138).

These two novels are not unique in their focus on matters considered here. One is reminded in varying degrees of Paule Marshall's *Praisesong for the Widow*, Gloria Naylor's *Linden Hills* and *Mama Day*, Alice Walker's *Meridian* and *The Color Purple*, Gayl Jones's *Corregidora*, Toni Morrison's *Beloved*, *Song of Solomon*, and *Tar Baby*, Merle Hodge's *Crick Crack Monkey*, Zee Edgell's *Beka Lamb*, Michelle Cliff's *No Telephone to Heaven*, and Brodber's *Myal*, all of which have numerous similarities in their treatment of female characters (and an occasional male) who experience an emotional, mental, and/or physical illness, who display similar symptoms, and who tend at some point to "go eena kumbla." They share also their exploration of the process of psychic healing that grows out of a community, is usually mediated through a female and/ or an ancestor figure, and moves each character toward a cleansing transcendence, a spiritual rebirth, a psychic wholeness, a revelatory discovery, a reclaiming of self within the black community, and a personal liberation. (Indeed, Marshall's *Praisesong* offers as many, if not more, points of comparison to *J&L* as *Salt*.) To emphasize these simi-

whispering into the ears of her elderly students, "Remember" (166–67); her repetition of "She might have died" as Velma recalls the numerous instances when she had a brush with death (7–8 and 269–74); and her repetition of "And she'd never been more cared for" as Velma catalogs the attention she got from family members after she ran away as a child (225–26).

12. In the essay "Music as Theme: The Jazz Mode in the Works of Toni Cade Bambara," Eleanor W. Traylor explicates *Salt* as "a modern myth of creation told in a jazz mode" (59). A comparable approach might be taken to *J&L*, in which Brodber introduces themes early in her work that are improvised and expanded in passages through which the same refrains echo. Each section of her work uses parts of a line of the lyrics of a popular Jamaican ring game of European origins (the order of the lines slightly altered for her purposes in the novel): MY DEAR WILL YOU ALLOW ME/ TO WALTZ WITH YOU/ INTO THIS BEAU-TIFUL GARDEN/ JANE AND LOUISA WILL SOON COME HOME. Brodber herself has called *J&L* "a concerto in four movements" (reading, Abington Friends, Philadelphia, May 6, 1988). And Bambara has referred to *Salt* as a "kind of jazz suite" ("Searching," 50), though she has also suggested that "sections of *The Salt Eaters* are closer to gospel than to jazz" (Interview, 29).

larities is not to deny that each of these works is important, unique, and exceptional with its own individual and distinctive concerns and style; none is a carbon copy of the other. Yet the many similarities they share are significant and are not, as Brathwaite reminded us, merely coincidental. They are indeed "part of a general cultural pattern" that demands the attention of us all.

Bibliography

Bambara, Toni Cade. Interview. In Claudia Tate, ed., *Black Women Writers at Work*, pp. 12–38. New York: Continuum, 1983.
———. *The Salt Eaters*. New York: Random House, 1980.
———. "Salvation Is the Issue." In Marie Evans, ed., *Black Women Writers (1950–1980): A Critical Evaluation*, pp. 41–47. Garden City: Anchor, 1984.
———. "Searching for the Mother Tongue" (Interview). *First World* 2, no. 4 (1980): 48–53.
Brodber, Erna. *Jane and Louisa Will Soon Come Home*. London: New Beacon Books, 1980.
Burks, Ruth Elizabeth. "From Baptism to Resurrection: Toni Cade Bambara and the Incongruity of Language." In Mari Evans ed., *Black Women Writers (1950–1980): A Critical Evaluation*, pp. 48–57. Garden City: Anchor, 1984.
Byerman, Keith E. "Women's Blues: The Fiction of Toni Cade Bambara and Alice Walker." In *Fingering the Jagged Edge: Tradition and Form in Recent Black Fiction*, pp. 104–70. Athens: University of Georgia Press, 1985.
Cassidy, F. G., and R. B. LePage. *Dictionary of Jamaican English*. London: Cambridge University Press, 1967.
Cobham, Rhonda. "Getting out of the Kumbla." Review of *Jane and Louisa Will Soon Come Home*, by Erna Brodber. *Race Today* 14 (December 1981–January 1982): 33–34.
Cooper, Carolyn. "The Fertility of the Gardens of Women." Review of *Jane and Louisa Will Soon Come Home*, by Erna Brodber. *New Beacon Review* 2/3 (November 1986): 139–47.
Dance, Daryl Cumber. *Folklore from Contemporary Jamaicans*. Knoxville: University of Tennessee Press, 1985.
"Delightful Jamaican Prose Poem." Review of *Jane and Louisa Will Soon Come Home*, by Erna Brodber. *Sunday Gleaner*, June 28, 1981, p. 7.
Durix, Jean Pierre. Review of *Jane and Louisa Will Soon Come Home*, by Erna Brodber. *Afram* 14 (1982).
Frye, Charles A., et al. "How to Think Black: A Symposium on Toni Cade Bambara's *The Salt Eaters*." *Contributions in Black Studies* 6 (1983–84): 33–48.
Hull, Gloria T. "What It Is I Think She's Doing Anyhow: A Reading of Toni Cade Bambara's *The Salt Eaters*." In Barbara Smith, ed., *Home Girls: A Black Feminist Anthology*, pp. 124–42. New York: Kitchen Table: Women of Color Press, 1983.
Kemp, Yakini. "Woman and Womanchild: Bonding and Selfhood in Three West Indian Novels." *SAGE (A Scholarly Journal on Black Women)* 2 (Spring 1985): 24–27.
Morrison, Toni. *Beloved*. New York: Knopf, 1987.

Naylor, Gloria, and Toni Morrison. "A Conversation." *Southern Review* 21 (July 1985): 567–93.

O'Callaghan, Evelyn. "Erna Brodber." In Daryl Cumber Dance, ed., *Fifty Caribbean Writers: A Bio-Bibliographical Critical Sourcebook*, pp. 71–82. New York: Greenwood, 1986.

———. "*Jane and Louisa Will Soon Come Home*: Rediscovering the Natives of My Person." Paper delivered at the Interdepartmental Conference, University of the West Indies, Mona, Jamaica, May 1982.

Parker, Dorothy. Review of *Jane and Louisa Will Soon Come Home*. *Black Books Bulletin* 7, no. 3 (1981–82): 57–58.

Rosenberg, Ruth. "You Took a Name That Made You Amiable to the Music: Toni Cade Bambara's *The Salt Eaters*." *Literary Onomastics Studies* 12 (1985): 165–94.

Traylor, Eleanor W. "Music as Theme: The Jazz Mode in the Works of Toni Cade Bambara." In Marie Evans, ed., *Black Women Writers (1950–1980): A Critical Evaluation*, pp. 58–70. Garden City, N.Y.: Anchor, 1984.

Willis, Susan. *Specifying: Black Women Writing the American Experience*. Madison: University of Wisconsin Press, 1987.

A female slave, a samboe, tied to a tree and beaten for having refused to submit "to the loathsome embraces of her detestable executioner." From John Stedman, *Narritive of a Five Years' Expedition against the revolted Negroes of Surinam*, 1796.

Father Sleeps with the Mudpies

GLASCETA HONEYGHAN

I was thirteen. I sat for an exam that lasted three days. It was strenuous, almost frightening, but I was glad my brain, void from cramming, was free to watch undistracted the days drag by until I would leave with Miss Odel. I had been too preoccupied to notice that Pa was quiet and had stopped eating.

Earlier, many times an idea came racing to my head that I could have invited Miss Odel to meet Pa—they had a lot in common. Both were foreigners, spoke Spanish, spoke unlike the villagers. They could have been each other's audience, but I felt terribly fearful of her seeing my situation—Pa's age, his one leg, the dilapidated one-room house, the filthy babies Ma watched, Ma's dirty clothes. Now I wasn't sure if Pa listened. Sometimes I speculated, based on pieces of information I gathered from villagers, that he was preoccupied, that his thoughts flashed across the waters, and I figured it was no pleasure for him to recall how he had prospered in his earlier years. He had no money, but he did have respect. He had never been to school, yet he once wrote articles for a local newspaper. He had taken up the preaching business and had done remarkably well. He worked with fine colleagues. His success had no limit. He had the power to marry virtually any woman, and he did marry a white woman. Then that foot got wounded in war. His career ended. Too haughty, he left his wife with his veteran benefits and took off without a trace. Here, he settled in a strange village with a wife and six children, and he seems to be a seventh child himself. Some times I reasoned Pa cracked a joke; other times I was certain his lamp went out and his night remained thick with blackness. Villagers claimed, "De ole man done lost his mind; de ole man is senile." Whatever was the matter with the old man had me restless and confused.

Pa continued his odd ways and progressively grew worse. One afternoon when I was returning home with a new undershirt for him, a curious darkening appeared in the sky. Soon the calm rain fell steadily, and I listened to other youngsters screaming, getting drenched, while I, in no hurry to get home and in fear of getting Pa's undershirt wet, sheltered at the Grindleys' shop. The shop had a half-faintish smell of white rum, salt fish, salt pork, kerosene oil, and Miss Iris's cooking all rolled into one.

Mass Edwin craned his neck, looked up at the emptying clouds, and spoke as if to God. "Well, it look like the good Lawd goin' bless de lan' dis night," he grinned, his hash-brown teeth blending with his dirty face, "look like we is in fo' some heavy rain dis evenin', an' I will be up at de crack o' dawn plantin' me few hole o' garden bean."

"Now," Mass Harold sent spittle flying on my arm, "my few head o' cattle will be in tip-top shape fo' market nex' mont'."

"All I care 'bout," Sparrow said wryly, "is jes to gets home to my baby. I jes wants her to fling her foots right 'cross my shoulder, an' I plays in her hair an' sings:

> Come back my darlin' an' dry up my tears
> Why did you leave for so many long years
> Where is dat love dat you promise me dear
> Come back my darlin' an' dry up my tear

Laughter shook the shop. I liked Sparrow. He was like a village joker, good at singing folk songs accompanied by his banjo. He could say anything about any well-to-do villager and get away with it because they claimed, "Sparrow lost a screw."

The rain held off. Mr. Frankweilder and his work crew drove up—he was the well-to-do fellow who set his bad dogs on us village children when we fetched firewood from his property. Fearful, I stuffed Pa's undershirt into my frock front and bolted home. I am not sure why I am including this shop scene—maybe back then I was running away from home, and maybe today I am using this scene as a way to postpone what I really want to say.

It was dark when I pushed open the unlocked door. It creaked, and a stench greeted me. I hopped out of my half wet frock and watched Pa. His body was bare, skinny, and languid. He had become unbearable since his mind had been affected. When he wasn't crawling on his hands and knees to nearby woods, he was scratching and clawing as though a demon were inside him struggling to be released. His behavior had put a terrible strain on Ma, but with the patience of a saint she bathed, dressed, and fed Pa. With homemade remedies, she tried fruitlessly to restore the old man's youth; uncomplaining, she carried out her routine, forgetting her anxieties in nursing him.

Over the flickering flame of our kerosene lamp with a smokey wick, I tried to engross myself in reading a Nancy Drew mystery and went to bed long past midnight. I was restless though, for there was something unsettling and even foreboding about falling asleep in an uncomfortable position in the crowded room. My space at the front of the smaller bed hardly afforded me room to lie on my side.

Across on the other bed Pa couldn't sleep either. We both stared intently at the ceiling, maybe each awake for different reasons. I dozed for awhile, but suddenly I felt some mushy stuff falling on me. The heavy wetness was falling all over me and my Nancy Drew book. I grabbed a handful and realized Pa was tossing his feces straight at me. He emptied his bowels, and, bit by bit, he threw chunks of wet feces all over me. I leaped up, crouched under the bed to gain shelter from the barrage, and as tears stung my eyes, I whispered to Jesus on the wall: "Why, why, why, is Pa doing this to me?" I have no memory of anything else that happened that night.

What Pa did to me that night continued to haunt me; I thought it would explode my brain. But now, after twenty-eight years I am still asking myself whether Pa's feces were a symbol expressing the bond that had existed between us. Could it be that even in his senility, he continued to love me, his "baby"?

Later that evening, Pa, in the night shirt I picked up at the dressmaker, sat cushioned against a pillow, motionless and unreachable, gaunt eyes peering at nothing. His new shirt was torn, shredded—the old-time tinsmith was beaten. Lines from Shakespeare were gone. Intellect was useless. I watched tearfully as Ma held his bony fingers, trembling, and brought a mug of water to his lips, which were white at the corners. I watched Pa wait to die and wondered whether he indeed had let go of everything, memories of defeats and successes. I imagined he felt nothing: no pain, no regrets, no burden, for he seemed unattuned to anything in his world, our world. His body seemed too light to contain any such thoughts. Ninety-one years of hardship and unfulfilled expectations had reduced him to a senseless, living corpse. The old survivor had lost.

On that hot July evening of 1962, the regular set-up crowd who could smell death started a vigil around Pa's bed to watch him breathe. They never missed. Pa died that night.

Shortly before Pa drew his last breath, Miss Cassie, a plump, cheerful lady, poured a little water in his mouth and said grimly, "Dis, my dear brodder, is to hep yuh on yuh journey into yuh lonely worl'." She stuffed cotton up his nostrils, then, skillful as a surgeon, she closed his mouth, and with a large piece of white cloth formed a bandage under his chin that she tied in a knot on top of his head. Quickly she used a smaller piece to tie his one and a half legs together. Normally, she would have tied his two big toes. Several other set-uppers hastily reversed the position of his body, laying his head at the foot of the bed to confuse any evil spirits lurking around. No member of his family could wash him so Miss Maggie and Miss Elita washed his body, one starting at his toes, the other at his head, finishing when they reached his middle. Betsy, belly bulging with six months' pregnancy, was forbidden to look at Pa lest her baby be born looking like the corpse.

The water used to wash Pa's body was carefully set aside, and family members who desired to be protected from evil spirits were encouraged to wash their faces in it. I had mixed feelings. I wanted to be protected, but somehow I felt Pa was right. He had told me all my life, "The dead knows nothing, my child; the dead can do nothing." This potent water was to be poured out just as Pa's body was on its way to the burial ground. Miss Katie stuck common pins into the bottom of his one foot so his ghost would not come back to haunt the village. This precaution made no sense to me since Pa could not walk when he was alive, but I kept quiet because here traditions were strong like the stones Miss Cassie arranged in the fireplace, as durable as the iron pot she set on the stones.

Pa's body, shrunken into a tiny bundle of dry skin, was wrapped in a huge white sheet. Our tiny mirror was turned to the wall lest the image of his corpse be reflected in it, causing more deaths in the family. Busy hands efficiently transformed our murky, foul-smelling shack into a clean, faint-smelling abode. When everything was in order, Miss Katie stood on our half-broken doorstep and with two sharp shrills and one prolonged holler summoned the other villagers. I blinked my eyes, and the yard was full of mourners.

Without orders, people assumed their duties as if directed by an un-written code. Six gravediggers with a bottle torch to light the roadway headed for one distant corner of our one-acre plot. Miss Cassie put bits of brambles in the fireplace, squatted, blew, and the fire a glaring yellow flame. Miss Katie parched coffee, and Miss Minnie, pestle in hand, beat the coffee in the mortar. Miss Bell grated coconut from which she would press milk to whiten the coffee. Meanwhile, Miss Pinkey, with a hurry-scurry, cut, basted, and hand-sewed red underwear for Ma so Pa's ghost wouldn't "play with" her when it returned. Likewise, Miss Maizie, a thin, wiry lady, armed all children in the family, tying scraps of red cloth around their necks and wrists. I felt somewhat repulsed by all this protection business, for Pa had said, "People don't understand you, child. You will be a fighter and nobody can trap you." So I dashed into the darkness and tossed my protection into the cornfield.

Other hands gathered mugs and cans and lit a lantern. Romel returned with a table he had borrowed, set it in the middle of our yard, and the requiem began.

Leonard dug out his sanky from his goatskin bag and started the tracking:

> Dere were ninety an' nine dat safely lay
> In de shelter ov de fold
> But one was out on de hills away
> Far off from de gate ov gold
> Away on de mountain, wil' an' bare
> Away from de tender sheperd care
> Away from de tender sheperd care

Now with the coffee parched, beaten, and brewed, women with heads tied in plaid bandanas reminisced over Pa.

"What is man?" Mis Cassie asked grimly, shaking her head. "We is here today an' gone tomorrow. De difference between life an' deat' is jes only one single breat'."

"Go on home go res' ole bwoy." Miss Katie spoke as if speaking to the corpse. "Yo takes care of t'ings up dere and till I come to join yo, fo' no matter how we t'inks we is bad an' powerful, we all gots to face deat'."

"Wise King Solomon say," Miss Louise flashed a disrespectful glance at Mr. Grindley, a well-to-do, "dat a live dog is better dan a dead lion, an' if I reads my Bible correc' Wise King Solomon also say, "We come here naked an' we leaves here naked, can't takes a fardin' to der grave wit' we."

"Yuh never miss de warter till de well run dry." Miss Cassie spoke with such intent grief as if her breathing depended on Pa. "It is not one or two times dat very man yuh see lying on his death bed dere save my chilvren life—quite a few time he hide a shillin' an' save my chilvren life."

I was astonished by this last woman's words. Where did Pa get money to loan others when we couldn't afford dinner many times?

Older girls and boys flirted and ran errands; younger children fooled around as if the occasion was part of their romping routine. Ma rummaged in the old cardboard trunk and prepared Pa's burial clothes. Lenard and his singing group sang "A Drunkard Reach His Cheerless Home." Men guzzled Red Stripe beer and white rum. I probably overlooked most of the details, for indeed they were many, and besides, I had started my own silent worrying—Miss Odel, the teacher who promised to take me away, would see my poverty-stricken family and house and would most likely change her mind. I felt a clumsy nervousness.

Villagers knew we had no reason to delay the burial, no need to wait for relatives coming from a distance, no need to prop blocks of ice on Pa's corpse. Without being told, villagers knew Ma couldn't afford to take Pa's already decaying body to the morgue in the city. They knew that after the set-up, Pa would be buried right quick.

As the group of women continued their chattering, calling up warning signs of Pa's death, my attention was directed to the solemn crowd stealthily singing "The God of Abraham Praised," and their voices ricocheted over the hills, piercing the black, faceless night. Standing behind a tree I watched the group doing the setting-up—their togetherness, the unbreakable bond in times of distress. I felt frightened yet safe because I recognized friendly gestures in those familiar faces, and a cold shiver ran down my spine. The set-up lasted until daybreak.

Now, I look back and I see very vividly the sun on its way over the Santa Cruz mountain, scattering rays into the leaves. A calm wind blows. Birds perched on branches blurt a chorus. A baby chuckles. It is a new day. But the yard is solemn, shaded in sadness, crying out emptiness and fear. Just yesterday Pa breathed. The sun, risen, would later disappear and would most certainly rise again, but for Pa all was ended. Once, like the sun, he shone radiantly, but a storm raged and only dark clouds remained.

Pa's body, dressed in his black burial suit in his wooden coffin, was carried out the front door which was the only door in the house. But Miss Vie cautiously reminded Ma, "Don't be surprise if de ole man come back to pay a visit, because him not supposed to go out de front door."

The last sight I remembered before dozing off was four men setting Pa's coffin on two chairs in the yard, where it would remain as mourners paid their last respects. Simultaneously, the house was swept with a crisp new straw broom, and two men demolished Pa's bed after they took it outside. There it would remain for the next nine days and nights, during which time set-uppers would welcome and entertain Pa's ghost till it retired on the ninth night.

I woke up suddenly and sat up scratching my head. I walked over to Pa's coffin. I stood there, glanced up, down, and sideways nervously and fought to keep my spirits up under the ordeal that was making a hollowness invade my forehead. Then with nerves on edge I gave a hard, long stare at Pa's artless body stretched out in his coffin. Somebody resketched him and forgot to paint him. He had survived the upheaval of World War I. Now he lay unmovable, unstirred, unruffled by what Pastor Black called "a passageway between two journeys." But my eyes rested on Pa's lifeless face, ugly, jaws sunk in, and he looked dead. He was cold, too

cold for a man on a journey. Still gazing senselessly at the body before
me, I saw Pa in one situation, then another. He had taken me on his lap
and lavished my bleeding wound with seaweed and some other stuff
from a bottle, though Ma couldn't care two pence about my misery. He
taught me Spanish, explaining the luxury of speaking more than one
langage. I was now an "A" student in Miss Odel's Spanish class and had
built a closer relationship with her because of Pa. When the others weren't
looking, Pa sneaked and fed me from his plate. Remembering these moments, I felt a slight tinge of sorrow. But, then, he had six children, one
leg, and not a farthing to feed his family, and the village children would
not have teased me had it not been for him. Why did he beget children
knowing he was not capable of feeding, clothing and sheltering them?

Then I recalled that dreadful day when Ma rended a branch from a
dogwood tree and was half killing me because I had told Betsy her face
looked like a hog hole. Ma claimed I said a swear word. Pa hopped over,
grabbed me, and because he was unstable on his one leg, we both fell,
him on top of me, shielding me from Ma. A tear inched down as I recalled
that maybe if it weren't for Pa, I might be the one in the coffin—stone
dead from Ma's blows. Then there were the zillions of times Pa rescued
me from the dreaded cassava and corn grating. Now, I know he grated
his pride and love for me in every root of cassava, in every ear of corn.
I know that now. I knew that then. And soon I began to feel guilty about
remembering his failures, and I cried, despising myself for not feeling
more sorrow for him. Then I recalled the terrible old man cleaning out
his little bony behind and flinging his feces not on the dirty cracked walls,
not on the unswept floor, but on me, all over me. I hated him, my skin
crawling with horrow and disgust—I felt like scratching out his two dead
eyes. My sorrow was now insincere, unnatural, and I began to feel sorry
for the way we all suffered, Pa too. I felt sorry for everything and everyone. That feeling smothered me with a heartbreaking sorrow, and I
walked away feeling weak and wobbly, slumped down next to the mango
tree, and wept bitterly.

Later that afternoon my family, Pastor Longworth, and the mourners
sang "We Shall Gather at the River" while six pallbearers hoisted Pa's
coffin on their shoulders and marched to the graveside. Clusters of church
members mingled with dirty gravediggers, and family members stood
solemnly around the grave. Ma couldn't afford to pay for Pa's body to
be taken to church so the entire ritual took place at the family plot. After
a song and prayer Pastor Longworth thundered his sermon across the
cornfield.

"Oh grave where is dy victry; oh death where is dy sting? I am de
resurrection an' de life, an' he dat hath fait' in me, though he were dead,
yet shall he live. We are gaddered here today on dis solemn occasion on

account ov one of our dear brodders." Pastor Longworth continued with his burial sermon full of quotes, misquotes, clichés, and pious sayings, ending as I anticipated: "Dust to dust, ashes to ashes. The Lord giveth and the Lord taketh. The spirit goes back to heaven." But Pa had told me all my life, "We die my child, melt, rot, but see, child, God will one day bring us back to life—those he feel like, that is." I like Pa's version of death. It has continued to pursue and puzzle me to this day, yet I am grateful for this hope to which I cling dearly.

Ma stood against a sweetsop tree and seemed barely able to remain on her feet. In her black crumpled frock and other fluffy white hat, eyes swollen and red, she sobbed ceaselessly, covered her face, and blew her nose in a piece of rag. Miss Odel and her junior choir sang "Marvelous Grace of Our Loving Lord," and as they sang the postlude Ma let out a piercing scream, followed by a rhythmic hollering. Some of Ma's friends held her up, while Miss Cassie, Miss Katie, and Sister Ginnette-Eve led off a muffled crying spell. These women made up the crying group that cried at all funerals out of respect for the dead person because he deserved to be missed. My brothers and sisters did not cry. I knew they were happy that Pa was gone.

I stood there unnerved, transfixed by the literalness of the event. Gradually feelings of joy, hurt, loss, and fear rushed to my head and flowed in gentle tears. Miss Odel hugged me. I clung to her, and only the joy remained.

They lowered Pa's body, in an unpainted pine coffin, into a six-foot grave. He was mud returning to mud. Like I played with mudpies, life was a mudpie game. You made a mudpie in the morning. Later that day the wind blew or the rain fell and the mudpie vanished into the earth, just like Pa. A lump of mud, he came from the dust. Now he was gone back and would melt. Six dirty gravediggers grabbed hoes and shovels and quickly packed the mound, obscuring Pa from a world that gave him little and took everything.

I Write Because . . .

BERYL GILROY

The war gave many colonial women access to opportunities in Britain. As a student in London in the 1950s, I was part of a small number of young "children of the empire" in pursuit of what was considered superior education. Within the confines of the various colleges at which we studied, we were students or learners, who, after suitable indoctrination, would return home and spread the word. The moment we went further afield, however, we were perceived differently and described, without any categorical doubt, by such names as immigrants, foreigners, natives, spades, and other congenitally British terms of derision. Not only did these names distance us, they also served as filters for our every word and deed. It was not unusual to be asked, "Where did you learn your English?" or alternatively to be told, "You foreigners must look and learn from us." The British took a reductionist view of us and maintained it by race bigotry.

Language and dress were taken as embodying special elements of the British culture with all its encapsulated "classisms," ethnocentricisms, and prejudices, and be they incidental or concealed, they had to be tolerated by us. Foreigners were sojourners, visibly and pathologically different. If we had even the most basic of rights no one mentioned the fact to us. The stereotype, although enfeebled and hoary, provided for the host society the crucial strands of an identity that had been historically constructed for us. This identity bore no relation to our feeling or interior lives or to our mobile young selves, as against the immutable and attributed selves through which some of us projected whatever helped us survive. In effect, black people in a racist society are two people—the facade and the real person who must exist in society.

By the mid-1950s, West Indians who had been recruited to do the work the British working class rejected increased in numbers. As I job hunted, I was given the opportunity to observe these women patiently engaged in the traditional jobs that the powerless and oppressed must perform. Alongside them were the Irish who had not yet learned to be "white" and were just as happy to do the menial work the war had spawned. But they too were so prejudiced they looked wholeheartedly for scapegoats among us. And when like other black women I was mocked, jibed at, and deliberately used as the butt of British humor, I learned to understand my own legitimate feelings of resentment and aggression and to understand theirs. In my world, magical thinking, aggression, anger, and resistance are for black people legitimate and healthy responses to racism. Whites, however, regard those responses as expressions of constitutional pathology.

Color prejudice has many faces, and in some people it is tucked away in a place of impenetrable darkness, to emerge and glow with irrational hate at the prospect of an encounter with someone different in creed, class, and especially race. Racism spawns the politics of terror to include both the racist and his victim. This terror is a specialty of the ethnocentric mind, which though it develops, can mature only in a gnarled or distorted way.

THE CHILDREN'S BOOKS

After I began to teach in a London primary school in 1953 I had many encounters with blatant and free-flowing racism. Any expectation of human rights and equality seemed in effect a stroll through "Cloud Cuckoo-Land." The books I found in my cupboard bore references so disparaging to black people that one wondered why they were written. On the playground the children skipped to various racist and antiforeign "traditional" rhymes.

This was a denominational school. The children, demurely repressed, prayed like two hundred compulsive parrots for the sick, the dying, and the heathen. When they prayed for the souls of the heathen, they peered at me from behind their grubby, tightly clasped pink hands. I realized that how I saw myself was not how they saw me. Religion helped the emergence of ethnocentricism in these children.

I heard my class read. Twelve out of forty-five could "bark at print." "They must be taught to read," said the head teacher. I shrugged. She meant I had to prove myself. I had come highly recommended.

I talked to the children about reading, its meaning and my expectations of them, and then I read to them. They listened with rapt attention, or so I thought. At the end of the story I was just about to congratulate myself when one said, "Don't they talk funny, them blacks!" Some of the children were still talking about and showing the trauma of evacuation. Others, on returning, had been unable to recognize their homes or their streets. For some, close relatives had vanished. The school readers bore no relationship to their lives. "Janet and John," the schoolbook children, lived in a pleasant bungalow with low-growing flowers around the door, a mother and father, and a lively little dog in the garden. The children in my class were still coping with the bomb-sites, which in some cases surrounded the wartime prefabricated houses or the hastily constructed apartment blocks in which they lived. When I presented the set readers to my class, I could see the terror in their eyes. Quietly I began preparing supplementary reading material. But methodology has its limits. I set aside periods of the day for talking. We called this "Problem Time," or "News Time," or "Story Time." Problem Time was the most productive because it allowed the children to talk about what they found problematic in the classroom or on the playground and what affected them en route to school or at home or anywhere in their environment. At News Time we heard about what was of interest to the children and what frightened or obsessed them.

These talks took me into the lives of the children, and in time our homemade books, which reflected their experiences, became therapeutic and meaningful to them. They sited themselves in situations in a recognizable world. The social familiarity of the texts released a desire to read. The success they experienced motivated them to approach material that was in dissonance with their day-to-day experience. The illustrations and language of our homemade books were naturally theirs and the narrative so sustained that their involvement was complete. The working classes, the black family, the Greek family all have their own valid cultures. These cultures must be made explicit. I used the strategy of discussion in a tutorial form time and again and built up a reservoir of stories. I offered them, although they consisted of a small number of words (fifty to two hundred), to several publishers, but they were considered too radical for publication. Among other things, I had written about real-life people and about powerless people, who had learned to express their anger and antagonisms. By strange chance, Leila Berg, a radical writer, incorporated the stories into the controversial series Nippers. I was determined not to be the puppet of the publishers and gentrify my readers. I firmly believe that two and a half-million of us blacks among sixty million of the others cannot set too much store by positive images. The children had to be helped to understand the psychology of difference by accepting it. Racism in Britain at that time was unacquainted with positive images and was trapped in historicist beliefs about the power of empire. Today prejudice has changed its form and has moved from the patriotism of empire to the burdens and conflicts of Common Market and Commonwealth. Attitudes to us have not changed. Foreigners are expected to adjust to the English value system, enter it, absorb it, and be grateful for the opportunity to do so. Cultural imperialism is the pivot of the system that breeds bigots, who in turn breed sturdier and more determined bigots.

These issues can safely be discussed, with reference to the behavior of children, through stories. Each family in some way mirrors society. In my writings, I try to say, "This is the way we are. This is a sample of our life. We are peripheral to your class structures. We are invisible when it doesn't suit you and visible when it does. I set out to tell the story as it is. Neither integration nor assimilation in the melting pot mode is the answer to our reality."

In the children's books I have written I have tried to give a psychosocial view of values and attitudes that affect the mental health of our children. My goal was tolerance, which comes from a wisdom obtained from self-knowledge. A writer's work is cast in time. No writer can cover all contingencies and all the nuances of culture and awareness that develop over time. I have tried to express the way a child's perceptions of herself, her family, and her psychosocial expressiveness must change under pressure from people who are important and significant but who ignore self-knowledge and cognitive capital.

ADOLESCENT WRITING

My concern with both of these strands compelled me to write five stories for older children. In the book *In for a Penny*, I tried to portray different incidents from the lives of "normal" black families and young people and explore the psychology of failure. Conflict and aggression are pointedly low-key, and everyone is "terribly nice and polite." Racism in the world of whites has not blunted the love of fathers for their families, and the men are loving and emotionally attached to their families. The harshness of the working life for a black man and the lack of caring it produces have been altered. But I like my characters to have emotional encounters with themselves and others in a story so that children can learn strategies with which to help themselves.

I allow my characters to monitor their perceptions and travel along the author's road, hearing her songs but singing their own. I like my characters also to understand the many faces of power and power-distance and to notice how racism mediates between man and woman, sister and brother, parent and child, of whatever race. I like my characters complex but sometimes linear and sometimes understated, bearing strands of our own racial uniqueness. Characterization to me is like a painting in which strong, clear colors or soft, subtle, elusive shades are used when necessary. Sometimes the painting is a gouache, sometimes an impression, at other times a bold still life. I think in colors. I even dream in primary colors, whatever the content of my dream.

ADULT WRITING

My autobiography resulted from a fit of pique. After hearing the older generation of blacks in Britain being pilloried as "Topsies and Toms," I decided to set the record straight. There had been Ted Braithwaite's *To Sir with Love* and Don Hinds's *Journey to an Illusion*, but a woman's experiences had never been published. As I wrote, my anger mounted when I recalled the experiences of my contemporaries—false accusations by the police, innocent people being beaten up, black men being offered drinks of urine disguised as beer, and expulsion from clubs and public places were day-to-day occurrences in their lives. There were no race-relations apparatus, no pressure groups, no media to bring the news into drawing rooms as it happened. Our women's concerns were with getting from A to B safely, without being assaulted by the Teddy Boys or chased by the grandparents of the National Front, the members of the League of Empire Loyalists. Until the Notting Hill Riots we were not really protected by the laws of this land although lip service was paid to equal rights. Women were adjuncts to men, and both were minimally considered and peripheral.

The English had gone to some of the colonies and seen deplorable poverty and therefore considered all Wogs lecherous, incontinent, and depraved. Some had gone to places where natives "lived in 'uts,'" and they believed all natives "live in 'uts.'" A parent said, "I'm not for 'er 'aving a black teacher. I was in India you know . . . Seen some sights. I did. None of them was teachers. Beggars yes. Loads was beggars" (*Gilroy, Black Teacher*, p. 54). The war took British working-class men and women farther afield than sentiment and kinship had previously done. They were so busy basking in their Britishness that their own persecution as a class and their humanity evaporated. So I wrote stories about prejudices similar to those the war had been about. The difference was that the British form was expressed in a jocular, nonauthoritarian manner. They used their tongues lightheartedly yet abrasively to strip away any idea of a confident whole or human self. For example, "You shouldn't trip over like that, a sturdy girl like you. Now, how many trees have you jumped out of in your life." A smile accompanied this remark, and you smiled back until struck by the implication of the words. Such statements were merely friendly space-fillers in conversation.

Black women were enigmas, especially to white men. They had seen black men "down by the docks. Other black men were villains and pimps. But the women! Aha!" We were mysterious to them, and they cloaked their fantasies about us in derision and renunciation.

In school, the extent of the ignorance of the teachers who should have known better made me feel ashamed of my colleagues. My colonial education was English in content, but they knew nothing about us. I often tested the images children carried around inside their heads about black people. When they painted my house they painted flats, sometimes with trees beside them for me to climb. They had not seen natives on TV as yet. Few owned television sets then. But my food was a different matter. "There were plates full of people for me to eat. Some were ordinary people, very frail and delicate and fully clad with salt, pepper, and tomato ketchup beside them" (*Black Teacher*, p. 98). These children were expressing what Thomas Tryon the vegetarian and mystic said about us in 1680 and what Edward Long said in 1772. In each generation prejudice against us, like physical traits, recurs.

My class progressed so well that parents who had formerly repudiated me as being a second-rate teacher were requesting that their children be placed in my class. I was different—a bit like them, but not quite. I felt a touch of professional pride until the ancillary worker pricked the bubble in which I floated. "The Mum's reckon you must 'ave something special—like I told 'em—you people from out of the bush can sometimes do wonders." She looked toward the ceiling in the most serious way. "There are things on this earth that we 'ere 'ave never 'eard of" (*Black Teacher*, p. 67). Juju was the essence of my success as a teacher.

In my work I try to capture the essential differences between us and other people. I use emotion to unite people. I try to incorporate a feeling of the poetic into the language I use. It is not easy to express how much my interior life is defined in my writing. I am hypercritical of my work and perfectionist in my expectations, and yet I exist in all my worst characters, even in Token (*Frangipani House,*) who has learned the callousness of the acquisitive society. I write swiftly and endeavor to help my reader hear her own internal thoughts. I need time alone. I spend great chunks of time alone. My family has always understood this need. I fight back like the characters in my books, and when I am satisfied that I have said what I want to say, that the reader and I would hear the same echoes and share the same emotions, I am content to think that I have drawn a good enough picture of contemporary reality. I write fact-fiction. As a psychologist I am given stories in plenty, but some are so surrealistic no one would believe them.

CONCLUSION

I write because there must be time for self-affirmation if what I write is to surprise and agitate the reader. Creativity includes the element of surprise. I write to say that whatever the conditions of my life, my spirit would lead me on in my desire to converse with others. When I write I say that I have never for one single moment of my life seen myself as a victim. I express my identity in the craft of writing.

Bibliography

Gilroy, Beryl A. *Black Teacher*. London: Cassells, 1976.
——. *Boy Sandwich*. London: Heinemann, 1989.
——. *In for a Penny*. London: Cassells, 1980.
——. *Frangipani House*. London: Heinemann, 1986.
Gilroy, P. C. *Ain't No Black in the Union Jack*. London: Hutchinson, 1987.

Challenges of the Struggle for Sovereignty: Changing the World versus Writing Stories

MERLE HODGE

My very dear friend Michael Anthony, one of the writers of the Caribbean for whom I feel a great deal of respect and affection, once said to me, expressing alarm at the activist role I seemed to have opted for: "But you have to devote your time to writing stories—you can't change the world!"

I am very confident that it is people who change the world and that people must continually engage in actions aimed at changing the world for the better. For me, there is no fundamental contradiction between art and activism. In particular, the power of the creative word to change the world is not to be underestimated.

Fiction has immense political power. Its power can be revolutionary or, of course, the opposite: it is a prime weapon of political conservatism. That is why it was important for us to study the literature of the British Isles during the colonial era; that is why today, in the era of independence, it is important to saturate the Caribbean people with American soap-opera and situation comedy and Rambo-style adventure.

I began writing, in my adult life, in protest against my education and the arrogant assumptions upon which it rested: that I and my world were nothing and that to rescue ourselves from nothingness, we had best seek admission to the world of *their* storybook. (I first began writing in child-hood, and those pieces which survive are a testimony to the power of the fiction to which I was exposed: namely, the power of the storybook.) The genesis of modern Caribbean writing lies, I think, in such a reaction, conscious or unconscious, against the enterprise of negating our world and offering us somebody else's world as salvation.

The protest against this imposition has developed, in my case, into an abiding concern with the issue of cultural sovereignty and beyond that, into an unapologetic interest in the political development of our region. Cultural sovereignty is an abstraction to a vagrant digging in dustbins for food on the streets of Port of Spain or a family that cannot send its children to school because there is no money for books.

For me, cultural sovereignty is part of the larger issue of Caribbean liberation—the struggle of the Caribbean people to finally inherit the Caribbean and its resources, the ongoing struggle of the Caribbean people for political power. In this struggle, cultural sovereignty is both a means and an end: we can neither achieve the liberation of the Caribbean without affirming and enthroning our culture, nor affirm and enthrone our culture in any real sense until we have won full political sovereignty.

And what, in all of this, is the use of writing stories? The potential of Caribbean literature for positively affecting the development of the Caribbean is an untapped resource. Caribbean fiction can help to strengthen our self-image, our resistance to foreign domination, our sense of the oneness of the Caribbean and our willingness to put our energies into the building of the Caribbean nation.

The cultural penetration of the Caribbean which we are witnessing today is a serious business. It is as serious as the invasion and continuing occupation of Grenada. It is perhaps even more serious, for you can recognize a military invasion when you see one. Invasion and occupation in the guise of entertainment are another kettle of fish.

And there are direct links between the continuing underdevelopment of the Caribbean and the continued—the renewed—suppression of Caribbean culture.

The culture of the Caribbean, the culture produced here on Caribbean soil by the ordinary working people of the region, has never gained full recognition in our society. It has never gained official recognition, and has never been fully recognized and valued by the very people who created it and who continue to create it every day of their lives.

Governments of the region recognize and pay attention to one aspect of the culture—the performing arts—not because they have any interest in the people who created the steelband and calypso and reggae and Carnival but because in the development of tourism and the quest for foreign exchange, these things can be turned into commodities, packaged, and sold. (Right now the government of Trinidad and Tobago is talking about "selling steelband to the world.")

But culture in its total definition—the full spectrum of responses that a people makes, collectively, to its specific environment, to ensure its survival in that environment—has yet to be properly addressed in the Caribbean context. Caribbean people suffer great ambivalence regarding their culture. We do not acknowledge or give value to our own most deeply rooted behavior patterns, our most intimate psychology. In the first place, we are not fully aware of what constitutes our specificity. We recognize our culture only in a negative, rejecting way: we see in our people tendencies and characteristics which we regard as aberrations to be stamped out—"aberrations" because they do not fit the norms suggested by storybook and television.

Let us take some very fundamental aspects of culture: language, family, and religion. Ninety-nine percent of Caribbean people, for 99 percent of their waking hours, communicate in a Creole language that is a fusion of West African syntax and the modified vocabulary of one or another European tongue. These languages have stubbornly survived generations of disrespect and active suppression in the home and in the education system. Possibly they have survived because they express *our* personality, our reality, our worldview in a way no other language can. Caribbean Creole languages have been fashioned to fit our communication needs, and they have not only survived but developed—and they continue to develop as our communication needs become, perhaps, more complex.

In the "English-speaking" Caribbean, statistics from the education system show that only a very small proportion of the population may be said to possess English. If we use as an indicator the passing rate for the English language examinations taken at the end of high school, we must question just how English-speaking the "English-speaking Caribbean" really is. In the Caribbean as a whole, only a small percentage of the population gains admission to high school, and only a small percentage of this percentage demonstrates proficiency in the English language upon graduation.

Creole is the main medium of communication in the Caribbean. Almost everybody uses Creole. But the attitude of the Caribbean people to the language they speak is incredible. Parents who speak nothing but Creole severely reprimand their children for speaking Creole. Educators at the highest level become too hysterical to argue rationally when they are presented with the very simple proposition that Caribbean people can be armed with *both* standard English and their mother tongue, Creole; that the teaching of English must never be accompanied by efforts to discredit Creole—just as the education system of, say, Denmark or Nigeria seeks to equip its people with an international language in addition and with no detriment to its mother tongue. Think of the implications for our mental health—we speak Creole, we need Creole, we cannot function without Creole, for our deepest thought processes are bound up in the structure of Creole, but we hold Creole in utter contempt.

The same goes for our family forms and the religions born on Caribbean soil. We live, very comfortably, in certain arrangements that perform all the functions of family—the socialization of the young, the provision of the material and emotional needs of all family members, the regulation of sexuality. Again, these arrangements do not fit the storybook prescription: in our family systems the head of the family can be female or male; legal marriage is not mandatory; the family spills beyond one household to include cousins, aunts and uncles, grandparents, and even godparents as functional members of a family.

These arrangements have survived for generations, despite official disrespect and attempts to force us all into the storybook family mold. And again there is ambivalence, a contradiction between our daily experience and the norms to which we subscribe, for we firmly believe that a "real" family consists of husband, wife, and children, with the husband as head, and that any variation on this model is an anomaly—even if it is an anomaly which we live.

In religion there is the same contradiction between "standard" religion—that is, Christianity—and a certain interpretation of the supernatural and styles of worship inherited from our African past which hold a strong attraction for us but which we are very careful to disown.

The culture of the Caribbean, then, has never gained validity in the eyes of Caribbean people. In the colonial era, Culture with a capital "C" was the culture of the colonizing country. Whatever we were practicing was not "real" culture. The colonial era came to an end and we moved into independence. Theoretically, we could now begin to build up a sense of our cultural identity. But we immediately found ourselves in a new and more vicious era of cultural penetration. Television, which is basically American television, came to Trinidad and Tobago in 1962, the year the British flag was pulled down. The same pattern can be seen all over the Caribbean—withdrawing the most obvious trappings of colonial domination and installing a Trojan horse instead.

Today we might be even further away from sovereignty than we were in the colonial era. Our already weak self-image continues to be undermined in an even more subtle way than before, and this paralyzes us, allows us to be manipulated and makes us less capable of taking our destiny into our own hands.

From the colonial era to the present time, one of the weapons used to subjugate us has been fiction. The proper role of fiction in human societies includes allowing a people to "read" itself—to decipher its own reality. The storyteller offers a vision of the world which is more coherent, more "readable," than the mass of unconnected detail of everyday experience. Fiction also brings to our attention and puts in place parts of our reality that are not visible to us or are normally overlooked, allowing us to form a more complete picture of our environment than our own observation allows. Paradoxically, the world of fiction appears more real to us, more *vital*, than the real world: it is more imposing and impressive than the real world. This is because of the greater coherence of the artist's creation, and also because of its greater intensity. The world of the story has a greater impact upon our imagination than does the diffuse scenario of everyday living.

When fiction draws upon our world, when it recreates our reality, it helps give validity to our world. It helps us to first make sense of our world, for it shows us underlying patterns and connections which give our reality a satisfying order. But also, in a way that is perhaps difficult to fully account for, *fiction gives substance to reality*. Beside the world of fiction, the real world pales in significance. For fiction (and perhaps all art) casts a redeeming and enhancing light back upon the reality from which it springs, endowing it with meaning, credibility, and authority. It allows a people not only to know its own world but to take it seriously. This is why an important element of the socialization of the young in every self-respecting society is exposing them to the fiction of their society. In preliterate societies this means teaching them the stories, songs, and poems of the tribe or enacting the life of the tribe through drama. In modern society it means putting the literary classics of a people on their school curriculum.

Caribbean people have only very limited exposure to their own literature. Caribbean literature courses are available at the University of the West Indies, and some texts have been introduced into the curriculum of secondary schools through the CXC (Caribbean Examinations Council) Exam. But access to secondary education remains limited, and the great majority of students study literature only in the first three years of secondary school, during which time they are likely to read all of three Caribbean texts, if indeed so many.

If we recognize the process by which fiction validates reality, it becomes clear that people steeped in imported fiction are not likely to develop a healthy relationship with themselves or their environment. They are more likely to reject the real, palpable world in which they live in favor of the world presented to them in fiction. Indeed, Caribbean people are capable of a kind of "mental desertion" of their own environment, which is not matched, I think, by any other people on earth.

Such was our situation during the colonial era, and such is our situation today. In this situation creative writing becomes, for me, a guerrilla activity. We are occupied by foreign fiction. Fiction which affirms and validates our world is therefore an important weapon of resistance. The most apolitical of writers becomes part of the struggle for Caribbean liberation— even a writer like V. S. Naipaul, whose vision of the Caribbean does not include anything as sentimental as "liberation" and who would be very alarmed if he were to be described as a Caribbean freedom fighter, has contributed enormously to sharpening our fuzzy self-image, if not to boosting our self-esteem.

For merely to portray Caribbean experience with the power of art is to pluck this experience out of limbo and give it a distinct shape and a name. And this, in our context, is potentially an act of guerrilla warfare. I am not talking about writers idealizing Caribbean reality. Literature contributes to a people's growth by portraying them both respectfully and *critically*, not by flattering them.

If we agree that Caribbean literature can contribute to the political process of empowering Caribbean people, then we must set about solving another problem: how do we deliver Caribbean literature to the Caribbean people? How do we compete with the great volume of foreign fiction that our people consumes?

One of the problems is that in speaking of Caribbean literature we are referring to a body of writing which is, in general, highly accomplished and very sophisticated, by any literary criteria. The Caribbean can boast of a relatively literate population, but our people are no more *literary* than any other. And the percentage of Caribbean people who will devote an evening to a novel of classical quality, Caribbean or otherwise, rather than to "Knots Landing" or Mills and Boone, is the same as elsewhere.

We might have to consider developing a modern tradition of popular literature, for which we have some precedent in, for example, the Onitsha market literature of Nigeria. There is not much in Caribbean literature to counterbalance the easily accessible paperback novel that comes to us from the United States, Canada, England, and even Australia. The idea of developing such a literature in the Caribbean may be fairly controversial. But I do not think that it necessarily involves a complete compromise of literary standards. A great deal of what is today revered as classical literature started out as fiction aimed at a mass audience rather than a highly educated elite. One example of this tendency is the work of nineteenth-century French novelists, which first appeared in serialized form in newspapers.

One of my specific concerns or ambitions is to one day be able to participate in the development of a strong popular theater. In Trinidad and Tobago—and, I think, in much of the Caribbean—the theater is perceived as an urban, middle-class activity. We have a duty, I think, to restore theater to its popular roots. We must take it out of the sophisticated urban theater building and into community centers, church halls, and school buildings around the country; we must also infiltrate the electronic media with a popular theater grounded in Caribbean experience.

The development of Caribbean children's literature is another of my concerns. One of the reasons why Caribbean literature has not yet fully invaded the school curriculum is that there is not a sufficient body of good fiction suitable for all age groups. Children in secondary school are exposed to Caribbean literature that is aimed at an adult audience; and at the primary school level, teachers seeking to bring Caribbean literature into the curriculum tend to rely heavily on folk tales.

Thus far I have said nothing on the subject of women. I am, of course, very interested in the redressing of imbalances, both in the projection of women in Caribbean fiction and in the participation of women in the creation of Caribbean fiction. I am not sure that feminism has always been a conscious concern or a motivating force in what creative writing I have done. When I wrote *Crick Crack Monkey*, I do not think that I knew the word *feminism*, and I may have been only vaguely aware of such a thing as a women's movement. What I did know was that there were types of women whom I greatly admired and other types for whom I felt a certain amount of disdain. I had developed these attitudes during the course of my childhood.

I later came to understand that as a child, I admired women who did not know their place—women who did not seem to pattern their lives after the rules laid down by nice Trinidadian society, by the church or by storybooks. These were self-possessed women who seemed to be operating by a different set of norms with regard to work, their under-standing of their own physical being, their sexuality, their relations with men, their family relations—women like the grandmother and aunt with whom I spent long periods of my childhood.

It is Caribbean women such as these who will continue to inhabit the world of my stories, for our struggle for Caribbean liberation will in-clude putting ourselves fully in touch with these everyday models of sovereignty.

Crick Crack Monkey:
A Picaresque Perspective

ENA V. THOMAS

A picaresque novel is essentially an ironic presentation of a chaotic society by an outcast of that society. Characteristically, the outsider gives a first-person perspective of his life experiences in the double voice of the experiencing "I" of the child and the narrating voice of the remembering adult. His aim in writing is twofold: first, to show how difficult it is for an outsider to gain respectability in a society that has only contempt for him and his culture, and second, to satirize the false values of a society of which he is a victim.

A picaresque vision is ironic because in attempting to satirize the false values of the dominant class, the narrator/protagonist inadvertently assimilates the very values he detests. The picaresque environment is marked by violence, brutality, and poverty and, as a consequence of the latter, by hunger and immorality as well. Frequently the minority group suffers discrimination at the hands of the ruling class because of differences of ethnicity, religion, and culture.

An indispensable ingredient of the picaresque novel is its humor, which often spans the range of the comic from crude farce to subtle wit. The humor is often a function of the struggle to survive; the protagonist uses the only weapon at his disposal, his wit and guile to outsmart his rivals, even though, ironically, he is usually outsmarted in the end. Humor in the picaresque may also be interpreted as a weapon of ridicule with which to attack institutions and individuals in the society that are perceived as supporting the injustices of the system.

The picaresque world view is amoral; the effort to overcome poverty and hunger and ultimately to move up in society makes morality a luxury the struggling outcast can ill afford. Finally, picaresque novels have an episodic structure, consisting of loosely related events, thereby underscoring the chaos and disintegration of the larger society.

To sum up, the term *picaresque* is a literary expression used to describe a social structure that keeps some of its members on its periphery, either because of race and color or religious affiliation. The author, who is invariably a member of the deprived class, examines the society from his position as an underdog to ridicule its institutions and supporters; this he does with irony and humor in episodes that trace the protagonist's materially rewarding but spiritually disastrous development.

A reading of Merle Hodge's *Crick Crack Monkey* leaves me with the conclusion that the novel has some distinctly picaresque characteristics.[1]

COLONIAL SOCIETY CREATES OUTCASTS

Crick Crack Monkey is the story of Cynthia Davis, nicknamed Tee, and told by Tee herself. The young girl grows up in colonial Trinidad in the 1940s in a society structured into three distinct classes based on race and color. The sociologist M. G. Smith has left us a vivid description of the class structure of British West Indian colonial societies:

> Typically and overwhelmingly, white (Europeans) and those able to assimilate closest to the white plantocracy in looks, colour, manners, language, dress, education and values, rank highest on every social, cultural and economic dimension and are legitimated as such; the coloured (mixed), again, typically and overwhelmingly occupy intermediary occupations and statuses, and are graded within the legitimation system in terms of their approximation to the dominant group; overwhelmingly and typically the poorer classes (Africans) are in the lower and more menial occupations in town and countryside, and the positions with least rank are occupied by blacks even where their ethnic inheritance is no longer "pure."[2]

In the colonial society described by M. G. Smith, Tee, Tantie, and the rest of the extended family belong to the bottom tier of the society because they are black and poor. By contrast, Aunt Beatrice, a descendant of the white ancestress Elizabeth Helen Carter, earns a place in the middle class through her mixed blood. Mr. Brathwaite, the French Creole planter, owner of Santa Clara Estate, is a member of the small, elite, landowning class. The divisions between the classes are so rigid and they are so

---

1. Merle Hodge, *Crick Crack Monkey* (1970; rpt. London: Heinemann, n.d.)
2. M. G. Smith, "The Plural Society in the British West Indies," in John Rex, ed., *Race and Class in Post-Colonial Society* (Suffolk, U.K.: UNESCO, 1977), pp. 166–67.

mutually contemptuous of one another that the lowest class functions in all respects as outcasts.

It is in the context of this hierarchical structure that Tee is motivated, in picaresque fashion, to strive to move out of her socially deprived, working-class group to assimilate the values and lifestyles of the middle class. Consequently, the journey that Tee makes is an inverse one from security and self-worth in the indigenous Afro-Trinidadian culture to alienation and disintegration of personhood in the urban metropolitan culture represented by Aunt Beatrice.

In the final chapter of her young adult life, Tee is a restless individual who can find no inner center either at Tantie's who represents the lot of Africa's dispossessed children; or at Ma's, symbolic of Mother Africa; or at Aunt Beatrice, the surrogate European mother. She is doomed to be on the run, and the chapter closes with her inevitable destiny of exile in England: "I desired," she confesses, "with all my heart that it was next morning and a plane were lifting me off the ground" (p. 111).

THE PICARESQUE ENVIRONMENT OF VIOLENCE

Crick Crack Monkey is a Caribbean version of the original picaresque novel, *Lazarillo de Tormes*, not because it imitates its Spanish ancestor but because colonial Trinidad reproduced the typical picaroon environment of violence and brutality and elicited picaroon responses from its most vulnerable citizens. V. S. Naipaul is the first person to recognize the picaroon nature of Trinidad's society when in *The Middle Passage* he writes: "Slavery, the mixed population, the absence of national pride and the closed colonial system have to a remarkable degree re-created the attitudes of the Spanish picaroon world. This was an ugly world, a jungle where the picaroon starved unless he stole, was beaten almost to death when found out and had therefore to get in his blows first whenever possible; where the weak were humiliated; where the powerful never appeared and were beyond reach; where no one was allowed any dignity and everyone had to impose himself."[3]

The inherent violence of the colonial environment is ultimately responsible for the rage that is evident in Manhatt'n's language: "Crick-crack yu mother! Is true whe ah tell yu—yu only blasted jealous it ain' you. Crick-crack? Ah go crick-crack yu stones gu yu!" (p. 7); it is responsible for Tantie's frequent habit of beating Tee: "She flew at me and battered me with the dishcloth she had in her hand, hitting out in furious relief" (p. 12); and it is to be blamed for the children's cruelty to Mr. Oliver, the caretaker, whom they stoned: "and Mr. Oliver was hoarse

3. V. S. Naipaul, *The Middle Passage* (Middlesex, England: Penguin, 1969), p. 79.

now and there was froth at the corner of his mouth and he was turning round and round and jabbing at the air with the broom as he shouted incoherently when suddenly his mouth stood open and the broom clattered to the ground at his feet" (p. 50).

THE WORM'S-EYE VIEW

Tee gives an underdog's perspective of what growing up in colonial Trinidad is like; her story would have been different had it been told by someone from the privileged middle class. For example, in *West Indian Perspectives*, Comitas and Lowenthal chronicled what they termed "the remarkable story played out on the doorstep of the North American continent from colonisation to self-government and from self-rejection to prideful identity."[4] In *Crick Crack Monkey* Hodge has her narrator give a different version of that experience, which contradicts Comitas and Lowenthal's interpretation. Her journey moves in reverse fashion from "prideful identity" to "self-rejection" because her perspective is the worm's-eye view that yields a characteristically picaresque *weltanschauung*.

THE PICARESQUE JOURNEY

Tee's journey in *Crick Crack Monkey* is not one of personal development but rather of psychological disintegration. The breakdown of her character begins imperceptibly in Tantie's home. Although Tantie's household provides an anchor for the sensitive infant, it is terribly flawed. The presence of a tantie marks the absence of a mother. Tee's first handicap is orphanhood. Chapter 1 ends with Tee's awareness of the absence of her mother and father, the former by death, the latter by exile: "Then Papa went to sea. I concluded that what he had gone to see was whether he could find Mammy and the baby" (p. 3).

The orphaned child has only her adopted home to serve her as moral exemplar and formal education at school to be her teacher. Both fail her. Tantie's world is a morally broken environment full of indecencies and obscenities. There is first the problem of Tantie's many lovers who offend Aunt Beatrice's sense of uprightness: "And then what about all those men, did we like all those men coming," Aunt Beatrice questions Tee and Toddan; and second there is the problem of physical and verbal violence that Tee has to endure.

On one hand, Tantie's world gives Tee negative moral values, and on the other the education system alienates her from herself and her culture.

4. Lambros Comitas and David Lowenthal, eds., "Editors' Notes," in *Slaves, Free Men, Citizens: West Indian Perspectives* (Garden City, N.Y.: Doubleday Anchor Press, 1973), p. xiv.

By the end of primary school, Tee has developed a schizophrenic personality characterized by self-hate and an admiration for all things foreign thanks to colonized teachers like Mr. Hinds and a British-oriented curriculum that symbolically starts with "A for apple." It is at this time that she creates her double, Helen, the epitome of the British child she would like to become: "Helen wasn't even my double. No, she couldn't be called my double. She was the Proper Me. And me, I was her shadow, hovering about in incompleteness" (p. 62).

Tee's journey through life, like the picaroon's, is marked by loss of innocence (as, for example, in the storing of her Oliver episode, p. 50), by petty theft (as in the episode with Mr. Brathwaite in Chapter 12), and finally by self-contempt. Having rejected self and family, she has no alternative but to flee her country.

PICARESQUE HUMOR

Humor in *Crick Crack Monkey* is verbal rather than physical and consists of amusing stories like the Manhatt'n anecdote and the Tantie/Ling incident. It may take picaresque delight in the scatological as when Tee finds pleasure in Mr. Hind's use of the word *nincompoops* or in the children's play: "When someone chose this situation of inescapable intimacy to emit an anonymous but very self assertive poops" (p. 17). Irony, however is the most characteristic form of humor in picaresque writing. The irony of Tee's life is total. It has what Ulrich Wicks calls "the ironic gap between the social non-status of the protagonist and the presumptuous act of writing his autobiography."[5] It is also ironic that education is the agent for Tee's upward social mobility and at the same time the cause of her self-hate and alienation. Finally, picaresque humor is satiric. In *Crick Crack Monkey*, the main target of criticism is the adverse effects of colonialism on one's cultural identification.[6] In her later writing, Hodge is very explicit on this topic. She writes: "In the colonial era the ways of Caribbean people were never seen as valid culture. What was promoted through all the formal channels of education was metropolitan culture."[7]

THE EPISODIC STRUCTURE

The anecdotes in *Crick Crack Monkey* take us into a world that is always collapsing and disintegrating. The story starts with death and ends with

5. Ulrich Wicks, "The Nature of Picaresque Narrative: A Modal Approach," *PMLA* 89 (1974): 244.
6. See Marjorie Thorpe, "The Problems of Cultural Identification in *Crick Crack Monkey*," *Savacou* 13 (1977): 31–38.
7. Merle Hodge, "Towards People Participation in Caribbean Development," in G. Beckford et al., *A Caribbean Reader on Development* (Kingston: Friedrich Ebert Stiftung, 1986), p. 92.

exile, and between these two extremities are numerous episodes depicting various degrees of death and exile. A typical foray into chaos is the chapter on EC/RC rivalry on the savannah, which sometimes ends in this way: "Sometimes men were caught. There would be a huge heaving pile on the ground . . . followed by a joyful throng" (p. 53).

Games played by children in the idyllic setting of Ma's country dwelling are wont to end with a disconcerting "poops"; holidays at Ma's would end with rivalry between two groups; a session of children learning arithmetic tables would come to a close with the bashing of slates in one another's faces. Moreover, the actual content of the episodes as well as the loose structure of an episodic plot tend to underscore the fact that things are falling apart.

In sum, *Crick Crack Monkey* is the narrative of an outsider struggling for social respectability, which she achieves ironically, at the expense of her integrity. The vision that it presents is both comic and tragic because of the peculiar double voicing of a child who experiences and an adult who remembers. But it is precisely the potential of the individual to remember his life that leaves the reader with the slim hope that all is not lost in a picaresque world.

Jamaica Kincaid and the Modernist Project: An Interview

SELWYN R. CUDJOE

This interview with Jamaica Kincaid was conducted on May 29 and June 3, 1987, in North Bennington, Vermont. It was translated by Cathy Boyle. This interview was conducted while Ms. Kincaid was writing A Small Place *(1988). She admits to reading Selwyn R. Cudjoe's* Resistance and Caribbean Literature *(1980) constantly while she wrote* A Small Place. *Since this interview was conducted, Ms. Kincaid has published* A Small Place *(1988). This interview is a valuable companion piece to the latter work and* Annie John.—S.R.C.

CUDJOE: Tell me a little about yourself. I know you were born in St. John's, Antigua, but I don't know when you left and so on.

KINCAID: I left Antigua shortly after my sixteenth birthday, in June of 1965. I came to America and became an *au pair* girl. I wasn't quite a servant, but almost. I was taking care of someone's children while I went to school. I lived with an American family, and I was going to school at night. I was supposed to go on and study nursing but I never did.

I eventually left the family and went to New York. I studied photography at the New York School for Social Research in New York, at night, as well as some other things—but mainly photography. How I got interested in photography is a roundabout story. I left the family and worked as a receptionist at various places, and then I went to school in New

This interview was originally published in *Callaloo* 12 (Spring 1989):396–411. Reprinted with permission.

Hampshire because I thought maybe I should go to college. So I went to Franconia College for at least a year—well, it was a little bit more than that—and then I came back to New York and found a job with a magazine called *Art Direction*, I think. I was fired for writing an article on black American advertising. It was very controversial because I said something—I can't really remember what it was—that made everyone upset, and so I was fired.

I thought I was entitled to unemployment insurance, but my unemployment checks never came, so I really had to try to find a job. I applied for a job at *Mademoiselle* and *Glamour*, but I couldn't type, so I didn't get these jobs. I submitted ideas to a magazine called *Ingenue*, and they didn't like any of them except one, in which I said I would like to ask Gloria Steinem what she was like when she was the age of the average reader of the magazine *Seventeen*. They thought that was a good idea, and Gloria Steinem kindly granted me an interview, and I wrote the article.[1]

It was a big success, and they turned it into a series of articles. They even sent me to Los Angeles to interview celebrities, asking them what they were like when they were seventeen. This was the first writing I did.

CUDJOE: And all the articles appeared in the same magazine?

KINCAID: Yes, *Ingenue*. One day, in the elevator, I met a man named Michael O'Donaghue. Well, I used to dress rather strangely in those days. I would wear a lot of old clothes and sort of looked like people from different periods—someone from the 1920s, someone from the 1930s, someone from the 1940s. I had cut off all my hair and bleached it blond, and I had shaved off my eyebrows. I really did look odd!

Anyway, this man seemed very taken by my appearance. He invited me to dinner and introduced me to a man named George W. S. Trow, who wrote for the *New Yorker*. He and I became very good friends, and he used to write "Talk of the Town" stories about me. One day he took me to dinner—I was very poor, so sometimes he'd take me to dinner. We were sitting in a Lebanese restaurant on Twenty-eighth Street. I had just said something, and he said, "That's so funny! Would you like to write for the *New Yorker*? I should introduce you to Mr. Shawn."

I said, "Sure—of course. I'd love to write for the *New Yorker*." So he arranged for me to have lunch with Mr. Shawn at the Algonquin. Mr. Shawn said that I should try writing some "Talk" stories. I don't think anyone really thought I could do it—I mean, I know I didn't think so. Well, that's how I began to write for the *New Yorker*.

CUDJOE: Tell me about your early education.

1. "When I Was 17," *Ingenue*, 1973.

KINCAID: I started in school when I was about three and a half years old, and the reason my mother sent me to school was that I gave her so much trouble at home! At that time, however, she had already taught me to read. You know, simple things . . . I knew how to spell *cat* and words like that. So she enrolled me in this school—it was a Moravian school—and she said, "Now remember, if anyone asks you, say you're five." You see, I was very tall.

Since I was five, school lasted only a half a day. I was supposed to come home and take a nap in the afternoons, but I'd come home and make so much trouble that when I was three and a half she finally had to let me go to school for the entire day.

From there I went to school in Antigua. I went to all the regular government schools. Then I went to one school, the name of which I absolutely hate. It was called, "The Princess Margaret School."

CUDJOE: You developed a great dislike for colonialism?

KINCAID: Yes. When I was nine, I refused to stand up at the refrain of "God Save Our King." I hated "Rule, Britannia"; and I used to say that we weren't Britons, we were slaves. I never had any idea why. I just thought that there was no sense to it—"Rule Britannia, Britannia rule the waves, Britons never ever shall be slaves." I thought that we weren't Britons and that we were slaves.

CUDJOE: No one ever told you this—it was just instinctive?

KINCAID: No, no one ever told me that. In those days—well, my mother used to be an Anglophile, but I realize now that it was just a phase of my mother's life. She was really a stylish person; it must just have been a phase in her development.

Anyway, I went to Princess Margaret School. I got a scholarship to go there, and my mother now tells me that I came in second on the island of Antigua to go to that school. I now realize that I left without taking the "O levels" of the General Certificate of Education. I came to America without taking them.

CUDJOE: Did you come to America intending to be a writer?

KINCAID: No, not at all. You see, the educational system in Antigua, well, Antigua has this incredible history. It went from colonialism to the modern world—that is, from about 1890 to 1980—in five years. When I was growing up, we still celebrated Queen Victoria's birthday on May 24, and for us England (and I think this was true for V. S. Naipaul, too) and its glory was at its most theatrical, its most oppressive. Everything seemed divine and good only if it was English.

So my education, which was very "Empire," only involved civilization up to the British Empire—which would include writing—so I never read anything past Kipling. Kipling wasn't even considered a serious writer.

CUDJOE: Who were the serious writers?

KINCAID: Well, the Brontës, Hardy, Shakespeare, Milton, Keats. . . . We were taught to read from Shakespeare and Milton when I was five. They were read to us while we sat under a tree.

CUDJOE: What induced you to write?

KINCAID: Well, as I was going to say, I didn't know that people were still writing. I somehow thought that writing had been this great "thing" and that it had stopped. I thought that all the great writing had been done before 1900. Contemporary writers just didn't exist. I mean, I read Enid Blighton and so on, but that wasn't really writing . . . it was something to entertain me. But I never wanted to be a writer because I didn't know that any such thing existed.

CUDJOE: Let us go on to your name. Why the name "Jamaica"?

KINCAID: That's not the name my mother gave me. The name my mother gave me was Elaine Potter Richardson, which was her family's name. I had always hated my name and then it turned out that my mother had named me after someone whom I particularly came to loathe—a Lebanese woman, one of these people who come through the West Indies to get something from it but they don't actually inhabit it. I know this sounds awfully racist, but I just can't stand those people.

At any rate, I had always hated my name and wanted to change it, but it was only when I started to write and actually started to sign my name to things that I decided I just couldn't do this. Since my family disapproved of my writing, it was easy for me to change names.

CUDJOE: What kind of family did you come from?

KINCAID: Well, we were poor, ordinary people. My mother's family comes from Dominica; they were land peasants. They had a lot of land, which they lost through my aunt making a bad marriage and my mother falling out with her family. My mother says that my real father can't even read, but he made a lot of money.

CUDJOE: This is your real father, as opposed to your stepfather?

KINCAID: Yes, but the man I speak of as my father [in my works] is really my stepfather. I grew up thinking he was my father.

CUDJOE: So you don't know your real father?

KINCAID: Well, actually I do, now. I know a sort of person who is my father. We see each other, but I can't get myself to call him "father." He's sort of typical of West Indian men: I mean, they have children, but they never seem to connect themselves with these children.

About my name, though: my mother disapproved of my writing, and all of my friends who had come to America had gotten respectable jobs and were building something for their families. They were sending something back home, but I just wouldn't hear of it. I lived in my own sort of poverty, and I thought I might come to something; but I didn't know, really.

At one point I thought I would never see Antigua or my parents again because I didn't like what they thought of me. At the time I didn't know I was thinking this, but now I realize that the convention of being this "well-behaved child" . . . I just couldn't do it.

CUDJOE: Are there echoes of that in *Annie John*?

KINCAID: Yes. It's very interesting for me to think about that. When I was writing that [*Annie John*], I was sort of giving voice to something which—well, I just didn't have any words for it. But if I had not been successful at anything I'd done, I probably wouldn't have seen my parents. First of all, they would have laughed at me.

I remember that when I was at Franconia College, it was much colder than I had ever thought possible. In one of my weak moments I had written to my mother telling her how cold it was—a pleading letter, I guess. At any rate, she wrote back very harshly, telling me that I was always trying to be something I wasn't. I thought, "Well, that's the last time I tell her anything about me."

CUDJOE: When I read *Annie John*, I sense that tremendous dislike for your mother.

KINCAID: Well, I hope it's an adolescent dislike, because now we get along very well. It's possible that as human beings we don't like each other at all but that as a mother and daughter we love each other. I think that if I were to meet my mother in a certain context, I wouldn't like her. She's an extraordinary person, there's no question about that.

CUDJOE: But you've never forgiven her for that letter that said you're always trying to be something you're not?

CUDJOE: Well, yes, I think that I have forgiven her—but I shall never forget that because what is so odd about that is that the way I am is solely owing to her. I was always being told I should be something, and then my whole upbringing was something I was not: it was English. It was sort of a middle-class English upbringing—I mean, I had the best table manners you ever saw.

CUDJOE: In your book there is a sense of revolt against these values.

KINCAID: Oh, yes. I never knew we were poor: we ate well; my mother was always grand in every gesture; I was very well brought up. I could never speak bad English in her presence.

CUDJOE: A kind of middle-class respectability that, as you look back, may seem repulsive, but which—for people trying to make something of themselves—is a saving grace, as it were. . . . But why did you choose the name Jamaica Kincaid?

KINCAID: It wasn't really anything meaningful. By the time I decided to change my name, that part of the world had become very remote to me. It was a kind of invention: I wouldn't go home to visit that part of the world, so I decided to recreate it. "Jamaica" was symbolic of that place. I didn't come from Jamaica. I changed my name before Jamaica became fashionable—at least, before I was aware of it. If I had been aware, I would probably have changed my name to "Scandinavia" or something like that, because I hate being popular.

CUDJOE: And "Kincaid"?

KINCAID: Well, it just seemed to go with it.

CUDJOE: What West Indian writers did you read before you came to America?

KINCAID: I didn't know anything about West Indian literature before I came to this country. I loved to read, which was something my mother encouraged. Later it grew to be a bone of contention between us because I liked to do nothing but read and would neglect my household duties. She could see that it gave me ideas, that it took me away from her influence.

CUDJOE: What kinds of things did you read?

KINCAID: I used to read novels, biographies. I would just READ.

CUDJOE: So is *Annie John* autobiographical?

KINCAID: The feelings in it are autobiographical, yes. I didn't want to say it was autobiographical because I felt that that would be somehow admitting something about myself, but it is, and so that's that.

CUDJOE: At what point did you begin to read West Indian writers?

KINCAID: Well, I've read very little. Years ago someone gave me *A Bend in the River* so I've read that, but really I've read very little West Indian writing. When you say you're having this conference on West Indian women writers I think, "God—I didn't know there were more!" That's wonderful.

CUDJOE: So you have no sense of a tradition in West Indian literature?

KINCAID: No. I just started to write. I never thought anyone would read it. Since I wrote for the *New Yorker*, I assumed that only white people in the suburbs would be reading it.

CUDJOE: I don't know how many black people read your work, but when you read your work at Boston University recently, most of your audience was white so I know that you do have a strong white following.

KINCAID: It's a strange thing to get letters from white women saying, "Oh, that sounds just like my relationship with my mother." In a way, I'd like to think that I could write in the universal, that if I say the oppression by the English was such-and-such, that I say it in such a way that any human being will say, "Yes, that was wrong." My father was this sort of person—someone who anyone could understand.

CUDJOE: You say that you would like to see your work as being universal. How do you see your works fitting into the contemporary emphasis on feminist writings?

KINCAID: I don't really see it, but that's only because I don't really see myself in any school. I mean, there has turned out to be a rise in West Indian literature, but I wouldn't know how I fit in it. I am very glad that there is such a thing, but on the other hand, belonging to a group of anything, an "army" of anything, is deeply disturbing to me. I think I owe a lot of my success, or whatever, to this idea of feminism, but I don't really want to be placed in that category. I don't mind if people put me in it, but I don't claim to be in it. But that's just me as an individual. I mean, I always see myself as alone. I can't bear to be in a group of any kind, or in the school of anything. I think I started to write a certain way because I just didn't like certain stories that were being written. I didn't like the way white Americans wrote—a deadpan way—and the way they always mentioned products and songs and supermarkets. They don't really write, they just mention things. They suppose that the reader is just like them, so he understands if you just use some brand name. I found that horrid—I mean, it was sort of like pop songs. If I wanted to have universal references, I'd listen to rock and roll for "universal teenage references." So I said I'd never write like that.

Of course, now I see that my writing had nothing to do with my not wanting to write like a young white American—I can't write like a white American. I'm not a white American, and I don't have the same experience. I don't have the luxury of longing to be a displaced person, that is, a person who doesn't fit into his parent's life, or a person who doesn't fit into the town he grew up in. I don't have the luxury of wanting that: it actually did happen to me. That I couldn't fit in was a real pain for me. It wasn't an act so I couldn't write like that.

CUDJOE: But to a certain extent your writing is against that ability not to fit in?

KINCAID: To me, when I read the writings of young white Americans, it's an invented pain. I would grant that the agony is real, that they really feel that way, but it's completely an invention. So I thought, I'm going to write this other way, but of course the way I wrote really had nothing to do with a reaction. It's just the way I wrote.

CUDJOE: My point in asking you whether you would fit into the mold of feminist discourse, whether you consciously intended it or not, is that the nature of feminist discourse is intensely personal, a very interior kind of writing, and your writing does seem to fit into that mold.

KINCAID: Yes, perhaps so. You could place my writings there, but I could not. I wrote that way because that was the way I could write, so it does not feel to me that this is the way women write. My second book, *Annie John*, is about a girl's relationship with her mother because the fertile soil of my creative life is my mother. When I write, in some things I use my mother's voice, because I like my mother's voice. I like the way she sees things. In that way, I suppose that if you wanted to say it was feminist, it can only be true. I feel it would have no creative life or no real interest in art without my mother. It's really my "fertile soil."

CUDJOE: We have spoken briefly about the notion of modernism. It may be part of the same question in that you may not be conscious of it, but some of it comes through in your works. Certainly at the creative level, things come through of which we are not entirely aware. In looking back, do you feel that modernism plays any part in your writing?

KINCAID: Well, I'm not conscious of it, but when I finally did get around to reading what the modern writing experience was—Virginia Woolf, James Joyce—I thought, "This is really it."
    There were two things that really got me interested in writing. One was a French film called *La Jetee*. It's very modernist and certainly avant-garde for its time. It's all still photographs, in black and white; it turns out it was made by an American living in France. Anyway, it's still photographs, and somewhere in the middle of this film there is actual move-

ment, and then it goes back to still photographs. I used to watch it over and over—I was incredibly moved by it.

The idea of a story—or anything—being realistic, the idea of representing something as it is, was absurd. I could never even imagine doing that here. And then I read Alain Robbe-Grillet. I can never remember the title of the book, but it was some of his short stories. I cannot describe them except that they broke every rule. When I read them, the top of my head came off and I thought, "This is really living!" And I knew that whatever I did, I would not be interested in realism. Whatever I became, I would not be influenced only by the things I read when I was growing up. I was very influenced by Dickens, Milton, Shakespeare, and the Bible; but after I read these other things I knew, for instance, that I would never go back to Antigua, that I would never be able to live comfortably in Antigua again. I somehow felt free of the West Indies, in a strange way, which is to say that I couldn't live there again in the way that I had lived there before, that if I did live there again it would have to be under some other terms. I thought that I could never go home because it would kill me, drag me down. It was a total act of liberation.

When I read Jones I thought, well, I will never write again. This is finished, this is everything that I would want to say. This was while I was writing my first book. I read about him in Stravinsky's memoirs—Stravinsky went to visit him. Also, when I read someone like Bruno Schultz, I think, "Now this is really writing." For instance, Nadine Gordimer is a wonderful writer, but the writing of hers that I like—particularly one short story—is completely weird. The title of the story is "A Lion on the Freeway." The collection is called *A Soldier's Embrace*. To me, it's the most wonderful thing.

I don't like realistic fiction, I almost never read it. I read history, a lot of history. I was just reading [Anthony] Trollope's *The West Indies and the Spanish Main*. He's so racist it's a joke! He hates the Spaniards so much that he can't even get to the black people. It's amusing to read.

I read over and over again books about the history of the Caribbean, and then I read *A History of England*. I love to read about the history of England. I have one book here about the history of England in which they talk in the mildest language about the atrocities they committed against each other—the War of the Roses, for instance—and then there are marvelous descriptions. The guy who lost France, for instance, was described as having had a "nervous collapse." After he lost France, he had a "nervous collapse." He went stark raving mad, he ruined his country, he was a complete asshole—but they have the mildest words for this, and so I love reading *A History of England*—but for a different reason.

Then I read about the history of the West Indies, all different books, because I keep thinking that someone will say it happened differently. I can never believe that the history of the West Indies happened the way it did.

CUDJOE: In terms of what?

KINCAID: Well, the wreck and the ruin and the greed. It's almost on a monumental scale. It's worse than Africa, really. The truth about it is that it erased actual groups of people—groups of people vanished, just vanished.

CUDJOE: It might be a good time to talk about your first story, "Antigua Crossings." There was one character, the grandmother, who was a Carib Indian. There was a real sense of dignity and of fierceness. There's one part in particular which I think is so wonderful, I'd like to read it and get your response to it:

> We live on an island, Antigua, and on one side runs the Atlantic Ocean and on the other side is the Caribbean Sea. The Atlantic Ocean does not matter much to us. It comes from too far away and it shares itself with too many other people who are too different from us. The Caribbean Sea is ours and we share it with people who live on islands like us, islands that are sometimes made out of coral, sometimes made out of dead volcanoes. All these islands surround the Caribbean Sea like a ring around the rosy pocket full of posey games, preventing it from spilling out into the larger world of seawater. I know there are other seas which seem more important and more special, but they exist for me only in books.[2]

I'm sure you haven't read it in a long time . . . what's your response to that?

KINCAID: I'm amazed. I mean, I actually like it. It was my first real attempt at writing a piece of fiction and completing it. In some ways I'm amazed at . . . oh, I don't know how to say this without sounding too . . . well, I think it's very beautiful and very true—the idea that the Caribbean Sea embraces the West Indies in this way. I'm amazed at that because I'm very stupid, and I always think that I don't get smarter from any time but my present. Also, the gentleness of it, and the generosity, surprises me, because I was much harsher then.

CUDJOE: The entire work seems gentle to me and lyrical. But it's written from the point of a view of a young girl of twelve years, so I think it captures how *she* sees the island. That vision, I think, is what created its beauty.

2. Jamaica Kincaid, "Antigua Crossings: A Deep and Blue Passage on the Caribbean Sea," *Rolling Stone*, June 29, 1978, p. 48.

KINCAID: Well, I'm amazed at that. You see, I spent all the time I had been away from the West Indies and from my mother building some kind of "literary monument" to it [the island of Antigua], and it was interesting that when I got back it had changed so radically. I was shocked that it had changed for the worse. All the things I had thought made it a bad place were gone—but it was worse, and it's not that things would be better should they go back in time.

When I look at what you just read, written in that naive way, and I look at the West Indies now, if I were to write that, I think I would have to say that I had been betrayed, and in fact the Caribbean Sea, which used to include us, which used to be only for us—well, we've rather assaulted [it].

In Antigua, the average Antiguan no longer owns the beach—it's all owned by foreigners. There's no seaside property in Antigua: only the foreigners can afford it, and so it's very rare that an Antiguan sees the Caribbean Sea. But it turns out that we're not interested in the Caribbean Sea—we're interested in New York. The Caribbean Sea is no longer ours; it cannot be observed in that way. It can't be observed as being so big and so blue and so beautiful anymore. It's now so much money.

CUDJOE: But it's probably also part of our innocence when we're younger. That's all we have and all we know.

KINCAID: But it turns out that coincident with the loss of innocence on my part, the description of the loss of the sea is true. Basically, it's owned by travel agents—you only have to look in the magazines—and it's not so big and so beautiful anymore. It accommodates millions of people who make much money so they can go on their holiday.

CUDJOE: When you speak of your grandmother—who was a Carib Indian, very tall and very dark—you say that she accepted Christianity but then went back to her own native religion. Were you trying to juxtapose the two worlds?

KINCAID: Well, I don't think I was trying to compare them, but if I were a person who did compare these things, I would obviously choose my grandmother's original religion because, to be quite frank, my grandmother's religion committed no crime against humanity.

She was pagan; her deep belief was not Christian, and then she married a man who, as it turned out, lived a really wild life. He was a policeman, but then he became rather pious. He owned some land and was a lay preacher. So she accommodated his beliefs while, I think, always keeping her own beliefs. Then there was the tragedy of my uncle dying. She felt her beliefs would have saved him, and he [her husband] felt that his beliefs—his beliefs being faith in God and Western medicine—would have saved him. Well, it turns out that his illness was of a type that my grand-mother's beliefs would have cured.

CUDJOE: What was the illness?

KINCAID: Well, he was possessed, and something was set on him.

CUDJOE: That's where the *obeah* just keeps coming up.

KINCAID: Yes, my family practiced, and now my mother is in this high state of excitement—what is it called? She's one of those Christians—they sing and clap—"the charismatics." She's a charismatic, and she embraces it the way she embraces everything that she's embracing at the moment. It's all for her, but before this stage in her life, she was really quite devoted—well, somewhat devoted, and, I think, more devoted than I was really conscious of—to *obeah* things. Every Friday she'd go and have her cards read, and it also has to be said that she felt she lived in a state of war with the other women my father had loved—or not loved but just had a child with—so she was always consulting people, with the memory of her brother in mind, I think.

CUDJOE: Her brother died? He was sick at home, during the rains.

KINCAID: Her brother John had died when she was a child, from *obeah* things. He had a worm crawl out of his leg. Now, this sounds odd, but it did happen.

When I came to America, among the many things I was glad to be in America for, one of them was to not be afraid of God anymore, of any God—to be so unafraid of God that I wouldn't even have to go to church, which is to say that I wouldn't have to admit the existence of such a thing as God. I had felt the overbearingness of God from every direction, top and bottom.

So I think that in this particular piece [that is, literary work] I wasn't making a comparison [between Christianity and *obeah*]. In any case, I don't think I had the skill to make a comparison: I didn't have the knowledge.

CUDJOE: But your grandmother, the Carib Indian, was she an *obeah* woman?

KINCAID: Well, yes. She was an *obeah* woman, perhaps not on the Haitian scale—they are very different—but she did believe in spirits.

CUDJOE: And she really did stop talking to your father?

KINCAID: Oh yes, they never spoke again. And she did have friends who were soucriants. For a while, I lived in utter fear when I was little, of just not being sure that anything I saw was itself.

CUDJOE: That's the modernist project, isn't it?

KINCAID: Yes, and I think that's why it confused me. In fact it is quite primitive. When I read these modernists I think, "This is great! This is like my reality!" I mean, the first time I saw modern art, I really got into it.

CUDJOE: I just recently completed an article ("Gateways to Submerged Consciousness: James, Melville, Harris and the American Imagination") that compares Melville, C. L. R. James, and Wilson Harris. The central point I wanted to make is that in our Americas, we have our own understanding of the subject that you don't have to go to Europe to discover. There's a great desire to go to France and look at what the French are saying. But we do have our own perception of that "otherness."

In other words, your work—perhaps even more than you may realize— is within the form of the modernist project because you're doing the things that strike at the physical core of the entire Americas.

KINCAID: Well, yes. I mean, at one point in my life I never knew whether the ground would hold, whether the thing next to me was real or not.

You see, in West Indian culture, things change so rapidly. In a conversation, you can go from laughing to quarreling, from deep enmity to deep friendship. When I left Antigua I thought: I'm free of this! But I couldn't be free of it in my head. I would carry it around with me—the thing that turned me into a writer, my mother, all of it. And I knew all of it through her: I saw the world through her.

CUDJOE: So in a sense, then, "Antigua Crossings" is just the beginning of that project. Some of the characters in that story seem to come up again and again in your other fiction. There are so many dimensions of *Annie John* in "Antigua Crossings."

KINCAID: I started to write *Annie John* then but I didn't have the stamina. It's funny how, as a writer, at some moments it works and at other moments it doesn't. So I wrote "Antigua Crossings"—and I didn't choose the title, and it's an awkward title, really—and I was not the person who could write anything else but that.

CUDJOE: What would you have called it?

KINCAID: I don't know, but I'm sure I would not have called it that.

CUDJOE: Let's talk a bit about *Annie John*. Annie seems to be very hardhearted at the end of the text. Is there any reason for that?

KINCAID: Well, it's a mask—she's not really hard-hearted. She really wants to break down and be taken back in, but there's a parting place.

She says she remembers that she's been told, "Once you start to do something, you have to see it through," and so she's got to see this thing through. But it's a hardness that has no substance, really, and if I were to continue to write this character—which I won't—you would see how the hardness is easily broken. She becomes enough of a woman to start imposing hardness on other people, but it's not a real hardness, and I think that the very last line shows that. It goes, "It's as if a vessel of liquid had been placed on its side and now was finally emptying out."

This is one of those hard-won victories that you have, I think, when you're an adolescent or when you're not quite an adult. You have all these little victories that you've won, and only you know how deep they go. The roots of them are just this big and can be washed away. Any slightly powerful force can uproot it; it doesn't really set, and for her to leave these people, she has to harden herself against them.

It's a very fragile "hard," and if they would just say, "Oh, don't go, we love you, stay here," she would be undone by it, even if she decided, "Well, no, I must." Though actually, looking at the chemistry of these things, if they had said, "Oh, do stay," she would have said, "No, I must go." The roots of her rebellion—well, it gets a little deeper. The more you can sustain your convictions or whatever, the better they are—I mean, the stronger they are. But it's not a real hardness, I don't think. And it couldn't be conciliatory.

CUDJOE: No, not at that point. If you had kept on writing about her long enough, there might have been a reconciliation.

KINCAID: Perhaps, twenty years later. But I think that one of the things you detect about this character when you read is that if you met her you would expect an interesting person, and you expect that it would work out. Some students from the West Indies with whom I've spoken have said they felt there should have been a reconciliation right then and there, before Annie left.

CUDJOE: Well, they want to impose their own romanticism on it. My wife says she wouldn't like to be a teenager anymore because it's such a very difficult period for a young woman. What the daughters do with their mothers is try to carve out their own turf—their own sense of independence—and it seems to be necessary in many cases.

KINCAID: But you know how unusual it is in the West Indies, the idea of carving out one's own territory. I don't really notice it being done; one lives very much the life of one's parents.

CUDJOE: What is the role of *obeah* in your work?

KINCAID: Well, until you mentioned it, I never thought it had any particular role. I was very interested in it—it was such an everyday part of my life, you see. I wore things, a little black sachet filled with things, in my undershirt. I was always having special baths. It was a complete part of my life for a very long time.

At night I would collect my urine in my little potty, and in the morning my mother would wash my feet in it. Then she'd put mine in with theirs in their pot—it's called a china-pot but it's not china—and then, after bathing her feet in it, she'd go and dribble it down the steps around the house. Sure enough, sometimes there would be fresh dirt dug up around the house, and there would be a bottle with things in it. So this was a part of my actual life, and it's lodged not only in my memory but in my own unconscious. So the role *obeah* plays in my work is the role it played in my life. I suppose it was just there.

CUDJOE: I'll give you an example from my life. My mother used to tell the story of this couple who fought and fought with each other from the first day of their marriage. They could never get along. One night in a dream, the wife was told to go and look below the front steps of her house—it was a house that was built slightly above the ground—and she would see a pin cushion with a ball of pins inside stuck all together. She was to take it, unravel it, and everything would be all right. The next morning she did just that and, as my mother told the story, all was well with the couple after that. There is no question that she believed the story.

One way to explain my mother's belief in that story is to postulate that there is another reality over which we, in our modernity, have no control—and certainly of which we know very little because we're too scientific.

KINCAID: Oh, yes, absolutely. Once I knew of a woman who wanted a man, but he would never look at her—and the next thing you know, they were married. They would say, "Oh, she tied him," and somehow it involved having him to dinner and all sorts of body fluids being used, but she was successful. Or somehow when he was asleep, she would rub something on his head and she would get the man. These stories were accepted; this was a part of my reality.

My mother would go to a woman every Friday who could tell if things were being done to us and if these women were having successes with my father. I'm pretty sure he was faithful, but that's only because he was old. But there were always these consultations, and really it was a sort of psychiatrist, someone keeping the unconscious all oiled up.

CUDJOE: Each society has its own means of coming to terms with that other part of its world. Call it what you may, one has to come to terms with it if one wishes to lead a healthy life. Each society constructs its own mechanisms: we tend to privilege the Western and call it "good" and "proper" and call ours "bad," "pagan," and everything else, but I guess it's how one looks at it. Many of these ideas come through in your work, more particularly in your first book, *At the Bottom of the River*. What about the function of dreams in your books? They seem to recur in both books.

KINCAID: Well, again, to be honest I don't really think I make these distinctions between dreaming and waking. This, again, goes back to my childhood, because there is little difference between dreaming and waking. Dreams could tell you things about your waking life—which turns out to be quite accepted in Western psychiatry. Your dream could tell you things about your waking life; it illuminates your waking life.

I used to be quite afraid [of dreams] because they would tell me things I didn't want to know, and I really believed all my dreams and took them very seriously. I still do, in quite the same way. So when I write about dreams, it's not really a dream, it's something that happens, but in this way.

And, as I say, this had to do with the strange perception about reality where I grew up. Reality was not to be trusted the thing you saw before you was not really quite to be trusted because it might represent something else. And the thing you didn't see might be right there—I mean, there were so many stories about people who were followed home by a dead person, and the dead person eventually led them into a pond. People would say, "Oh, the *Jablesse* are out tonight."

My mother had this experience, and I've written about that—I think it's in "Antigua Crossings." If I haven't, I will have to write about it. They were going to school and saw a beautiful woman bathing in the river— Dominica has so many rivers. In those days they didn't have many bridges, so they had to cross this river—which was particularly full because it had rained a lot. At the mouth of this river they saw a woman, a beautiful woman, surrounded by these mangoes, wonderful mangoes. In fact, my mother has shown me the mango trees and the place where this happened. Well, they were about to swim to her, but some people realized that this was not real—it was too beautiful, the mangoes were too beautiful. One boy swam to her, and he drowned. His body was never found. He vanished; everything vanished. My mother didn't tell me that story as a folktale; that was an illustration to me of not believing what I saw, of really not being deceived by appearances, of really being able to tell that it was really a woman and not someone who would drown you.

CUDJOE: If you wouldn't call it folklore, how would you call it?

KINCAID: I would say it was my mother's experience with life.

CUDJOE: Which, to her, was real.

KINCAID: Yes . . . it's not more folkloric than if, say, a child was walking to school here in America and was kidnapped and never found. In that case you would say to your child, "Don't stop for anybody to pick you up." I thought that all of these things were a way of making me understand that the world was not what it seemed—which is true.

CUDJOE: In light of this view of the other world, how do you explain the symbol of light in one of your books? It appears quite often. Perhaps you're not conscious of it . . . but what are these lights?

KINCAID: That I can see . . . I think I have an explanation for that. It must be the obsession with these "things" because they all seemed to happen in the dark and to be part of darkness. (Apart from the fact that I grew up in this extraordinary light, this blinding, thick light of the sun, that seems to give off a light that makes things transparent.) But the sun is almost hellish, really. Sometimes it would turn from something wonderful, the light of the sun, into a kind of hell.

I think that at some point I became obsessed with things being not that unclear, that things could not just vanish, that there could be some light that would show the reality of a thing, that this was false and this was right. I think it was my obsession. I think I really get obsessed sometimes with the idea that there could be just ONE undeniable truth, something that is so true, not for any purpose—it's just true. "This is true, and you can't deny it. . . ." It's very childish. That section on the river, I understood when I was doing it that it was very naive, that only a child, really, would ask, "Well, can't you just give me one answer, and that's that, and it stays there and it doesn't move, and it doesn't do anything except . . . what it does, and it's just itself. And it's not two-sided, and it's not full of this-and-that." I think the image for light—I know it always comes up in my writing—is just my hope that there will be just one true thing.

CUDJOE: And isn't that the charm of your work?

KINCAID: Well, I don't know. . . .

CUDJOE: It's certainly uncomplicated at one level.

KINCAID: Yes, that's the "one true thing." I hope for that. I want for there to be just one true thing that doesn't come and go, and I think that's how the light functions. I think that some parts of At the Bottom of the River are really very simple. I had sort of gone through a lot—not in terms of anything personal—I had hoped to write something, and that part of it was a sort of yearning for something.

There's a part of it where I write about the green color of the grass. In that piece, I suppose I just want things to stay still, just something that won't perish or won't go away; that it would remain just sort of paradisical. Not eternal . . . but just the possibility of . . . well, maybe three minutes of the day one could enter that sort of place. Just absolute peace, not happiness. I decided that happiness is too much activity, too busy. I don't really yearn for happiness; I yearn for an absence of anxiety. I don't yearn to be happy, because I don't know what it is, really. I don't really understand the phenomenon. . . .

CUDJOE: So you aim for peace?

KINCAID: (laughs) Yes. . . .

Adolescent Rebellion and Gender Relations in *At the Bottom of the River* and *Annie John*

HELEN PYNE TIMOTHY

Perhaps the most puzzling moments in Jamaica Kincaid's *At the Bottom of the River* and *Annie John* are those involving the emotional break between the mother and daughter and the violence of the daughter's response to her mother after that break. In the early stages of the narrative, Kincaid, chronicling the intense emotional bond in which they are wrapped, is at pains to detail the warmly affectionate upbringing Annie received from her mother. To the child the relationship was so satisfying that the father was almost shut out; in fact he operated on the periphery:

> As she told me the stories, I sometimes sat at her side, leaning against her, or I would crouch on my knees behind her back and lean over her shoulder. ... At times I would no longer hear what it was she was saying: I just liked to look at her mouth as it opened and closed over words or as she laughed. How terrible it must be for all the people who had no one to love them so and no one whom they loved so, I thought. My father for instance. (*Annie John*, pp. 22–23)

Indeed, Kincaid creates such a perfect world of strongly nurturing mother figure and dependent child suffused with primary love that there can only be agreement when Annie says, "It was in such a paradise that I lived."

Nancy Chodorow, in her revealing study of psychoanalytic theory as it may be applied to the relationship of mother and daughter, has documented the pattern of absolute dependence in a primary love relationship that links the child to the nurturing mother figure. In the early years

233

the mother is central to the focus of the child, idolized and idealized. Chodorow shows that the apprehension of the mother figure can be so strong that the child has to go through a period of rejection to separate subject/self from object/mother before development of the individual consciousness is possible. For the female child, this split comes at puberty and must, therefore, have important ramifications for the expression of her sexuality.

Annette Insanally has also illustrated the relevance of Jacques Lacan's theory of psychic development in her reading of *At the Bottom of the River* in commenting on "the mother/daughter figure in a strange inseparable love/hate syndrome where the father figure is tangential and indistinct but important." There can be no doubt that the findings of psychoanalytic theory form an important framing and structural device that shapes the particularities of the works and therefore strongly illuminates the workings of the inner life of the protagonist. All the elements of the classic stages of development of the girl from what Kincaid describes as a possible "life as predictable as an insect's and I am in my pupa stage . . . primitive and wingless" to the woman who must be confident in her own person, her selfhood, and her sexuality: "I shall grow to be a tall, graceful and altogether beautiful woman, and I shall impose on large numbers of people my will and also for my own amusement, great pain."

Both *At the Bottom of the River* and *Annie John* are primarily concerned with intense mother/daughter relationships, the psychic development of the girl child, the teaching and learning of appropriate gender roles, and the breaking of the strongly imposed image of the mother for the development of individuation in adulthood.

Obviously, these stages of psychic development take place within any culture, and presumably they provide evidence for a metatheory that has universal application. The concern of this essay is therefore to inquire whether, and in what ways, Kincaid has anchored the imaginative reworkings of these experiences within the particular culture of the Caribbean in such a way as indelibly to infuse the development of Annie and the nameless "girl" of *At the Bottom of the River* with a "local habitation and a name."

The stages of Annie's psychosocial development are all amplified within the context of Caribbean cultural practices and beliefs. In the early stage of intense primary love and involvement with the mother, the first hint of separation comes with the child's awareness of death and her understanding that the perceived integrated personality of the two might be split by the loss of one individual. Annie's perception of her mother begins to change when she realizes that her mother has links with a community outside of her own perception:

One day, a girl smaller than I, a girl whose mother was a friend of my
mother's, died in my mother's arms. I did not know this girl at all...I
heard my mother describe to my father just how Nalda had died...My
mother asked my father to make the coffin for Nalda, and he did, carving
bunches of tiny flowers on the sides. Nalda's mother wept so much that
my mother had to take care of everything and since children were never
prepared by undertakers, my mother had to prepare the little girl to be
buried. I then began to look at my mother's hands differently. They had
stroked the dead girl's forehead, they had bathed and dressed her and laid
her in the coffin my father had made. My mother would come back from
the dead girl's house smelling of bay rum—a scent that for a long time
afterward would make me feel ill. For a while, though not for very long, I
could not bear to have my mother caress me or touch my food or help me
with my bath. I especially couldn't bear the sight of her hands lying in her
lap. (Annie John, pp. 5–6)

Here Annie's mother is closely involved in a momentous happening in
which she was not the center. She could clearly envisage the possibility
of her dying and leaving her mother as well as the possibility of her
mother betraying the primary love tie and dying herself and leaving
Annie, like her classmate, "such a shameful thing, a girl whose mother
had died and left her alone in the world."

Furthermore, the details of the death rituals as delineated are
strongly indicative of Caribbean cultural habits. Annie's mother must
of necessity be available to her neighbor in times of sickness and
death; she must assist in transporting the child to the doctor, must
help with the laying out of the body, must support and nurture the
mother through the time of grieving. The father assists by carving the
handmade coffin. This act is his personal involvement, but the male
figure is not central to the emotional ritual. Thus the death is reported
to him by the mother; but it is she who is central to all its demands,
and her involvement is personal. Of course, Annie's feelings toward
death are ambivalent: she is deeply aware of the understanding that
death could rob her of the most intensely loved person, her mother.
Yet in her attempts at role-modeling she wishes to become schooled
and to penetrate the secrets of the ritual so she can be like her mother,
an important person in a gender-binding ritual.

The burgeoning perception of subject/self, object/mother reaches the
moment of separation, as expected, at puberty. Annie begins to see everything about her mother in a negative light and, typically, transfers the
intensity of her emotion to a friend, Gwen. Her sexual urges are beginning
to develop, as is the awareness of her physical presence and that of others.
What is interesting about the presentation here is the way the mother is
portrayed as relating to her daughter's developments:

The summer of the year I turned twelve, I could see that I had grown taller; most of my clothes no longer fit. . . . My legs had become spindle-like, the hair on my head even more unruly than usual, small tufts of hair had appeared under my arms and when I perspired the smell was strange, as if I had turned into a strange animal. I didn't say anything about it, and my mother and father didn't seem to notice, for they didn't say anything either. (*Annie John*, p. 25)

But in fact the parents had noticed, and the change in behavior manifested itself most violently in the mother, not the father. Kincaid seems to be making the statement here that in the Caribbean context, the mother is unable to continue successful role-modeling after the child reaches puberty. Up to this point, Annie's mother has been a strongly loving, caring, nurturing mother figure. Annie receives no beatings, only minor punishment. "I ate my supper outside, alone, under the breadfruit tree, and my mother said that she would not be kissing me goodnight later; but when I climbed into bed she came and kissed me anyway."

Moreover, Annie had been encouraged to model herself in every detail on her mother's conduct and behavior so as to become a perfect woman. Kincaid is at pains to show the mother's involvement with every detail of the child's development. The mementos of important stages in her prepubescent development are locked in a trunk to be taken out and lovingly recalled from time to time. But this Caribbean mother is unable to speak about the later stage of the child's development; she "didn't seem to notice." Kincaid's message seems to indict the Caribbean mother: she does not know how to communicate openly about the girl's development into a sexual being.

The contrast between the mother's attitudes in the girl's pre- and postpubescent periods is almost shocking. In her relationship with Annie there had previously been a highly pleasurable integration of the child's body and the mother's as part of the relationship of loving and caring; and the child displayed an acutely sensitive response to her mother's body shape, touch, and smell. In this Caribbean family there is a lot of touching, hugging, and caressing between mother and daughter: the mother swims with the daughter on her back, they bathe together in an extended ritual which is firmly rooted in the bush-bath African-derived cultural habit where the body becomes almost a temple of good, but where the function and pleasure of sensation are not ruled out.

Up to puberty, then, the mother's role-modeling signals affirmatives about the body, sensation, and sensuality. These affirmatives are further reinforced in Annie's school life. Her friends in a girls' school, cut off from boys, are almost hysterical in their desire to "prove" their womanhood by growing breasts and menstruating. Annie's description of her first period is full of drama and emphasizes the emotions of awe and reverence, beauty even, in this event, and in the response of the other girls to whom it is revealed:

> At recess, among the tombstones, I of course had to exhibit and demonstrate. None of the others were menstruating yet. I showed everything without the least bit of flourish since my heart wasn't in it. I wished instead that one of the other girls were in my place and that I were just sitting there in amazement. How nice they all were, though, rallying to my side, offering shoulders on which to lean, laps in which to rest my weary, aching head, and kisses that really did soothe. (*Annie John*, p. 52)

Annie's personal response betrays the uncertainty of the moment engendered by the fear of the future which this watershed must of necessity entail. But the fear is devoid of any suggestion of shame or secrecy; rather, it is a fear of adulthood, of uncontrollable changes in her life.

The wild abandonment and pleasure in their physical personhood which the girls display is contrasted with the mother's attempts to suppress her own and Annie's after Annie entered puberty. What can be her motive, why does she deliberately cut herself off from the closeness of touch and caress, from wearing the same dresses, from accompanying her daughter on walks with her father? Is her desire to push Annie away into the perception of herself as other ("You just cannot go around the rest of your life looking like a little me") motivated by psychological primes, sexual jealousies, and uncertainties or social mores? Perhaps her actions arise out of a mixture of all these; but the discussion here will primarily consider the latter as part of a network of complex structures perceived by the child.

This child is an extraordinarily sensitive participant/observer of her mother's life; and at this stage her acuity is trained toward the asymmetrical aspects of her behavior which can now be negatively assessed. The most obvious and, for the child, the most confusing and searing are concerned with questions of sexuality between mother and father.

In *Annie John* the figure of the father is peripheral to the intense absorption that links the daughter to the mother. Nevertheless, to the preadolescent, he is an important love object. Interestingly enough, however, when Annie begins to assess her mother negatively, she also transfers her negative viewpoint to her father, who is then seen as being more a part of her mother's universe than of her own: "They were eating away as they talked, my father's false teeth making that clop-clop sound like a horse on a walk as he talked, my mother's mouth going up and down like a donkey's as she chewed each mouthful thirty-two times . . . I was looking at them with a smile on my face but disgust in my heart" (*Annie John*, p. 136). Even if there are adjustments for Annie's tendency to an overwrought sensibility in her emotional assessment of her parents, there is a suggestion of sexual jealousy in her perception of the mother's physical closeness to the father. Alexander's relations with other women, although they occurred before his marriage, also appear to have had some impact on Annie. Although this description that the father has had affairs and "outside children" which he does not acknowledge represents a social truth of Caribbean society, the fact that he has been intimate with women whom he now passes by without speaking in the street invests sensitive young Annie with a subliminal sense that there is something shameful in a sexual relationship. Kincaid seems to be indicating here that male sexuality has no consequences, whereas for females the consequences are severe.

But more important is the mother's ambivalence about her own sexuality; she has suppressed this aspect of herself in her role-modeling although she does at one point recommend marriage and motherhood to Annie. But these concepts seem divorced from any sexual involvement. Heterosexual involvement is seen by the child as sin and shame, not joy or pleasure.

It is therefore totally understandable that when Annie unexpectedly sees her mother joyfully engaged in a sexual act with her father she is thrown into an emotional turmoil that causes the split and antagonism of daughter and mother with its consequent consuming negative assessments of the mother's role and behavior. These negative assessments begin strongly with the inability of the mother to negotiate the meaning of the girl's burgeoning sexuality.

Indeed, the ambivalence of the Caribbean mother is reinforced by Annie's mother's extreme reaction to a most innocent meeting and greeting of three boys which Annie engages in on her way home from school. Kincaid describes:

> On looking up, she observed me making a spectacle of myself in front of three boys. She went on to say that after all the years she had spent drumming into me the proper way to conduct myself when speaking to young men it had pained her to see me behave in the manner of a slut . . . in the street and that just to see me had caused her to feel shame. The word "slut" (in patois) was repeated over and over, until suddenly I felt as if I were drowning in a well but instead of the well being filled with water it was filled with the word "slut," and it was pouring in through my eyes, my ears, my nostrils, my mouth. As if to save myself I turned to her and said, "Well, like father like son, like mother like daughter." (*Annie John*, p. 102)

Of course, behind Annie's impudence lies the understanding that she has discovered a serious weakness in her erstwhile strong, dominant, and correct mother. Moreover, this weakness points to a deep-rooted ambivalence, an insecurity that brings into question the very basis of the mother's existence and can be read further as the mother's inability to transmit to her daughter a coherent value system that embraces the various aspects of her role as woman in a Caribbean society.

Indeed, "Girl," in which the mother is the classic transmitter of culture and her function in the learning and teaching of the female role, overt within the context of the particular Caribbean society, demonstrates the uneasy mix between the two streams of Africa and Europe through which the mother has to thread her way and that of the child in her interpretations of the Creole world of the Caribbean.

Wash the white clothes on Monday and put them on the stone heap; wash the color clothes on Tuesday and put them on the clothesline to dry; don't walk bare-head in the hot sun; cook pumpkin fritters in very hot sweet oil, soak your little clothes right after you take them off; when buying cotton to make yourself a nice blouse . . . it is true that you sing benna in Sunday school? always eat your food in such a way that it won't turn someone else's stomach; on Sundays try to walk like a lady and not like the slut you are so bent on becoming; don't sing benna in Sunday school; you must'nt speak *to wharf-rat boys, not even to give directions* . . . this is how to hem a dress when you see the hem coming down and so to prevent yourself from looking *like the slut I know you are so bent on becoming* . . . this is how you sweep a corner; this is how you sweep a whole house; *this is how you sweep a yard*; this is how you smile to someone you don't like too much; this is how you smile to someone you don't like at all; this is how you smile to someone you like completely; this is how you set a table for tea; this is how you set a table for dinner . . . this is how you set a table for breakfast; this is how to behave in the presence of men who don't know you very well, and this way they won't recognize immediately the slut I have warned you against becoming; be sure to wash every day, even if it is with your own spit; don't squat down to play marbles—you are not a boy, you know; don't pick people's flowers—you might catch something; don't throw stones at blackbirds, because it might not be a blackbird at all. . . . This is how to make a good medicine for a cold; this is how to make a good medicine to throw away a child before it even becomes a child; this is how to catch a fish; this is how to throw back a fish you don't like, and that way something bad won't fall on you; this is how to bully a man; this is how a man bullies you; this is how to love a man, and if this doesn't work there are other ways, and if they don't work don't feel too bad about giving up. *(At the Bottom of the River,* pp. 3–5)

This quasi-monologue of the mother with the occasional indignant interjections of the daughter is strongly revelatory of the ambivalences that invest the role-modeling of the Caribbean mother, particularly since she herself has serious conflicts. As we have already seen, sexuality is almost instantly related to sluttishness, possibly because of the mother's fear that her daughter will become the exploited female of "wharf-rat boys" or even of the father's former lovers, who view her with hate, in other words, will lose her chance to rise in class, in the world. There is also the possibility that, with the male who is acceptable in class, sexuality is possible, even desirable: "this is how to love a man, and if this doesn't work there are other ways." The girl is being urged to use her womanly wiles to accomplish results from an act she is simultaneously being taught is shameful. Included here is also a recognition that a woman's sexuality must be used to accomplish a rise in social status—possibly an unconscious explanation for the beautiful, strong, young mother's marriage to a much older, weaker, far less beautiful husband, who offered her marriage and a comfortable home.

Moreover, the Caribbean mother who is bent on seeing her daughter rise from the lower classes to the middle ranks must not only teach her useful housekeeping tasks, cleanliness, good manners, and practical knowledge of her environment but also European norms and the need to desist in the practice of African ones. The girl perceives these paradoxes inherent in the mother's relationship to her own Caribbean culture, and they become part of the negative features that help reinforce the split between the egos of mother and daughter and the daughter's subsequent rebellion. Thus in the mother's perception, Christianity, Sunday school, good manners (the ability to curtsy), and piano lessons are all essential to her daughter's acceptability and respectability. Consequently she must not sing benna songs (folk/African songs) in Sunday school; but Christian training becomes far less important when dealing with the real problems of life. Here the mother falls back on the belief in folk wisdom, myth, African systems of healing and bush medicine, the mysteries of good and evil spirits inhabiting the perceived world of nature. "Don't pick people's flowers—you might catch something; don't throw stones at blackbirds, because it might not be a blackbird at all. . . . This is how to make a good medicine for a cold; this is how to throw away a child before it even becomes a child."

It is therefore significant that Kincaid juxtaposes the event that causes Annie's awakening to this dimension of her mother's life with her return from Sunday school. For the child there is a complicated clash of eschatological systems which she cannot articulate. She can only feel that some important principle has been violated which she attributes to her mother's hypocrisy.

Annie's rebellions are directed primarily against her mother's notions of respectability—being "a lady" in her sense of what would be required for the socially ambitious in a European context: the battle of wills takes place over Annie's lessons in good manners ("how to meet and greet important people in the world"), piano lessons, Christianity, and a good

European-style secondary education. The emotional split leads to a clash and finally an isolation of Annie that becomes so burdensome it leads to a mental breakdown.

The signals given during this period of mental and emotional collapse confirm the insecurity of the search for a coherent cosmology in which the child's social ambition, her intellectual and romantic yearnings, gleaned from European books (Blyton, the Brontës) and a European education, her moral, spiritual, and cultural landscape, and her sexual urges can all be accommodated.

Such complexities can never be completely resolved, but Kincaid is careful to guide the reader. There is the obvious sexual symbolization of the washing of the photographs (all of the people in white) of herself at her First Communion, her Aunt Mary at her wedding, and her father in cricket gear (white) "to remove the dirt from the front of my father's trousers." Next, the episode with Mr. Nigel is instructive. Mr. Nigel, his fishing partner, and Miss Catherine, the woman they share harmoniously, are firmly anchored in a world free of pretensions or intrusion from any imported system of value. Their untrammeled security provides a wholeness, a kind of truth for which Annie longs.

But the most important influence on Annie at this time is the formidable figure of Ma Chess, the grandmother. Kincaid has cast her in a fully African world. She inhabits the world of the African spirits and, as long as she remains true to that vision, is able to control life and death. Her beloved son dies when she defers to the unbelief of Pa Chess and gets a doctor about an illness which "the doctor knew nothing about, and the obeah woman knew everything about." After that irretrievable and distressing error her commitment to the African-Caribbean spiritual universe is total and unwavering. In her Kincaid has provided a portmanteau figure of African myth and reality: Ma Chess is African healer, bush medicine specialist, and Caribbean obeah woman, extremely conscious of the presence of good and evil in life and able to ward off evil. She is also the mythological "flying African" able to cross the seas without a boat, and the flying "soucouyant" (female witch) who lives in a hole in the ground. Her world, however, is not threatening to the child but comforting and healing because of its coherency, its validity, and its verity. As Annie describes the healing relationship,

Ma Chess is on the floor at the foot of my bed, eating and sleeping there, and soon I grew to count on her smells and the sound her breath made as it went in and out of her body. Sometimes at night, when I would feel that I was all locked up in the warm falling soot and could not find my way out Ma Chess would come into my bed with me and stay until I was myself—
. . . I would lie on my side curled up like a little comma, and Ma Chess

would be next to me, curled up like a bigger comma, into which I fit. *(Annie John,* p. 126)

This tension-free relationship is typical of a grandmother/granddaughter link, but it also records the sense of security the conforming world of Ma Chess exudes. A valid sociological point emerges here: for some of the older generation of Caribbean women, the penetration of European cultural values into the African cosmology was not so intense or so desirable. Most of these systems of belief, syncretism, are beginning to appear in Annie's mother's universe. Annie herself is going to "somewhere; Belgium," the heart of Europe, far away and in rejection of "obeah women" (African systems of belief). But there is a recognition that like her grandmother and mother before her, she must carry a trunk, that is, the cultural baggage of a race, a country, and a class, although for each generation, the trunks are packed with different contents.

What a complex moral cosmology Caribbean girls must inhabit and how ambivalent are the signals passed on to them. But even in the act of rebellion Kincaid strongly shows that the break between mothers and daughters can never be final or complete, that the women are linked irrevocably to each other by ties that are finally inextricable.

An African mother holds her infant to her breast as an English slave ship approaches the coast. From *Poems of the Abolition of the Slave Trade*, 1809, by James Montgomery, James Grahme, and E. Benger.

Initiation in Jamaica
Kincaid's *Annie John*

DONNA PERRY

Two recent studies attempt to trace the mythic patterns contained in women's fictions, particularly those written by white, middle-class, Western women: Annis Pratt's *Archetypal Patterns in Women's Fiction* (1981) and Rachel Blau DuPlessis's *Writing beyond the Ending* (1985).[1] These studies are significant not because they can help us better understand *Annie John* (or the work of other black women writers) but because they so clearly outline the parameters of the so-called Western tradition in literature. A short summary of the texts will demonstrate what I mean.

Annis Pratt singles out two dominant patterns in novels of development written by women. The first, the "growing down" story, is the conservative extreme, a model of how to prepare for marriage, behave, and learn humility, stoicism, and self-abnegation. The message is that submission to suffering and sadism prepares one for life; an example is Fanny Fern's popular *Rose Clark* (1856). The more common pattern in women's fiction, according to Pratt, is the move from the green (matriarchal) world, which is restorative, positive, and nourishing, to the enclosed patriarchal world. The message here is that the world of nature belongs to women, but no other world does. Nature keeps women in touch with their selfhood, but this state of innocence is usually destroyed with the onslaught of the patriarchal world. Often there is a "green world" lover (who is

1. Annis Pratt, *Archetypal Patterns in Women's Fiction* (Bloomington: Indiana University Press, 1981); Rachel Blau DuPlessis, *Writing beyond the Ending: Narrative Strategies of Twentieth-Century Women Writers* (Bloomington: Indiana University Press, 1985).

more desirable than the socially acceptable one), and a rape trauma is necessary to overturn the matrilinear society. Examples would be Emily Brontë's *Wuthering Heights* (1847) and Margaret Atwood's *Surfacing* (1972). These nature myth narratives are rooted in Greek mythology in which the woman, raped by the gods, turns herself into another life form (Daphne becoming a laurel tree after her rape by Apollo, for example). Sometimes the women find solace, companionship, and independence in nature.

DuPlessis explores the way Western women writers subvert the marriage plot of the novel through themes of reparenting, female bonding, mother-child dyads, and brother-sister pairs. She studies a number of modern texts in which women "find themselves" in ways other than through romance (Dorothy Richardson's *Pilgrimage*, the fiction of Virginia Woolf, the poetry of H.D. and Adrienne Rich). But, as she demonstrates, often the cost for these women is great—the female protagonist may remain isolated, commit suicide, or go insane.

The problem with these two studies is that they look, for the most part, at the writing of white middle- and upper-middle-class women who saw themselves as part of a literary tradition that glorified marriage and romantic love. DuPlessis spends only fourteen pages out of two hundred on Zora Neale Hurston, Gwendolyn Brooks, Toni Morrison, and Alice Walker, and Pratt cites Paule Marshall, Margaret Walker, Hurston, and Morrison only in passing.

I am suggesting that fiction by women of color and Third World women offers new myths of female development and new definitions of success. As Paule Marshall and Alice Walker have demonstrated, black women have been forced outside the "happily ever after" world of white middle-class privilege to find the story of their lives closer to home. Both describe turning to their mothers for those stories. Marshall recalls learning from "the poets in the kitchen," her mother and the other women from Barbados, who urged one another to talk ("Soully-gal, talk yuh talk!") and gained power through their language ("In this man world you got to take yuh mouth and make a gun!").[2] Walker found her mother's life to be poetry, and the "ambitious" gardens she grew were her daughter's legacy. As Walker generalizes: "And so our mothers and grandmothers have, more often than not anonymously, handed on the creative spark, the seed of the flower they themselves never hoped to see: or like a sealed letter they could not plainly read."[3]

2. "The Making of a Writer: From the Poets in the Kitchen," *New York Times Book Review*, January 9, 1983; rpt. in *Reena and Other Stories* (Old Westbury, N.Y.: Feminist Press, 1983), p. 7.
3. "In Search of Our Mothers' Gardens," *Ms.*, May 1974; rpt. in *In Search of Our Mothers' Gardens* (New York: Harcourt Brace Jovanovich, 1983), p. 240.

Novels by women of color, particularly women from outside the United States, draw on different traditions and reflect a different set of cultural assumptions from those that writers like Pratt and DuPlessis define as universal. In many cultures (West Indian, with its roots in Africa, for example) images of strong, autonomous women abound; women are often seen as powerful, even awe-inspiring. African tradition featured women as tribal leaders and *obeah* women, trained in witchcraft and knowledgeable about herbal medicine and cures. Older women were revered as storytellers and keepers of the family history. In short, a woman functioned in other ways than solely in her relationship to men.

I am suggesting that in fiction by women of color, particularly that written by women who have lived or live outside of the industrialized West, there are other development patterns for women. The "green world" harmony that Pratt describes can survive, if transformed, but DuPlessis's romance plot will wither away. A close study of Jamaica Kincaid's novel *Annie John* (1985) suggests a possible paradigm for female development that represents an alternative to the victim models we find in most recent fiction (and in life).

Annie John, Kincaid's only novel, began as a series of short stories and sketches in the *New Yorker*. It is an initiation tale about a young girl's movement from childhood to maturity—from life in lush, fertile Antigua to her eventual move to London at seventeen, when the novel ends. In one sense, Annie's life is just beginning as she leaves her island home for "civilized" Europe, but her apprenticeship in Antigua has prepared her adequately for the world she will face beyond it.

Three aspects of West Indian culture contribute to Annie's development and empower her to leave home and create an independent life: the storytelling tradition; the tradition of the obeah woman who reads nature's signs (storm, cuts that won't heal) and who curses and cures using the materials of nature (herbs, dead animals); and matrilinear bonding—the strong blood tie of women through the generations.

The storytelling tradition among people connects the present with the past (thus suggesting timelessness and immortality), establishes a sense of community, and testifies to the power of language not only to record but to transform reality.

At an earlier time, an enslaved people had to depend on this oral tradition to transmit and maintain their cultural heritage. The tradition of storytelling is an integral part of African culture and was continued in the West Indies among Africans brought there by British, French, and Dutch colonizers. Its continuation in the United States among West Indian immigrants is clear from Paule Marshall's *Brown Girl, Brownstones* (1959), in which young Selina Boyce learns her ethnic identity from her mother and the other Barbadian immigrant women as they talk in her Brooklyn kitchen. In "The Making of a Writer: From the Poets in the Kitchen" (1983), Marshall says that she first learned the power of language through hearing stories.

Storytelling plays a central part in *Annie John*. In an interview, Jamaica Kincaid said, "Clearly, the way I became a writer was that my mother wrote my life for me and told it to me."[4] Significantly, Kincaid claimed that she never read twentieth-century writers until she left Antigua at age seventeen. Her models were stories she heard—ritual retellings of her own and her people's pasts.

There is very little in *Annie John* about the influence of "traditional" writers Annie studied in school, probably because they had little meaning for her. She is forced to copy out Books I and II of *Paradise Lost* as punishment for her rebelliousness—an example of the Western tradition being used punitively—and the novel she cites as her favorite, *Jane Eyre*, is about a woman who is a rebel. The tradition—predominantly white, male, middle-upper class—could not speak to her as her mother's stories could.

What are the effects of this African storytelling tradition? First, Annie becomes the hero of her own life, in sharp contrast to the fate of Western heroines, who are usually forced into prescribed roles and scripts as Pratt and DuPlessis suggest. Significantly, it is Annie's mother who is the weaver of the tale. In the often-repeated ritual of going through Annie's baby trunk, Annie Senior goes through the contents, piece by piece, holding up each item and recreating her daughter's past through vivid accounts of its significance. The christening outfit, baby bottles (one shaped like a boat), report cards, first notebook, and certificates of merit from school become both relics and omens—symbols of the girl she was and the woman she would become—through her mother's transformative language. The narrator remembers: "No small part of my life was so unimportant that she hadn't made a note of it, and now she would tell it to me over and over again."[5]

But there is method in the telling. The stories woven were designed to stress Annie's assertiveness, her accomplishments, and her independence: the slipped stitch in the christening dress happened when Annie, still in her mother's womb, kicked. Annie's mother creates the myth of Annie for her so that her past becomes as real to her as her present. Like Greek heroes who chanted the litanies of past glories to prepare themselves for battle and to awe their opponents, Annie's mother sings her daughter's praises and empowers the child.

Another function of storytelling in the novel is to provide an impetus

---

4. Quoted in Patricia T. O'Conner, "My Mother Wrote My Life" (interview with Jamaica Kincaid), *New York Times Book Review*, April 7, 1985, p. 6.

5. Jamaica Kincaid, *Annie John* (New York: Farrar, Straus & Giroux, 1985), p. 22. All references are to this edition and are given in the text.

for Annie's emergence as a writer. At twelve, she is asked by her British schoolteacher to write an "autobiographical essay." She tells the story of the time she went swimming with her mother and her mother disappeared from view. She recreates the panic she felt when her mother disappeared and the joy when she reappeared. But Annie changes the ending both to suit her audience and to please herself. In life Annie's mother shrugged off the event's significance; in Annie's imaginative reconstruction, mother embraces daughter lovingly. Annie wins the adoration of her classmates and her teacher—teary-eyed, Miss Nelson adds the story to the class's library of books. And Annie manages, through telling and transforming her story, to begin the imaginative reconstruction process that is auto-biographical fiction.

The most significant implication of storytelling, the power of language in the book, is that it gives Annie a potential source of resistance. From childhood, Annie uses her imaginative versatility to make up elaborate lies to tell her mother when she disobeys. But, more important, stories become a way to rewrite the history of an oppressed people. In *Resistance and Caribbean Literature* (1980), Selwyn Cudjoe says, "The purpose of colonial education was to prepare obedient boys and girls to participate in a new capitalist enterprise."[6] He quotes Sylvia Wynter, who adds, "To write at all was and is for the West Indian a revolutionary act."[7]

The revolutionary potential of language is dramatically illustrated in an episode entitled "Columbus in Chains," depicting the navigator's ignominious return to Spain after he offended the representative of King Ferdinand and Queen Isabella. The narrator remembers: "How I loved this picture—to see the usually triumphant Columbus brought so low, seated at the bottom of a great boat just watching things go by" (pp. 77–78).

Having seen this picture in her textbook, Annie connects Columbus with patriarchal tyranny in general when she overhears her mother talking about Annie's grandfather. The old man who once dominated her life has now become infirm, according to Annie Senior's sister, who still lives in Dominica. Reading her sister's letter telling her of her father's ill health, Annie's mother laughs and says, "So the great man can no longer just get up and go."

Echoing her mother's scorn of patriarchal privilege, Annie writes under the Columbus picture: "The Great Man Can No Longer Just Get Up and

---

6. Selwyn Cudjoe, *Resistance and Caribbean Literature* (Athens, Ohio: Ohio University Press, 1980), p. 21.

7. Sylvia Wynter, "We Must Learn to Sit Down Together and Talk a Little Culture: Reflections on the West Indian Writing and Criticism, Part I," *Jamaica Journal, Quarterly of the Institute of Jamaica* 3 (December 1968): 31; cited in Cudjoe, *Resistance*, p. 3.

Go." For this rebellious act she is stripped of power (she is removed as class prefect) and made to ingest a heavy dose of Western culture—Books I and II of *Paradise Lost*, which she is forced to copy.

Although neither Annie the child nor Annie the narrator focuses on the full implications of colonization, the racism that was a part of West Indian life, the confusion and anger it caused are evident. The narrator remembers:

> Sometimes, what with our teachers and our books, it was hard for us to tell on which side we really now belonged—with the masters or the slaves— for it was all history, it was all in the past and everybody behaved differently now; all of us celebrated Queen Victoria's birthday, even though she had been dead a long time. But we, the descendents of the slaves, knew quite well what had really happened, and I was sure that if the tables had been turned we would have acted differently; I was sure that if our ancestors had gone from Africa to Europe and come upon people living there, they would have taken a proper interest in the Europeans on first seeing them, and said, "How nice," and then gone home to tell their friends about it. (p. 76)

The narrator's political consciousness is still in an embryonic state, however, since this childish perception is neither challenged nor commented on. Although there are hints of outrage at colonial oppression, the book, for the most part, emphasizes Annie's personal growth, not the political situation in the West Indies. Jamaica Kincaid is not a "political" writer in the sense that the Jamaican writer Michelle Cliff is, although these references to oppression suggest that in later works she might more fully explore the political implications of colonialism. (See note at end.)

A second source of strength for Annie lies in the obeah tradition. Two facts about obeah deserve note: the obeah was believed to be in communication with the devil and other spirits, and she was thought to have full power to exempt one from any evils that might otherwise happen.

Annie's mother consults the obeah woman (as well as her own mother and a friend) when ominous signs appear—a small scratch on Annie's instep does not heal, a friendly dog turns and bites her, a prized bowl suddenly slips and breaks. The obeah woman reads and interprets: one of the many women from her husband's past is putting a curse on them. The cure would be a ritualistic bath in water in which the barks and flowers of special trees had been boiled in oils.

As a child, Annie fantasizes about such supernatural power when she is in love with her secret friend, the unwashed, barefoot, tree-climbing "Red Girl." When this friend moves away, Annie dreams of rescuing her after a shipwreck and escaping with her to an island where they can get their revenge on the adult world: "At night, we would sit on the sand

and watch ships filled with people on a cruise steam by. We sent confusing signals to the ships, causing them to crash on some nearby rocks. How we laughed as their cries of joy turned to sorrow" (p. 71).

Like her mother's stories, the obeah woman's charms have the power to transform reality: they can undo curses, heal wounds, even destroy enemies. From this obeah tradition Annie learns the power of working with nature, of trusting in signs and symbols, of trusting one's instincts.

The matrilinear bond between Annie, her mother, and her grandmother proves to be the most empowering force of all. The two women present striking generational contrasts: Ma Chess, the grandmother, who lives in Dominica, more skilled in obeah than anyone Annie knows, appears in person only once in the novel, though her influence is felt throughout. When Annie becomes seriously ill at age fifteen, her grandmother mysteriously appears "on a day when the steamer wasn't due" and nurses Annie back to health. As Annie's mother had done before, the grandmother feeds and bathes Annie, literally taking her granddaughter back into the womb: "Ma Chess would come into my bed with me and stay until I was myself—whatever that had come to be by then—again. I would lie on my side, curled up like a little comma, and Ma Chess would lie next to me, curled up like a bigger comma, into which I fit" (pp. 125–26).

This image of Annie as a fetus protected by its mother is an apt description of the "paradise" of the early part of the novel, when Annie and her mother lived in harmony. With the onset of adolescence came inevitable mother-daughter tensions, and Annie struggled to free herself from life in her mother's shadow. It is as though the maternal sheltering is surfacing again—symbolically—through the nurturance of the grandmother. This nurturance does not smother the adolescent girl but serves as a source of strength, for she has already become a separate being. Her mysterious illness at the end of the novel corresponds to the death of her child self—a dependent self that must grow into freedom. But her grandmother's nurturing clearly suggests that she is not to break away from her past, as most male artist-heroes do (we think of James Joyce's Stephen Daedalus or D.H. Lawrence's Paul Morel). Instead, she must grow into her new, freer self, with maternal blessing. Remember, it was Annie's mother, earlier in the novel, who encouraged her daughter to become independent.

Annie's mother remains her strongest role model. The older woman left Dominica at sixteen to escape a domineering father and gave birth to Annie, her only child, at thirty, after marriage to a man thirty-five years her senior who already had grown children older than she was. This is no romance plot, at least not in the conventional sense, but one based on mutual respect and admiration.

Like all mothers in all cultures, she tries to train her daughter in proper sexual conduct, respectful behavior, and appropriate customs and rituals, but Annie's mother knows the importance of independence and is strong enough to force her child out of the nest: when Annie is twelve her mother stops their communal baths, dressing alike, and being inseparable. She wants her daughter to become a woman.

In "The World and Our Mothers," in the *New York Times Book Review*, Vivian Gornick claims that mother-daughter struggles are more complex than those between fathers and sons because they are fraught with more ambivalence. Speaking of the child's struggle, she says: "Our necessity, it seems, is not so much to kill our fathers as it is to separate from our mothers, and it is the daughters who must do the separating."[8]

Gornick's thesis is borne out in the recent pioneering work by Nancy Chodorow and others, but she is mistaken when she claims that "nowhere in literature is there a female equivalent of the protagonist locked in successful struggle, either with the father or with the mother, for the sake of the world beyond childhood" (10). This may be true of the fiction of white women, but several women of color have immortalized "successful struggle(s)" between mothers and daughters in fiction and autobiography: I think of Paule Marshall's *Brown Girl, Brownstones* (1959), Maya Angelou's *I Know Why a Caged Bird Sings* (1970), Maxine Hong Kingston's *The Woman Warrior* (1975), and Toni Morrison's *Beloved* (1987), as well as *Annie John*.

But the paradigm here is different: in a racist society in which the world beyond the family denies her autonomy, the female hero of color looks to her mother—and the world of women—to find models of strength and survival. As Mary Helen Washington explains the situation of the black woman writer in America:

> The literature of black women . . . is about black women; it takes the trouble to record the thoughts, words, feelings, and deeds of black women . . . and few, if any, women in the literature of black women succeed in heroic quests without the support of other women or men in their communities. Women talk to other women in this tradition, and their friendships with other women—mothers, sisters, grandmothers, friends, lovers—are vital to their growth and well-being.[9]

Whereas Gornick and others, following the lead of modern psychoanalysis, claim that our greatest source of tension and conflict resides in the family, black women writers (and many writers of color) recognize that these familial tensions cannot be seen apart from the broader reality

8. Vivian Gornick, "The World and Our Mothers," *New York Times Book Review*, November 19, 1987, p. 52.
9. Mary Helen Washington, Introduction, *Invented Lives: Narratives of Black Women, 1860–1960* (Garden City, N.Y.: Doubleday Anchor Press, 1987), p. xxi.

of racism. Thus, for the woman of color, her mother and the women in her family and/or community provide strength, self-confidence, an individual and communal history, and heavy doses of reality. For whatever the tensions these characters encounter at home are minor annoyances compared to their oppression in a racist culture.

Annie John is not an overtly political novel, but it challenges us to reexamine old models of what autonomy means for women. At the end of the novel, seventeen-year-old Annie leaves for London and a career as a nurse. Some readers might say that her initiation has not yet begun— that Antigua has been a womb, a paradise from which she must escape— but I disagree. Annie John is as developed as her mother was at sixteen when she packed her belongings into a single trunk and left home alone. And like her grandmother, she has magical powers—her language can transform her life into art.

Since this essay was written, Kincaid has expressed her political convictions in a nonfiction study of Antigua past and present: *A Small Place* (New York: Farrar, Straus & Giroux, 1988).

Bra Rabbit Meets Peter Rabbit: Genre, Audience, and the Artistic Imagination: Problems in Writing Children's Fiction

JEAN D'COSTA

> Perhaps it is only in childhood that books have any deep
> influence on our lives. In later life we admire, we are
> entertained, we may modify some views we already
> hold, but we are more likely to find in books merely a
> confirmation of what is in our minds already. But in
> childhood all books are books of divination, telling us
> about the future, and like the fortune teller who sees a
> long journey in the cards or death by water they
> influence the future.
>
> GRAHAM GREENE, *The Lost Childhood*

Every culture produces literary genres that serve culture-specific purposes. This function is a given, an obvious cliché. Genres pass from culture
to culture, are modified, absorbed, and reabsorbed. Such transference is
also cliché, a given. Certain kinds of transference and absorption, however, produce a unique pattern of acceptance and adaptation. In these
transactions the peculiar nature of genre to control the expectations of
the audience and the audience's complementary hunger for the security
of genre may precipitate insecurity, confusion, experimentation, and finally, the emergence of new-made art forms.

In the meeting of Peter Rabbit and Bra Rabbit (or his equivalent, the
Caribbean spider-hero and trickster, Anancy)—a meeting that is still in
session—one may explore the demands genre makes of the would-be

fiction writer who has listened closely to both voices. The writer's tensions echo those of the audience, which in this instance includes any Caribbean child who goes to school, who listens to the radio and watches television, and who responds to the languages of the media and of black culture.

As a writer, I have been aware of the difficulties of moving between the languages that represent the worlds of Anancy, of *Little Women*, and, latterly, of *Dallas*. It is only in recent time that the gravitational pull of genre has made me realize that, for example, a science fiction tale set in Jamaica creates conflicts between plot and characters: rockets and reggae? Rastas in space suits? The maker's imagination seems poised between two irreconcilable worlds. Yet the truth is that writer and audience make use of the genres of both, the languages of both, and the history of both.

THE HISTORICAL CONTEXT

The colonial migrations from Africa and Europe into the supposedly empty spaces of the Western Hemisphere produced first a seeming silence, then a division (on one hand) into the "high" culture of print and simultaneously (on the other hand) into the "low" oral tradition of an underclass. The slaves and indentured servants created a folklore that preserved forms other than those of the "high" culture, forged new types (the Jamaican Anancy story), and influenced the "high," imitative level, first decoratively and then profoundly.

During the early period of apparent silence, the colonial world produced no printed literature even where printing presses existed. Jamaica in the nineteenth century boasted several newspapers with a respectable standard of literary style. The presses turned out pamphlets and the occasional volume of prints or studies of local scenes but no novels, poems, or plays. Such texts came only from the metropolitan world. No one expected to find anything comparable to Jane Austen or Charles Dickens in a colonial capital. No one expected a Jane or a Charles to be born in such a place, but in the period of silence the Creole Janes and Charleses absorbed the tales told around them, the graphic, vulgar songs heard on street and back veranda, and the stories in books from abroad, that vast and mighty world to which the colonial imagination yearns—if it is literate in the language of that world.

In this group of literates we first see the meeting of "high" and "low" genres, which later produced the written literature of the new culture. Silent themselves, the literates of the nineteenth-century Sunday schools brought up a generation that rewarded its parents with earnest imitations of metropolitan literary forms: the fantasy school essay "A Day by the Seaside," satirized by Naipaul in *A House for Mr. Biswas*, finally comes true by the end of the novel when Mr. Biswas's son becomes a part of the middle-class, metropolitan world of picnic hampers and cars that calls its parents "Daddy" and "Mummy."[1]

In the period of imitation characterized by Mr. Biswas, the reader versed in the high culture may become the aspiring writer of a new fiction. This new writer must contend with a generic conditioning that affects the narrative voice, the moral argument, the gestures and behavior of characters, the interplay of action, characters, and setting, and (most obviously), the nature of the language. Here we find the creators of such early twentieth-century works as *The White Witch of Rosehall* and *Under the Skin*, both sensationalist romantic adventures full of derivative postures.[2]

Here too we find those Caribbean voices that assert the necessity of writing in standard English, that claim the Creole languages are inadequate to express serious ideas, and that perceive only an artistic vacuum in the low culture, dismissing its depth, variety, and energy.

But the writer who succeeds the imitator suddenly seems to bend *all* inherited genres into new shapes: Derek Walcott fuses oral folk tale, choric verse drama, and the morality play to produce *Ti Jean*. Jean Rhys takes gossip, voice, and viewpoint to extraordinary lengths to fashion a new form: the multiple first-person narratives that make up the account of the first Mrs. Rochester in *Wide Sargasso Sea* have no precedent other than the necessity of a new sensibility and imagination.

Genre as a Way of Seeing and Acting

Let us look briefly at some of the provisions a genre offers to a maker. In the oral tradition of Old English heroic verse, the maker benefits not only from the inherited accounts of tribal victory and disaster but from the "word hoard" of previous makers. The proper gestures for greeting a victorious thane, for mourning a kinsman at the funeral pyre, and for sharing drink in the meadhall stand out in the poetry of the Anglo-Saxons and form its characteristic diction and imagery. In the same way, the Anancy story offers the gestures proper to the tricking of an opponent, the wooing of a lady, and the adoption of disguise. It also offers characteristic diction and imagery: Anancy's lisping "bungo" talk marks him as a uniquely Caribbean figure.

Even the endings of the heroic poem and the Anancy tale are highly formulaic in language and in dramatic outcome: the Old English poet ends with a moral summing up of the outcome of the warplay, celebrates the doomed who fell in the place of slaughter, and commends their names

1. See V. S. Naipaul, *A House for Mr. Biswas* (New York: Random House, 1984), pp. 356–57, 440, 504.
2. H. G. DeLisser, *The White Witch of Rosehall* (London: Ernest Benn, 1929); and William F. Vassall, *Under the Skin* (New York: S. Stone Williams, 1923).

and deeds to the lips of those who shall come after, who shall sing their praise. The "Jack Mandora me no choose none" distances narrator and audience from Anancy's lies, tricks, and unscrupulous self-interest. His survival requires no celebration beyond the fact of itself, a Caribbean miracle. Both patterns of events, gesture, moral commentaries, and character types constitute distinctive genres. It is hard to imagine what the interaction of these very different genres would be, once they have come into contact. I have chosen the examples to point up the role of genre in the history of a people as well as to show how the model of tale or heroic lay becomes a self-perpetuating force, drawing the maker's imagination toward the world it portrays.

THE MAKING OF THE WRITER

In the Caribbean situation, the writer deals with the demands of genre both privately, within her imagination, and publicly, within the expectations of the audience. A great change in the nature of the colonial imagination occurred when the artist began to see herself and her group as her primary audience; at this stage the new imagination separates itself finally from the colonial bond. It is no accident that large metropolitan publishers have set up offices in places like Jamaica and Trinidad within the lifetime of Rhys and Walcott. It is also significant that the greatest stock in trade of these publishers consists of school texts and children's books. The new writer is the child of the reading audience, one who heeds the call of the low tradition while practicing the high.

The making of a writer derives from the making of a reader. In the genre of children's literature, generic influence from the literary, high culture may well be stronger, more conservative, and more pervasive in the audience than is the case in adult genres. Education and literacy exert a strong influence on the meeting of low and high literature, or, to be more exact, on the meeting of oral and printed literature in a Caribbean Creole culture. For example, a child raised on oral folktale in which the hero is a cunning, duplicitous, amoral survivor (Anancy/Bra Rabbit) meets in school and in the public library the heroes and heroines of the metropolitan, high culture: Little Red Riding Hood, Peter Rabbit, the Bobbsey twins, Lassie, Alice, and later on the heroes of Roald Dahl, Kipling, and Jack London and the heroines of L. M. Montgomery, Judy Blume, and Frances Hodgson Burnett.

The influence of the latter group (the adventure stories for the ten-to-thirteen-year-old group) tends to be more intrusive than that of the folktale because such fiction becomes part of schooling and social mobility, whereas the printed folktales (Grimm, Andersen, and Perrault) have to compete directly with the local oral tradition and may form less of a classroom staple. I have, for example, read or heard European folktales at home along with Anancy stories; my peers at primary school heard a few of the European tales in school and, typically for a small rural community, heard none at home.[3] Instead, these friends had a wider exposure to the local oral tradition and did not meet much fiction of the high culture until later in their schooling.

Throughout colonial times, the beginning grades of primary school drew on the European tradition, using poems, tales, riddles, and songs that contrasted sharply with the oral tradition. Jamaican individualism (which can sometimes reach the level of a social behavior) has often been identified by Jamaicans themselves with the Anancy ethic of willful self-interest. The moral of the Little Red Hen differs critically from that of Anancy stealing Bra Alligator's eggs, yet certain moral patterns do converge.

In the European folk fairy tale, some of the same generic patterns of survival and cunning exist: Jack (with his Beanstalk), Ulysses, and Puss-in-Boots all use lies, deception, and tricks to survive, to prevail against terrible odds, and to win. But at the end of the Anancy story, unlike at the end of the European folk fairy tale, the hero's great triumph usually consists in staying alive. One step ahead of his adversaries, Anancy lives, but not "happily ever after." Instead, the conteur disclaims responsibility for the hero's behavior: "Jack Mandora, me no choose none."

In one of the few tales in which Anancy wins a king's daughter as wife (and the kingdom as well), the conteur ends: "Anancy is the wickedest King ever reign. Sometime him dere, sometime him gone run 'pon him rope an tief cow fe him wife."[4] These generic actions symbolize both the literal spider and the magical spiderman: spiders get about by swinging on their webs, and Anancy gets about cunningly so as to mystify others, to rob and trick, and to enrich himself and his family.

The classic Anancy story stands indeed as a symbol for any lie, fantasy, trickery of words, or deception: "don tell me no Nancy 'tory," is a favorite command of anyone suspected of lying.

In contrast to the Anancy story, the Beatrix Potter story carries a different message expressed in different gestures. While defying human authority and power as exemplified by Mr. McGregor, Peter Rabbit lives within the authority and firm moral code of his parents. Like Anancy, the Beatrix Potter hero may act out of pure self-interest and greed; he may delight in killing and eating smaller creatures if he is Mr. Tod, and the narrator may grant him the right to do so. But the

3. European folktales adapted into the Creole cycle change so much in form that even "Mr. Bluebeard" resembles the original only in the basic plot outline; see Walter Jekyll, *Jamaican Song and Story* (Kingston, Jamaica: Sangsters, 1966), pp. 35–37.
4. "Yung-Kyum-Pyung," ibid., p. 12.

action remains framed in the safety of Edwardian middle-class childhood: being tucked in bed, having tea, going shopping, and being rescued by one's parents. All the action covertly leads toward the happy ending celebrated in Victorian children's literature and inherited by the Caribbean child audience.

One need not go much farther to see that the genre represented by Anancy and that practiced by Beatrix Potter do not fit well together. Even though many of Potter's characters and plots show the triumph of the weak over the strong and the joyous amorality of gratification, her writing expresses a world that *acts* differently from that in which Anancy thrives. The worlds of Potter and of *Lear* are essentially one. The children's writer prepares the sensibility which, at the adult stage, will comprehend M. Poirot, Lady Macbeth, and Eliza Doolittle. Writing on Beatrix Potter, Graham Greene makes the point, perceptively and deliciously, when he classifies her works under such titles as "the great comedies" and "the great near-tragedies." Peter Rabbit and his cousin Benjamin Bunny belong with the "great (paired) characters of history" such as "Quixote and Sancha."[5] The challenge to the writer of Caribbean children's fiction lies in the creation of a world that will prepare the young Caribbean mind for Antoinette Cosway and Lady Macbeth, for J. R. Ewing and Anancy, and for Bob Marley, Dylan Thomas, and Lewis Thomas.

In large part, the differences between these genres emerge in the ability of language to summon up assumptions, moral attitudes, and cultural associations that frame any single text. The fusion of differing linguistic and generic codes thus becomes the primary challenge to the new writer.

Every literary genre belongs within a code of language usage. The narrator operates within that code, and the audience expects the code. Not to hear Jamaican Creole in an Anancy story disappoints the audience and thins the effect of the telling or reading. The hero speaks in "bungo talk," through his nose, and must do so to remain in character, just as he must also "work his head" to exploit those around him.

On the other hand, Peter Rabbit's narrator can tell the audience that "lettuce is very soporific" and get away with it. On the page facing this statement the audience sees Peter fast asleep in Mr. McGregor's garden, in great danger of capture and death. In the folk tales of the Western Hemisphere, Bra Anancy and Bra Rabbit define themselves by language type as well as by language behavior: they can speak the high form if they need to, but using it forms part of their deceptions and cunning.

If every genre carries with it a unique diction, plot, narrative, and

---

5. Graham Greene, *The Lost Childhood* (New York: Viking Press, 1951), pp. 106–11.

characterization, then the audience brought up on dissimilar genres and conflicting cultural assumptions must contend with the mixed signals reaching it from different sources. The old solution lay in supposedly denying the low genre in favor of the high. I say "supposedly," for Caribbean audiences have remained consistently attached to the low genres in spite of the efforts of generations of teachers and cultural missionaries. But this attachment has not prevented the "divided child" of Derek Walcott's *Another Life* from feeling a deep uncertainty when confronted with what it believed to be a choice between the high and the low.

I can make the situation plainer by referring to my own work as a "divided child" and a new writer. I was brought up in both traditions, and my pleasure in Anancy stories and local folktale was as acute as my appetite of English adventure stories. When I began to consider writing, my ambition focused on the pleasure and entertainment I had found in these literary worlds. I wanted to entertain and console other children of my own world: a literate and bilingual Jamaican world. But I also hoped that my work could slip into oral lore by the agency of tellers, dramatizers, and the friend who reads aloud.

To reach this audience, the tale or story would have to capture the generic expectations of an audience keyed to the voice of Anancy as well as that of Peter Rabbit. Its plot and gestures would have to reflect a Jamaican world view, if not a Jamaican reality (the two are not the same).

How easy it would have been in the writing of *Sprat Morrison* to have lapsed into the code of the English school story. And how impossible. Sprat must live in terror of the common entrance exam, he must jostle for patties in the schoolyard, and he must carry his mother's market basket, and even though he goes to the beach for an outing, he goes as a Jamaican lower-middle-class child might: in a broken-down car patched together by his father.

As a maker of fiction, I have become very aware of how strong are the dictates of a culture in the shaping of a story. None of my novels could have come into being without the social setting that shapes them. Instead of being silenced by the existence of the high and low traditions, I rely on both to provide my material and direction. For example, Jamaican ghost stories and family lore play an important part in *Voice in the Wind*. In this novel, the plot and diction mirror the behavior and life histories of a Jamaican social type, the poor but respectable farm family of the early and mid-twentieth century. As I have been tempted by other genres, such as fantasy science fiction, I have found my imagination fired as much by the possibilities of drawing on the low tradition as by the high.

A fantasy science fiction tale, however, could present extreme difficulties of a purely generic kind: what technology, for example, should underlie the central conceit of such a tale? Robots and rockets have no place in Jamaican life at present. Time travel might work. A past utopia would not, unless one wished to honor the Arawaks. Although certain genres present obvious difficulties, we would be making a great mistake to assume that the world of reality and of the imagination must remain unreconciled.

For a long time the historical novel also seemed to present insuperable generic difficulties. The past was closed, dark, frightening, and shameful. Yet Vic Reid has been able to thrill a generation of children with his recreations of the 1831 and 1865 uprisings in Jamaica.

Perhaps the most difficult problem for me lies in the moral imperative that invades children's fiction. All societies expect a certain didacticism in children's fiction even if they allow children the right to pleasure and delight. Because of the strength of the British tradition, the moral message it carries can easily penetrate Caribbean fiction. Assumptions of class slip in, even if one overcomes those of race. Only by staring the audience in the face can one make sure that the values expressed by the new work remain true to the world for which it is intended.

Yet in spite of the contradictions and tensions that these different genres create in me as reader and as writer, I have found that they allow for a wider range of narrative, for the creation of many more voices and characters, for much irony, satire, pathos, and excitement, and ultimately, for a long and happy meeting between some of my closest friends: Bra Tiger and Mr. Tod, the rolling-calf and the Wizard of Oz, the shark hunters of Montego Bay and the cowboys of Texas, Dickon of *The Secret Garden* and Anancy himself.

If the history of the Caribbean tells us anything, it is that in dire need we can create new language forms. It tells us that the will to survive cannot be destroyed. It tells us that the imagination works on "what is past, and passing, and to come" to shape new forms. Anancy becomes Uncle Time, no simple trickster but—in Dennis Scott's vision—

> a ole, ole man...
> All year long 'im wash 'im foot in de sea,
> long, lazy years on de wet san'
> an' shake de coconut tree dem
> quiet-like wid 'im sea-win' laughter
>
> scrapin' away de lan'[6]

6. Dennis Scott, *Uncle Time* (Pittsburgh: University of Pittsburgh Press, 1973), p. 32.

In Olive Senior's poem "Nansi 'Tory,'"[7] he becomes "somebody's grand-father" and "Heaven's doorkeeper" whose

> atomised
> heart on a
> beach
> reassemble[s]
>
> Awaiting
> return.

7. Olive Senior, *Talking of Trees* (Kingston, Jamaica: Calabash, 1985), p. 28.

Clare Savage as a Crossroads Character

MICHELLE CLIFF

The first piece of writing I produced, beyond a dissertation on intellectual game-playing in the Italian Renaissance, was entitled "Notes on Speechlessness."[1] In these notes I talked about my identification with Victor, the wild boy/child of Aveyron who, after his "rescue" from the forest and wildness (and, presumably, the she-wolf who nourished him) by a well-meaning doctor of Enlightenment Europe, became tamed, "civilized," but never came to speech.

I felt with Victor when I first read his story. My wildness had been tamed, that which I had been taught was my wildness, which embraced imagination, emotion, spontaneity, history, memory, revolution, and flights of fancy. Flesh was replaced by air; Caliban by Ariel. But, as Roberto Fernandez Retamar has observed,

> There is no real Ariel-Caliban polarity; both are slaves in the hands of Prospero, the foreign magician. But Caliban is the rude and unconquerable master of the island, while Ariel, a creature of the air, although also a child of the isles, is the intellectual.[2]

Victor's name, the name given to him by Dr. Itard, lives in odd juxtaposition to his fate. The victory is not his, really, it belongs to his

---

1. Michelle Cliff, "Notes on Speechlessness," *Sinister Wisdom*, No. 5.
2. Quoted in Gayatri Chakravorty Spivak, "Three Women's Texts and a Critique of Imperialism," in Henry Louis Gates, Jr., ed., *Race, Writing and Difference* (Chicago: University of Chicago Press, 1986), p. 245.

civilizer, tamer, colonizer, he who would erase Victor's history before his indoctrination, assume the forest was merely brutish, and tell the tale entirely from his own point of view.

Then, too, Victor is speechless. Do we understand this speechlessness as an act of self-erasure or one of rebellion? Or both?

I use Victor here as a metaphor for a colonized child, who is chosen to represent the colonizer's world, to peddle the colonizer's values, ideas, and notions of what is real, alien, other, normal, supreme. There are, of course, different brands of colonization; some colonized children will turn a profit for the colonizer and perish in defense of his boundaries; some may one day slit his throat. But all are washed in the notion that life before discovery in the forest, the Middle Passage, civilization, represents only brutishness and therefore he or she must forget, deny, be silent about that part. The child is not allowed to become whole under such stringent taming.

These thoughts serve as an introduction, explaining that part of my purpose as a writer of Afro-Caribbean (Indian, African, and white) experience and heritage and Western experience and education (indoctrination) has been to reject speechlessness by inventing my own peculiar speech, one that attempts to draw together everything I am and have been, both Caliban and Ariel and a liberated and synthesized version of each.

Caliban speaks to Prospero, saying: "You taught me language, and my profit on't / Is, I know how to curse."[3]

This line immediately brings to my mind the character of Bertha Rochester, wild and raving ragout, as Charlotte Brontë describes her, cursing and railing, more beast than human. It takes a West Indian writer, Jean Rhys, to describe Bertha from the inside rather than from the outside, keeping "Bertha's humanity, indeed her sanity as critic of imperialism, intact," as Gayatri Spivak has observed.[4]

And what a fine phrase to describe the character we all encountered as girls as the madwoman in the attic.

Rhys said in an interview when speaking of Bertha and The Wide Sargasso Sea, "I thought I'd try to write her a life."[5] It is a statement at once moving and sensible.

It makes one (at least, this one) wish another Caribbean writer would take on the character of Heathcliff and write him a life.

The protagonist of my two novels is named Clare Savage. She is not exactly an autobiographical character, but she is an amalgam of myself

3. Houston A. Baker, Jr., "Caliban's Triple Play," quoted in ibid., p. 391.
4. Spivak, "Three Women's Texts," p. 249.
5. Quoted ibid.

and others, who eventually becomes herself alone. Bertha Rochester is her ancestor.

Her name, obviously, is significant and is intended to represent her as a crossroads character, with her feet (and head) in (at least) two worlds. Her first name means, signifies, light-skinned, which she is, and light-skinnedness in the world in which Clare originates, the island of Jamaica in the period of British hegemony, and to which she is transported, the United States in the 1960s, and to which she transports herself, Britain in the 1970s, stands for privilege, civilization, erasure, forgetting. She is not meant to curse, or rave, or be a critic of imperialism. She is meant to speak softly and keep her place.

Her surname is self-explanatory. It is meant to evoke the wildness that has been bleached from her skin, understanding that my use of the word *wildness* is ironic, mocking the master's meaning, turning instead to a sense of non-Western values which are empowering and essential to survival, her survival, and wholeness, her wholeness. A knowledge of history, the past, has been bleached from her mind, just as the rapes of her grandmothers are bleached from her skin. And this bleached skin is the source of her privilege and her power too, she thinks, for she is a colonized child.

She is a light-skinned female who has been removed from her homeland in a variety of ways and whose life is a movement back, ragged, interrupted, uncertain, to that homeland. She is fragmented, damaged, incomplete. The novels *Abeng* and *No Telephone to Heaven* describe her fragmentation as well as her movement toward homeland and wholeness.[6]

At the end of *No Telephone to Heaven*, Clare Savage has cast her lot, quietly and somewhat tentatively, but definitely. She ends her life burned into the landscape of Jamaica, literally, as one of a small band of guerrillas engaged in a symbolic act of revolution.

Many readers of this novel think this an unhappy ending; they do not want the character to die. Though essentially tragic, for her life has been so, I see it, and envisioned it, as an ending that completes the circle, or rather triangle, of the character's life. In her death she has complete identification with her homeland; soon enough she will be indistinguishable from the ground. Her bones will turn to potash, as did her ancestors' bones.

This ending and the sense it conveys is reminiscent of the work of the Cuban artist Ana Mendieta. I was inspired by the work of Mendieta, who died in 1985 at the absurd age of thirty-six. Like Clare Savage, like me,

---

6. Michelle Cliff, *Abeng* (Freedom, Calif.: Crossing Press, 1984); *No Telephone to Heaven* (New York: E. P. Dutton, 1987).

Ana Mendieta was a child-exile. She had been sent from Cuba by her parents, in cahoots with the Catholic church and the U.S. State Department, which devised a plan to rescue children from growing up under the auspices of a Marxist government. Under this plan, fourteen thousand children were shipped out. Ana and her elder sister Raquel ended up in Dubuque, Iowa, when Ana was about twelve. The children spoke no English at all.

The critic Elizabeth Hess commented on Mendieta's work:

> Mendieta's art took shape in performance, earthworks, sculptures, and photographs. Again and again, she carved a haunting iconic figure into the ground, onto the side of a cave, or even into a stream of water by defining the form with ripples and rocks. On occasion the figure was born in flames, literally exploding into existence, then burning up. All that was left of these pieces, called the Silueta Series, was a scar . . . a shadow-image. The earth owns these works, which eventually will disappear over time.[7]

The artist herself said that her work was "a direct result of having been torn from my homeland during my adolescence."[8] Some of Mendieta's etched landscape exists today in Cuba, where she worked in 1981.

Her work, like mine, has been a movement back to homeland, to identity. She represents this homeland, this landscape of her identity, as female, as womb, the contours of a woman's body, at times filling the contours with blood, other times fixing the silhouette to the earth by gunpowder. In other work besides the Silueta Series, Mendieta uses this landscape of her identity, as in her series of drawings on tropical leaves, for example.

At the end of No Telephone to Heaven, Clare Savage is burned into the landscape of Jamaica, by gunfire, but she is also enveloped in the deep green of the hills and the delicate intricacy of birdsong.

Both Mendieta and I understand the landscape of our islands as female. For me, the land is redolent of my grandmother and mother, it is a deeply personal connection. The same could be said of Clare Savage, who seeks out the landscape of her grandmother's farm as she would seek out her grandmother and mother. There is nothing left at that point but the land, and it is infused with the spirit and passion of these two women.

Looking back over Abeng and No Telephone to Heaven I find the theme of the grandmother repeated. I try in both of these novels to show the power, particularly the spiritual authority, of the grandmother as well as her victimization. Hers is a power directly related to landscape, gardens, planting when the heavenly signs are right, burying the placenta

7. Elizabeth Hess, "Out of Body," Village Voice, December 8, 1987, p. 119.
8. Ibid.

and umbilical cord, preparing the dead for burial. This powerful aspect of the grandmother originates in Nanny, the African warrior and Maroon leader.

At her most powerful, the grandmother is the source of knowledge, magic, ancestors, stories, healing practices, and food. She assists at rites of passage, protects, and teaches. She is an inheritor of African belief systems, African languages. She may be informed with *àshe*, the power to make things happen, the responsibility to mete justice.[9]

She appears in several places in my work. Most prominently she is Miss Mattie, the grandmother of Clare Savage. With her brown arms furiously, sensuously working as she pounds the beans from her coffeepiece into dust in her carved mortar with her smoothed pestle, she embodies power, the life force she represents. When she appears as the grandmother of Christopher, a character in *No Telephone to Heaven*, she inhabits the Dungle, all but bereft of power except for the power to judge, to assess the worthiness or unworthiness of others. The vestige of her African power source, its symbol, is the thunderstone that sits in her enamel water jug, purifying the water she draws from a dripping standpipe.

The theme of the grandmother, specifically the Jamaican grandmother, her tradition, her history, embraces both of these women. Finally, it is her death in the almshouse fire in Kingston that impels Clare to Jamaica once and for all.

There is one grandmother who stands apart from the others in *No Telephone to Heaven*. She is the woman Hart Crane envisioned as the flesh of America, Powhatan's daughter Pocahontas.[10] She becomes grandmother in death, whereas in life she was daughter and mother. Pocahontas is buried in Gravesend, having died on the Thames at the start of her return home in 1616, in her twentieth year. On board also were her infant son and English husband, who returned to Virginia.

Pocahontas's name has often been considered synonymous with collaborator, traitor, consort of the enemy. The truth is more complicated. The daughter of Powhatan, she was kidnapped by colonists and held against her will. She was forced to abandon the belief system of her people and to memorize the Apostle's Creed, Lord's Prayer, and Ten Commandments. She was taken to England in 1616 and there displayed—a tame Indian, the forest behind her, cleansed by civilization. She became known as the "friend of the earliest struggling English colonists whom she nobly rescued, protected, and helped," as is written on her memorial

9. For a definition of *àshe*, see Robert Farris Thompson, *Flash of the Spirit* (New York: Random House, 1983), esp. pp. 5–9.

10. Hart Crane, *The Bridge*, Part II, "Powhatan's Daughter" (rpt. New York: Liveright, 1970).

tablet in St. George's Church. She is memorialized as Rebecca Rolfe; her real name, translating as Bright Stream between Two Hills, erased.[11]

She, like Victor, has been rescued from wildness, a colonized child who exists in history, speechless.

When Clare Savage recognizes Pocahontas in that graveyard in Gravesend she makes a choice, begins a series of choices, which will take her from the mother country back to the country of her grandmother, her own.

11. St. George's Church is in Gravesend. Information about Pocahontas is found in Beth Brant's brilliant essay, "Grandmothers of a New World," *IKON*, no. 8 (1988).

Leh We Talk See

JEANNETTE CHARLES

De abeng is one conch shell we run away slaves use fe
use fe signal to de odders when de white man wuz
cuming fe hunt we down. It is a symbol of de oppression
we face and de fight we fought.

Columbus sail de ocean blue in fourteen hundred ninety two, an when
he did he discover de Caribbean. I just whan fe know how he could ah
discover someplace dat already had people pon it. I does check tings out
yuh know, so I pik up dis here Oxford American Dictionary, an I see dat
to discover mean to be de fust to obtain site or knowledge of. When
Columbus did lan', de Indian dem had don' set up a society pon de
islands. So I don' see how anybody in de right min' can say dat Columbus
discover de Caribbean. So leh we geh one ting straight from de beginin',
dis here Columbus wuz an interloper an not a discoverer as we are led
to believe.

(Schoops) Dem Europeans wih dem high an mighty self enslaved an
eventually kill off dem Indians dem. Dey rob dem Indians of dey own
lan' an force dem fe wuk till dey drop dead. Well now, after dey done
kill off all de Indians, dey still needed somebody fe wuk de lan' an so.
Well guess wha, thirty-eight years had pass since Columbus cum an dem
start importing my people from Africa fe do dey dirty wuk. Tis like Marley
say "Ole Pirates yes dey rob I, sold I to de merchant ships, minutes after

269

dey took I from de bottomless pits." Buh guess wha, de song does go on fe say, "But my hands were made strong by de hands of de Almighty, we forward in dis generation triumphantly."

Yes sah, in all dere greed fe de riches of de Islands, de white man rob us from we home an bring we fe wuk fe dem. Lawd, de white man had we in chains, buh fe we hearts wuh strong. Yuh see struggle is both physical an psychological. Tis one hard struggle we had fe loose de white man chains, buh we loose dem tho'. Ih jus goes fe prove dat where deres a will deres a way. We black people jus cyar be held down fe long. We is truly a strong race.

Man we couldn' stan fe be in dem chains. Ah wha dem tink we is animals? From de very beginnin' we decided we wuzn' goin stay in no chain, so we resist! We use fe bun down de massas Plantation an run way to de hills. We ain' only run to de hills fe hide yuh know, we use fe attak de white man dem all de time. We destroy so much of de property an so till dem had no odder choice buh fe set we free. We wuh bad meh son! Eh-eh, hear me say we we like if I wuh dere. I guess I feel dis way becaus we is all black an dem wuh fe me ancestors. An yes Lawd we are all one in de spirit. Alright, den, now dat yuh understan' where I cumin' from I goin go ahead an say WE. Anyway like I wuh sayin' before, we show dem dat we no whan fe adopt no culture of deres, we whan fe keep we heritage alive. We no whan no vanilla in de cawfee. De white man try fe make we believe dat black is sinful, so we fe hate weself an wuk hard fe dem fe better weself cause dem is we salvation. I know fe sure I ain' goin wurship nobody who does treat me as bad as de white man treat we. I know we never sen' call dem. Dem jus whanted fe geh we fe slave fe dem so dey make up dis lie bout tryin' fe help we fe fool dem moomoo dem in dey homelan'. Den when we geh here dem make everybody believe we no human buh savage.

Anways dis here lightenen of de cawfee is wha *Abeng* by Michelle Cliff is all about. Leh me start off by saying dat she call dis abeng fe symbolize de oppression an resistance of we black people. I hope yuh remember wha me say about de abeng before. If not den turn back an educate yuhself meh son. Anyway dis here novel stars one buckra Pickney name Clare Savage. Clare mamma is one buckra jus like she, buh fe she puppa is one vanilla white man. She mamma does expose she to she black heritage by tracking through de bush with she an partaking in som obeah rituals an so, buh she fadder forever tellin' she she white. Ah wha here tall. I don' know how one pickney wih as much color in dey skin as she can be white. Ah who him tryin' fe fool? Dis could only make de poor chil' real mix up. Yuh see Clare does love fe be in de bush with she granmodder an dem, but when push cum to shove she does act like one white gal quick.

Clare story is dat of Michelle Cliff an odder light skin blacks. Take note on how de chil' name Clare Savage. Dis poor chil' no gah no love from de white or black man. De white man no like dem becaur dey gah dat black savagery runnin' through dey veins. De white man don' believe dat de black man is a wild animal, so dem no whan no half black near dem. Tis dem own wuthless appetite wha create buckra yuh know, buh dem still see we as savages. On de odder side of de coin, de black man no like buckra becaur dem too close to white.

Yuh se de white man is one clever fox. When he did'n whan fe dirty he hand in de hot sun with de black man blood, he puh dese buckra in charge of we. So ih wha dese half-an-half who use fe whip we. Dem use fe geh treated better than we becaur of dem lightness, buh dey white man no love dem no more dan he love us. So now look wha happen! When de slavery did end we as people did fin' ih hard to geh very far becaur we wuh facing hatred from within an without. So instead of gettin' lighter de struggle geh harder since we had try not only fe resist de white man buh also fe try fe bring de race togedder fe better weself.

Lissen no brodder man, we hav fe ban togedder as one fe uplif' de race. We hav fe make it so dat we pickney dem will be proud to be black, no madder wha shade dey is. We really cyar afford fe be fighten' each odder. Enough people out dere does hate we jus becaur we black, we really don' need fe be generating no extra hatred fo weself.

Dis here book *Abeng* really geh me tinkin'. Ih does show dat ih don' pay fe try fe imitate de white man. Fe as long as yuh goh sum color in yuh skin dem goin' hate yuh. Anyway why should we try fe imitate de white man? Black is beautiful! We no need fe adopt de policy of nobody dat does like fe enslave odder people. Ah wonder wha would ah happen if we had try fe enslave dem. We would have probably been attacked from all sides. Wha we hav fe do fe survive in dis white man's world is STRUGGLE! Fight de oppression. Look out fe yuh brodder in need. Leh we live like one no man!

We wuz rob from we modder Africa an mos' of us don' know a ting bout she, so now we does consider weself more as West Indians. Dis don' mean dat we is supposed to forget we heritage. Love yuh black brodder, whether he be in Ghana, Trinidad, or Harlem. One ting we mus' always remember is dat deres strength in numbers. If yuh have a goal in min', yuh can attain it. Like de sayin' go "no pain no gain." Sure it's goin' be hard, buh wih enough determination we can make it. Remember struggle is both physical an psychological. If yuh tink yuh can't, yuh won't. Live wih de white man buh hold fast to yuh heritage. Be proud to be an Ashanti or whatever descendant. We cyar leh de "civilized" people keep we in chains forever, we hav fe stan up fo we rights. As

Marley say, "Won't yuh help fe sing dese songs of freedom,/Cause all I ever heard,/Redemption song./Emancipate yuhself from mental slavery/ None buh ourselves can free our minds." Dem goin' try fe keep we down, buh we ah goin' keep uprising. Love yuh brodder man, an walk Good.

Parang

MARION PATRICK JONES

Rodney Alleyne, Woodbrook recalled, was *acting* permanent secretary in a ministry whose political head was Ursula Dyer's husband. That Woodbrook remarked this on verandas and in burglar-proofed bedrooms had little to do with Rodney Alleyne and less to do with Hayes Street, as the ministry was popularly called, and nothing to do with education, which is what the ministry was about. It had to do with that continuing cycle of rebirth which Jack Dyer and Buddha discovered. Woodbrook prided itself that cycle after cycle nothing changed. The streets, Rosalino, Carlos, Luis, and Alfredo, were named after the numerous children of some planter, Butler and Roberts after the victorious Boer war. The quadrangles of streets remained bordered by pavements swished clean before five in the morning. At regular intervals there were miniature parks, their concrete paths across grass. The low houses remained with their front gardens, their backyards narrowly walled in, broken bottles from overgrown sewerage tracks. The flat green sea spread somewhere behind a docksite that once had been an American base and was now the site of a flour mill designed, Woodbrook said, to sprinkle dust on polished floors. To the north stood opulent St. Clair. Beyond, the mountains were blue, green, or gray according to the mood of the petulant weather. Rodney Alleyne was mentioned with that indulgent affection Woodbrook kept for those who were always Woodbrook, who remained Woodbrook, who created neither the scandal of great achievement nor the scandal of non-

This is an excerpt from Marion Patrick Jones, "Parang" (unpublished).

achievement. Rodney Alleyne's wife, Rachael, was a MacIntyre, they whispered from their rocking chairs; Mac-Ti-*Ar* they pronounced it. Everyone understood. Paused. *Poor Rachael.* Jocelyn, Melina Rodriguez, and Sister Magdalene of St. Joseph's Convent were Rachael's nieces. Hm, they were something else. *Anna's* children.

Poor Rachael. Looked at their television sets or placed a glass with Dewar's whiskey on a veranda wall. . . .

"Now that Anna is gone," Rachael said sitting up in bed, "the children have no one but me."

"Um," he had replied.

"Stanley doesn't count," Rachael went on, "he left them of his own free will, didn't he? He can't blame them now for not looking back at him. I wonder what he thought he was doing at Anna's funeral today, eh? Do you remember how Anna wept when he left? The glass she just dropped broke, eh? And now *pramps* he is there at the funeral crying. Is the children I am sorry for. Just at the time that they really need a mother Anna up and dies. Anyway, they still have me to hold on to. In a way I am nearer to them than Anna ever was. It is strange the people God gives children to. I suppose His ways are not ours."

"Um," he said. He remembered thinking that he and Rachael were linked by the make-believe of things neither could whisper.

It was the night after the funeral. They had all gone back to Anna's house. Jocelyn ran up the stairs, turned the key in the door, and turned on the lights.

"Something to drink?" Jocelyn asked in a matter-of-fact way. There was a tray on the table with glasses, a bottle of whiskey, and some fashionable pastries Jocelyn had bought from Jacqueline's that morning.

"I am soaked through," she added. "What an awful day for a funeral. Who else is having whiskey?"

"You all should come over by me," Rachael said, declining the whiskey with a nod of her head. "This house without Anna is really like walking among jumbies. Let's all go over to my place. I have a pelau waiting. You'll stay, won't you Magdalene? Tonight," she added sharply, "is a time for the family to be together."

"Do you know what I want?" Jocelyn turned around defiantly, hugging her waist with one hand, a glass in the other. "I wish to stand at the edge of the cliff near to the Toco lighthouse and watch the waves come in, by myself, with a choice to return or to disappear." Her eyes were swollen.

"You must be really stupid," Magdalene said. "Who is going to drive you up to Toco at this hour and in pouring rain?"

"Jocelyn always thinks of herself." Melina was sniffing. Her handkerchief was a ball in her hand. "I've never seen anything like it. Here we all are after a funeral and all that Jocelyn can do is to act as a tourist. Can't you even wait until Mama is cold in the grave?"

"Look, Melina," Magdalene laughed, "here, take some more whiskey and stop your nonsense. If Mama did make a difference, would it be any use now?" She smoothed her blue dress again and crossed her feet one over the other. The black moccasins were slightly worn.

"But you agree that she made a difference." Melina intervened quickly, sticking one forefinger into the air to make a point. She had on silver chains, long, short, thin, fat. They hung from her neck to her waist. "You accept the principle that she made a difference?"

"What Anna did or did not do is finished," Rachael said with a firm, final note. A black and white striped dress ballooned over her waist. "It's no use quarreling over it. She tried her best, poor thing, and now she is gone. Come, let's go over to my place."

Rodney turned to look at Rachael. There was hope in her voice as if she felt the way he had hoped to feel—that something magnificent was starting now that Anna was dead.

"It is Jocelyn," Melina insisted. "She wasn't interested in the way Mama suffered, she never thought of me with Peter likely to grow up as nothing, she never thought of Magdalene lonely in a convent. All she thought about was seeing the island in grand style. Do you think that I have forgotten, eh? Jocelyn went to London to get away from work and responsibility, then she comes back as a queen."

"I am not lonely in a convent." Magdalene tilted her head in the air. "You always say that as if it must be so. I am no more lonely than anyone else is anywhere. So don't bring me into it, Melina. You don't know a thing about the convent anyway."

"You are only saying that to save Jocelyn. She says Toco, and everyone runs to take her to Toco. Why should she impose herself on the rest of us?"

"I am fed up with Melina," Jocelyn shouted, the calm, practical air before Anna's death disappearing. "You would think that I was with strangers the way she gets on. I should never have come back."

"Who do you think took care of Mama when you were enjoying yourself in London?" Melina asked her.

"And how do you think she lived?" Jocelyn snapped. "On your occasional big, big gifts? Or Magdalene's prayers?"

"How do you know I prayed for her?" Magdalene looked at Melina out of the corner of her eyes while speaking to Jocelyn.

"Yes, I knew that you would throw it in our face. All this talk about

Toco was only to say you supported Mama, you did this, you did that. I know you Jocelyn. No thought for any of us. Mama spoiled you and you used Mama to get at me." Melina was crying.

"Spoiled me. That's a joke." Jocelyn laughed a little. Rodney noticed for the first time that she had fine lines around her eyes and her cheeks hollowed in before curving under her sharp jawbones. "I had just arrived in London, catching my tail in Brixton, traveling to hell to work, freezing in a bedsitter, and what is the news I get? Melina is getting married and must have a nice wedding at St. Theresa's with six bridesmaids and a hell of a list of things she needs from panties to stainless steel. I lived on bloody apples and coffee when I wasn't haunting Marks and Sparks so that you could have that wedding. You think I've forgotten? Who the hell did you think did it? Daddy had a sudden conversion? Magdalene had given up her blasted comfort, or Mama had won a sweepstake?"

"You all like to go over past history, eh. You would think that there was never a present or a future, never a . . . forget it." Magdalene got up and stood before the window. Its curtains starched, newly ironed, hung halfway down to the floor.

"Aunt Rachael was talking about what people want. All I want is to. . . . "

"Yes, stand at Toco lighthouse," added Melina, "and see the waves come in just as you did before you left Trinidad. Right? You have no heart, man."

"I know what Jocelyn means to say," Rodney began.

"Oh shut up, you," Rachael shouted, "this is going to end up in a quarrel. Anna wouldn't wish us to quarrel tonight."

"Just like Jocelyn," Melina continued. "I really don't know why she always provokes a quarrel. She just waits to come home to start a quarrel. This is the time to talk about going to Toco?"

"Oh I will take you to Toco if you really want to go." Magdalene pulled her navy blue dress straight over her knees. "Right to the Toco lighthouse, where you can decide freely and in grand style that it would just be too much trouble to jump off into the sea. I'll sit in the car and give you ten minutes to make up your mind."

"At this time of night? Do you see what Jocelyn is like?" Melina appealed to them all. "She knows Magdalene can't be out alone in the nun's car at this time of night? See what I mean?"

"What has my being a nun got to do with it? If Jocelyn wants to go to Toco at eight at night to watch into the great darkness, why not?

"Because," Melina said making loud noises with her nostrils, "Jocelyn can't always get her own way. Mama spoiled her, and I don't see why we should continue it."

"Me?"

"Yes, you, Jocelyn. Mama always made a difference. If you're honest, Magdalene, you'll tell Jocelyn that Mama always made a difference. I hope she takes that into account when she throws herself into the sea."

"Continue it, Magdalene," Melina nodded, "Jocelyn has to be told the truth some time."

"Never a confession," Magdalene said, "never the wiping out of the yesterdays to permit us the todays. Just never."

"You see, Jocelyn is never wrong. Who asked Magdalene about confession? You think I wished that huge wedding? John and I planned twenty guests, we had two hundred. Some of them I never laid eyes on before—like the Wellingtons from San Fernando—and have never seen since. I wanted a bouquet of red roses and ended up with stephanotis, not to talk about having to carry a whole layer of my cake to some Indian man who used to keep cows. So don't blame it on me, Jocelyn. It was you who wished it to be that way. Don't blame it at all on me, eh. Stop standing there, John, and say something."

"It is none of John's business," Rachael intervened sharply. "Why must you all rake up old things so? Think of Anna for once, all of you."

"That's what we are thinking of, what else? It was she who spoiled Jocelyn, and she preferred Magdalene to me, too. I was always the one left out."

"You left out? You're making some strange jokes today, Melina. I was the one left out. I was in London not even knowing Mama was ill or that Peter wasn't normal, nothing. All I got was an invitation to the funeral, all."

"Ah, that was because Mama didn't want her sweet dear Jocelyn disturbed. She didn't mind disturbin' me, and she knew she couldn't disturb Magdalene, but here I was with Peter, with John away on one of his damn business trips and everything on me. I bet you were having a good time in Mayfair, Jocelyn, I bet you."

"Christ, Melina, how often do you think I see Mayfair? Magdalene, I thought you were driving me to Toco? I am fed up with Melina, fed up. All I do when I come here is work, work, work; all I do when I am away is work, work, work. Then Melina says that it is I who wished the five-hundred-guest wedding. It's a helluva thing. It could have been the registry for all I cared."

"It was a nice wedding," Rachael put in, her eyes wide, dreaming, "but I don't see what it has to do with now. Why should you all bring up Melina's wedding now? I couldn't understand the cake to the coolie man though."

"Simple." Magdalene's eyebrows were heavy black lines on a clean shining face. "Your cigarettes are at your side, Melina, and here's an ashtray. Weddings are like funerals, are like confession, the end and the beginning. Didn't you know?"

"Ah, we are in for a sermon," Melina lit a cigarette, "a great piece of Magdalene's philosophy. You don't have to spout it to us Magdalene, I have heard it all before. God created Peter as he is because in some special way he loved him enough to grant him eternal innocence. Remember that? Fancy telling me that crap when I had a dream of his being a doctor or an engineer or a prime minister! Now Mama is dead, we all get a soaking in Lapeyrouse, Jocelyn is lending me hell, John as usual doesn't say a word, silent as the blasted cemetery itself, and what do I hear funerals and weddings same khaki pants. Chrise, Magdalene. Enough is enough. Jocelyn wanting to kill herself from Toco lighthouse, have mercy, eh!" Her hand fiddled with a lighter, turning it off, on, off, on. Wondered if that was a real diamond on Jocelyn's hand?

"Did Anna ever explain to you, Rodney, why she wanted a whole lift of Melina's wedding cake taken to the Indian man who used to cut grass in the square for his cows? I never understood it. There are a lot of things about Anna I never could make out, could you, Rodney?"

"Uh," he told her, "uh."

"I swear it's Stanley," Rachael hissed between almost closed teeth, "and did you see him this afternoon? Long tears, you know, the widower in fine style, big black tie and all. *Scamp.*"

"Has it ever occurred to you, Aunt Rachael, that perhaps he meant it?" Magdalene asked.

"Ah, forgiveness!" Melina blew her smoke into the air. "I told you that Magdalene was in a preaching mood. Do you have to proclaim your damn righteousness all the time, Magdalene? Daddy treated Mama like hell, you know it, what are you pretending?"

"Oh God, Melina, who was speaking of forgiveness?" Magdalene asked her. "All that I meant was that we don't ever know what anyone really thinks when faced with the grave. That's all, that's all! I am not proclaiming a thing and I didn't say that he didn't treat Mama like hell, that isn't the point. What does it matter now anyway?"

"Yes, it does matter." The lines stretched near Jocelyn's tight nostrils. "I watched Daddy today, and all I could think was that I hoped it all hurt him. I never knew that I hated him as much as I do. He made Mama what she was and if I was in London working for Melina's wedding it was because of that bastard."

"My wedding? Damn it, Jocelyn, if you were going to bring it up forever and ever why did you do it? It's like Aunt Rachael and those damn dolls we couldn't play with because she'd come and ask Melina where is the doll I gave you? As if I had asked for the doll at all. You were right in a certain way about Peter, Magdalene. Anyway, I wanted a train with a real engine."

"Ah." Jocelyn's lipstick was a dull brown melting into her face. "At last someone is right for Melina. We shouldn't be drinking whiskey; this calls for champagne. I can't be hearing correct."

"Thanks be to God that Peter hasn't and never will have the calculating hierarchy of wants that I've had to live with all my life. At least if I give to him I give quite freely. He can't return a damn thing. I know that from the start. There's your innocence for you, Magdalene. He won't be an engineer, nor a doctor, nor a prime minister, which is only to say that he won't be the son of a bitch like the whole damn lot of you starting with Jocelyn and thanks for things I never wanted and now must be grateful for."

"Poor Dad." Magdalene turned around the gold band of a ring on her finger. Her hands reminded him of Rachael's. Anna's had large knuckles locking on the fussy woven gold Stanley had given her. "Whatever he does I remember him waylaying me on the road with a pair of skates in a Glendinning's bag. It was my birthday, and I wanted skates. Today we were on one side of the grave, he on the other, and I thought to myself how I wish we could bury Mama's pain and our pain with her, a sort of reconciliation, that's what I meant, Melina. Why is it that some things are allowed to mark us forever?"

"Because they do," Melina said firmly. "I am the only one in this joint that is prepared to recognize that. You think that you can join a convent, change your name and emerge like Saul turned into Paul. Nice. Put on a veil, wear a little cross, and it's all over. You're on the way to eternal life and to hell with the past. Jocelyn quits, goes to London, has a ball of a time with the family only something to come back to, Trinidad a hell of a holiday. So she can talk of sailing off the cliffs at Toco as free as a blasted bird and you can talk of reconciliation."

"Ah, poor little sister, carrying the burden alone in a backwater of a country. Give her some sympathy, Magdalene," said Jocelyn mockingly with a flip of her head and a frozen, bitter smile. What was it about Jocelyn that reminded him of the bare branches of the purple poui still in Adam Smith's square after a night of April rain had swept away the flowers? Or of La pique jagged, disappearing with the patient scoop away of quarried stone? "John, you persuade her, we from the heights of success are all sorry for poor little Melina, poisoning us all with smoke, dropping cigarette ash on the floor I polished this morning, and Mama hardly dead yet but dear, sweet, long-suffering Melina is bubbling with hellfire like the Devil's Woodyard in person."

"Not me, nuh, not me," John laughed. "You'll never catch me with that one, Jocelyn. I know the sisters. Do you think I wish to jump in and

have you all turn on me afterward? I don't know a damn thing about all
this back history, and to tell you the truth I'm not about to find out. Not
intervening, man. Know my wife too well."

"But she's right, isn't she?" Melina asked him sharply. "Or are you on
Jocelyn's side, too, like Magdalene? John, do you love me or *don't* you?"

"Choices again. How we all come back to it? You know, Melina, with
all this about Jocelyn and Toco, there isn't much difference between you
two. What, Aunt Rachael, don't tell me that you're going to break down
now? Here, take my handkerchief." Magdalene took it out from the pocket
at her side. The handkerchief came out with a rosary and a little flat blue
book with a gaudy cross on it. The handkerchief itself had a corner of
lace that Rodney had not expected. It was as though Magdalene was
taking off her veil.

"Well," she added, "must be about hurts we hold on to eroding what
we were created to be."

"Don't make me laugh! Aunt Rachael, why are you crying now that
it's all over? And who is asking dear Sister Magdalene to inflict her heaven
and her hell on the rest of us? John, I demand an answer."

"Of course I love you, Melina, what do you wish, another grand dec-
laration?" John asked her.

"I haven't heard you say that ever since Peter was born. Do you know
what that man said then, *him!*" Melina pointed with her thumb at John.
"He said there are two things we always promised that we'd do: go in a
flat-bottomed boat up the mangrove swamps, watch the birds come in at
sunset, and go down the hidden caves behind Wright's jade plant place
to see the blind ugly oilbirds belonging to another evolution. Why did
you tell me that, John?"

"Why, why, why? My God, Melina, do you realize that since Peter was
born you've spoken to me only in question marks? We had promised to
see both. Satisfied?"

"No, I'm not. Why then, John? Why did you bring it up then. Why
pick on those?"

"Why not? Lord, you do keep things in your craw, eh. I can't even
recall when I said it. You're really at your best this evening. What next
will you remember?" John stretched his long legs. His socks were an
absurd green above black shoes smudged with the red dirt of the cemetery. Jocelyn had made the cushions when she came, yellow, brown,
orange, scattering them on Anna's morris couch.

"Because you never reply to me, that's why."

"I'd reply if I knew what the question really was, but since I don't,
silence is the best line of defense. Seriously, Melina, if you'll tell me what
you want me to say, I'll say it, anything to make you happy." He moved
his foot around in little circles.

"That's new, hear him?" Melina raised her voice. "Someone wants to make me happy, to take me on a boat for a romantic ride into the sunset to see birds flying in with the darkness, or down beautiful caves to watch birds that go blind with the light. How about that, huh?"

"You really are a plague, Melina," Rachael whooped between her tears, "a, a, p-p-plague. When it isn't Jocelyn, it is Magdalene; when it is not Magdalene, it is John. Can't you behave yourself for once?"

"Can't you behave yourself for once," Melina mimicked. "That again. I'm the only one left to misbehave. You won't know what Jocelyn does since she's quit, the bastard, and Magdalene became a saint at one fell swoop. It's easy for them to behave."

"It's not, you know," Magdalene said irritably. "Why do you always tell me that, Melina? As if it was I who were buried?"

"Because you are, that's all. Jocelyn is at least tempted by Toco and your free will. You," Melina laughed again, "what the hell do you know of anything? Let's face it, Magdalene. You ran away from it, shrouded yourself in yards of righteousness, and left the rest of us to deal with the real world, the flesh and the devil. Talk about first-class selfishness. First-rate *Sister* Mary Magdalene, I had to live with it. Behave yourself, Melina, don't shame Magdalene, remember we have a nun in the family now. As if I asked for that either, that or the blasted wedding when anyway, Jocelyn, your champagne ran out before half the guests came to the house and I spent my time terrified that I'd trip up a veil stretching from here to Frederick Street. I couldn't even use the thing for mosquito netting afterward!"

"All right, Melina, you wish to have it out with someone," Magdalene said. "Right, I joined the convent. Right, I left home at nineteen, left you and Jocelyn with Mama. Good. Accept. No problems. But if you think that arranged everything for me you must be jokin'! What do you think? You go in, put on a veil—you called it yards of righteousness—and that's it. Well, it isn't, eh, just that, not contesting, but, ah, forget it, Melina, we're in for one of your storms. Mama is dead and even if there wasn't eternal life she is happier where she is, and I say to myself, God, I believe in the resurrection, but even if it didn't happen I'd believe in the greatness of death."

"I knew Anna had something up her sleeve yet," Rachael whispered to him. "What do you think she was looking up wide awake out of the coffin for? And that awful spiteful thing she had us read. This is what she really wanted. Cats and dogs and everyone at everybody's throats. Poor John, I hope Melina isn't going to repeat that Stanley business, and, Rodney, I swear that when I hear Magdalene almost saying that the Lord didn't rise from the dead, I wish we could call old Finbar Ryan back to hear her. He'd straighten her out in *one*. Talk

about pagans walking around in veils and calling themselves nuns.
Sisters my eye."

> $ Sisters drunk mass wine-coconut devil water rum and
> coconut water
> $ Whores treading corn between candles
> Cemetery closing in
> Working $ overtime
> White Jesuits $

The Battle with Language

GRACE NICHOLS

As a writer I feel strongly multicultural and very Caribbean. If I have to describe myself as coming from a particular part of the world, I like to think of myself as coming from the Caribbean. Most of my work is created out of that culture which embraces so much. The Caribbean has one of the richest, most fascinating cultures one can hope to find anywhere; though this may sound like a cliché, for me it is true. It has its poverty and backwardness, but just thinking about all the different cross-influences and mixtures—Amerindian, African, Asian, European—gets me high.

I am constantly amazed at how much of Africa still remains in the Caribbean, considering the disruption caused by slavery and the European colonizing experience. The presence and influence of the indigenous people are evident in the region too. I feel a kinship with the Amerindian people of Guyana, for example, with their myths and legends. I have used some of their legends in my children's stories. The Guyana hinterland is very much in my psyche so that part of me feels a bit South American and the incredible destruction of the Aztec/Inca civilization also informs our heritage.

Then of course there are the influences of the different immigrant groups who came out to the Caribbean: East Indians, Chinese, and Portuguese. My voice as a writer has its source in that region. I feel a concern for the Caribbean and its economic and political future.

> Wake up Lord
> brush de sunflakes from yuh eye

Back de sky a while Lord
an hear dis mudder-woman cry
on behalf of her pressure-down people

God de Mudder / God de Fadder / God de Sister
God de Brudder / God de Holy Fire . . .

As a writer and poet I am excited by language, of course. I care about language, and maybe that is another reason why I write and continue to write. It is the battle with language that I love. When writing poetry, it is the challenge of trying to create or chisel out a new language that I like. I like working in both standard English and Creole. I tend to want to fuse the two tongues because I come from a background where the two worlds, Creole and standard English, were constantly interacting, though Creole was regarded, obviously, as the inferior by the colonial powers when I was growing up and still has a social stigma attached to it in the Caribbean.

I think this is one of the main reasons why so many Caribbean poets, including myself, are now reclaiming our language heritage and exploring it. It is an act of spiritual survival on our part, the need (whether conscious or unconscious) to preserve something that is important to us. It is a language that our foremothers and forefathers struggled to create and we are saying that it is a valid, vibrant language. We are no longer going to treat it with contempt or allow it to be misplaced.

I do not think the only reason I use Creole in my poetry is to preserve it, however. I find using it genuinely exciting. Some Creole expressions are very vivid and concise and have no equivalent in English. And there comes a time when, after reading a lot of English poetry, no matter how fine (I love the work of many English poets), I want something different; something that sounds and looks different to the eye on the page and to the ear. Difference, diversity, and unpredictability make me tick.

I have a natural fear of anything that tries to close in on me, whether it is an ideology or a group of people who feel that we should all think alike because we are all women or because we are all black, and there is no room to accommodate anyone with a different view.

I cannot subscribe to the "victim mentality" either, which seems to me like wallowing in "Look what they've done to us." It is true that black women have carried much more than their share of hardships along the way. But I reject the stereotype of the "long-suffering black woman" who is so strong that she can carry whatever is heaped upon her. There is a danger of reducing the black woman's condition to that of "sufferer," whether at the hands of white society or at the hands of black men. I know too many black women with a surmounting spirit and with their own particular quirkiness and sense of humor to know that this is not true.

In the early days when I first started reading my poetry, a few women who wanted to know why I didn't write about or focus on the "realities" of black women in Britain—racial discrimination, bad housing, unemployment—and this poem came as a response to that:

Of Course When They Ask for Poems
About the 'Realities' of Black Women

they want a little black blood
what they really want
at times
is a specimen
whose heart is in the dust

a mother-of-sufferer
trampled/oppressed
they want a little black blood
undressed
and validation
for the abused stereotype
already in their heads

or else they want

a perfect song

I say I can write
no poem big enough
to hold the essence

of a black woman
or a white woman
or a green woman

and there are black women
and black women

like a contrasting sky

of rainbow spectrum

touch a black woman
you mistake for a rock
and feel her melting
down to fudge

cradle a soft black woman
and burn fingers as you trace
revolution
beneath her woolly hair

and yes we cut bush
to clear paths
for our children
and yes we throw sprat
to catch whale
and yes
if need be we'll trade
a piece-a-pussy
than see the pickney dem
in the grip-a-hungry-belly

still there ain't no
easy belly category

      for a black woman
      or a white woman
      or a green woman

and there are black women
strong and eloquent
and focused

and there are black women
who always manage to end up
frail victim

and there are black women
considered so dangerous
in South Africa
they prison them away

      maybe this poem is to say

that I like to see
we black women
full-of-we-selves walking

      crushing out
      with each dancing step

the twisted self-negating
history
we've inherited

crushing out
with each dancing step

I am also very interested in mythology. It has created certain images and archetypes that have come down to us over the ages, and I have observed how destructive, however inadvertently, many of them have been to the black psyche. As children we grew up with the all-powerful male white God and the biblical associations of white with light and goodness, black with darkness and evil. We feasted on the world of Greek myths, European fairy tales and legends, princes and princesses, Snow Whites and Rapunzels. I am interested in the psychological effects of this on black people even today and how it functions in the minds of white people.

Once when I was taking part in a discussion on this subject, a white woman in the audience made the point that darkness was frightening. Children were afraid of the dark because they couldn't see in the dark. I agreed with her. I myself put on lights if I am feeling a bit uneasy for some reason. But what the white imagination has done is to transfer this terror of darkness to a whole race. I am fascinated, to say the least, how whenever white people—whether writer, painter, or dramatist—portray an evil, ugly, or monstrous character they inevitably make that character black. It is as if the white imagination cannot help depicting this because it is the image that comes to mind in relation to evil or terror.

I think that white people have to be aware of this in their psyche and question whether they want to be trapped in this clichéd vision.

I feel we also have to come up with new myths and other images that please us.

Although *The Fat Black Women's Poems* came out of a sheer sense of fun, of having a fat black woman doing exactly as she pleases, at the same time she brings into being a new image—one that questions the acceptance of the "thin" European model as the ideal figure of beauty. The Fat Black Woman is a universal figure, slipping from one situation to the other, taking a satirical, tongue-in-cheek look at the world:

Shopping in London winter
is a real drag for the fat black woman
going from store to store
in search of accommodating clothes
and de weather so cold

Look at de frozen thin mannequins
fixing her with grin
and de pretty face salesgals

exchanging slimming glances
thinking she don't notice

("The Fat Black Woman Goes Shopping")

Literature is not static. The myths of the old were created by the poets
of old and remain powerful sources of imagination, to be drawn on again
and again. Odysseus in his rolling ship did a lot for mine as a child and
I am grateful. But we have to keep on creating and reshaping. We have
to offer our children something more than gazing at *Superman 1*, *Superman
2*, *Superman 3*, and possibly *Superman 4*, so that when they look out on
the world they can also see brown and black necks arching toward the
sun so they can see themselves represented in the miraculous and come
to sing their being.

In *i is a long memoried woman*, the woman is something of a mythic
figure. She breaks the slave stereotype of the dumb victim of circumstance.
She is a woman of complex moods who articulates her situation with
vision. Her spirit goes off wandering, meeting women from other cultures. She is a priestess figure and employs sorcery when necessary.

I require an omen, a signal
I kyan not work this craft
on my own strength
alligator teeth
and feathers
old root and powders
I kyan not work this craft
this magic black
on my own strength
Dahomney lurking in my shadows
Yoruba lurking in my shadows
Ashanti lurking in my shadows
I am confused
I lust for guidance

("Omen")

It is not easy talking about myself as a writer. I believe that my feelings
on a range of issues come out much better in my poems and writings.
Poetry, thankfully, is a radical synthesizing force. The erotic is not separated from the political or spiritual, and a lot gets said.

It is difficult to answer the question "Why I Write" because writing is
not a logical activity. It is a compulsion like a disease that keeps you alive.
At a simple conscious level I would say that I write because writing is
my way of participating in the world and in the struggle for keeping
language and the human spirit alive (including my own). It is a way of
sharing a vision that is hopefully life-giving in the final analysis.

In writing, I feel that I have some control over the world, however erroneous this might be. I do not have to accept things as they are but can recreate the world a little more to my own liking. I do not have to accept a world that says that the black woman is invisible, for example, or a world that tries to deny not only black women but women on the whole the right to participate in the decision making necessary for change and an improved quality of life. I can introduce my own values. I can write against stereotypes as I have done with *The Fat Black Woman's Poems*.

Questions such as "How do you see yourself? Do you see yourself as black first or as a woman first?" sometimes asked by other women freeze up the brain and become irritating because they seem like arbitrary cross-examination. It is not something you even sit down and think about—"Now am I black first or am I woman first?" These make up one's essential being, whatever that might be. "Am I a committed writer?" I think I am committed to my own truth. "Which is more important to me, the women's struggle or the fight against neocolonialism and political repression?" I can't compartmentalize myself. I hate all forms of oppression. South Africa makes me feel chronically ill inside. I can't shut it out. And if a woman is being oppressed, say by her man at home, then that personal immediate oppression is just as hateful as the one by the state.

"Do I write as a 'woman' or simply as a writer?" I don't really know but I believe that my perceptions cannot help but be influenced by my sex, race, cultural background, and a heap of other factors, like my childhood. Life is a mystery to me too. I am still working toward clarification. Maybe if I had all the answers I wouldn't be writing at all.

How I Became a Writer

LORNA GOODISON

I was born on August 1, 1947, in Kingston, Jamaica. I am the eighth of nine children. I was born in the heart of the city of Kingston at 117 Orange Street. Actually, I was born at the Victoria Jubilee Hospital, or "lineen" as it was and is known to Jamaican people. It was only a few years ago that I discovered that "lineen" meant "lying in," which was something that genteel ladies did when they took to their rooms to give birth. Lineen was and is the public maternity hospital where poorer women go to give birth, often lying more than one to a bed. This double language, which is part of my heritage, is one of the main influences on my work as a poet and sometime short-story writer.

The yard I grew up in had no trees. It had one breadfruit tree that had no head. A flying sheet of zinc had decapitated it during the 1952 hurricane so it was a tree trunk that led up to nothing. The lack of trees in my early memory gave me a great love for things pastoral. When I first went to visit my mother's country—that is, the district of Harvery River in the parish of Hanover—I was overwhelmed by the beauty of trees and green things growing. As soon as I could have a say in where I lived, I chose to live outside of cities. I fell in love with the country, especially with the river in which I had my first true baptism. The family river, Harvery River (town and river) is named for my mother's family. I remember the feeling of being completely submerged in a deep body of water for the first time as opposed to standing under the shower in Kingston.

The one flaw in the country was that there were no electric lights. When night fell I became hysterical. I had never seen darkness so dark. During the day the river would flow in a graceful movement outside the house, the trees would offer up whatever fruit or flowers they bore, kindly, easily. The breadfruit trees had heads and bore full-scale backed fruit that when roasted tasted better than any bread. There was even one breadfruit tree that grew about two feet up from the ground, then proceeded to extend itself horizontally to form a seat for children to sit on. All this was during the day. When night fell and my aunt and cousins tried to ward off the thick darkness with some pot-bellied kerosene lamps, I was terrified. That wonderful light green and white foaming river had turned into a hissing serpent, and the friendly trees that dropped mangoes and plums and flowers were now moaning and shaking their heads, sobbing in the night wind in the darkness.

From that time, I was obsessed with light and darkness. No matter how splendid something was, if it was shrouded by darkness, it was terrifying. I longed for light; I would press my knuckles against my eyeballs till two spots of copper-colored light appeared there, then I'd pray to fall asleep before they went out.

I never knew anybody who was a poet when I was growing up. I thought all poets were men and that they wrote poems like "The Daffodils." I grew to resent that poem. I thought it was stupid to go on so much about a flower I had never seen. Something in me wanted to read about people and things that were familiar to me. Growing up, I read comics, the *Daily Mirror*, a weekly British tabloid with a saffron-yellow cover, which my sister (who was a journalist) bought, and I read some of her books, which I was not supposed to read.

For example, I read most of James Baldwin's *Go Tell It on the Mountain* when I was nine or ten, and I read Truman Capote's *Other Voices Other Rooms*, but I hated his description of the black maid. And I read and grew to love poems for their danger and power, especially the poems in *The Oxford Book of Modern Verse* edited by W. B. Yeats. I found "In a Green Night" by Derek Walcott when I was attending high school and read it. For the first time I began to see poetry that seemed powerful and spoke about themes and landscapes that were familiar to me. I also read Paule Marshall's *Brown Girl, Brownstones*, which had a great influence on my late teenage years. Selema was the heroine I most identified with in all the books I had read.

I never thought I would be a poet. When I was very young I wanted to be a floorwalker in a department store because it seemed to me that floorwalkers could just walk up and down and think their own thoughts and get paid for doing that. That's what I wanted to do—to think my own thoughts.

I wrote my first poem when I was eight or nine. It was about rain and its regenerative qualities. It contained such lines as "the trees lift their heads again, after a shower of rain." I did not keep it or any of the early poems I wrote because I never thought I would be a poet, but many of my poems contain references to rain. My first collection, *Tamarind Season*, was my attempt to release some of the ideas and experiences that had been backing up on me in my late teenage years. Many of those poems are a crying out. Rabindranath Tagore, whose work I found and was drawn to when I worked on the bookmobile for the school library service, speaks about souls that have been wounded trying to find expression through poetry. Jewish mystics speak of seven bands binding the heart. In my case, *Tamarind Season* was the release of at least one band binding my heart.

I still was not sure I could call myself a poet even after *Tamarind Season* came out. I wasn't sure what poets did except write poems occasionally, and there was a part of being a poet I did not like. I was beginning to sense that to be a poet you had to feel a lot more than most people and you could never be completely or fully absorbed in whatever you were doing because you were always writing a poem in your head.

I was brought up in the high Anglican church, which was really Henry VIII's excommunication step away from the Roman Catholic church. All the ceremony and the ritual, incense and candles (which I loved) were part of my childhood church experience, but I always had the feeling that something big should happen to me in church and it never did. The most exciting thing that happened in my church in all the time I went there was the day the minister lay down across the aisle of the church to illustrate to us just how laid low was that unfortunate traveler from Jerusalem to Jericho.

I always wanted a great inner soaring thing to happen to me in church. It never did, but it happened to me with poetry, and now I think much of the religion (for me literally being rebound to the source) that has come to me through Sufism has gone into my later writing. For this influence I am much indebted to the Egyptian writer Ali Darwish.

My second collection of poetry came about in a different way than *Tamarind Season*. The poem "Bedspread for Winnie Mandela" showed up a small clipping from the *New York Times* floating on the ground as I was walking somewhere. The South African police had done the ultimate— they had arrested a bedspread for daring to be in the colors of the African National Congress. It became a poem. The other poems were often like endlessly taking dictation, making sure I was accurately taking down what I heard. I think all those poems speak to the themes of love and justice, and quite a few of them speak to the conditions of women.

My third collection, *Heartease*, began to stretch me as a poet. I remember being taken over by some of those poems to the extent that I was glad I was not driving a car. These poems are about the internal journeying to a place where the heart can find a measure of ease. Some of these poems, such as "Ceremony for the Banishment of the King of Swords," attempt to heal people who make bad choices in love.

I remember writing the last lines of "Heart Ease New England" in my room at the Bunting Institute, Radcliffe, in May 1987. I was writing from a gracious place inside me, looking out on the Bunting yard, thinking that spring was coming, that I had had a very good year in Boston, that I would be going home soon to Jamaica, and that *Heartease* (the manuscript) was finished. It was a great feeling.

Months later, when I realized I had not written anything after *Heartease*, I began to feel troubled. Was *Heartease* my last book? Did God take me seriously because I had written another poem called "My Last Poem Again" in which I was moaning about the tyranny of poetry? For many months nothing happened. Then I found myself reading a book by the theologian Henri Nouwen on the desert fathers and mothers, and I was overcome with the idea that mortals could possess a peace so deep, a peace born of extended union with silence, that it could be transferred to others. This gave birth to a poem called "Benediction of a Desert Mother," and that seemed to clear the way for the collection I am now working at. It is called "Amber" at this point, but I don't know what it will be called in the end. This work reassures me that there is still more truth and light to be revealed from the word. On my good days I think I can call myself a poet, and I think poets are the ones who should write about truth and light.

An African family awakens to find their home ablaze as they are ambushed by "ruffians on their prey." From *Poems on the Abolition of the Slave Trade*, 1809, by James Montgomery, James Grahme, and E. Benger.

Managing the Unmanageable

MARLENE NOURBESE PHILIP

European thought has traditionally designated certain groups not only as inferior but also, paradoxically, as threats to their order, systems, and traditions of knowledge. Women, Africans, Asians, and aboriginals can be said to comprise these groups and together they constitute the threat of the Other—that embodiment of everything which the white male perceived himself not to be. Where the latter was male, the Other was female; where he was rational, the Other was irrational; where he was controlled, the Other was uncontrolled—a slave to his or her emotions; where he was white and therefore the repository of all that was good, the Other was black and the repository of all that was evil. If left unchecked, western European thought suggests, these qualities—of the Other—could undermine the social order; for this reason these groups are considered potentially, if not actually, unmanageable. At all times they must be managed.

Historically, dealing with the unmanageable has run the gamut from the actual destruction of peoples when necessary—genocidal practices in the Americas, for instance—to management: putting the unmanageable into preordained places within society so that they can be more easily controlled.

A telling example of how management works to control that which is considered different and representative of Otherness may be seen in the early responses of European artists to the plastic arts of Africa and Oceania. Contact between the European artist and these areas of the world was a part of the colonial conquest by Europe; many works of art from Africa and Oceania were in fact acquired by Western museums as a direct consequence of colonial wars of conquest. As Hal Foster argues in "The 'Primitive' Unconscious,"[1] before contact with the art of Africa and Oceania, European art, having exhausted its traditions, was at an impasse. Contact with, and the influence of, the African and Oceanic aesthetic, particularly in the plastic arts, was indispensable to the revitalizing of European art traditions. Without these influences the modernist art movement would not have been possible.

The essentially spiritual and ritualistic nature of the African and Oceanic cultural aesthetic which the European artist either misunderstood or was uncomfortable with would eventually lead to the invention of the concept of primitivism, which became a conceptual tool to manage those very cultures and societies.

In working on the poems that comprise the manuscript *She Tries Her Tongue*,[2] I came up hard—to use a Jamaican expression, I "buck up" against the weight of Eurocentric traditions and became aware that even poetry and the way it was brought to, and taught in, the Caribbean was a way of management. I was, in fact, working in a language which traditionally had been yet another tool of oppression, a language that has at best omitted the reality and experience of the managed—the African in the New World—and at worst discoursed on her nonbeing. The challenge for me was to use that language, albeit the language of my oppression, but the only one I had, to subvert the inner and hidden discourse—the discourse of my non-being.

How does a writer who belongs to one of those traditionally managed groups begin to write from her place in a language that is not her own? How does she discover or uncover a place and language of empowerment? These were some of the questions that faced me. The power I sought was not the same power the white European male/father has used to manage, control, and destroy the other, but a power directed at controlling our words, our reality, and our experience.

"You better know your place." In the Caribbean this expression was often used to remind children of their essentially inferior position in society or to chastise someone who had been perceived to have stepped out of his or her social position. In *She Tries . . .* I set out to be unmanageable. I refused to "know my place," the place set apart for the managed peoples of the world. I intended to define my own place and space and in so doing I would come up against the role of language and the issues relating to that. I was also to discover that I could not challenge the language without challenging the canon that surrounded the poetic genre. The following is a quotation from notes I made as I worked on the poem

1. Hal Foster, *Recodings* (Port Townsend: Bay Press, 1985), p. 181.
2. Winner of the 1988 Casa de las Americas prize for poetry.

"Discourse on the Logic of Language," which contains many of the themes and issues already mentioned:

To take the poem one step further and re-embed it, re-encrust it within its context—to put it back in the mire of its origins. So in *Discourse on the Logic of Language*, the poem is sculpted out of the colonial experience—exploitation of peoples, destruction of mother tongues—to become "a work of art"—objective and, according to the canon of Literature, universal. The next step, for me, is to deuniversalize it—make it specific and particular once again. Eliot talked of the objective correlative—the arousal in the reader of the exact emotion the poet felt as *he* wrote. This assumes the existence of certain universal values that would or could prompt the reader to share with the writer *his* emotions. This assumption is never articulated and the so-called universal values were really a cover for imperialistic modes of thought and ways of acting upon the world. The patterns of culture, the images, the forms of thinking, the Literature that were being imposed around the world on different peoples were very specific to a very specific culture (Western/European), and a very specific class within that culture—they were however propounded as universal. So the little Black girl in the West Indies was supposed to conjure up the same feeling that Eliot had when he wrote of fogs and cats and Prufrock.

In *Discourse*, by cramping the space traditionally given the poem itself, by forcing it to share its space with something else—an extended image about women, words, language and silence; with the edicts that established the parameters of silence for the African in the New World, by giving more space to descriptions of the physiology of speech, the scientific legacy of racism we have inherited, and by questioning the tongue as organ and concept, poetry is put in its place—both in terms of it taking a less elevated position—moving from centre stage and page and putting it back where it belongs—and locating it in a particular historical sequence of events (each reading of such a poem could become a mini drama). The canon of objectivity and universality is shifted—I hope permanently disturbed.[3]

She Tries . . . was the result of my refusal to "know my place." Since completing that manuscript I have become aware of certain shifts. As a writer, I had been aware for some time of a reader over my right shoulder: white, Oxford-educated, and male. Over my left shoulder—in the shadows—was an old wizened and "wisened" black woman. *She Tries* . . . succeeded in pushing the reader to the right further into the shadows, and the reader over my left shoulder has emerged more clearly from the shadows into the light. *She Tries* . . . has also taught me my place.

One of the unexpected results of being unmanageable in my writing life has been that many of the poems in *She Tries* . . . have become unreadable in the traditional sense; in my being unmanageable, the poems

3. Notes from Working Journal (Ms. *She Tries her Tongue, Her Silence Softly Breaks*—a work in progress).

themselves have also become unmanageable. One aspect of allowing the poetry to become unmanageable arises from my giving in to the urge to interrupt the text. One can hazard many reasons for this urge. It may arise from a need to reflect a historical reality: the African in the New World represented a massive interruption of both the European text of the Old World and the African text of a more ancient world that had continued uninterrupted for millennia, as well as the text of the aboriginal world of the Americas and the Caribbean.

A friend with whom I raised this issue of interruption of text suggested that the urge was probably the result of Caliban/Prospero relations: wanting both to be in the space of power long dominated by the white European father *and* to return to our lost paradise.

Whatever the reason, the urge to interrupt the text is there and I have acted upon it time and again in both poetry and fiction. The result is that the poem no longer reads as it ought to; it becomes unreadable both because of the interruptions and because so many things happen on the page or pages, as the notes from the working journal reveal. However, in making the poem unreadable, it becomes a more accurate description and expression of what our experience as managed peoples in the Caribbean has been. The African's encounter with the New World was catastrophic and chaotic: how does one and how ought one to manage such an experience in poetry or in writing? How does one make readable what has been an unreadable experience?

The form of the poem becomes not only a more true reflection of the experience out of which it came, but also as important as the content. The poem as a whole, therefore, becomes a more accurate mirror of the circumstances that underpin it.

Another unexpected result of the attempt to allow oneself to be unmanageable within and without the text was the eruption of the body into the text—tongue, lips, brain, penis—the body insisted on being present throughout *She Tries* . . . .

When the African came to the New World she brought with her nothing but her body and all the memory and history which body could contain. The text of her history and memory was inscribed upon and within the body which would become the repository of all the tools necessary for spiritual and cultural survival. At her most unmanageable, the slave removed her body from control of the white master, either by suicide or by maroonage—running away, where the terrain allowed, to highlands, there to survive with others as whole people and not as chattels. Body, text, history, and memory—the body with its remembered and forgotten texts is of supreme importance in both the larger History and the little histories of the Caribbean. I believe this to be one of the reasons why the body erupted so forcibly and with such violence in the text of *She Tries* . . . .

There is a second reason, which has to do with the fact that for the black woman a double managing is at work. Historically for her there was the management of the overseer's whip or gun, but there was the penis, symbol of potential or real management in male-female relations. Today the overseer's whip has been replaced in some instances by more subtle practices of racism; the penis continues, however, to be the symbol of control and management, used to cow or control. The ultimate weapon of management and control for the female is rape; this knowledge and the consequential fear is, I believe, latent in all female bodies.

In the poem "Universal Grammar," I appended an excerpt from *Mother's Recipes on How to Make a Language Yours, or How Not to Get Raped*: "Slip mouth over the syllable; moisten with tongue the word. / Suck Slide Play Caress Blow—Love it, but if the word / gags, does not nourish, bite it off—at its source— / Spit it out. / Start again" I was suggesting in this excerpt from the imaginary *Mother's Recipes* the link between linguistic rape and physical rape, but more than that the potential for unmanageability even when faced, as a woman, with that ultimate weapon of control—rape. *Mother's Recipes* was an attempt to place woman's body center stage again as actor and not as the acted upon.

Working through the poems contained in *She Tries* . . . resulted in an epistemological break for me; my relationship with Western European traditions, particularly as they relate to literature, and systems of knowledge has been irrevocably ruptured. The understanding of how the underpinning of knowledge is often nothing but power—power of the white European male to define his knowledge as absolute—was a painful but liberating experience. An excellent example of this exercise of power may be seen in how the roots of classical Greek civilization, which are embedded in Afro-Asiatic civilizations, have been erased over the centuries. Where this erasure was not possible, the African source of Greek civilization, most notably Egypt, was Europeanized and Egyptians make to appear light-skinned and a part of Mediterranean rather than African culture. The rupture to which I have referred has resulted in my becoming an epistemological orphan; how to construct a replacement for the old epistemological order is a task which is both challenging and difficult but which is essential.

All of this, however, brings me back to language and power, for as Noam Chomsky, the linguist, has noted, language is nothing but a dialect with an army. Someone, at some time, established the linguistic rules that govern us today: that the noun should agree with the verb, for instance, and that person had the power to enforce that rule. This is not to say that we should ignore those rules; in some instances they are useful. But understanding that the foundation of much European thought and knowledge systems is power enables us all to be more unmanageable. For those of us who use the demotic languages of the Caribbean—dialect— to express our reality in writing or in speech, an understanding of the underpinnings of power enables us to challenge what has been until very recently the linguistic hegemony of Western Europe in the Caribbean.

We, the managed, historically the object and focus of much management activity, often think of ourselves as marginalized in relation to the larger culture—Western European or American. Often, however, the words we use to describe ourselves collude in our management. To think of ourselves as marginal or marginalized is to put us forever at the edge and not center stage. The word *margin*, however, has another meaning which I prefer to think of when it is used as a descriptive term for managed peoples—it also means frontier. And when we think of ourselves as being on the frontier, our perspective immediately changes. Our position is no longer one in relation to the managers, but we now face outward, away from them, to the undiscoverd space and place up ahead which we are about to uncover—spaces in which we can empower ourselves.

From margin to frontier—is a deceptively simple act requiring no movement or change, but only the substitution of one word for another. It is an important and liberating first step, this substitution of words and meanings, but to make that authentic leap from margin to frontier demands nothing less than a profound revolution in thinking and metamorphosis in consciousness.

As women writers we each attempt in our own way to write and rewrite our experiences; in my own case it often is the Caribbean experience in its myriad forms. In this act of writing we too are being unmanageable, for the managers have not traditionally thought of us as thinkers, or writers, or keepers of memory and history. By far the majority of Caribbean women remain hewers of wood and drawers of water, women who, like my mother, grew strong out of a severe lack of choice. These women, by being in their own way unmanageable, have allowed us to stand on their backs to provide us with more choice than they had. In changing the margin to frontier, we continue the long tradition of unmanageability, which has permeated our experiences here in the New World and, I hope, hasten the demise of all managers and systems of management.

Finding My Voice

AFUA COOPER

The act of writing came naturally to me. As a child I loved books. In books I could live other lives, be like the heroines in the books, and live in their enchanted world. Books expanded my horizons and released my imagination.

I first came to literature by listening to stories, riddles, and jokes being told by family members and neighbors. The culture in which I spent the first eight years of my life was an oral one (there was no television) and storytelling was one of the principal forms of entertainment. An uncle, for instance, used to tell duppy stories.[1] From him we learned of the rolling calf, the three-foot horse, and the old hige.[2] He told these stories with great embellishment: speaking like the duppy, behaving like the duppies. Needless to say, when I was a child, these stories filled me with great fear, but I remember to this day how fascinated I was by them.

An aunt narrated 'Nancy stories while a younger cousin would tell us the notorious "big boy" stories far from the ears of grown-ups.[3] My parents, aunts, and other family members and neighbors told us factual stories, myths, and legends about my own family. Through an aunt I learned of my great-grandmother who was famous (or infamous) for using

---

1. Duppy: Jamaican for ghost
2. The rolling calf, the three-foot horse, and the old hige are monster characters in duppy stories. The rolling calf breathes fire from his mouth and pulls a long iron chain with one of his hind legs. The three-foot horse is a terrifying horse with three feet. The old hige is an old evil woman who comes out of her skin, puts it aside, and flies away to do bad magic.
3. 'Nancy is a derivative of Anansi. Other forms are 'Nansi and Anancy.

her head to butt (in Jamaica we say "buck") anyone she had a physical fight with. I found this story so fascinating that I used to ask my aunt to tell it to me over and over again. Later I learned that my family's history and legends were woven into the general history of the district where I was born and spent my early years. From my elders I also learned national history. It was my paternal grandmother who first told me of the 1938 riots that took place in Frome and all over the island.[4]

In Kingston, where I moved at age eight, the forms of entertainment were different. There was television even though the aunt and uncle I lived with did not own one. But my aunt and uncle had a shop, and every evening men from the neighborhood gathered there to play dominoes, ludo, and other games. After these games, the conversation invariably turned to politics, world affairs, and so on. The men (and the women, who inevitably joined in) argued back and forth with great passion. Listening to them reinforced the sense I had already developed for words, language, and riddims.[5]

The church, too, played a role in my literary development. At Sunday School we had to memorize Bible texts, discuss their meaning, and recite them at the beginning of service. In Sunday School class I developed a love for the Psalms. The church service itself, the preaching, the singing with the handclapping, the playing of the tambourines and the organ, had an exhilarating effect on me. During religious holidays the appropriate dramas were enacted. I was usually an angel, a wise man, or a disciple. For such occasions lines, songs, and verses had to be memorized by the actors. Not only did participation in these dramas enhance my self-confidence but it also instilled in me a love for drama, poetry, song, and the written word. I still cherish that background, even though I am no longer a churchgoer, for its rich oral and literary influence. Rastafari tradition and culture with its symbology and imagery has also influenced my work.

I started writing poetry in primary school. One of the first pieces I wrote was on Jamaican national heroes. This was not a coincidence given my love for history and biography. During high school I was given a lot of encouragement for my poetic endeavors though I never really thought that I could be a writer. I did not know of anyone who made her living as a writer. I think my ambition then was to study history and literature in some postsecondary setting but I was not sure. What I knew for certain was that I would write no matter what.

I had a solitary teenage life. Poetry, the reading and writing of it, helped

4. Frome is a town in the parish of Westmoreland in Jamaica. At Frome sugar estate in 1938 workers demonstrated against their working conditions and the cost of living. Several were eventually shot and killed by soldiers who were called in to put down the riot.
5. Riddims: Jamaican for rhythms

me survive my adolescence. Poetry was my exorcist, my therapist, my witch doctor.

On coming to Canada I continued to write. Again, writing served as a survival tool. My immigrant experience brought with it a new urgency. I started to read my work publicly. Poetry in its printed form can sometimes be very restricted. Through reading I was able to lift the words from the paper and release them. Many of my poems are oral as opposed to literary. While writing them I hear distinct riddims and chants. Other poems are written with a literary bent. At times both these aspects of the art are represented in many of my pieces.

I can say I write because I am a black immigrant woman living in a white, male-dominated, racist, and classist society. But I write primarily because of a spiritual compulsion which demands that I put pen to paper and open my mouth and chant. I would write regardless of where in the world I lived and who I was. Certainly what I write has a lot to do with my sex, race, and status. These factors definitely inform my worldview.

Three main energies are evident in my work. These are the lyrical, the spiritual, and the historical.

Sometimes when I compose a poem it sounds like a song charged with riddims. Some of my poems, for example, Marie Joseph Angelique and Christopher Columbus, are part song and part poem.[6] In many of my pieces the boundaries between the poem and the song are unpatrolled. I never consciously set out to break down the barriers between poetry and song, but the more I write the more I see what my subconscious is doing. This points to the fact that we as Africans in the New World never lost the essence of our cultural heritage, which I believe is coded in our genes, because in African villages poetry was sung, recited, and chanted. The Griots of West Africa are today a living example of this tradition.[7]

By spiritual I mean delving into the inner consciousness. This consciousness provides me with imageries and symbols that manifest themselves in my work. Poems like "The Upper Room" and "She Dance" are filled with biblical and orisha imageries.[8]

> Baptism of fire
> baptism of fire
> baptism with your voice Mahalia
> as you take me to the Upper room to meet my Lord.
> HalleJah![9]

6. These poems are in my new book of poetry, *Womanpoem* (forthcoming).
7. Griots (pronounced gree-o) are West African "bards" who recite from memory stories about important historical events, natural phenomena, great families, and even lesser ones. These stories take the form of the epic poem and are always performed.
8. From *Womanpoem*.
9. Ibid.

My love for history came from listening to my own family history. In my later life I realized that the country I lived in was once colonized (it still is) and that I belonged to a race that was enslaved and despised. I was filled with a thirst to know more about myself, my family, my country, my race, and, later on, my gender. History presented itself as the medium through which to discover these things. Poems such as "Roots and Branches" and "The Underground Railway" are examples of my using history as a rich poetic source. The following is from "Roots and Branches":

> I hear that Congo Nancy
> my grandfather's mother, was
> black as coal and she was
> a fighter, a warrior woman who used
> her forehead to butt her adversary
> yes, she was Nanny's daughter herself.

And from "The Underground Railway":

> Harriet Shepherd had enough of slavery. She gathered her five children, seized massa carriage and horses and rode to freedom.[10]

I consider myself to be not only a poet but a cultural and community worker as well. When I read and write poetry I am engaging not only in literary production but in cultural and community work as well. The plight of the poor, the status of women and children, racism, world peace, and global hunger are some of my concerns. I am also the mother of a man-child, a black male child. Because of the nature of the society I live in, being a black parent of a black child has its own particular stresses. I see discrimination in the school system against children of color and the determination of the powers that be to fail these children. Cocaine and crack have invaded our communities, and the young men in particular have fallen victim to these drugs. Unemployment in the black communities is probably the highest for any ethnic group, with the exception of native Canadians, and it is the young in our community who are most affected. As a writer, as an observer, I am responsible for giving voice to these maladies.

What do I hope to achieve in and with my poetry? To say one is working for social change has become passé these days. But I do hope through my work to make a change. There is so much pain in this world, and through my poetry I attempt to give people some hope and healing energies. For some of the pain to cease we have to have a radical reallocation

10. Ibid.

of the world's resources. I believe the meek and the poor shall inherit the earth. I realize that though I hope to change society through my work, the change has to start with me. This process has to begin with myself. On a more personal level, through my work, I hope to bring my outer and inner life into harmony and unison.

Mirror, Mirror on the Wall

CLAIRE HARRIS

The Blue Room at Marty's is hot and crowded. Smoke hangs in layers between the audience and the writers on stage. The questions are quick and probing. When the lights fail, members of the audience pass cigarette lighters back and forth in a determination to be recognized. Finally, the question comes. I can't say it's a surprise. I've been expecting it from the moment I stood up at the microphone and pointed out that if one lives in Toronto, one is a Canadian poet. To live in Alberta, however, is to be designated a prairie poet, an Alberta poet, or as in my own case, a feminist poet, a black poet, or an immigrant poet. I am all these things; but the people who use these terms, consciously or unconsciously, define areas of exclusion from the mainstream.

"What more do you want?" demanded the questioner. He went on to point out that I had eastern publishers, had been reasonably widely reviewed, had won an international award, and was involved in many areas of the literary scene in Calgary.

"What more could you possibly expect?"

It was a good question. It has made me think a great deal about Canada and why, though I have lived and worked here for twenty-two years, I still am considered an outsider. The question deserves a detailed answer.

In a nutshell, I want the horns of the dilemma on which immigrant writers are so fearfully poised to recede a little. If this is to happen, there must be some recognition that the dilemma exists. For it is inescapable;

it is inherent in any attempt by an outsider to merge with an established social construct. It is no less real because its barriers are as vague and shadowy as the dilemma itself may appear to be to those who do not face it. To put it crudely, either one must abandon personal experience and personal myth to adopt the mythology and aesthetic of the larger society, or one must accept marginalization. In either case the bedrock of personal truth is replaced with shifting sand. Unfortunately, the horns of this dilemma are sharper because the national policy of multiculturalism creates the illusion that every effort at cultural integration is being made. In fact it is merely a smoke screen, money thrown at a problem that requires education. What it does do, very effectively, is to brand the views of "others" and their work as "exotic." No challenge to the self-concept of the larger society need be taken seriously. The society is relieved of the responsibility to decode the signs and patterns of 20 percent of its people; relieved too of the responsibility to measure these expressions and the reality they illustrate against the cherished myths of the dominant group.

Let me attempt a practical example, the writing instructors "show, don't tell." A poet reads in the *Herald* that an immigrant businessman has had an arm broken while he was being forced into the police car and that far from resisting arrest, he was attempting to get assurances from the police concerning his two children, both under ten, who were in the back of his car. The judge throws the case out of court and blasts the police behavior as totally unacceptable. The day's editorials strongly support the verdict and suggest that the behavior of the police is un-Canadian. But the "immigrant poet" knows that this is merely an extreme example of the sort of psychic insult that occurs over and over again. She knows that the community is rife with such stories. She knows that few members of visible minority groups who have come into contact with the police do not suffer from a well-founded fear of incipient racism. She understands that such fears are bound to change, ever so subtly, the way one is. What the poet has personally experienced and what she has read flow together, and she begins to write.

She begins to weave the details of the incident with details of landscape embedding the poem in its Canadian setting. She addresses the poem to the general reader, the "you" of modern poetry. She challenges the vision of her humanity that forms the bedrock from which such violence arises. "Ah!" says the editor, the critic, "this is not the matter of poetry, and these are not poetic feelings." "These are not the themes of Canadian poetry," says another. "This is not poetic feeling, lyrically expressed." "Who are you writing for, or to?" she is asked.

She could, of course, point out that this particular version of the aesthetic is merely post-Wordsworthian. More important, however, is the idea that the Canadian realities of her life are acceptable only if she excises important segments of them. She is accused of a lack of lyricism and transcendence; code for a softening romanticism that would deny the strength and accuracy of her emotions. In the final analysis, what is being objected to is her assertiveness, her refusal to play the role of victim. Such poems challenge the Canadian compact: the idea that overt racism is crude and unacceptable; contempt, hatred, and attitude are private matters. The other side of the coin is that it is okay to charge that officer with violence, but it is not okay to point out the racism that is at its root. No poem can cry, "You must change your life." Such critics are not interested in the poem as object, as process, or as possibility. They are instead, though they would doubtless deny it, guardians of an ideology.

You must not think that such a poet is silenced. She is not. On the contrary, she may find a home among the large feminist press. If she is lucky, she will meet an enlightened editor, or editors; she will find a home in Commonwealth literature or in the ethnic press.

If the stars are right for her, she will become relatively well known. But she will always be hyphenated. In this society based on immigrants, where immigrants remain 20 to 30 percent of the population, she cannot expect the symbiotic relationship of ideas that ought to be possible. In fact, talent may take her a great distance, almost to the mainstream, provided she does not reveal the deepest truths about her life in Canada.

Still sitting at the typewriter, our poet is, after all, a poet. She may face the even more insidious temptation to write in a genuinely extreme manner for those political groups who welcome such work. Our poet may therefore find herself expressing values, using language in ways that are no less limiting but will win the approval, the publications, and the invitations to read. Such a situation not only limits her but forces her to adopt the caricature of impotent rage that the values, codes, and symbols of the dominant group have woven for her. Without her own truth, her own sign, she can neither reclaim nor transcend her reality. Instead, movement-cliché and positive feedback of true believer to true believer threaten to reduce all but the hardiest to cant. Because the marginalized need not be taken seriously, such work is seldom subjected to rigorous criticism, except, of course, from the point of view of its politics. Worst of all, marginalization in a particular group, say a radical women's group or a radical black group, is comfortable, especially if the politics of the moment make the group fashionable.

And a place will have been found for her. She will be appointed Jeremiah. People will say to her as they have said to me, "You must write about South Africa," or more revealing, "I'm so glad you're writing about racism and police brutality. Now I don't have to write about it."

One can, of course, refuse the offer. One can, one should, write in the desert, on the edges. There one may find sunlight or darkness, make both one's own, part and parcel of the essential humanity we all seek. But when all is said and done, our poet should be able to come in from the tundra, and speak, and be heard in her own image and her own language. She should become part of, and her realities, her values, and codes should find their legitimate place in what David Donnell in "Poetry, Music, and Ethnic Differences" in *Poetry Canada Review* calls the national landscape.

Neither in the Blue Room at Marty's nor at the First International Conference on Women Writers of the English-speaking Caribbean was there time for all this. But I should have emphasized that not publication, nor readings, nor requests for one's views, nor even prizes won make one mainstream. To quote Donnell, "Poetry and fiction still experience a considerable English pressure here, a pressure more fundamental (than discrimination), more a matter of concept." Nevertheless it is worth acknowledging that the concept is the concept of the colonizer with its historical use of dehumanizing exclusivity as one of the tools of power. As such within a national community it is an exercise in bad faith. That this practice is implicit rather than explicit does not make it any less tragic. In fact, it may hinder the thoroughgoing exploration of this subject. It is the lack of this exploration that makes it possible to consider as Canadian the works of Irish or Czechoslovakian immigrant writers and to exclude the works of visible immigrants that challenge the prevailing myths.

Miss Flori's Flowers

OLIVE SENIOR

Hand-picked flowers from the loveliest gardens.
Catering for elite gentlemen.

From Miss Flori's business card

Like the other dwellers in the lane, Delia Morales couldn't help but be aware of Miss Flori's girls. Although Miss Flori's rambling three-story establishment had its entrance on Hanover Street, and its elegant curved double staircase led directly to the second floor, where the reception area—which she liked to call the salon—was located, the girls were never allowed to come or go through the front.

Miss Flori's business was based on illusion, and the principal one was that she was running an exclusive gentlemen's club. She wasn't afraid of the law, or the police, or even being denounced by the church. She wasn't afraid of anything, for her clients (or members, as she preferred to say) included lawmakers, high-ranking police and army officers, top government officials, merchants, and professionals, well-known country planters, and even a clergyman or two—in short, all the men in society who mattered. They came openly to dine, for she served excellent meals, to drink or play cards and billiards, to sit in the library and read the English newspapers and magazines to which she subscribed as part of the service. She offered one or two rooms for overnight stays by her country members. What else went on there was nobody's business.

Miss Flori was rather like a frustrated theater director (indeed, she had had a brief and unsuccessful fling on the English music hall stage). She liked to arrange, to stage everything, to bring off surprises for her gentlemen (she would have had her girls bursting out of cakes had she thought

Excerpt from a novel in progress.

of it). Each year she staged a marvelous tableau called "The Secret Language of the Flowers," which starred all the girls (revealing more than we are prepared to do, except to say that being a talented costume designer, she prefigured Frederick of Hollywood by at least two generations). More than anything else, she had never lost the childhood habit of pretending and liked to think that she could get everyone pretending along with her. One of her most transparent pretenses was that she was part French.

Despite what she considered to be her modern outlook, for she kept up with current events (her gentlemen could tell you), she would deplore the school of contemporary theater which believes in revealing everything on stage. Miss Flori, a protector of womanhood, would never have allowed any of her girls to see anything that passes for theater today, for subtlety, decorum, and decency were her watchwords.

Like a good director, she knew that for her audience to enjoy the scene unfolding, for the illusion to be complete, the setting had to be right. That the rambling wooden structure with its windows protected and obscured from passing eyes by coolers and its front and side verandas shaded by a husky bougainvillea had in fact three entrances was a tribute to the foresight and thoughtfulness of the owner.

Miss Flori's property took up the entire corner lot, and in addition to the main entrance, there was a discreet little gate on the side street through which the shyer of her members, such as the clergymen, could pass without being seen (she amused herself by calling it the eye of the needle). At the rear of the premises, there was a gate in the high brick wall which could open wide enough to allow entrance to delivery carts or any of the gentlemen's coaches that needed to be parked off the street. The girls made their graceful entrances and exits through this back gate.

The habitués of the tenements and small craft shops on the lanes were great admirers from afar of Miss Flori's girls—and of Miss Flori herself, for that astute lady widely patronized the nearby craftsmen, employing the shoemaker, the locksmith, or the cabinetmaker whenever she wanted work done. She gave employment to the tenement dwellers when she could or interceded with one of her members to assist a bright and promising lad. She gave the children treats at Christmas and could be relied on to help out in dire emergencies. She was known as a fair but exacting employer, and even those lane dwellers she fired bore her no grudge. In a place where people were judged on the basis of how they treated others rather than what they did, Miss Flori was regarded as a benefactor, a highly respected businesswoman. Miss Flori also knew that in courting the goodwill of the yard dwellers, who included some notorious criminals, she was ensuring the protection of her property and the safety of her girls.

She did have critics, of course, the ones who plagued the whole society, such as the Warner woman, who would appear out of nowhere dressed in tattered and shapeless clothes, her head wrapped in red, her staff in her hand. From time to time she materialized on the street in front of Miss Flori's place and created a dreadful commotion. "Hearken ye dwellers of iniquity. Blood will flow on the streets when the sevens clash. Take heed. Take heed. Repent. Judgment is coming," she would scream. (The more superstitious girls, usually the ones from very strict religious homes, would take this as a reference to Miss Flori's establishment because it was number 77 and get hysterical and hide under their beds trembling in anticipation of judgment, which would arrive in the form of Miss Flori dragging them out and administering a good slap and a brandy.)

And, of course, there were the ordinary religious people (one to every tenement yard), who went to their noisy little clap-hand, tin-roofed churches every night and kept aloof of their neighbors because they were unclean (spiritually, in this context) and who stood in their yards and loudly declaimed against the den of iniquity on Hanover Street when the spirit moved them, usually to the shouts and curses and laughter of other yard dwellers. But such bad-minded shouts had no effect on the general routine at Miss Flori's.

Her girls came and went, picking their way daintily for some distance down the garbage-strewn, foul-smelling lane, and came out on to the main street some distance from Miss Flori's, for the illusion had to be maintained that none of these girls lived and worked there. They walked with one hand lifting their long skirts above the filthy mud tracks, showing off their elegant high-buttoned boots. With the other hand they held their parasols (for Miss Flori liked her flowers to be closer to hothouse camellias than tropical hibiscus) as well as tiny lace handkerchiefs soaked with Kananga Water or Khus Khus perfume, which they daintily touched from time to time to their delicate temples and noses. Crafty Miss Flori also knew that having to use the lanes kept the girls at home and out of mischief even when they weren't busy, for they so hated walking on these back streets that they left the house only out of dire necessity.

But if Miss Flori's girls hadn't been seen on these lanes, what visions of beauty, what trailing scents would the dwellers of these warrens have to tantalize them? In a world before the cinema, what inaccessible elegance would the young men who lived in wappen-bappen have to fantasize about? What ideals of womanhood would the young girls who slept curled up on the floor with eight or ten other family members to a room acquire?

It was seeing Miss Flori's girls go past the tenement from the time she was a little girl that had inspired young Delia Morales with her own dreams of beauty and with the possibilities of escaping from the yard. Not that she had harbored any dreams of becoming one of Miss Flori's girls. She would never have entertained such an elevated notion. It was obvious that Miss Flori's girls did not come out of the tenements; they were high-born ladies, every one of them. But young Delia could still copy them, their dress, their manner, and their style, for unlike the other yard dwellers, she was every bit as pale as the passing flowers were.

Miss Flori would not have dreamed of looking into the tenements either. She would have been appalled at the thought that anything good or desirable or wholesome could come out of those rank, darkened doorways, which only the vilest of creatures would choose to enter, much less live in. In any event, Miss Flori hardly needed to look. She had girls begging to be taken in, some brought by their mothers, and was able to pick and choose to fill the few places left by girls wanting to leave (very few of them) or wanting to set up on their own in other towns (as she encouraged the older ones to do) or being set up in their own little homes as the mistresses of rich men. It was also not unknown for one of her girls, especially the country ones, to find a husband among her clients, to Miss Flori's great joy, for like the headmistress of the best girls' school, she shared vicariously in her girls' achievements and was confident that the chosen one would discharge her duties as chatelaine to the most exacting standards. After all, they had been coached in that new role and given a new name and a new identity by that director of renown, Miss Flori.

Miss Flori, regretfully, would have to get rid of a girl from time to time, for her rules were as strict as those of any boarding school and she expected them to be adhered to. And there had been one or two cases she never liked to talk about, failures that brought a faraway look of sadness to her eyes, of girls who actually abandoned her home for some passing and low tradesman or worse—an early Mignonette, for example, who had run off with the sign painter who had decorated the salon with the beautiful trellises and trailing flowers. How was Miss Flori to know that in years to come he would be revered as one of the island's leading artists?

Despite her discretion, word of Miss Flori's establishment traveled by circuitous routes, satisfied flowers brought their sisters and cousins, and she had a steady stream of little seamstresses fleeing their prisons as apprentices to hard Kingston mistresses. Once a year, Miss Flori left her establishment in the capable hands of Columbine, the oldest of her girls, who, feeling like the last rose of summer, had opted for administrative duties. Miss Flori traveled for several days, by stages, until she arrived on the south coast, to take the waters at the Black River Spa.

As she went horseback riding or took soothing boat trips up and down the river and its many tributaries, she scanned the horizon for any fresh new wildflowers she might spot in these arid and unpromising surroundings. Some of her sophisticated clients had a passion for the little red-skinned St. Elizabeth girls, who were as wild and untamed and nervous as the horses that flourished on their hot savannas. Their parents were always willing for the elegant visiting lady from Kingston to take one or as many as she wanted of their spare daughters, for what purpose they never thought to inquire, and the little girls themselves were usually unbelieving of their good fortune, happy to abandon their only prospects: having babies and making cassava bammies and straw baskets and hats in the dusty yards around their wattle and daub huts for the rest of their lives (which were usually mercifully brief).

When Miss Flori arrived home with her freshly gathered bouquet, her clients would be excited by their rawness, their smell, their ignorance of everything, and the way they spoke so they could hardly be understood, their naive wonder at the new world. She would allow the older girls to take them around and show them the marvels of the city, like gas lamps and electric tramcars, allow them to act like themselves until their novelty wore off, and then begin the complete training course in being one of Miss Flori's flowers.

Miss Flori's training was as exacting as that of the modeling schools, which in later generations would pursue lofty standards, taking the raw clay of girls just like Miss Flori's from all over the island and molding them into sleek, sophisticated beauties, whose faces and bodies projected from every newspaper and television screen, billboard and barroom calendar, were what every little schoolgirl wanted to emulate.

Miss Flori's girls operated on a much smaller stage, of course. For the most part, her establishment was their world, and because they confronted their publics not from a runway where they could isolate themselves with haughty poses, not from the distancing effect of a camera lens, but usually in a one-to-one relationship, always close up, they required a deeper and more convincing education. This was the education to which Delia Morales was subjected when Miss Flori unexpectedly one day plucked her from the street exactly opposite her own back door in a part of the city where the only uncultivated flower ever known to bloom was the prickly yellow Kingston Buttercup (also known as Police Macca), which astonishingly sprouted on every bit of wasteland whenever the rains fell.

"The Uprising," a batik by Valerie Belgrave.

On Combining Batik Art and Novel Writing

VALERIE BELGRAVE

At present I am working as a batik artist and fabric designer. I am also awaiting the publication by Heinemann Books of England of my first novel, *Ti Marie*. The novel is not incidental to my work in batik, so I will talk briefly about it before exploring why I have come to be doing batik.

My artistic purpose in both writing and doing batik is a deliberate attempt to ennoble my country and its people, to promote racial tolerance, not so much by condemning racism as by promoting positive images of West Indians, and to challenge the corrosion of our psyche and culture caused by the foreign mass media, not so much by condemning it as by creating a greater self-appreciation. My method is to start with what appeals to the people, with what people can relate to, what is the least alienating to them or what is alluring in popular culture.

In the novel, I have used themes that, though generally unpopular with West Indian writers of fiction, are very popular with West Indians who read for entertainment or for escape. I chose to write a historical romance. This is a very familiar genre to us. Ironically, though, we are not familiar with seeing ourselves portrayed there, especially not with dignity and commanding respect. By using the familiar in an unfamiliar way, I have tried to heighten reality and to give us a sense of a living history in which we participated.

The history of the development of Trinidad, fortunately, lent itself to this approach because Trinidad, with its relatively short history of slavery (only fifty years), its population of free blacks and free coloreds, its direct contribution to changes in colonial administration, and its significant con-

317

tribution to the demise of the slave trade, can easily be interpreted as an area where black people experienced freedom early. The area of romance was chosen because West Indians love romances but are starved for local ones. Too often the West Indies is portrayed as a crude, basic place and love stories as bawdy and bacchanalian. I feel that by neglecting a theme the people like, by neglecting to romanticize our people, we as artists inadvertently strengthen the stranglehold of foreign popular entertainment.

In the novel I have followed the format and flavor of the typical historical romance with the deliberate aim of showing how stereotypes operate in our environment, of heightening reality by not making the circumstances so unique that they become unbelievable. The stereotype to which I refer is not that of the plantation novel. I have also deliberately created liberal white characters to ensure that in exposing the horror of slavery I do not exploit the norm, especially when dealing with Trinidad, where abuses under slavery were fairly subtle. I should point out that in the West Indies we are fed sympathetic white characters. In attempting not to stray from the prototype, I have made my hero, for example, sympathetic, but not because he is brave or strong or just because he loves his grandmother, but because he becomes politicized into our concerns.

I have also incorporated in the novel the elements that permeate my visual work. In addition to the expected strong sense of nationalism and racial pride and concern for the oppressed, I have used powerful female characters, I have emphasized the landscape, and I have combined the abstract, in this case idealism and symbolism, with the practical.

Now, how did I arrive at batik? Batik is generally considered a craft, but the distinction between art and craft is being challenged. My involvement in batik is partly aimed at contributing to that debate for I am trained as a painter. I have studied art since my high school days. This is more significant than it may appear for a West Indian because not many schools offer art or treat art seriously. In Trinidad, as in most of the islands except Jamaica, there are no art schools. I was fortunate that although my school did not take a modern approach to art or employ highly trained teachers, the teachers were concerned and farseeing and not rigid in their approach. In my high school class there were three girls, including me, who were "good" at art. The other two were, in my opinion, far better than I was. Their drawings were always perfect, whereas mine were wild, to say the least. Yet I always got the highest marks. It was embarrassing, and it was not fair. These girls were my friends. I remained puzzled about this throughout my high school career. Looking back, I can see that skill in execution is not what makes an artist but the ability to convey meaningful, personal expression. I am exceedingly grateful to those early teachers. I was also very fortunate that my parents were willing and able to buy materials for me to use because this is a serious problem for West Indians. Materials that North Americans take for granted from nursery school are expensive to us, and so the chance to work in art is open only to the fortunate. This also explains why most of our artists execute large pieces only after they have left home and gone abroad. It is not necessarily the narrowness of their vision but the lack of funds for materials. It is not surprising that our "fine art" has lagged behind our native arts. Most of our native arts, for example the steel pan, began by using discarded or inexpensive materials. Therefore, our fine art has been available only to the privileged.

After leaving high school, I studied painting at Sir George Williams University (Concordia), Montreal. This was in the late 1960s and early 1970s, and I think the time and place exerted lasting influences on my work.

At the university the approach to art was much more inclined toward the abstract than my high school training, and this was a time of tremendous social upheavals (the civil rights and black consciousness movements in North America and the mass movement for social change in my own country of Trinidad). My interest in alleviating the plight of oppressed peoples and in promoting their right to fulfillment was awakened. This interest also became part of a deeper and wider sense of the need for all people to be liberated into a higher degree of consciousness and to a sincere conviction of our common humanity.

With the latter influence, my approach to art, though never one of art for art's sake, became fully committed to art as a social force and a means of communication. With the heavy emphasis on abstract art and my new consciousness, my style of painting grew in two directions, which for a long time seemed to be in contradiction with each other. First, an exacting "pointillist" style that concentrated on color, movement, and feeling led to a series of successful paintings in acrylic on small and large canvases. These I simply called "Vibrations."

In addition to following this abstract style, I was determined to make my work relevant to my roots and ideals. I had grasped the value of abstract work to express ideas, perhaps better than representational work, yet I felt that the abstract, although acceptable to colleagues and art connoisseurs, would seem obscure to the wider audience to whom I was committed. I began working toward developing a "primitive" style that I hoped could incorporate both the abstract and the representational.

I also began to explore "naive" painting and made it the subject of my art history papers. Far from flinching at the flaws in naive paintings as I half expected I would, I found myself very moved by them. To quote from one of my university papers, "Naive painting can be described as having a general sense of simplicity, a delight in linear qualities, an almost abstract sense of form, a lack of well articulated perspective, an emphasis on shapes and flatness, a general use of rich and deep coloring as well as an insistence on covering the entire surface with a design." I believe I intuitively formed an instant bond with the "naive." This tendency can still be seen in my work in my concentration on form, my sometimes flippant treatment of exactness of representation, the boldness of my colors, and the emotive quality.

I began to do paintings with simple lines and broad areas of flat color, simplified my approach, eliminated "painterly" concerns, and concentrated on form and composition. By composition, I mean the way of putting the work together or of ordering and distributing form and space on the surface in a harmonious fashion. By form, I mean shapes that have an inner life and energy. This new approach was probably also influenced by the graphic work I was doing at the time. By contrast, it may be worth pointing out that this "naive" influence may also have affected the success of my graphic work, as can be seen in my prize-winning dry point etching *Dirge of the Indian Women*, which has very simple lines.

Although my primitive style was initially semiabstract, it became more and more recognizably representational, although different from the realism of my high school landscapes, portraits, and still lives, it was a realism that seemed more economical and directed toward form and feeling in the sense I described above. Looking back on it, I feel that at that period I was unknown to myself, preparing myself for batik. My formal training in batik lasted about an hour. I have taught myself everything that I know about it. My conscious preparation for it did not last over a long period. It may be said that I was worked on by a catalyst.

The first time I ever saw a batik was in my advanced painting class at university, when a fellow student from Singapore brought one in to show me. It was like the usual batik, stylized and static, but I was overwhelmed by its exotic quality. I do not think I said much, but I knew instantly that that medium held tremendous possibilities for me. I had no idea how to do it, and the little I had seen on a TV program seemed jumbled and confused. After I left the university I went back to Trinidad and continued painting with growing success, but I still bore the image of that batik in my mind. I happened to return to Montreal on holiday one summer, and I bought a book on batik and the tools and wax and came back home planning to begin one day. By chance, since I worked at the university, I was invited to drop in on a course in batik that was being offered at the summer school. After an hour I knew I had it down pat. I wanted to make a gift for a friend's wedding so I drew a picture and showed the teacher and said this is what I'm going to do in batik. He said to me, "That's impossible to do in batik." I took up the challenge. I did it, and by the end of the two-week summer school, I had done about three more complex pictures and sold every one at the students' turning out exhibition. That was how I started.

I should now describe the process of batik a little more closely. Batik is wax resist dyeing. The process, which is very simple in principle, entails drawing or painting with molten wax on natural fabric and then submerge dyeing of the fabric, that is, dunking and soaking the fabric in a container of dye.

For a complex picture I have first to draw the picture either directly on the fabric with something like charcoal on paper and transfer it to the fabric. Usually I use a light table so the drawing will seem more natural than if it is traced with carbon. I work out a plan for the colors on paper. Color sequence is extremely important in batik, much more than in painting because with batik each color takes on the characteristics of the former color. I therefore mix my colors on the fabric. Next I start applying the molten wax to the washed and dried fabric. This wax will retain the first color, which is almost always white. I can also use white in any other areas which I need to dye in a color that will conflict with the colors I am about to dye. Those areas can be dealt with after the fabric is dewaxed and rewaxed. Then when I am sure that I have all of this done and have not forgotten even the tiniest spot, I dye the first color. In batik one virtually cannot correct a mistake.

Once I had discovered batik I felt immediately that my style of painting was tailor-made for this medium. I saw that works that were not necessarily "painterly," that concentrated on composition, with broad areas of color, would lend themselves to that medium. I started off boldly, with "naturalistic" batik pictures as my first attempts. I found in this medium exactly what I had been searching for: the earthiness, the primitive ambience that is intrinsic to batik. If that was not enough, the mere fact that fabric is an everyday item struck me forcefully. Here was a medium that could break down the alienation that my people often displayed toward formal painting. It was a medium that could actually cross class barriers and, better yet, could be sold at prices low enough to accommodate the middle and lower income brackets.

Without further hesitation I set to work freely composing pictures with social, political, and nationalistic themes, pictures that endorsed the beauty of the island and the people and that affirmed black dignity. The medium seemed to me to capture the flavor of Trinidad.

A reviewer of my first exhibit in 1974 seemed to grasp my intent. The title of the review in the *Trinidad Guardian* was very significant. It said, "batik art, the medium is also the message." The reviewer recognized a number of important points, among them, "Trinidadian art has too long been a shadowy and shabby half sister of European art. One wonders whether the Trinidadian artist is not forcing his vision into a foreign idiom and an irrelevant medium." The reviewer spoke of the exhibition as a "vibrant departure from both traditional media and traditional themes." The reviewer also seems to have understood the significance of the choice of materials. "Dye wax and cloth are made the tools by which the artist works a truly Trinidadian atmosphere," and she saw that "our experience in the West Indies and our 'local' color needs a medium which is as much part of our experience as the subject matter. It is not sufficient to transfer local scenes to canvas. The very surface and the tools must have evolved from our multi-cultural past."

This first exhibition in batik was entitled "Batik as Craft and Art Form." It was held at the Trinidad Hilton in Port of Spain, 1974, and its theme was "Two Cultures, One People." (In Trinidad there are two major racial groups, Africans and East Indians.) The themes of the pictures emphasized racial unity and nationalism, and the fabrics were cottons and silks designed for dresses, wraps, and saris.

Recently, in addition to exhibitions, I have held and participated in many fashion shows. Sometimes I display dresses, but the most exciting part of the show to me is the wraps. I try to drape the models in styles that are reminiscent of the exotic places from which our people originated. In the last few years, too, I have been drafted into the theater to design sets and costumes for local plays. I custom design the batik fabric for the particular play. For Trinidad's Central Bank's Christmas 1987 production of an original West Indian fairy tale (*Ti Jean and Mariquite*), the set was the biggest challenge. I used three delicately colored sixteen-foot batik panels as my main stage background. By throwing lights behind the panels I was able to exploit the stained-glass effect of batik and conjure up a fairy-tale world of spires "stabbing the sky" or by dimming the lights I could achieve an effect of haunting forests, whereas with frontal lights the effect was that of architectural columns.

Since that 1974 exhibition, I have kept on experimenting with the aim of developing greater and greater control of the medium. There are many variables to be contended with in batik. In the process it has occurred to me that the two styles of my early paintings have come together in some of these experiments. I can see the discipline of my pointillist style in the painterly, detailed batik landscapes. The detailed pictures are more difficult to execute than they may appear. When doing them I have to think in a roundabout way, almost like working in the negative, retaining color but never directly painting on color. To say the least, it is a bit nerve-racking. It is also quite strenuous. In these painterly pieces I sometimes dye one piece as many as twelve or fourteen times, usually dewaxing once or twice in between. By the end the picture is not only covered with wax but with discolored wax so that it is hard to see what one is achieving. I am led on by blind faith until the unveiling, when the piece is finally dewaxed. Of course, this is what makes batik such an exciting medium to work in. The surprise at the end is always a big thrill.

In 1980 I held my biggest and perhaps my best exhibition to date at the National Museum in Port of Spain. It was clear then to me that there were three tendencies in my pictures: that is, the scenes from everyday life, the political or social commentaries, the genre and the Acadian scenes. In the Acadian landscapes the emphasis was on lushness. *The Bathers*, for example, captured three brown-skinned nudes in a pool surrounded by Trinidad's flora of wild lilies, orchids, philodendrons, bamboos, and ferns. There were several pictures with similar themes because I thought it significant to present a change from the tourist brochure stereotype. It is still all too rare to find West Indians glorifying or ennobling their native landscape and native people in a lyrical, unashamed, and positive manner.

Alongside these Acadian pieces were semiabstract political pieces such as the very large *Caribbean Explosions of '79*, which touched on many tensions of that year, including the Grenada revolution. There was also *The Eviction*, which was a comment on the destruction of squatters' shacks and the plight of the landless and homeless. There was *Wondering*, a statement on the International Year of the Child and the confusion of futureless children, and there was *The Calling*, a statement of women's struggle for equality and justice. A reviewer in the *People's Magazine* (Trinidad) of May 1980 stated in reference to *The Calling*: "Valerie is deeply concerned with women's problems universally but with particular emphasis on the Caribbean woman. In *The Calling* a woman stands symbolically nude and free calling out to all women who are oppressed by the roles and situations assigned to them by their society."

This same reviewer also commented on the attempt to give full and complimentary play to the racial characteristics of our women, which were much derided in the past. She wrote, "In order to clearly establish their Caribbean identity, characteristically large bottoms are purposely projected as part of the 'West Indian self' Valerie sees necessary for self-acceptance."

In recent years I think my pictures have been weighted toward the genre form. They have also become less semiabstract in the sense that figures are more clearly representational, but I have not as yet given up the freedom to use semiabstract approaches. My "swirling, all-embracing line," of which one reviewer wrote in the *Trinidad Homemaker Magazine* in 1974, is as much in evidence in my most recent piece on the plight of our youths (*On Rites of Passage*) as it was in an important piece from my 1985 exhibition, *On Grenada*, a lament on the Grenada tragedy of 1983.

My enthusiasm for batik as a medium remains undaunted, but I would like to indicate that I am not intrinsically prejudiced against working in other media. For although batik best captures the flavor that I need, I feel that my visual experience with batik can only serve to enhance any work I may do in another medium.

Finally, I would like to add that although I have given great emphasis to my batik pictures in this essay, the mainstay of my livelihood in batik is my utilitarian fabrics. Throughout the years I have always persisted in doing these because I feel that the fabric enhances the feel of an exhibition, helping to create a space that is in itself a sensual experience to enter. More than this, the mere presence of lengths of fabric in a display lends an informal attitude to the work, because no one is intimidated by cloth. Doing these lengths of cloth helps me to stay on a down-to-earth plane, and I find it very gratifying to contribute to the growing sense of identity and the resultant desire for self-expression in clothes evidenced by today's woman. Finally, it is great for my freedom of expression as well and a relief from the exhausting precision and the concentration required to do the complex pictures. I try not to fall victim to the bugbear of commercialism and to insist on bringing out the integrity of each design using as much raw material and dyeing as many times as necessary to make the particular piece a satisfying creation.

Thoughts on the Choice of Theme and Approach in Writing *Ti Marie*

VALERIE BELGRAVE

I wrote *Ti Marie*, a historical romance, because that genre is popular.[1] I like to think that my work appeals directly if not exclusively to the masses of people. From the start I intended that this novel would be as close as possible to others in this genre and still remain faithful to progressive ideas and reflect black consciousness. The logic of the novel will be understood intuitively by most readers. Here I will briefly describe my thoughts and intentions when I wrote it, which were not meant to distract or dissuade the reader from the pure entertainment of the novel.

In the harsh reality of slavery, a typical scenario more often than not involved a white man (the hero) and a beautiful black girl (the victim). She was his mistress or bed wench and filled in the time until he met "Miss Right," that is, "Miss White" (the heroine). Although such a story is typical, it would neither be truly romantic nor ennobling to black readers; nor would the hero be a positive white role model. But the popular reading audience sustains itself on white heroes and characters who are treated sympathetically and are forced to ignore glaring deficiencies in their personalities.

Therefore, it was necessary to treat the hero sympathetically so that he would be recognizable and, at the same time, establish and emphasize positive contrasts with the prototype. In part, the book represents a conscious effort to counteract, by use of similarity and contrast, the ills of similar popular novels. I realized that my hero could not be sympathetic

---

1. Valerie Belgrave, *Ti Marie* (London: Heinemann, 1988).

325

in the usual way. Instead, I would make him respond to the valid concerns of black people, and this would also assist in bringing these concerns to center stage.

Having made this decision, I faced the next question: how was I to find such a hero during slavery? It is difficult to conceive of such a person. I realized that I was not going to reconstruct a typical version of the past. In fact, as I stated in the preface to my book, I was going to write a fairy tale, a story that, though not attempting to change historical reality, would be an "as it might have been" or "as you like it" story. And why not? We are sufficiently familiar with the characters and characteristics of eighteenth-century slavery that we need not rehash them. In any case, in its purest form, historical romance is essentially a grown-up fairy tale, written in the spirit of a fairy tale although it sometimes reflects questionable motives and messages from the author.

I decided I would draw on the fact that it was the age of the French Revolution, radical ideas, and active abolitionist movements and that the very history and reality of Trinidad made it a land of unusual tolerance and unusual promise. Therefore, people who were the products of these circumstances could have existed and may even have met.

So why not create an entire cast of progressives, black and white? Why not allocate the villains to the background for a change? I also decided that an exploration of liberalism, idealism, and humanism (both as they relate to the island and to the characters), struggling to assert themselves in a world as inhumane as the eighteenth-century slave society, would be interesting and relevant for a modern reader. This also gave me a chance to scrutinize the relevant modern questions of the limits of liberalism and the development of revolutionary consciousness. This approach also allowed me to remove the idea of revolutionary consciousness from the negative, nihilistic, and ethnocentric mode into which it is usually cast and which distracts from its essential value and importance in the advance of the human race.

So although *Ti Marie* is set in an insistent historical reality, it is partly "a gossamer world . . . a fairy tale spun to amuse a child's fantasy." If the probing reader does not realize this, the romance may become partly incomprehensible. Like many fairy tales, it is set among beautiful people in a land of compelling beauty. It deals with some of the rudimentary stuff of fairy tales such as aristocrats, and the protagonists are essentially enchanted. But they are enchanted in a special way. It is their liberalism, their enlightenment, and even their futuristic interrelations in the given historical period that make them so.

The enchanted protagonists include innocents, liberals, rebels, radicals, visionaries, and even revolutionaries. There is a hierarchy of developed personalities in the book derived not just from a personal struggle against oppression, as in the case of Fist, or from the privileges that were enjoyed by the advantaged class such as education. Thus in spite of her limited formal education, Yei is as high in the hierarchy as is M. Louis, who is there because of his education, revolutionary zeal, and active search for truth. The absence of marked sex-role typing also shows the futuristic orientation of the characterization.

Among these characters there is a hierarchy of victims—the very title of the romance and the accompanying native rhyme ought to prepare the astute reader for this. Perhaps Tessa is the most victimized, but there are others: Diego, Elena, and the island itself. But none of the main protagonists are victims in the stereotypical sense, that is, because they have botched a struggle against oppression or because of the sadism of the villains. They are victims because of the contradictions of humanism, trying to assert itself in an inhumane world. What is important is that even if they have to go through a period of vengeful rebellion (Fist) or disillusionment (Elena), their plight leads them to political and social consciousness.

In my book I try to reinforce the concept of global humanism, which is the central point of my romance. At the same time, my authorial position is designed to avoid alienating any reader. In fact, any reader (barring literary critics, of course), who chooses to read a novel that is about a white hero and a black heroine is already predisposed, no matter how tentatively, toward liberalism. I can safely court such readers and address their best instincts in the same spirit that I have addressed them through the main protagonists. The reader is an essential ingredient in the novel. It is his or her humanness that endorses the rightness of the struggle in the novel for humanism. As the postscript shows, that struggle has met with significant if not complete success. The reader must take up the gauntlet and continue to struggle in the present.

"Rasta Queen," a batik by Sharon Chacko.

Batik: An Ancient Craft as an Expression of Contemporary Jamaica

SHARON CHACKO

Batik is the ancient craft of resist dyeing of fabric, involving the application of fluid substances such as wax, cassava, or bean paste and half-fluid mud, which solidify on the cloth, rendering it impervious to dye. Although it is one of the most widespread techniques of fabric decoration, many are ignorant of the process.

In wax resist dyeing, designs are created on cloth by applying molten wax with a brush or tjanting (Indonesian metal pipe) before the cloth is immersed in a dye bath for a set period. Only the unwaxed areas are dyed, and successive waxings and dyeings result in the creation of batik pictures. Because wet cloth cannot be waxed, the cloth has to be dried completely, without disturbing the waxed design. The most convenient way is to peg it to a clothesline in the sun. Usually lighter colors are dyed first and the darkest shade last of all. A chemical reaction between the coloring agent and the fabric occurs, so the color becomes a permanent part of the cloth rather than merely pigment applied to a surface. The characteristic veining of dyed lines, which radiate like webbing in the background of many batiks, is created by the crackling of the wax during the process. Rivulets of dye snake along these tiny gullies in the waxed surface when the fabric is immersed in the dye solution. This effect can be controlled or prevented, depending on the type of wax used. Beeswax, with its high fat content, crackles reluctantly, whereas paraffin is extremely brittle and crackles readily. Eventually, the wax is removed by boiling or by ironing with newsprint.

The technique is thought to have originated and developed to a so-

329

phisticated level of design and content in the Far East. It was known in China in the seventh century A.D., even earlier in India, and later on in Southeast Asia and West Africa. One prevalent theory suggests that batik originated among a set of non-Chinese hill tribes known as the Miao, who came under Chinese influence. The Chinese adopted the technique and developed it to a higher standard. The export of silk batiks spread the skill to surrounding areas in Central Asia and the Far East and even farther afield to the Middle East and southern India. Important secondary sources developed where the art was further elaborated and disseminated. Eventually, batik techniques came to be practiced in at least some regions of all continents except for Australia and the Pacific Islands. In the Americas, pre-Columbian cotton fabrics found in archaeological remains of Inca Peru appear to be batik, but this has not been scientifically verified. There were a few fairly old centers of batik production in eastern Europe, but their influence was localized. Generally, the great centers of batik were remote from the industrialized West. Europe proper became exposed to batik fairly recently in the history of the art as a result of imperialism and trade expansion. Dutch penetration of the Far East in the seventeenth century initiated the importation of Javanese batiks, which prompted European imitation of the method. Eventually manufacturing centers developed in Switzerland, Holland, and England, which by the late nineteenth century were producing machine-made imitations of Javanese batiks, mainly for export to Asian and African markets.

Batik, along with other traditional art forms, played an integrating role in traditional societies. Fabrics for everyday and ceremonial use were decorated with symbols and designs embodying communal religious beliefs. Each region and grouping had its own distinct patterns and colors, which were transmitted from generation to generation, uniting the living with the dead, the spiritual with the material. This is in direct contrast with the western European cultural tradition that has removed art from the normal world and left it to languish on a pedestal or wall. I consider myself an inheritor of an integrating aesthetic expression, and I trust that while continuing it, I might expand it.

Through force of circumstance, I am self-taught, having come upon batik rather fortuitously, and have developed it through a process of trial and error for over a decade. From early childhood I had always drawn and colored on any surface I could reach. But there were no artists in my immediate family and network of friends, and the schools I attended lacked art programs. My drawing skills were sustained by constant urges to illustrate literature texts in their margins, to shade all scientific diagrams for biology lessons (to the great annoyance of the tutor), and to scribble wicked cartoons of oppressive teachers for classmates' entertainment.

I continued the academic direction charted by high school and went on to obtain a B.A. degree in history and Spanish from the University of the West Indies, Mona campus. In the course of academic toiling, I recall frequently being sidetracked by reference books containing art reproductions. I was particularly susceptible to Gauguin's glowing Tahitian idylls, and pictures of Mayan temple murals and jade gods automatically transported me from dusty library stacks to overgrown ruins in the Yucatan rain forests. Nevertheless, I was awarded a UWI postgraduate scholarship and spent two years researching the social history of early twentieth-century Jamaica. During this period, I interviewed elderly survivors of earlier times and combed through old newspapers and books in the National Archives. But a growing dissatisfaction with the restrictions of sharing my research with a narrow, specialized group made the rigors of academic discipline seem onerous. (Ironically, in the course of developing my art, I often have to isolate myself to foster the concentration necessary to produce my batiks. And the structural discipline inherent in the process can be even more tyrannical than slavery.)

During my apprenticeship as a historian, I found myself reverting to drawing images when dealing with emotional experiences, whether stressful or joyful. And the visual appreciation of my human sources and their habitat generated much of my enthusiasm for the fieldwork. While interviewing an aged, retired schoolteacher, for example, half of me would mentally catalog his memories. The other half would admire the lines mapping his eyes, the shadow of his curved form in the rocker, the outline of his silhouette against the square of the open window. And in the background was always bright yellow light, green and brown shadows, sometimes scarlet flashes, and purple recesses. Eventually, I abandoned my academic research and for an interim involved myself in handcrafts, including tie-and-dye and batik, and soon became preoccupied with the welding of dye and cloth.

The nature of the batik process facilitated the development of my sense of color and form. Now my faithful friend the pencil was being used on cloth to outline the pattern to be waxed. From the routine use of dyeing skills, I acquired a store of knowledge of dye combinations and shades. The basic technique was available in "how-to" primers, and supplies were household materials, available in small, economic quantities in supermarkets and pharmacies. Having just left one institution, I was reluctant to restrict myself to the framework of another, so I did not enroll at the art school. Without the intimidating expectations of teachers, I constructed a foundation of skills for a more advanced art. A very important part of my development was that I sold many of my early efforts to individuals who were among the exodus of professionals from Jamaica in the 1970s and wanted mementos of home to take into exile. My batiks were much cheaper and more easily transported than bona fide gallery art. But I developed in virtual isolation from the formal gallery structure, which excluded craftworkers such as myself, and the meager response of a few professional artists, "nice colors," did not encourage me to declare myself. I relied on the appreciation of other untutored craftworkers and my family, who were outside the gallery milieu, to feed the need for an audience. It was not until I had lived away from Jamaica for three years that I began to submit my batiks to professional art shows. I am grateful to those new friends who virtually dragged me, protesting all the way, toward public display. The opportunities to view my work alongside that of other artists' helped me to sharpen my perspective on my art, and valuable critical feedback from a more sophisticated audience encouraged me to extend my boundaries even further.

The fact that I was able to develop my art to a considerable degree of skill without the incubating benefits of gallery patronage reflects largely on Jamaica's creative vibrancy. In spite of the rigors of slavery and colonialism, artistic self-expression has been prolific, and we have a rich legacy of dialect verse and storytelling, music and dance, pottery and straw-weaving, influenced mainly by African roots but modified by Caribbean experience. I left the rigid academic structure to expand creatively in a wider, informal ambience of artistic activity, with an audience already responsive to virtuosity in any form, whether it be intricate handwork or inciting dub poetry. The fact that reggae, our contemporary music, originated among the untutored and disadvantaged and expanded to become an international musical force best exemplifies the extent to which Jamaica is a birthplace for innovative art.

Rastafarian culture was the particular catalyst in my artistic unfolding, with its aggressive promotion of cultural self-reliance and African identity, reinvigorating a long-standing Jamaican tradition of resourcefulness in creativity. The brethren's use of hand knitting and fabric decoration produced clothing imbued with cultural symbols, and their immediate environment exemplified the natural, with domestic paraphernalia made from coconut and calabash shell, wood, straw, and earthenware. The Rasta vision also came to dominate reggae in the late 1960s and 1970s, and the driving beat underlined Jamaica's social and political pulse, with outcries for social justice and spiritual regeneration. In short, an entire subculture developed to give distinction to contemporary Jamaica and even farther afield in the Caribbean. Developing societies face the danger of becoming creatively passive in their growing dependence on foreign capital, technology, and markets for material survival. Already, many of us are "mimic men," echoing the compulsive consumerism of Western, industrialized society. The Rasta insistence on cultural integrity and practical application of still valid ancient traditions offers a forceful counterbalance to the psychological damage of modernization.

Accordingly, most of my early batiks featured Rastafarians and the emblematic colors of red, gold, green and, black. The batik *Rasta Queen*, used to embellish the program booklet for this conference, represents the culmination of the early "underground" development of my art and was the last picture completed before I left Jamaica for a spell in the late 1970s. It was very meaningful to me when it was chosen in 1980 to symbolize the exhibition of Women's Art from Developing Countries at the First International Women Artists' Festival, held in Denmark to coincide with the U.N. Forum on the Decade for Women. It was also crucial encouragement to pursue my obsession with batik.

Generally, my art is a record of my response to Jamaica, exploring human and geographic experience with a good measure of personal fantasy thrown in. I often depict women in their various dimensions, with motherhood being a dominant theme. The Jamaican madonna is not a sentimental icon; rather, she is a survivor who struggles to nurture her children on limited material resources. Two batiks displayed at the conference reflect the archetype: the *Orange Seller* with her sleeping child and *Elaine* standing fiercely over her family.

Environmental protection is another preoccupation. As we develop our economy, we seem to be repeating the mistakes of industrially advanced societies, and pollution in all forms threatens our well-being. Industrial waste is slowly killing the once beautiful harbor of our capital, and effluence from vehicles and factories is discharged continually into the atmosphere. Perhaps it is this uncontrolled urbanization that leads in part to the violence that has become a regular feature in Jamaica and the wider world. This is not merely a reference to the murderous drug and political "posses" at home and abroad. It also includes the possibility of universal, man-made destruction as the political behemoths confront each other with deadly weapons aimed at the heart. At the same time they feed the smaller nations with genocidal toys, and the entire globe seems to be at war. *The Tree of Life* batik in this exhibition is a meditation on this theme. The primordial landscape with icons representing all forms of life is threatened by an obscene explosion ripping the sky apart.

Naturally, I revel in the beauty and geographic distinctiveness of Jamaica. The dyes on cotton echo the blue-green mountains and outline the nestling shapes of rural cottages emerging from a mat of leaves: breadfruit and mango, banana and croton, cocoa leaf and fern. At other times they sound the harmony of humble structures in a tenement yard, dwelling on the shades of rust on zinc and the muted patina of weathered board, as in *Daybreak*, exhibited here.

In the course of my artistic career, I have encountered myopic, self-appointed arbiters of Jamaican aesthetics, who would nullify the worth of batik pictures. They consider the medium to be a lowly, decorative craft because it is not part of the academic art tradition of Western Europe, which dominates our bustling gallery scene. Consequently, it is often ignored in art critiques or referred to in a condescending fashion. By consistently producing and showing batik, however, I am contributing to its recognition as a valid art form, although this has not been a conscious aim, for it seems to have adopted me, rather than vice versa. It is heartening to know that there are several of us working in batik, both in Jamaica and the rest of the Caribbean, as well as farther away in North America and Europe and in the Far East. The more batik artists emerge, the more likely it is that there will be a system of evaluation based on the art's unique form, rather than on prevailing lazy comparisons with conventional oil painting on canvas.

Finally, my modest contribution to the debate on art and gender is the thought that sometimes women artists are their own worst enemies. Some of us seem to have accepted a notion of there being a limited space available to artists who happen to be women. Accomplishment by other women seems to threaten our own little slice of the pie, and we draw apart in unhealthy rivalry. It would be better to welcome and encourage more women to the ranks so that we would actually expand the space, whether real or imaginary. True strength cannot be based on unnatural monopoly, and we only stand to benefit from the ferment of increased creativity. In conclusion, it has been inspiring to have been included in a gathering of creative writers. This integration of the written and spoken word with the visual image runs counter to the debilitating tendency to divide reality into separate and isolated aspects. I read widely and greedily, and literature fuels my imagination and creative discipline. My exhibition at the conference is another way of celebrating the writers whose works have kept me company. I look forward to maintaining and strengthening preliminary contacts and to exploring the many new authors whom I encountered.

Bibliography

Brandon, Reiko Mochinaga. "Country Textiles of Japan. The Art of Tsutsugaki." New York: John Weatherhill, n.d.
Gittinger, Mattiebelle. "Master Dyers to the World: Technique and Trade in Early Indian Dyed Cotton Textiles." Washington, D.C.: Textile Museum, n.d.

Kent, Kate P. "Introducing West African Cloth." Denver: Denver Museum of Natural History, 1971.
Larsen, Jack Lenor. "The Dyer's Art." New York: Van Nostrand Reinhold.
Lu Pu. "Designs of Chinese Indigo Batik." Beijing, China: New World Press, n.d.

A female quadroon slave of Surinam. Most of the slave women of Surinam were reputed to be very beautiful. Hence the saying, "The samboe dark, and the Mulatto brown, the Maesti fair, the well-limb'd Quaderoon" (during slavery, a Maesti was the offspring of a European and a Quadroon).

WOMEN WRITERS OF
THE SPANISH-, FRENCH-,
AND DUTCH-SPEAKING
CARIBBEAN: AN OVERVIEW

Women Writers of the Spanish-Speaking Caribbean: An Overview

MARIA CRISTINA RODRIGUEZ

If we agree that the Caribbean is a fragmented, small region because of its political, economic, and language differences, we must also agree that even within so-called common language sectors, great differences exist. The countries of this region were formed by European economic enterprises in the fifteenth and sixteenth centuries: Spain, England, France, and Holland determined the ethnic groups, the economy, and the political system that would prevail in the twentieth century.

After Spain had lost the last of its colonies in the New World in 1898, the legacy of the plantation system, the economic interest of the United States, and the international power games between first and second world countries further determined the fragmentation of the Spanish-speaking Caribbean region. Simón Bolívar's project to make the Antilles part of the Latin American countries and José Martí's and Eugenio Maria de Hosto's attempts to form an Antillean federation remained idealistic endeavors never to become reality.

During the nineteenth century the Dominican Republic was torn by internal power struggles and by political leaders who at various times wanted to join the United States or rejoin Spain or become an independent nation. Invasions by Haiti and the United States and long-ruling dictatorships such as that of Rafael Leonida Trujillo from 1930 until his assassination in 1961 hampered progressive economic and political development. Cuba went from being the puppet state of United States sugar interests to long and bloody dictatorships under Gerardo Machado from 1925 until 1933 and Fulgencio Batista on and off from 1940 until

1958. Puerto Rico remained in the hands of the United States from 1898; it went from a military government and governors appointed by the U.S. president to a populist movement led by Luis Muñoz Marín, which culminated in 1952 with the recognition of a particular relationship with the metropolis called a free associated state, a sophisticated term for colony.

The 1950s were decisive years politically for the Spanish Antilles. Since then the Dominican Republic has become more and more dependent on U.S. investments while maintaining a very fragile democracy sustained by consent of the military and the large landowners. To the chagrin of the United States and Latin American dictatorships, Cuba is the first socialist country in the New World. Puerto Rico holds elections every four years to debate its present political status and the economic benefits of becoming part of the most powerful country in the world or of establishing a socialist democracy in peace and friendship with all countries. The result is always the same: the free associated state remains with little political power but apparent economic gains.

Because of the power play, Cuba and Puerto Rico, which enjoyed good neighbor policies in the 1930s and 1940s, now seem as far apart as Grenada and Australia. No goods from Cuba (including books) can be circulated. Cultural exchanges have been limited to the whims of U.S. governments— more in Carter's time, less and less in the last seven years. Puerto Ricans have become alienated from the island of Cuba, and the only contact has been the so-called true stories brought back by the exiles who came to Puerto Rico in large numbers in the 1960s and 1980s. According to these "witnesses," Cuba is an enormous prisonhouse where no one eats, plays, or reads. All they do is work; they never speak for fear of being imprisoned or killed. Groups such as the Puerto Rican Socialist party and the Antonio Maceo Brigade, universities, and cultural organizations are responsible for presenting the Puerto Rican people with another view of Cuba. Singers such as Pablo Milanes, Sylvio Rodriguez, and Amaury Perez and writers such as Nancy Morejon, Miguel Barnet, and Cinthio Vitier have shown that Cuba is alive and well despite the blockade and the lies. Still, to acquire books or records from Cuba is a very difficult and costly task. Traveling to an island that is so close is legally impossible or so expensive it is easier for the average citizen to travel to the Dominican Republic or New York or Disney World.

Because of the growing influence of the United States in the Dominican Republic, that country has become closer to Puerto Rico. Thousands of illegal immigrants live in Puerto Rico and have established their own ghettos working in the jobs that Puerto Ricans refuse because of low wages and living in run-down places abandoned by working-class families. To encourage tourism, the Dominican government has made it easier to enter the country. For example, during Trujillo's reign and while the military ruled the country, even if there was a civilian government, a blacklist of people belonging to or associated with leftist groups existed. Puerto Ricans can now enter with no passport, only a birth certificate; the plane fares are cheap; several airlines serve this route; and there is even a ferry from the west coast of Puerto Rico. Yet literature does not flow in the same way.

Dominican Republic presses are known for ignoring copyrights and publishing anything they think will sell well. Publishing a book in the Dominican Republic is very cheap compared to Puerto Rico or Spain. Yet books by Dominican writers seldom if ever circulate in Puerto Rico unless they are published by a Mexican, Argentinean, or Spanish press. An exiled Cuban press in Spain is one of the few that has published literature from the Dominican Republic, either as a whole book dedicated to this national literature, *Lecturas Dominicanas*,[1] or in Caribbean anthologies.[2] The only way to get books from this country is to bring them out personally. Ironically, Cuba and the Dominican Republic have better access to Puerto Rican literature than this island, which is always cited as a model of democracy and freedom but never receives books from neighboring countries.

From the moment that Spanish Antilleans were defined as Cubans, Dominicans, and Puerto Ricans, a sense of nationhood was established which identified a distinct culture separate from that of Spain. By the 1840s writers born on these islands were writing poems, describing customs particular to the region—*jibaros* and *guajiros* took the place of *peninsulares*. Interestingly enough, women were always present in cultural groups dedicated to the promotion of the arts, literature, and progressive ideas like abolition and independence. An example is Lola Rodriguez de Tio in Puerto Rico.[3] Most of these women were wives and daughters of landowners, who were able to move about because of their wealth and status in society. Gertrudis Gomez de Avellaneda from Cuba was a very outspoken woman who lived many years in Spain and became a prominent romantic novelist.[4] These women were able to become a part of struggling political or intellectual groups because they were brave enough to tolerate society's attacks on their behavior. Many had to endure exile for voicing their political convictions.

During the nineteenth century the number of women writing novels in the Antilles was minimal, but their voices were heard in poetry. Fiction

1. Carlos Fernandez-Rocha and Danilo de los Santos, *Lecturas Dominicanas* (Madrid: Playor, 1977).
   2. Eliseo Colon Zayas, *Literatura del Caribe: Antologia* (Madrid: Playor, 1984).
   3. Lola Rodriguez de tio, *Posias Patrioticas, Poesias Religiosas* (Barcelona: Ediciones Rumbos, 1968).
   4. Gertrudis Gomez de Avellaneda, *SAB* (1841); *Guatemozin* (1846).

has been a difficult realm for women to enter. Those few who have, have seldom been able to pursue a writer's career and publish more than one novel or collection of stories. For Puerto Rican women, this situation has changed dramatically in the last fifteen years.

In the Spanish Antilles, literary movements have excelled in poetry. Some of the best poets of the time have belonged to the modernist movement and its branches. Later La Poesia Sorprendida and the Generacion del 48 in the Dominican Republic, the Minoristas and the Origenes group in Cuba, the writers who founded the magazine *Indice* and later *Asomante*, promoted poetry in which women participated if on a small scale. Carmen Natalia Martinez and Aida Cartagena Portalatin were Dominican women who were very active in political and literary groups.[5] Mercedes Torrens de Garmendia and Dulce Maria Loynaz from Cuba were women poets who, if not part of the established poetic movements, were at least recognized by these intellectuals.[6] Fina Garcia Marruz was the only woman in the group Origenes.[7] Julia de Burgos from Puerto Rico was a poet who moved away from various closed literary groups to become a lone voice of feminine consciousness.[8] In Puerto Rico the literary magazine *Asomante* was edited by two women, Nilita Vientos Gaston and Monelisa Perez Marchand.

In the past fifteen years, women have continued to write poetry and to publish their work in book form or as contributions to various magazines. In the Dominican Republic Jeanette Miller and Sherezada (Chiqui) Vicioso are two poets whose development continues with every new poem.[9] Both women seem to write poetry in the very few seconds they are able to steal from lives dedicated to other aspects. Miller is an art critic and Vicioso has traveled as far as Africa as a consultant for UNESCO. Both now reside in the Dominican Republic and are very active in the country's cultural life. Women poets are very numerous in post-revolutionary Cuba. Their works have won prizes from UNEAC (the Writers and Artists Union) and from Casa las Americas. Nancy Morejon has continued writing poetry and growing and changing her work as her

---

5. Carmen Natalia Martinez, "Oda heroica a las Mirabal," and Aida Cartagena Portalatin, *Vispera del Sueño* (1944); *Del Sueño al Mundo* (1945); *Una Mujer Esta Sola* (1955); *Mi Mundo, el Mar* (1956); *Una Voz Destada* (1962); *La Tierra Escrita* (1967).

6. Mercedes Torrens, *Fragua de Estrellas* (1935); *Jazminero en la Sombra* (1942); *La Flauta del Silencio* (1946); *Fuente Sellada* (1956). Dulce Maria Loynaz, *Versos* (1938); *Juegos de Agua* (1947).

7. Fina Garcia Marruz, *Transfiguracion de Jesus en el Monte* (1947); *Las Miradas Perdidas* (1951); *Visitaciones* (1970).

8. Julia de Burgos, *Poema en Veinte Surcos* (1938); *El Mar y Tu* (1953).

9. Jeanette Miller, *Formulas Para Combatir el Miedo* (1972); Sherezada (Chiqui) Vicioso, *Viaje Desde el Agua* (1981); *Un Extrano Ulular Traia el Viento* (1985).

country and her own perception of life have changed.[10] She has published seven books of poetry beginning with *Mutismos* in 1962. Her most recent book is *Piedra Pulida* published in 1986. She is a black revolutionary woman, and her poetry goes from intimate revelations to the cry of protest for the invasion of Grenada. In Puerto Rico, Aurea Maria Sotomayor has just published a book entitled *De Lengua, Razon y Cuerpo* (About language, reason, and body) in which she gathers the work of nine recent women poets whom Sotomayor believes express a new voice. Among them, Rosario Ferre and Olga Nolla have written fiction but continue to write poetry.

Angela Maria Davila, Etna Iris Rivera, Luz Ivonne Orchart, Nemir Matos, Lilliana Ramos, and Vanes Droz write poetry in spite of holding demanding jobs. Each has published at least one book, and some have been involved in editing literary magazines such as *Reintegro*.

Aurea Maria Sotomayor states that it is more difficult to publish poetry than fiction because publishers believe that poetry does not sell well. This is true in the Caribbean, where publishing can be a very expensive enterprise. Yet there is no doubt that more women write poetry in the Spanish Antilles than stories or novels. In the Dominican Republic, Aida Cartagena, a critic, historian, and poet, published a novel in 1970 hailed by critics, *Escalera para Electra*. But it was a voice in the desert because this publication did not encourage other women to publish fiction, it was not followed by a second novel by Cartagena. Lately another Dominican woman, Hilma Contreras, has published two books of fiction: a novel, *La Tierra Esta Bramando* (1986), and a collection of stories, *Entre Dos Silencios* (1987), which have become available to readers outside the country through special distributors such as the Bilingual Publications Company in New York.

The absence of women in fiction is most noticeable in today's Cuba, just as their absence as film directors draws attention because of other radical changes in this society. Women have been recognized for their storytelling capability throughout the years in children's literature. At some time in their lives, Dora Alonso and Rosa Hilda Zell have written for children, but they have been slow to achieve recognition as adult storytellers. Dora Alonso, who is now seventy-eight, overcame the limitations imposed on a woman writing in male literary circles. Her first stage was in the novella criollista o "de la tierra" with *Tierra Adentro*. She was part of the Minorista group and changed her style as Cuba went from dictatorship to revolution. Her excellent collection of stories, *Ponolani*,

---

10. Nancy Morejon, *Richard Trajo su Flauta* (1967); *Parajes de una Epoca* (1979); *Octubre Imprescindible* (1983); *Cuaderno de Granada* (1984); *Piedra Pulida* (1986).

won a Mencion Especial from the jury of Casa de las Americas in 1966. Since then she has published stories, *Once Caballos*, memoirs, essays, and children's stories. Aida Bahr is only thirty-eight years old, but she is one of the few women fiction writers in Cuba today. Her collection of stories, *Hay un Gato en la Ventana*, published in 1984, is an impressive first work in which technique and theme blend to create a particular style that stays away from the well-known, almost standardized, male narrative modes. Women have written some of the best literature in recent years. Rosario Ferre is perhaps the most prolific with a collection of stories in 1976, *Papeles de Pandora;* three children's books for adult readers, *El Medio Pollito, La Mona que le Pisaron la Cola, Los Cuentas de Judn Bobo;* a collection of essays, *Sitio a Eros,* and a book of narrative poems or poetic narratives, *Fabulas de la Garza Desangrada.* In 1986 she published her first novel, *Maldito Amor,* which, although she calls it a novel, is more a long story or novella. Other women writing stories who have only published one book are Magali Garcia Ramis, *La Famila de Todos Nosotros,* Carmen Lugo Filippi, *Virgines y Martires,* a collection she shares with Ana Lydia Vega; and Carmen Valle, *Diarios Robados.* Of the women who have decided to dedicate their souls to the writing of stories, Ana Lydia Vega seems to keep her promise with *Virgenes y Martires, Encancaranublado,* and the 1987 collection, *Pasion de Historia.* Language is the essence of her writing, and her books are very popular in Latin America, especially in Argentina, where a Buenos Aires publisher is responsible for this last collection of stories.

Just as Rosario Ferre has tried her hand at writing a novel, Magaly Garcia Ramis published *Felices Dias Tio Sergio,* which seems more a recollection of childhood than a bildungsroman. The one writer who has been able to tell a story using all the techniques available to a novelist is Mayra Montero. In her novel, *La Trenza de la Hermosa Luna,* she sets a story of love, political dilemma, and internal struggle in a setting of turmoil: Haiti a few weeks before Duvalier fled to France.[11] Montero has not only written a superb novel, but she has made it a Caribbean novel. It is interesting that Montero's protagonist is not a woman, as is the case with the other women writers mentioned. Jean Leroy is a man with a particular sensitivity—perhaps a "feminine" feeling. Yet this character is baffled when the woman he has loved for years rejects him to live with an old and ugly man—in Leroy's view, of course.

The Dominican Republic, Cuba, and Puerto Rico are islands with so much in common that we are amazed at the little knowledge that exists about contemporary Caribbean writers. These three countries are experiencing a cultural awakening and an awareness that women's voices have a distinct style and a very particular narrative discourse. It seems that

---

11. Mayra Montero, *La Trenza de la Hermosa Luna* (Barcelona: Editorial Anagrama, 1987).

literature and the performing and fine arts are dangerous to those who play power games. We notice that there is no problem in listening to and purchasing records of the latest merengue or salsa number. As long as lyrics deal with sex, games, and women as objects, all is well in Puerto Rico and the Dominican Republic. Protest songs from these countries are known only in their own backyard. Cuba, on the other hand, has been isolated in every respect because even a popular song or a cartoon supposedly carries a revolutionary message that could endanger the freedom enjoyed by the Dominican Republic and Puerto Rico.

I believe women can take advantage of the negative way they are perceived in the Spanish Antilles. Women are seen for the most part as harmless, emotional, almost hysterical if pushed too far, unable to make a reasonable argument, and playing at being independent just to come home running to a man who will offer security in exchange for submission. So when women write, they are not taken very seriously. It is all right if they want to compete in a woman's writing contest (*letras femeninas*). They can be tolerated if they are relatively good and make us laugh. When they get too serious, like Rosario Ferre and Aida Bahr in their stories, they become dangerous and must be closely watched. There is more tolerance of women poets because they tend to deal with intimacies— their own, not men's. But fiction is a problem; it resembles life too closely.

Women share common experiences; they establish bonds based on mutual help and understanding. Their writings deal with themselves and their rituals. They are not out to destroy but to find a meaning that will guide them in their childbearing and rearing, in their love relationships, in the fulfillment of their abilities, and in their social and political involvement. Women writers must explore this common bond and in that way break the barriers that have fragmented the Caribbean.

Women Writers of the French-Speaking Caribbean: An Overview

MARIE-DENISE SHELTON

The concept of Caribbean literature is relatively recent, validated by the growing awareness in the Caribbean of a common historical, cultural, and geopolitical experience that transcends national diversity. To state that there is a Caribbean literature is to recognize the existence of a certain relationship with language and the world which constitutes what some have called the Caribbean discourse. This discourse as defined by Edouard Glissant is produced within a space that has been shaped by slavery, colonialism, creolization, and insularity. It also assumes the specific social and political forces within and outside the islands which threaten them with assimilation or annihilation. "The idea of Caribbean unity is cultural re-possession. It reinstates us in the true essence of our beings: it cannot be assumed for us by others."[1] When we speak of Caribbean literature we speak of a threatened utterance which a certain "regime of truth" represses or attempts to neutralize. Paradoxically, these antagonistic forces have served to mold Caribbean literature and ensure its intelligibility.

The literature by women in the Caribbean is inscribed in this general discursive space. Isolating feminine expression does not imply that it can be detached from the conjuncture sketched above. Rather, the attempt here is to determine, within the field of competing voices, what women say and how they say it. A different "knowledge" of being Haitian, Martiniquan, or Guadeloupean is expressed in the works by women. At

1. Edouard Glissant, *Le discours Antillais* (Paris: Editions du Seuil, 1981), p. 18.

the level of thematics, feminine writing tends to expose conflicts and mutilations that characterize the being-in-the-world of women in the Caribbean. The development of literature by women has been thwarted or at least retarded by the prevailing social order in Haiti, Martinique, and Guadeloupe, where literature has traditionally been viewed as a male prerogative. The number of women writers is therefore small relative to that of their male counterparts. Women's literature also tends to be more vulnerable to the pressures or aberrations of literary production in the Caribbean. The lack of viable literary institutions places the writer (female and male) in a negative situation. Either the difficulty of being published forces the writer to silence or she/he must submit to the requirement and priorities—often fanciful—of foreign literary establishments. There is little happiness for the Caribbean writers who have repeatedly deplored the precarious conditions in which they must operate: lack of institutional support; absence of a real reading public; high illiteracy rate among the majority of their countrymen; cultural biases of the minority, who more readily consume the literature of France and Europe; indifference of the foreign readership. All this is compounded by the malaise felt by the writer in the presence of the two languages of unequal status, French and Creole. The emergence of numerous feminist presses in Europe and Canada has not affected the situation of the Caribbean woman writer. As Liliane Devieux, a Haitian novelist residing in Quebec, remarks: "When a work is written by a Haitian woman, I think that it is the Haitian society which is behind her, and in that sense it is not only or simply a woman issue, it is the problem of the Haitian society as a whole, and that does not interest the people in Quebec (men or women)."[2]

Here I will not retrace the history of feminine literary expression in the Caribbean or examine specific texts in detail. Rather, I will attempt to isolate certain thematic currents and identify certain narrative practices that can permit the mapping of feminine literary imagination in the context of Caribbean societies. Of course, the inevitable disadvantage of such a cursory investigation is that it overlooks the internal coherence, the texture, and the density of individual works. I hope this brief examination will disclose the pattern that generates what Michel Foucault terms "cette parole qui pourtant faisait la différence,"[3] in this context, the differential language used by women writers of the French-speaking Caribbean. I have limited the scope of this study to the novel, because of the absence of a representative body of works by women in other genres.

One of the most pervasive themes in the Caribbean novels written by

2. In Jean Jonassaint, *Le pouvoir des mots/les maux de pouvoir* (Montreal: Presses de l'Université de Montreal, 1986), p. 50.
3. Michél Foucault, *L'ordre du discours* (Paris: Gallimard, 1971), p. 14.

women is the problematic of feminine exclusion and dispossession. Generally, the narrative in the first person by a female character presents itself as a frustrated enunciation which affirms and denies, creates, and dissolves the female sense of self. These novels written in an autobiographical or monological mode recite the interminable drama of a female protagonist whose self-identity is so severely compromised that she becomes engulfed in a web of neuroses and phantasms. No other voice comes to interrupt the unfolding of the neurotic episode because the female character as subject/narrator is the sole legislator of the order and content of the discourse. The self projected in these works is enclosed in a stifling and unaerated space. Everything happens as if the narrative sought to experience the limits of opprobrium, to denounce an evil that corrodes from the inside. Without home or country, or rejecting both home and country, the female protagonists are deported outside of their bodies, which they experience as alien and hateful. Michèle Lacrosil with her novels *Sapotille et le Serin d'argile* (1960) and *Cajou* (1961), Marie Chauvet in *Fille d'Haiti* (1954) and *Amour* (1960), Maryse Condé's *Heremakhonon* (1976) and *Une Saison à Rihata* (1981), or Myriam Vieyra's *Le Quimboiseur l'avait dit* (1980) and *Juletane* (1982) express this feminine pathos.

Michèle Lacrosil illustrates with disarming frankness the alienation of her female characters. *Sapotille et le Serin d'argile* has no story line. The novel is written in the form of an impressionistic journal kept by a Guadeloupean woman named Sapotille while on a journey to France on a ship named the *Nausicaa*. In this journal, Sapotille undertakes an inner journey to her past, depicting a life filled with shame, humiliation, and self-doubt in the prejudice-ridden society of Guadeloupe. As a pupil at the Pensionnat Saint-Denis directed by French nuns, Sapotille craves solitude and invisibility. Under the gaze of her white teachers and light-skinned classmates she feels irremediably ugly. Nothing can exorcise her fear of being visible. She finds a strange enjoyment in being confined alone in a dark cell "like a wild beast in its hole." In her adulthood, Sapotille feels the same urge to fade away from the world's sight, wishing to live in a big city, where she can remain invisible to those who pass by her. The discovery of her slave ancestry only confirms her certainty of her inferiority, of belonging to a race doomed to remain at the bottom of the anthropological scale. Cajou, the protagonist of Lacrosil's second novel, *Cajou*, is likewise torn with anguish, consumed by an unbearable feeling of ugliness. She also yearns for total invisibility and is unable to bear her own sight: "I was Narcissus in reverse ashamed of myself and deploring my own reflection,"[4] she writes in her diary, which is, like Sapotille's, the repository of morbid thoughts. Trapped in the fortress of her skin,

4. Michèle Lacrosil, *Cajou* (Paris: Gallimard, 1961), p. 64.

convinced that she is repulsively ugly, Cajou sinks into pathological despair and finally commits suicide. Sapotille and Cajou both feel marked with an indelible stain, guilty of an unforgivable sin.

In depicting these tragic female figures, Lacrosil illustrates the ravages of a psychological condition that can be called autophobia. It is explained in part by the psychologist Erik Erikson on the structure of shame: "Shame is an impulse to bury one's face or to sink, right then and there into the ground. But then it is essentially rage turned against the self. He who is ashamed would like to force the world not to look at him, not to notice his exposure. He would like to destroy the eyes of the world. Instead he must wish for his own invisibility."[5] These remarks are all the more pertinent when compared to Cajou's own explanation of her malady: "When a little girl discovers, in the dim light of her experience, that all the ugliness of the world has gathered in the mirror she consults, instead of viewing herself as a monster, she at first directs her anger at the mirror."[6] Sapotille's and Cajou's militant self-hatred explains their rejection of motherhood. Sapotille feels relieved when she loses her child. "It was dead, it had not come to existence. It had not suffered; it would not suffer. What a luck! If no one understands, too bad! she exults."[7] By committing suicide, Cajou intends to destroy herself and the child in her womb, a child who, she reasons, would only relive her agony. Michèle Lacrosil reproduces the language of her characters' despondency. The first-person narration gives her novels an autobiographical coloration that places her in the lineage of Mayotte Capecia, the author of a book entitled *Je suis Martiniquaise* (1948), which receives Franz Fanon's psychiatric attention in *Black Skin White Masks*. In this autobiography, Capecia furnishes one of the first testimonies of the Caribbean "mal féminin." She recounts without inhibition her state of utter alienation. Considering her blackness a malediction, she awaits through her whole life liberation in the form of a sudden whitening of her skin and redemption through the love of a white man.

The feeling of inhabiting a body that is a perverse envelope of death is equally felt by the heroines of Marie Chauvet, Lotus of *Fille d'Haiti*, and Claire of *Amour*. Their existence is threatened from the inside by an anguish of worthlessness and from the outside by a climate of social and political violence in Haiti. An extremely puzzling character, Lotus is caught in a web of social and personal contradictions. Daughter of a "successful" prostitute, she belongs nowhere. To the masses, she is a mulatto who enjoys the amenities of bourgeois life; in the eyes of the

---

5. Erik Erikson, *Childhood and Society* (New York: Norton, 1963), p. 252.
6. Lacrosil, *Cajou*, p. 30.
7. Michèle Lacrosil, *Sapotille et le Serin d'argile* (Fort-de-France, 1960), p. 187.

bourgeoisie, she is a pariah who bears the mark of her mother's infamous trade. Lotus cannot claim a private space either, privacy being for her the source of her social calamity. In the villa inherited from her mother, she leads the obscure and improbable life of a virgin whore. She allures men only to reject them when they try to possess her. She hates men: "Because they had stolen my mother away from me, men were my worse enemy."[8] Unable to find a place in society, failing to define who she is, Lotus finds a sort of liberation in madness: "I am a madwoman, but a madwoman who reasons," she concludes.[9] Madness is also the solution chosen by Claire, the protagonist of Chauvet's *Amour*, another extremely complex and confused personality. Claire feels she is abnormal, a misfit. "Why am I black, why?" she asks in despair. Like Lacrosil's characters, she fears the gaze of others. She dreams of becoming as elusive as a "shadow" or as imperceptible as a "flea." Claire is an "old maid" in a society that considers marriage a woman's natural vocation. Feeling unloved and rejected, she withdraws into an obscure world of fantasies and voyeurism against the backdrop of violence and political repression. Her revolt against the society she loathes is the diary she keeps with religious regularity. In it, she unveils the sordid dramas being played behind the closed doors of the self-proclaimed elite. She also exposes the cruel reality of Haitian society, in which the majority suffers under the grip of chronic poverty and the yoke of tyranny. Claire takes her revenge against the reign of political terror by killing one of its satraps, the military commandant, Caledu. This act seems to offer her provisional liberation, but she vacillates between opposite ideological and emotional poles and cannot glue together the parts of her fragmented self. Caledu for her is an object of both irrepressible attraction and violent repulsion. She criticizes the bourgeois society of which she is a member (although marginalized) but accepts its values and defends the class/color structure that ensures its privileges. The plight of the masses elicits her compassion, but she can hardly mask her disdain for the common people. The Haitian woman as portrayed in Chauvet's fiction is a being in exile from society and from herself. A recent novel by Jan Dominique of Haiti, *Memoires d'une amnesique* (1986), is also illustrative. It is a story of the disorientation suffered by a woman who tries to break the silence to which amnesia has forced her. She undertakes a search that leads her to diverse places in her vain attempt to reconstruct some meaning from her shattered life. Here again, as in Chauvet's novel, political and social violence furnishes the background to the protagonist's crisis.

A desire for oneness moves the feminine figures although they fail to

8. Marie Charvet, *Fille d'Haiti* (Paris: Fasquelle, 1954).
9. Ibid., p. 82.

define themselves. They seek refuge in madness, suicide, or symbolic self-annihilation. Zetou, the tragic character of Myriam Warner-Vieyra's *Le Quimboiseur l'avait dit* (1982), recounts her tale of slow disintegration from her small Caribbean village of Karura to the psychiatric asylum in France where she has been committed. Uprooted, living under the constant fear of imminent catastrophe, Zetou, an adolescent abused by a cynical mother and her lover, unleashes her insane rage against the irrational order of life as she experiences it. *Juletane* (1982), Warner-Vieyra's second novel, is in the form of an intimate diary. It recounts the "passion" in the sense of suffering and martyrdom of a Caribbean woman in Africa. Juletane, the protagonist, is married to an African whom she met in Paris and, when she arrives in Africa, she must share conjugal life with her husband's two other wives. The novel is a dark tale of the exile, solitude, and despair of a woman for whom madness becomes the principle of liberation and survival. She is known in the African community as "the mad one," and she herself dreams of "waking up in another world where insane people are not insane, but wise people who defend justice."[10] A similar theme is explored in Maryse Condé's *Une Saison à Rihata* (1982), which offers yet another image of the spiritual deterioration of a Caribbean woman married to an African, who considers herself an unassimilable foreigner, a "stranger" in Africa. The redemption which Veronica, the heroine of Condé's *Heremakonon*, seeks from her existential disease of belonging nowhere, of being deprived of identity, only leads to a deeper sense of dispossession. She leaves her native island of Guadeloupe to seek redemption in France and Africa but finds only emptiness, disillusionment, and depression.

To return to the island is impossible. For Veronica, Guadeloupe is a carceral place inhabited by a contemptible humanity, a place that has robbed her of identity and pride as a black woman. For Marie-Hélène, the protagonist of *Une saison à Rihata*, the island has become "sterile, a deserted matrix which can no longer envelop a fetus."[11] From the depth of their despair, Warner-Vieyra's characters see it as a very remote spot of light that flickers as if in a hallucination. The relation with Africa is even more problematic and gives rise to intense but paradoxical emotions. On one hand, Africa is viewed as a promised land to which one goes to find personal redemption and plenitude. On the other, Africa is experienced as an alien, even hostile, place, where the dream of self-discovery gradually shrivels. Images of dark holes and bottomless pits, sensations of dampness and viscosity, as well as a feeling of total unbelonging transform the return to the ancestral land into a nightmare filled with pain

10. Myriam Warner-Vieyra, *Juletane* (Paris: Présence Africaine, 1982), p. 141.
11. Maryse Condé, *Une saison à Rihata* (Paris: Laffonte, 1981), p. 77.

and horror. The encounter of Condé and Warner-Vieyra with Africa stands in sharp contrast to the pious sense of communion felt by proponents of the Negritude movement in their "return to the sources." One is tempted to speculate that this disparity in vision is in part related to a changed ideological climate in the Caribbean over the past few years. Indeed, today, for a number of intellectuals and writers, the concept of "Antillanité" tends to take precedence over the notion of "Africanité" in the definition of Caribbean cultural identity.

There is a fatal resemblance among the female figures described in all these stories of individual bankruptcy and pessimism. Their psychological functioning is characterized by the institution of "an internal police state" that impedes all "normal" life activities. The characters who experience the world as threatening are drawn into a solipsistic existence in which there is no other reality but the self, yet withdrawal into the self does not produce a sense of security. It transports them into a spiral of delusions and ritualistic behavior in which the self slowly weakens until it ultimately disintegrates. The thematics of exclusion and expatriation developed in these novels cannot be considered as a mere literary formula. Given its persistence and centrality, one could view it as the reactualization of a problematic, which has its origin outside of the text. These stories could well be read as metaphors of the contradictions and tensions characteristic of feminine existence in the Caribbean. Written in the same language of violence, they describe a morbid rupture, a catastrophic separation. If the female protagonists adopt the same syntax, it is no doubt because they feel a similar psychosocial internment. They reenact through tales of alienation the gesture that excludes them as women from the recognized realm of debate. To employ Luce Irigaray's terminology, one could say that feminine logos in the Caribbean is produced "outside this volume circumscribed by the meaning articulated in [the father's] discourse, [in] a zone of silence."[12]

One should not leap to the conclusion, however, that the literature by women about women in the Caribbean is the complacent transcription of female neuroses. These texts constitute within the framework of Caribbean expression a counterdiscourse that actively criticizes the social reality that so oddly disorganizes the female sense of self. At the heart of this seemingly egocentric discourse is a call, implicit or explicit, for the transformation of the structures of society and the system of values that destroys freedom. The language of contestation is sometimes diffuse or ambiguous. Lacrosil's novels, for instance, in spite of their obsessive nature, constitute an indictment of a still prevailing Caribbean world view inherited from the slave/colonial era that equates "being" with white and

---

12. Luce Irigaray, *Ce sexe qui n'en est pas un* (Paris: Les Editions de Minuit, 1977), p. 111.

"nothingness" with black. The illness of Cajou and Sapotille is not on-togenic. It is sociogenic, rooted in the island's class/color hierarchy. The psychological disorganization of Marie Chauvet's female characters cannot be understood outside of Haiti's repressive social and political institutions. The panic of Warner-Vieyra's heroines can be conceived as symbolic of the Caribbean people's situation in front of the destructive play of forces they experience but cannot yet control.

The literary confrontation with society can sometimes be too direct, as in Nadine Magloire's *Le mal de vivre* (1968) and *Le sexe mythique* (1975). The didactic intention is hardly hidden in these two works written in the strident language of pamphleteers. Magloire's tone is naively provocative when denouncing the conditions in Haiti, where "women never reach maturity and remain all their lives minors."[13] The novel is for its author a pretext for reflecting on the problems of language, readership, and cultural support which writers inexorably encounter in a country like Haiti. These considerations obfuscate the already very tenuous story line.

For most of the novelists considered in this study, writing is a praxis, a commitment to social reality. Marie Chauvet, for instance, finds the pressing accent of the indigenists to decry the dire misery of the Haitian peasantry in her novel *Fonds des Nègres* (1961). Although Chauvet's social vision is often blurred by sectarian concerns, she always adopts an antithetical posture in face of the unjust order of things in Haiti. It must not be forgotten that Chauvet died in 1982 in exile, forced out of Haiti after the publication of her trilogy, *Amour, colore et folie*, which contains a virulent denunciation of Haiti's tyrannical regimes. Marie-Thérèse Colimon in *Fils de misère* (1973) depicts the condition of the masses in the manner of the nineteenth-century French social novelists: powerless victims of an indifferent or brutal social structure. With Lamercie, the protagonist, she portrays the struggle of woman to lift the poverty that condemns her and those of her condition to a subhuman existence. The conclusion of the novel, however, leaves little hope for change as Lamercie dies, felled by the bullets of defenders of the status quo.

In *Le chant des Sirènes* (1973), Colimon exposes the contradictions of the exodus of Haitians to foreign lands in search of economic or personal salvation. In this collection of short stories, Colimon, with a mixture of humor and gravity, shows that the attraction of "over-there" (là-bas) is as delusive and maddening as the song of sirens heard by disoriented seamen. The logic of modern reality that transports Haitians to the most remote parts of the world explains why there are echoes of the Vietnam War in Liliane Devieux's *L'amour oui, la mort non* (1976). Marie Chauvet's posthumous novel, *Les Rapaces* (1986), offers a horrifying image of Haiti's

13. Nadine Magloire, *Le sexe mythique* (Port-au-Prince: Editions du Verseau,) p. 58.

misery: police terrorism, famine, the wholesaling of Haitian blood on the international health care market, and so on. In the society Chauvet depicts, all human values have vanished and violence has reduced both oppressed and oppressors to a semibarbaric state. Maryse Condé's latest novel, *La vie scélérate* (1987), erases all boundaries in its attempts to incorporate fragments of the black experience throughout the Americas and indeed throughout the world. The text gives the appearance of a patchwork seemingly conceived to translate the reality of the diaspora. In this saga of a Guadeloupean family over several generations, Condé undertakes a journey through contemporary black history. She evokes those Guadeloupeans and Martiniquans recruited for the construction of the Panama Canal. We are transported to the center of Marcus Garvey's movement, to the San Francisco of the 1960s with the Black Panthers, to the upheavals of the civil rights struggle with Malcolm X and Martin Luther King. Condé takes her characters to Jamaica and Haiti. There are even references in this novel to the political events that shook Haiti at the fall of the Duvalier regime. In *Segou I* (1984) and *Segou II* (1986), history constitutes the strategic point from which Condé unfolds her dense and less than neutral African saga. With *Moi Tituba* (1986), Condé undertakes the project of filling in a blank page of history. Following the example of the Afro-American novelist Ann Petry, Condé reconstructs the life of the black witch of Salem, the forgotten one whom history remembers only as "a slave from Barbados, who practiced Hoodoo." The novel is written in the first person. It is Tituba herself who claims her right to existence. She recounts her struggle for survival under the system of slavery in Barbados and against religious bigotry in Massachusetts. In exalting the will to live and the resilience of her heroine, Condé no doubt sought to propose an inspiring model in the context of today's debate for independence in Guadeloupe and Martinique. Her Tituba, however, who remains essentially a toy in the hands of fate and her oppressors, can hardly be considered a mobilizing symbol. She does not reach the stature of a figure such as Solitude, the legendary maroon, who in Caribbean lore incarnates resistance and invincibility.

Some works in Caribbean feminine expression can be viewed as breaking the chain of alienation. They propose images of women who find a voice to claim a parcel of power over reality and destiny. These works provoke interesting questions and uncover uncharted domains for women and the Caribbean as a whole. Such is the project of Simone Schwarz-Bart in *Pluie et vent sur Télumée Miracle* (1972), strangely translated under the title *The Bridge of Beyond*. Schwarz-Bart affirms the forces of life against those of death and destruction. She articulates a poetry of presence and plenitude against absence and fragmentation. With her, the notions of

Caribbean self and Caribbean history become thinkable. Télumée, her heroine, like the other women of the Lougandor family to which she belongs, expresses all that is possible to express in spite of the adverse conditions threatening her resolve to live. A system of liberating myths is elaborated in this novel, which celebrates the regenerating power of love and the possibility of conquering what in the brutal logic of realism seems impossible: freedom. To the reality of the plantation, of conditions of the Antilles, Schwarz-Bart opposes the indomitable spirit of women who refuse to be subjugated. Télumée draws her energy from the language and the culture of the island which mediates her entrance into the world of identity, presence, and continuity. Télumée is not extradited outside of her body, whose beauty she offers to her lover, Elie. She feels "right in her place where she is," that is, in the island. The island in Schwarz-Bart's fiction is not a place to be fled nor a prison in which one slowly dies; it is the locus of self-discovery and human realization. One can speak of Schwarz-Bart's aesthetic practice as a veritable "poetic of space." There is a certain solemnity in this novel, which celebrates the reappropriation by the islanders of their territory. Schwarz-Bart introduces her own creolized language to take possession of the landscape. She selects a precise vocabulary to name familiar sites, trees, flowers, and plants of the island. It is as if the legitimate occupation of the Caribbean soil by its inhabitants depended on the act of naming. Time is reconquered as the Caribbean existence is replaced in its historical continuum. The quest for the African source is central in Schwarz-Bart's reconstruction of reality. Other dimensions are conquered as the author undertakes a bold exploration of the magical realm that lies beyond empirical reality. In this perilous enterprise, Schwarz-Bart never succumbs to sterile and factitious imagery. The point of departure and the point of arrival of her narrative is always the human experience.

In *Ti-Jean l'Horizon* (1979), her second novel, Schwarz-Bart executes one of the most accomplished Caribbean literary compositions. In this daring epic, history converges with the marvelous, playful notes alternating with grave tones, and vivacious spirit blends with an introspective mood. It is a polyphonic construct in which the author harmonizes different voices to tell a tale of indestructible love, the love of Ti-Jean for Egee, a "négresse sans fard ni pose," whom he calls his "Little Guadeloupe." It is also the fantastic tale of the hero's search for the sun, symbol of freedom, which has disappeared, swallowed by a monstrous Beast from "elsewhere." At the end of his long journey through the present and the past, the realms of reality and surreality, Ti-Jean, the hero, feels "old as the mountains" but convinced that "everything is intact." The end, for him, is only the beginning because "already, life was being reinvented, passionately, in

light of torches simply painted in the soil."[14] Schwarz-Bart in her fiction
brings to an apotheosis the creative force already illustrated in the remarkable works of Jacques Roumain, Jacques S. Alexis, or Edouard Glissant. Like these writers, she concretizes through a conscious aesthetic
practice a *Weltanschauung* that recognizes the urgency of collective liberation. Her recently published play *Ton beau capitaine* (1987) also deserves
mention here. In this piece, Schwarz-Bart, with an economy of words
and brilliant insight, succeeds in relating the struggle of man and woman
to forge a language to communicate over the waters that separate them.
It is the story of a Haitian migrant worker in Guadeloupe and his wife,
who remains in Haiti. It is a story of dreams shattered but unceasingly
reformed, of truth emerging from lies, of desire indefinitely postponed,
of two people searching for unknown words to formulate their love. A
masterpiece of conciseness and vision, this play is significant not only
because of the themes it explores but also because it suggests the development of a dialogue between the Caribbean societies. It signifies that
Guadeloupe is aware of Haiti in an eminently urgent manner. It implies
that a cross-discursive space has been created where a new debate on the
destiny of the Caribbean is taking place.

Women writers in the Caribbean have been involved in an active in-
terrogation of reality, past and present. Their preoccupations and their
responses are diverse. Their voices are not interchangeable. The investigation of works by women reveals that the spectrum of their concerns
is as broad as that of their male counterparts. They come from diverse
ideological perspectives and remain enmeshed in the relations that define
social and cultural reality in the Caribbean. There are, of course, as I have
attempted to demonstrate, certain striking parallels and similarities in
Caribbean women's fiction: the internal position of the female subjects/
narrators in several novels tends to be the same, their relations with or
disconnections from others seem to be determined by similar categories
of experience, the narrative is often motivated by an urgent personal crisis.
My examination also reveals that Caribbean women's fiction is not solely
centered on the self. It is structured on the multiple contradictions and
potentialities within Caribbean societies. The literature by women writers
in Haiti, Guadeloupe, and Martinique is not a marginal phenomenon;
neither is it an innocent practice. It brings us into direct confrontation
with the experiences and aspirations of the Caribbean people. Women
writers are fully engaged in the verbal and aesthetic process through
which literature institutes its connection with reality.

14. Simone Schwarz-Bart, *Ti-Jean l'horizon* (Paris: Editions du Seuil, 1979), p. 286.

Women Writers of the Dutch-Speaking Caribbean: *Life Long Poem* in the Tradition of Surinamese *Granmorgu* (New Dawn)

INEKE PHAF

In recent months, a controversial and polemical discussion in the Dutch press has centered on Astrid Roemer, born in 1947 in Paramaribo, Surinam, and a resident of the Netherlands for the last ten years. The points in this public debate are certainly not unlike those raised in similar discussions in the United States that touch on the humiliation of a so-called black female person who refuses to let herself be classified under an exclusively black, feminist, lesbian, nationalist, or other label because it seems to condemn her never to develop in any other direction. The variety of Astrid Roemer's points of view—although always based on the same cultural and creative conflict—causes her to be the subject of attacks by Surinamese colleague-writers as well as by Dutch journalists, who accuse her of the incorrect use of the Dutch language, superfluous metaphorical involvement, opportunism in sexual relations with press representatives to make herself famous, and the product of a momentary fashion in Dutch culture, not to mention more indecent points they make to damage her publicly. All of this does not prevent her readers from buying her books, and although the professional criticism of her literary work is still relatively poor, her theater texts, poems, short stories, and novels are discussed in schools, free universities, and creative writing courses of spontaneous reading circles, not only in the Netherlands, but to a lesser degree in her native country as well.

This debate is not as innocent as it seems at first sight because nearly half of the Surinamese population currently lives in the Netherlands, following and trying to interpret the inside political strategy of the military government of Desi Bouterse since 1980, which forever changed all ex-

357

isting stereotypes about Surinamese identity as a "happy multicultural society." This reflective process disturbs the production of literary clichés and deeply influences the creative expression of Astrid Roemer, as is shown especially in her last book, *Life Long Poem*, published in November 1987 in Haarlem.[1]

To anyone familiar with the cultural tradition and complexity of Caribbean society, it seems inexplicable that Surinam and the so-called Dutch Antilles (the islands) are undiscovered spots, not only in women's literature but also in the general panorama of world culture. Although located at the border of the American continent, these lands hardly seem to belong to it, despite their linguistic treasures of Papiamento, Sranan, Sarnami, Javanese, Saramacca, Djuka, Dutch, English, and at least ten more living languages.

The history of this part of the world is closely related to the slave trade— Korsou was the harbor that slaves were brought through if they came from Africa and thence into the whole of the Americas—and at the same time it had the best organized opposition against any form of colonizing centralized government, the villages of Maroons and Indians in Surinam having remained intact up to the present time. Slave trade and rebellion are crucial issues in modern history since the time of Cristobal Colón, the birth of present-day American society, which reveals all the traces of the archetypical prejudices in the Caribbean area, where they have often survived in their most elementary form because of long socioeconomic stagnation.

One could understand the task of a present-day writer to break through this isolation of nonparticipation in an American context, especially in the twentieth century, as these areas begin to define themselves as modern nations (Surinam has been independent since 1975; the Dutch Antilles are negotiating autonomy for the 1990s) which cannot completely share the ideas of the French Revolution, American independence, or Simón Bolívar's dreams at the end of the eighteenth century. History has proven to be more complex, in that political ideas can resolve the limitations on the more dynamic process inside sociocultural structures. This conscience characterizes the structure of the recent book by Astrid Roemer.

Life Long Poem deals with historical facts within a Surinamese perspective during the 1970s and 1980s only in an indirect way; history does not seem to influence the action but lies at the base of the narrative plot, which is shaped as an autobiographical novel. The protagonist speaks in the first person, the *I* as the subject and center of the novel in her dialogue with the opposing *you*—Surinamese persons of different gender, age, and cultural background. The protagonist searches for the reasons for her own existence as the writer experiencing it, and thus the reader, as the continuous

---

1. Astrid Roemer, *Levens-Lang Gedicht* (Haarlem, the Netherlands: In de Knipscheer, 1987).

interlocutor, shares the writer's feelings. The obvious struggle in dialogical form between the centralizing *I* and the decentralizing *you* elaborates on the resistance of the Surinamese against their past within a modern and metropolitan world. In this sense, the nation-perspective is transmitted through confusing personal experiences with family members, friends, servants, and others, all belonging to something that is called Surinam, with its smells, vegetation, atmospheric events, and historical facts.

If we accept this nation-orientation as a conscious concept in Roemer's book—and there is no reason not to—the narrative construction she chooses refers immediately to what the Russian linguist and literary theorist and critic Mikhail Bakhtin is speaking about in his essay "On the Prehistory of the Novelistic Word,"[2] published in 1941 in the USSR, which underlines the relationship between national identity and the novel as a genre. Bakhtin traces the birth of the novel in the seventeenth century back to its predecessors in the classical period of Greek culture, in which the inner structure of what would later be called a novel was present in the ironic capacity of parodizing nation mythologies, showing them with their "hidden" or "forbidden" sides up instead of the sides that dogmatic tendencies would normally allow. This laughing about or "carnivalization" of popular nation dogmas found its written expression in the democratic Greek world in a fourth theater performance, after the public had consumed the tragic trilogy, in a comical relativization of all the serious conflicts represented in this classical theater form.

The revival of classical culture in the Renaissance and the redefinition of national perspectives with the discovery of the New World gave birth to the novel, which internalizes this classical literary technique to reflect nation reality as a changing and changeable process. This historical development has an impact on how the language of novels can be understood in a specific historical situation. The simultaneous presence of a tragical reality and its paradoxical ironization prevents any dogmatic one-line explanation and shows the novel as a working hypothesis about this issue, which reflects only one possible view of this phenomenon expressed through the writer in his historical setting. On the basis of this working hypothesis, the capacity of different language levels which refer to social contexts is tried out to test the efficacy of this dialogical function of literature in opening space for a complex and differentiated world. In the interpretation of Bakhtin this dialogue is basically self-critical and must be understood as such. Otherwise, any interpretation would miss the sense of debating cross-cultural historical issues through the style of novelistic dialogue, which goes far beyond the grammatically correct expres-

---

2. Mikhail Bakhtin, *Esthétique et théorie du roman*, trans. from the Russian by Daria Olivier, preface by Michel Aucouturier (Paris: Gallimard, 1978), pp. 441–73.

sion of situations and intends to shape them in the archetypical setting as a part of cultural communication through written texts.

These reflections on the irreplaceable style of the novel, relating it to modern history in a much wider scope than a sociology of the novel usually does, focusing almost exclusively on the author's inner rebellion against bourgeois society, seem to account for everything the *Life Long Poem* of Astrid Roemer is calling for. The 340-page novel is written mostly in Dutch, although the linguistic complexity of Surinamese society is accentuated by Sranan and Saramaccan quotations, the English of gospels and spirituals, and a frequent use of biblical expressions, sometimes in church Latin.

The four large parts, each one introduced by an astrological reference of the *I* or by a description of the dry and wet seasons in Surinam, are divided into three small chapters each. This structure, at first sight very regular, betrays the eye by giving the impression of an action which develops tragically in the first three parts and then adds a counterpart in the fourth, creating an ironic, parodizing interpretation of the former narrated drama. Yet it is not so simple. The *I* goes from one profound experience in a relationship to another, apparently without a rigid chronological scheme of action, letting anyone make his own logic out of the reading. Her life is described as that of a divorced woman in the Netherlands with several relationships to women of the family or friends, which show a way back to the first childhood memories in Paramaribo when she was three years old. This is the function of the constant dialogue of the *I* with the different *you*'s, persons who have been of importance in her life. Through this procedure, a hundred years of family history become transparent as a reflection of a crucial part of history in a land scarcely existing on the margin of history of the American continent since the end of the eighteenth century.

The reference to this Age of Enlightenment is recorded by an often-repeated children's song, which describes the indifferent reaction of streetfolk to the English invasion of Paramaribo in 1799 in their interpretation of the official attitude to it: "Perun Perun mi patron san'wani kon'mek a kon'[Perun Perun my chief lets come what has to come]."[3]

Like other recent novels about a hundred years of family history in American nations, such as *A Hundred Years of Solitude* by Gabriel García Márquez or *The House of Spirits* by Isabel Allende,[4] to mention only those influenced by Spanish-American and Caribbean cultures, Roemer's history accentuates the cyclical structure of her narrative, from which she gives a way out by breaking the stereotypes that determine personal as

3. This is a constantly repeated verse throughout the entire novel, in which the writer elaborates on one variation.

4. Gabriel García Márquez, *Cien años de soledad* (Buenos Aires: Losada, 1968); Isabel Allende, *La casa de los espíritus* (Mexico City: Edivisión), 1985.

well as social reality. The Chinese and Arabic-Moorish great-grandfathers who came to Surinam at the end of the past century and had many children with different women, of which the official one was very religious, are the criminal and immoral commercial forefathers of the decent, urban, middle-class family of the *I*, established and relatively prosperous in the capital of Surinam, Paramaribo. The late grandfather was the most famous baker in town, and the five children of his legal marriage are a pharmacist, a sports teacher, a classical organist, a dancing-school director, and an importer of foreign consumer goods. All of these professions fit into the perspective of a proper social standing, considered to be much more civilized than dependence on only a bakery. The bakery is inherited by the illegitimate children of the grandfather, and the two parts of the family do not share their respective destinies. The fact that the grandfather lived till his death with a woman without any education, who helped him with his work in the bakehouse and gave birth to daughters, does not fit the image of a happy, united, middle-class front so the respectable descendants banned him from their memory.

Such a doomed past cannot be overcome by a demonstration of family ties which respond to social expectations or by the formation of a united front of the colored population in politics, presuming that the differences in culture and education simply will disappear. These social structures, profoundly marked by racial prejudice, can be mobilized only by an individual effort accompanying the social ones in the aspiration to change. In this sense, the *I* shows her marriage as an act of rebellion. At the moment that she becomes independent by finishing her last exams, she falls in love with an infamous seducer of women in Paramaribo, a black lawyer and representative of the united political front. He is sent to the Netherlands as a diplomat, and she goes with him as his official wife.

In spite of her not completely accepted marriage, the *I* keeps a solid relationship with her mother and grandmother, two women she is very close to, even though she recognizes, criticizes, and tries to overcome in herself their legacy of racial prejudice, insensibility, and middle-class arrogance toward persons descended from other sociocultural traditions. This continuous social and individual rebellion against the violence characterized by bloodshed is symbolized in the tiger dance as a cornerstone to initiate a dynamic concept of a nation. As the conditions for the independence of Surinam are negotiated by the united government front, the mother of *I*, as director of the dancing school and respected member of the urban community of Paramaribo, is asked to prepare an official dancing event during the visit to the colony of the Dutch queen and her prince consort. As a representation of the disappearance of old traumas, the tiger dance announces a new beginning, but its symbols do not express the real situation. This situation changes slowly and when, some years later, children play the ghost dance at masked parties, an old popular singing game comes up: "Mi de kon' mi de kon' spoke'dans bigi sensi wan'luku spoke'dans (He is coming, he is coming, the dance of the ghosts, one big cent to look at the dance of the ghosts)."[5] The persons identified with a slave past return, such as the miserable lebas who clean the streets of dirt, the bakrus or beggars, the jorkas or shadows of the forefathers, and the azimas, religious men dressed in women's clothes.

The presence of a father plays an important role in social as well as personal life. It determines the neurotic relationship of *I* with her memories. Only in the fourth part does a solution appear for a possibility of public and individual happiness in the future. The female black child of an intimate friend of *I*, her first lover, gave his adopted daughter her name. The name acquires a symbolic meaning because this child is the only one who does not wear masks during the children's party with the ghost dance. Having a father permits her to live without masquerades, as opposed to her older namesake, *I*. The protagonist then discovers that her own—to her unknown—father is a Cuban stardancer who visited her land and wanted to take her mother with him to his country, that now pagan and proud nation of Castro, a plan which the grandmother sabotaged because she did not want to lose her only daughter. It is in this sense that the presence of the Havana-yellow emotional experiences filled with blood references imply the longing for more peaceful alternatives in the search for democratic identity in this novel.

The message of opening up national perspectives, already present in two other novels by the same author, *About the Madness of a Woman* and *Nowhere, Somewhere*,[6] is shown in this recent work in a classical novelistic conception of modern world literature, in which a strong engagement against racism and participation in debates about feminist and gay rights is elaborated in the knowledge that literature is a powerful medium in the struggle to overcome social prejudices imposed by Western culture:

> Literature can be for us a powerful medium if we reject the models which Western literary history dictates and if we are conscious of a specific paradigm that the historicity of our country and our people imposes on us. Only when we are rescued from the mirror image of the material rulers of the world and search for what are our essential values, as individuals and as a collective, as lettered and as unlettered persons, literature will speak for us, because only then the language will have found its originality again: in the beginning was the word.[7]

5. This verse is repeated twice at the end of the third part in the novel, the tragic end.
6. Astrid Roemer, *Over de gekte van een vrouw* (Haarlem: In de Knipscheer, 1982); Astrid Roemer, *Nergens ergens* (Haarlem: In de Knipscheer, 1983).
7. Astrid Roemer, "In the Beginning Was the Word and After That the Illiterates: About

With this biblical reference to the beginnings of written tradition in the New Testament, it must be stressed that Astrid Roemer unconsciously looked back to the oldest democratic literary style simultaneously to confirm and criticize nation myths, proposing that the existence of concrete symbols in relation to Surinam is proven without any doubt. In this tradition one could look back on the history of women writers in her home country and the Antilles to see where they used their accents to express themselves, to show their interpretation of the Surinamese/Caribbean female "image" of one who "refused to have children, refused to confess to men and refused to work for her landlords."[8]

As they started publishing around the time of World War II, some women writers did not know anything about the books of European women in Germany, England, or the Netherlands, who wrote about plantation society in the West Indies in the seventeenth and eighteenth centuries after having traveled to this region or because of an intensive correspondence with their family and friends located there. They were oriented to the primary tradition of women (and men) as centers of a rich oral history, flexible toward any public and personal event that happened and therefore the nearest historical expression to the feeling of the different social groups. Over the course of modernization, these mostly poetical beginnings became elaborate literary products including short stories, theater plays, and novels, and the list of important women writers is already long, although not studied within its own traditional line. A few of these writers are Lydia Ecury, Oda Blinder, May Henriques, Sonia Garmers, and Diane Lebacs from the Antilles and Sophie Redmond, Bea Vianen, Trudy Guda, and Thea Doelweit from Surinam, as well as at least fifteen others who began to publish in the last five years. Attention to Astrid Roemer, who characterizes herself as a publicist and not as a professional writer because of the elitist connotation the Western world has given to this expression, and her work by no means lessens the value of the work of the others. Because of lack of investigation and out of solidarity with Astrid Roemer in reference to the polemic around her at this time, I hope to give a more objective, female support from the side of the literary critics, revealing her classical importance within literary history. At the same time, I am proposing a framework within which the entire literary tradition of women writing about changing expectations in the national orientation of their home region may be studied in stylistic and cultural expression as well, to sensitize this effort to open space for textual reflection in a Caribbean context.

the Power of Literature," in Ulrich Fleischmann and Ineke Phaf, eds., *The Caribbean and Latin America/El Caribe y América Latina* (Frankfurt am Main: Vervuert, 1987), pp. 210–30.
  8. Ibid, p. 234.

To give an impression of how closely related they are with Roemer, I end this essay with a poem written by the oldest known poetess of Surinam, Johanna Schouten-Elsenhout, born in 1910 in Paramaribo, who noted her verses down on paper "amidst the aromatic fragrances of her cooking pots," in a Sranan without punctuation or versification:

GRANMORGU

Ini a pikin alen-ten dropu

ay mi lobi
a tapu a dyamanti pasi fu a neti

mi si taki yu de
nanga dyomp'ati f'den dungru yari
f'mi libi I dyompo tanapu
lek wan owru dren di kon tru

Wan krioro di ben e sribi
a mindri dungru pasi f'libi
frey opo lek wan kopro-prin
maskita
fu suku a libi di kibri en srefi
a mindri son nanga alen
a ondro den tranga rutu f'den
bon-taki
fa den e way fu tron draywinti

fu kanti den bigi bon ala sey

Anu na anu ati e doro gron f'ati

Brudu e katibo yu skin

Ke mi krinfesi sranan uma

nanga yu trutru granlobi
yu sor i srefi a tapu a gowtu
pasi
granmorgu
a mindri den fayalobi bon

NEW DAWN

In the drops of
the rainy season
oh my love
On the diamond-studded path of
the night
I see that you shrink
from the dark years
of my life. You have arisen
like a long lost dream which
comes true
A Creole who slept
midst the dark alleys of life
startled like a malarial mosquito

to look for life hiding itself
amidst the sun and rain
under the strong roots dangling
from the branches of a tree
how blow they not to be a wind
that whirls
and causes huge trees to sway
from side to side
Slowly the heart reaches the
bottom of the heart
The body becomes a slave to
blood
Oh my open-faced woman of
Surinam
with your real deep love
you've dared to show yourself on
the gilded path
new dawn
amidst the fayalobi trees.[9]

9. Johanna Schouten-Elsenhout, "Granmorgu," in Jan Voorhoeve and Ursy M. Lichtveld, eds., *Creole Drum: An Anthology of Creole Literature in Surinam* with English translations by Vernie A. February (New Haven: Yale University Press, 1975), p. 235. This poem may belong to the tradition of the "lobisingi" (love songs), which are a completely feminine affair. They originated "after the time of slavery. Lesbian love is more or less institutionalized in Creole society" (ibid., p. 18).

Caribbean Women Writers:
A Selected Bibliography

Selected Critical Works Dealing with West Indian Women's Literature

Bandara, S. B. "A Short Bibliography of Caribbean Fiction." *World Literature Written in English* 18 (April 1979): 181–234.

Barratt, Harold. "Shuttered Cleavage: Marion Jones' Tormented People." *World Literature Written in English* 19 (Spring 1980): 57–61.

———, ed. *Critics on Caribbean Literature*. London: Allen & Unwin, 1978.

Baugh, Edward. "Goodison on the Road to Heartease." *Journal of West Indian Literature* 1 (October 1986): 13–22.

Bennett, Louise. "Bennett on Bennett." *Caribbean Quarterly* 14, nos. 1 and 2 (1968): 98.

Brathwaite, Edward. "Creative Literature of the British West Indies during the Period of Slavery." *Savacou* 1 (June 1970): 46–70.

Brathwaite, Edward, and Lucille Mair. *The Caribbean Woman*. Special issue of *Savacou* 13 (1977).

Boyce-Davies, Carol. *Out of the Kumbla*. Trenton, N.J.: Africa World Press, 1988.

Breiner, Laurence A. "Lyric and Autobiography in West Indian Literature." *Journal of West Indian Literature* 3 (January 1989): 3–15.

Cooper, Carolyn. "Disarming Women." *Journal of West Indian Literature* 2 (January 1987): 55–66.

———. "Noh Lickle Twang: An Introduction to the Poetry of Louise Bennett." *World Literature Written in English* 17 (April 1978): 317–27.

———. "The Oral Witness and the Scribal Document: Divergent Accounts of Slavery in Two Novels of Barbados." In Mark McWatt, ed., *West Indian Literature and Its Social Context*, pp. 3–11. St. Michael, Barbados: English Department of University of the West Indies, 1985.

Coulson, Sheila. "Politics and the Female Experience: An Examination of *Beka Lamb* and *Heremakhonon*." In Lowell Fiet, ed., *West Indian Literature and Its Political Context*, pp. 92–105. Río Piedras, Puerto Rico: University of Puerto Rico, 1988.

Cudjoe, Selwyn R. *Resistance and Caribbean Literature*. Athens: Ohio University Press, 1980.

Dance, Daryl Cumber, ed. *Fifty Caribbean Writers: A Bio-Bibliographical and Critical Sourcebook*. Westport, Conn.: Greenwood Press, 1986.

Fayad, Mona. "Unquiet Ghosts: The Struggle for Representation in Rhys' *Wide Sargasso Sea*." *Modern Fiction Studies* 34 (Fall 1988): 437–52.

Fido, Elaine Savory. "The Construct of the Self: Jean Rhys' Work and the Concept of Autobiography." Paper Presented at the Eighth Annual Conference on West Indian Literature, May 1988.

———. "Island and Overseas: Visions." *Journal of West Indian Literature* 1, no. 2 (1987): 58–64.

———. "The Politics of Colours and the Politics of Writing in the Fiction of Jean Rhys." In Lowell Fiet, ed., *West Indian Literature and Its Political Context*, pp. 61–78. Río Piedras, Puerto Rico: University of Puerto Rico, 1988.

Gilroy, Beryl. "The Woman Writer and Commitment: Links between Caribbean and African Literature." *Wasafiri*, no. 10 (Summer 1989): 15–16.

Harris, Wilson. "The Question of Form and Realism in the West Indian Artist." In *Tradition, The Writer and Society*, pp. 13–20. London: New Beacon, 1967.

Hawthorne, Evelyn. "Power from Within: Christianity, Rastafarianism, and Obeah in the Novels of Roger Mais." *Journal of West Indian Literature* 2, no. 2 (1988): 23–32.

Herdeck, Donald E. *Caribbean Writers: A Bio-bilbio-critical Encyclopedia*. Washington, D.C.: Three Continents Press, 1979.

Hill, Errol. "The Emergence of a Caribbean Aesthetic." *Bim* 17 (June 1983): 101–9.

———. "An Interview with Olive Senior." *Kunapipi* 8, no. 2 (1986): 11–20.

Insanally, Annette. "Sexual Politics in Contemporary Female Writing in the Caribbean." In Lowell Fiet, ed., *West Indian Literature and Its Political Context*, pp. 79–91. Río Piedras, Puerto Rico: University of Puerto Rico, 1988.

James, Louis, ed. *The Islands in Between: Essays on West Indian Literature*. London: Oxford University Press, 1968.

Jonas, Joyce. "Wilson Harris and the Concept of Threshold Art." *Journal of West Indian Literature* 1, no. 2 (1987): 29–34.

Kemp, Yakini. "Woman and Womanchild: Bonding and Selfhood in Three West Indian Novels by Women." *Sage* 2 (Spring 1985): 24–27.

King, Bruce, ed. *West Indian Literature*. London: Macmillan, 1979.

Leigh, Nancy J. "Mirror, Mirror: The Development of Female Identity in Jean Rhys' Fiction." *World Literature Written in English* 25 (Fall 1985): 270–84.

Lawrence, Leota S. "The Historical Perspective of the Caribbean Woman." *Negro Historical Bulletin* 47, nos. 1 and 2 (1984).

———. "Women in Caribbean Literature: The African Presence." *Phylon* 44 (1983).

Luengo, Anthony E. "*Wide Sargasso Sea* and the Gothic Mode." *World Literature Written in English* 15 (April 1976): 229–45.

Mellown, Elgin W. "A Bibliography of the Writing of Jean Rhys." *World Literature Written in English* 16 (April 1977): 179–202.

Ngcobo, Lauretta, ed. *Let It Be Told: Black Women Writers in Britain*. London: Virago, 1987.

Niesen de Abruña, Laura. "Twentieth Century Women Writers from the English-Speaking Caribbean." *Modern Fiction Studies* 34 (Spring 1988): 85–96.

Norris, Jerrie. *Presenting Rosa Guy*. Boston: Twayne, 1988.

O'Callaghan, Evelyn. "Feminist Consciousness: European/American Theory, Jamaican Stories." In Lowell Fiet, ed., *West Indian Literature and Its Political Context*, pp. 27–51. Río Piedras, Puerto Rico: University of Puerto Rico, 1988.

———. "Journals, Letters and Stories—Early West Indian Narratives by Women."

Paper Presented at the Eighth Annual Conference on West Indian Literature, May 1988.

———. " 'Outsiders' Voice': White Creole Women Novelists in the Caribbean Literary Tradition." *Journal of West Indian Literature* 1 (October 1986): 74–88.

———. "Thriller! Some Observations on Recent Popular Fiction in the West Indies." In Mark McWatt, ed., *West Indian Literature and Its Social Context*, pp. 148–62. St. Michael, Barbados: English Department of the University of the West Indies, 1985.

O'Connor, Teresa F. *Jean Rhys: The West Indian Novels.* New York: New York University Press, 1986.

Pollard, Velma. "Cultural Connections in Paule Marshall's *Praise Song for the Widow.*" *World Literature Written in English* 25 (Fall 1985): 285–97.

Poynting, Jeremy. "East Indian Women in the Caribbean: Experience and Voice." In *India in the Caribbean.* London: Hansib Publications, 1987.

Ramchand, Kenneth. *Introduction to the Study of West Indian Literature.* Middlesex: Nelson, 1976.

———. *The West Indian Novel and Its Background.* 2d ed. London: Heinemann, 1983.

Rheddock, Rhoda. *Elma Francois.* London: New Beacon Books, 1988.

Rohlehr, F. G. "West Indian Poetry: Some Problems of Assessment." *Bim* 14 (January–June 1972): 80–88, continued in 14 (July–December 1972): 134–43.

Sander, Reinhard W. "Short Fiction in West Indian Periodicals: A Checklist." *World Literature Written in English* 15 (November 1976): 438–62.

Scafe, Suzanne. *Teaching Black Literature.* London: Virago Education Series, 1989.

Thorpe, Marjorie. "The Problem of Cultural Identification in *Crick Crack Monkey.*" *Savacou*, no. 13 (1977): 31–38.

Tiffin, Helen. "Mirror and Mask: Colonial Motifs in the Novels of Jean Rhys." *World Literature Written in English* 17 (April 1978): 328–41.

Troester, Rosalie Riegle. "Turbulence and Tenderness: Mothers, Daughters, and 'Othermothers' in Paule Marshall's *Brown Girl, Brownstones.*" *Sage* 1 (Fall 1984): 13–16.

Walker-Johnson, Joyce. "Autobiography, History and the Novel: Erna Brodber's *Jane and Louisa Will Soon Come Home.*" *Journal of West Indian Literature* 3 (January 1989): 47–59.

Williams, John, trans. "Return of a Native Daughter: An Interview with Paule Marshall and Maryse Condé." *Sage* 3 (Fall 1986): 52–53.

Wilson, Betty. "Sexual, Racial and National Politics: Jacqueline Manicom's *Mon examen de blanc.*" *Journal of West Indian Literature* 1, no. 2 (1987): 50–57.

Works of Poetry by English-Speaking Women Writers of the West Indies

Adisa, Opal Palmer, with Devorah Major. *Travelling Women.* Oakland, Calif.: Jukebox Press, 1989.

Alexander, Francine, Candyce Kelshall, and Laila Haidarali. *The Aftermath.* Port of Spain: Privately printed, 1988.

Allfrey, Phyllis. *In Circles.* Middlesex: Harrow Weald, 1940.

———. *Palm and Oak II.* Roseau, Dominica: Star Printery, 1973.

Alt, Daisy. *Dedications on Turning Thirty.* Kingston, Jamaica: Mode Printery, 1971.

"An Anthology of West Indian Poetry." *Caribbean Quarterly* 5, no. 3 (1958), also in *Kyk-Over-Al*, no. 22 (1957).

Antoine, Jean. "The Artist's Dream," "On Unspoken Love," and "On Work Well Done." *New Voices* 3, no. 5 (1975): 26, 12–13.

Augustus, Stella. *Steps Along the Way.* Port of Spain, Trinidad: Imprint Caribbean Ltd., 1977.

Bain-Mottley, Janice. "Casual Meeting." *Voices* 1, no. 4 (1965): 5.
———. "Effects of M.J.Q." and "Invitation." *Voices* 1, no. 3 (1965): 3, 20.
Bennett, Louise. *Dialect Verse.* Kingston, Jamaica: Herald, 1942.
———. *Jamaican Dialect Poems.* Kingston, Jamaica: Gleaner, 1948.
———. *Jamaican Humor in Dialect.* Kingston, Jamaica: Jamaica Press, 1943.
———. *Jamaica Labrish.* Kingston, Jamaica: Sangsters, 1966.
Bloom, Valerie. *Teach Mi, Tell Mi.* London: Bogle l'Ouverture, 1983.
Brand, Dionne. *Chronicles of the Hostile Sun.* Toronto: Williams and Wallace, 1984.
———. *Earth Magic, Winter Epigrams and Epigrams to Erneste Cardenal in Defense of Claudia.* Toronto: Williams and Wallace, 1983.
———. *'Fore Day Morning.* Toronto: Khosian Artists, 1978.
Brathwaite, Jacqueline. *A Tribute to All.* Scarborough: Tobago Printery, 1989.
Breeze, Jean Binta. *Riddym Ravings and Other Poems.* London: Race Today, 1988.
Brown, Beverly E. *Dream Diary.* Kingston, Jamaica: Savacou Co-operative, 1982.
Brown, Lloyd. *West Indian Poetry.* London: Heinemann, 1978.
Burnett, Paula, ed. *Penguin Book of Caribbean Verse in English.* Harmondsworth: Penguin, 1986.
Bynoe, Irene. "Illusion." *Bim* 1 no. 2 (1943): 6.
Caesar, Oris. "Fools' Gold" and "What the Night Says." *New Voices* 3, no. 5 (1975): 7.
———. "Uncle Sammy." *New Voices* 2, no. 3 (1974): 7.
Clarke, Elizabeth. "Signs and Wonders." *Savacou*, nos. 7 and 8 (1973): 120–21.
Collins, Merle. *Because the Dawn Breaks.* London: Karia Press, 1985.
Collymore, Petra. "Humming Bird." *Bim*, no. 44 (1967): 287.
Comma-Maynard, Olga. *Carib Echoes: A Collection of Poems.* Port of Spain, Trinidad: Guardian, 1957.
———. *Carib Echoes: Poems and Stories for Juniors.* Port of Spain, Trinidad: Columbus Publishers, 1972.
Cooper, Afua. *Breaking Chains.* Toronto: Sister Vision, 1984.
Cromwell, Liz. "All the People of the World," "As Birds Sing," "Crucifixion," "Diary of a Three Year Old Black Princess," "Fairy Tale," "Rosary," "Singer," "Time Shook Its Head," and "Victim." *New Voices* 4, nos. 7 and 8 (1976): 44–50.
———. "Canadian Jungle Tea." Toronto: Hosian Artists, 1975.
Cudjoe, Vera. "I'm Hungry." *New Voices* 4, nos. 7 and 8 (1976): 51–52.
Das, Mahadai. *Bones.* Leeds: Peepal Tree Press, 1989.
———. *I Want to Be a Poetess of My People.* Georgetown: National History and Arts Council, 1976.
———. "My Finer Steel Will Grow." *Samisdat* 31, no. 2 (1982).
De Lima, Clara Rosa. *Dreams Non Stop.* Ilfracombe, Devon: Stockwell, 1974.
———. *Reminiscing.* Ilfracombe, Devon: Stockwell, 1973.
———. *Thoughts and Dreams.* Ilfracombe, Devon: Stockwell, 1972.
Evelyn, Phyllis. "Catmospheries." *Bim* 1, no. 2 (1943): 10–11.
Gill, Margaret. "Lovesong of a Canecutter." *Savacou*, nos. 7 and 8 (1973): 117–18.
Gomez, Ivy M. *Roses in the Rain.* Port of Spain, Trinidad: Privately published, 1975.
Gonzales, Maria. "Alma" and "Apparition." *New Voices* 3, no. 6 (1975): 22–23.
———. "Deep Down" and "Falling." *Corlit* 3, nos. 1 and 2 (1976): 19, 29.
———. "The Masquerade of Life." *New Voices* 3 (1974): 14.
———. "Sea Creatures." *New Voices* 3, no. 6 (1975): 33–34.
———. *Step by Step.* Diego Martin, Trinidad: New Voices, 1974.
Goodison, Lorna. *Heartease.* London: New Beacon, 1988.
———. *I Am Becoming My Mother.* London: New Beacon, 1986.
———. *Lorna Goodison* [excerpts from above works]. New York: Research Institute for the Study of Man, 1989.

————. *Tamarind Season.* Kingston, Jamaica: Institute of Jamaica, 1980.
Grenada Independence 1974: A Cultural Pot-Pourri. St. George's, Grenada, 1974.
Hamilton, Aileen. "Quinine." *Bim* 10, no. 39 (1964): 220.
Hamilton, Doreen. "And It Will Put Trinidad on the Map." *Voices* 1, no. 1 (1964): 10.
Harris, Claire. *Translation into Fiction.* New Brunswick, Canada: Gooselane Editions, 1984.
————. *Travelling to Find a Remedy.* New Brunswick, Canada: Gooselane Editions, 1986.
Hearn, Joy. *Collection of Poetry.* Port of Spain, Trinidad: Horsford Printerie, 1973.
————. *Poetic Trinidad: A Book of Poems.* Port of Spain, Trinidad: Horsford Printerie, 1973.
————. *Trinidad, the Gem of the Caribbean.* Port of Spain, Trinidad: Privately published, 1975.
Hinds, Patti. "The Coming Storm," "Identity," and "Progress." *New Voices* 3, no. 5 (1975): 14–15, 24–25, 29–30.
————. "Cry Out." *New Voices* 4, nos. 7 and 8 (1976): 88.
Hitching, Pamela. "Child." *Bim* 11, no. 43 (1966): 188–90.
————. "Poets." *Bim* 11, no. 42 (1966): 105.
Hosten, Pamela. "Forever April" and "Harlem." *Voices* 1, no. 2 (1964): 10.
Iniss, Esther. "A Cry from Back Clouds." *Bim* 14, no. 53 (1971): 25.
Iniss, Phyllis. "Archie and Bert" and "Gloggania." *Bim* 2, no. 6 (1945): 29, 56–57.
————. "Concerning Gragoons and Groots and Grubious Grobs." *Bim* 4, no. 13 (1950): 24.
————. "Gloppery" and "Hounddog." *Bim* 4, no. 16 (1952): 250, 288.
————. "Gumrum." *Bim* 3, no. 11 (1949): 256.
————. "Lamentation," *Bim* 7, no. 27 (1958): 182.
————. "Non-entity" and "Poem." *Bim* 2, no. 8 (1947): 14, 39.
————. "P.P.P." *Bim* 3, no. 10 (1949): 110.
————. "Pelicanalia" and "Ponki Poo." *Bim* 3, no. 9 (1948): 16, 48.
————. "Pseudo-Spurious and Specious Species." *Bim* 1, no. 4 (1944): 20.
————. "Sir William Wartsby." *Bim* 2, no. 5 (1945): 14.
————. "Spring Song." *Bim* 6, no. 21 (1954): 55.
————. "Two Poems of Doom." *Bim* 12, no. 45 (1967): 57.
————. "The Witchdoctor of Banjanbadram." *Bim* 2, no. 7 (1946): 22–24.
Jackman, Joan. "The Egrets Remind Me." *Corlit* 3 (1974): 25.
Jackman, Maria. "Confidentially," "The Return," and "To the Child within You." *New Voices* 3, no. 5 (1975): 10–11, 18.
————. "Slow Rush Hour." *New Voices*, no. 4 (1974): 26–27.
————. "To Open the Window." *New Voices*, no. 2 (1973): 10–12.
Jennings, Lucy. "Steel Drum." *New Voices*, no 3, (1974): 6.
Johnson, Carol. "To Kiss a Slave." *New Voices* 3, no. 5 (1975): 19–21.
Jones, Barbara Althea. *Among the Potatoes: A Collection of Modern Verse.* Ilfracombe, Devon: Arthur Stockwell. 1967.
————. "Escapist's Dream." *Voices* 2, no. 3 (1973): 7.
————. "West India." *New World Quarterly* 3, nos. 1 and 2 (1966–67): 68. For an untitled poem by the same author, see *Voices* 1, no. 6 (1966): 20.
La Fortune, Claudette. *Poems and Short Stories.* Port of Spain, Trinidad: Horsford Printerie, 1970.
Macdonald, Hilda. "Dawn" and "Evensong." *Kyk-Over-Al*, no. 22 (1957): 47.
Marson, Una. *Heights and Depths.* Kingston, Jamaica: Gleaner, 1931.
————. *The Moth and the Star.* Kingston, Jamaica: Gleaner, 1937.
McLean, Rachel. "Poem." *New Voices* 4, nos. 7 and 8 (1976): 50.
McTair, Dionyse. "Conference Jan. '71." *Caribbean Quarterly* 18, no. 4 (1972): 56.

Merrin, Annette. "The Child" and "Loneliness Is . . ." *Corlit* 3 (1974): 28.
———. "Faces." *New Voices* 3, no. 5 (1975): 26.
Miles, Judy. "Aerosel Falls in Love," "America on the Line," and "Why Six Isn't a Magical Figure." *Savacou*, nos. 9 and 10 (1974): 28, 82–84.
———. "At Two O'Clock" and "The Holocaust." *Voices* 1, no. 4 (1965): 2–3, 13. See also *Bim* 11, no. 42 (1966): 112.
———. "Blackout," "Empathy," and "Lunch Hour." *Bim* 12, no. 47 (1968): 187–89.
———. "Heavy Water" and "Litany." *Bim* 14, no. 54 (1972): 92–93.
———. "Joke," "Knot," and "Summer and Kitsilano Beach." *Voices* 2, no. 1 (1969): 12–13.
———. "Party." *Bim* 13, no. 50 (1970): 80.
———. "The Room." *Voices* 1, no. 6 (1966): 16; also in *Bim* 12, no. 45 (1967): 15–16.
———. "Season's Greetings, Love and Revolution." *Caribbean Quarterly* 18, no. 4 (1972): 53.
———. "Suicide?" *Bim* 11, no. 44 (1967): 267.
———. "Venetian Blinds." *Voices* 2, no. 3 (1973): 61.
Morris, Mervyn, ed. *Selected Poems of Louise Bennett*. Kingston, Jamaica: Sangsters, 1982.
Nichols, Grace. *The Fat Black Woman's Poems*. London: Virago, 1985.
———. *I Is a Long Memoried Woman*. London: Karnac House, 1983.
———. *Lazy Thoughts of a Lazy Woman*. London: Virago, 1989.
———. *Poetry Jump Up*. Harmondsworth: Penguin, 1989.
Nobbee-Eccles, Grace. *For Small Fry*. Port of Spain, Trinidad: Guardian Commercial Printery, 1957.
Pawan-Taylor, Daphne. "Songs of the Delta" and "Sun Shower." *New Voices* 3, no. 5 (1975): 9–10, 91.
Philip, Marlene Nourbese. *Harriet's Daughter*. London: Heinemann Education, 1988.
———. *Salmon Courage*. Toronto: Williams Wallace International, 1983.
———. "She Tries Her Tongue." Manuscript collection of poetry. 1989.
———. *Thorns*. Toronto: Williams Wallace International, 1980.
Pindar, Yvonne. *Some People Will Never Learn*. Port of Spain, Trinidad: Ministry of Education and Culture, 1973; privately published, 1974.
Poems and Stories of St. Christopher, Nevis and Anguilla. Basseterre, St. Kitts: Extramural Department, University College of the West Indies, 1960.
Radford, Wendy. "The Beautiful Years." *Bim* 14, no. 53 (1971): 19.
Ragoonanan, Veronica. "Underprivileged." *Corlit* 3 (1974): 33.
Rampaul, Fareeda. *Poems and Musings*. Trinidad: Privately published, 1974.
———. *Verses, Rhymes and Jingles for Infants*. Port of Spain, Trinidad: Ministry of Education and Culture, 1974.
Rostant, Lorain. "My Boy, Willie." *Voices* 1, no. 2 (1964).
———. "The Promise." *Voices* 1, no. 1 (1964): 141.
———. "A Sunday Morning." *Bim* 11, no. 41 (1965): 13.
———. "Unmasked Maladie." *Bim* 10, no. 40 (1965): 285–86.
———. "Ward, Mental Hospital." *Bim* 10, no. 39 (1964): 218.
———. "Where There is Memory." *Bim* 11, no. 43 (1966): 197.
Saint, Margaret. "Birdsong" and "Reptile." *Bim* 2, no. 7 (1946): 51, 53.
Scott, Rowena. "Across the Table." *Voices* 2, no. 1 (1969): 18.
Sealy, Anna. "Atomic Power." *Bim* 2, no. 7 (1946): 59.
Searl, Diana. "Fertility." *Voices* 2, no. 1 (1969): 10.
Seerattan, Joyce. "For Amy Jacques-Garvey." *New Voices*, no. 3 (1974): 8.
Senior, Olive. *Summer Lightning*. London: Longman, 1986.
———. *Talking of Trees*. Kingston, Jamaica: Calabash, 1985.

Shah, Zorina. "The Wind My Lover" and "Touch the Wind." *Corlit* 4 (1974): 27, 35.
Southwell, Alma. "Queries." *Bim*, no. 40 (1965): 266.
———. "A Sanctuary." *Bim* 10, no. 39 (1964): 222.
Springer, Einton Pearl. *Out of the Shadows.* London: Karia Press, 1988.
Springer, Rhonda. "Wishing on an Unborn Child." *Savacou*, nos. 9 and 10 (1974): 85.
Themes: Verse and Prose from U.W.I., St. Augustine. St. Augustine: University of the West Indies, 1970.
Themes III: Verse and Prose from U.W.I., St. Augustine. St. Augustine: University of the West Indies, 1972.
Themes IV: Verse and Prose from U.W.I., St. Augustine. St. Augustine: University of the West Indies, 1973.
Toppin, Christine. "Visions." *Bim* 11, no. 44 (1967): 288–89.
Tucker, Agnes. "Discovery." *Bim* 8, no. 31 (1960): 196–97.
———. "The Sparrow Tree." *Bim* 8, no. 30 (1960): 70–71.
Vuurboom, Toni. *The Field Are White.* Maracas, Trinidad: College Press, 1976.
Walrond, Linda. "Fisher of Man." *Bim* 15, no. 58 (1975): 142.
———. "The Magic Bow." *Bim* 12, no. 47 (1968): 202–3.
———. "Poem." *Bim* 12, no. 45 (1967): 51.
———. "A Woman's Agony." *Bim* 11, no. 44 (1967): 285.
Worrell, Patricia. "Death of a Labourer" and "Power." *New Voices* 3, no. 5 (1975): 27–28.
Writing. Port of Spain, Trinidad: Ministry of Education and Culture, 1967.
Wyke, Marguerite. "Calypsonian." *Voices* 1, no. 6 (1966): 8.
———. "Guyana." *Voices* 1, no. 1 (1964): 12.
———. "History Leaves No Memorials to the Poor." *Voices* 1, no. 2 (1964): 12.
———. "Last Lap." *Bim* 15, no. 57 (1974): 34.
———. "A Note on Becoming a Foreigner." *New World Quarterly*, nos. 1 and 2 (1966–67): 67.
———. "On Remembering Immortelles." *Bim* 7, no. 27 (1958): 126–27; also in *Caribbean Quarterly* 5, no. 3 (April 1958): 224–26, along with the poem "A Plume of Dust."

Prose Works by English-Speaking Women Writers of the West Indies

Adisa, Opal Palmer. *Bake-Face and Other Guava Stories.* Berkeley: Kelsey Street Press, 1986.
———. *Pina, the Many-Eyed Fruit.* San Francisco: Julian Richardson Associates, 1985. [children's literature]
Audrey Alleyne. "Light Over Darkness: An Easter Story." San Fernando, Trinidad. 1970.
Allfrey, Phyllis Shand. *The Orchid House.* London: Constable, 1953; London: Virago, 1982.
Archibald, Kathleen. "The Answer." *Trinidad* 1, no. 2 (1930): 75–78.
———. "Beyond the Horizon."' *Beacon* 1, no. 3 (June 1931): 29–31.
Ashtine, Eaulin. *Crick Crack: Trinidad and Tobago Folk Tales Retold.* St. Augustine, Trinidad: Extramural Department of the University of the West Indies, 1966.
———. *Monkey Liver Soup and Other Tales from Trinidad.* London: T. Nelson, 1973.
———. *Nine Folk Tales, Retold by Eaulin Ashtine.* Port of Spain, Trinidad: Ministry of Education and Culture, Publications Unit, 1968.
Barteaux, Marion. *Grandmother's Stories from the Sugar-Cane Island of Barbados.* 2d ed. Bridgetown, Barbados: Cole's Printery, 1964.

————. *More Grandmother's Stories from the Sugar-Cane Island of Barbados*. Bridgetown, Barbados: Cole's Printery, 1965.

Belgrave, Valerie. *Tia Marie*. London: Heinemann International, 1988.

Bennett, Louise. *Anancy and Miss Lou*. Kingston, Jamaica: Sangsters, 1979.

————. *Jamaica Labrish*. Kingston, Jamaica: Sangsters, 1966.

————. *Laugh with Louise*. Kingston, Jamaica: City Printery, 1961.

Brand, Dionne. and Krisantha Sri Bhaggiyadatta. *Rivers Have Sources, Trees Have Roots*. Toronto: Cross-Cultural Communication Centre, 1986.

Brodber, Erna. *Jane and Louisa Will Soon Come Home*. London: New Beacon Books, 1980.

————. *Myal*. London: New Beacon Books, 1988.

Brown, Beverly. *Dream Diary*. Kingston, Jamaica: Savacou Co-operative, 1982.

Bryan, Beverly, Stella Dadzie, and Suzanne Scafe. *The Heart of the Race*. London: Virago, 1985.

Burford, Barbara. *The Threshing Floor*. London: Sheba Feminist Publishers, 1986; Ithaca, N.Y.: Firebrand Books, 1987.

Chee, Valerie Lee. "Birds of a Feather." *Corlit* 3, (July 1974): 11–13.

Cliff, Michelle. *Abeng*. Trumansburg, N.Y.: Crossing Press, 1984.

————. *Claiming an Identity They Taught Me to Despise*. Watertown, Mass.: Persephone Press, 1980.

————. *The Land of Look Behind*. Ithaca, N.Y.: Firebrand Books, 1985.

————. *No Telephone to Heaven*. New York: Dutton, 1987.

Cobham, Rhonda, and Merle Collins, eds. *Watchers and Seekers: Creative Writing by Black Women in Britain*. London: Women's Press, 1987.

Collins, Merle. *Angel*. London: Women's Press, 1987.

Comma-Maynard, Olga. *Carib Echoes: A Collection of Short Stories and Poems*. Port of Spain, Trinidad: Uyille's Printerie, 1944.

————. *Carib Echoes: Poems and Stories for Juniors*. 9th ed. Port of Spain, Trinidad: Columbus Publishers, 1972.

D'Costa, Jean. *Brother Man*. Kingston, Jamaica: Longman's West Indian Authors, 1978.

————. *Escape to Last Man Peak*. Kingston, Jamaica: Longman Caribbean (Blue Mountain Series), 1975.

————. *The Hills Were Joyful Together*. Kingston, Jamaica: Longman's West Indian Authors, 1978.

————. *Over Our Way*. London: Longman, 1980.

————. *Voices in the Window*. London: Longman, 1980.

————. *Sprat Morrison*. Kingston, Jamaica: Collins, Sangster, 1979.

De Lima, Clara Rosa. *Countdown to Carnival*. Devon: Arthur Stockwell, 1978.

————. *Currents of the Yuna*. Devon: Arthur Stockwell, 1978.

————. *Kilometre Nineteen*. Devon: Arthur Stockwell, 1980.

————. *Not Bad, Just a Little Mad*. Devon: Arthur Stockwell, 1975.

————. *Tomorrow Will Always Come*. New York: Ivan Obolensky, 1965.

Dominican Short Stories. Roseau, Dominica: Arts Council of Dominica Writers' Workshop, 1974.

Duffy, Maureen. *The Passionate Shepherdess: Aphra Behn, 1640–89*. London: Jonathan Cape, 1977.

Edgell, Zee. *Beka Lamb*. London: Heinemann, 1982.

Fergus, Howard A., ed. *Dreams of Alliouagana: An Anthology of Montserrat Prose and Poetry*. Montserrat: University Centre, 1974.

Ferguson, Moira, ed. *The History of Mary Prince, a West Indian Slave, Related by Herself*. London: Pandora, 1987.

Fonrose, Veronica. *The Evil Spirit*. Port of Spain, Trinidad: University of the West Indies, Extramural Department, 1966. [drama]

Fraser, Ruth. "The Mango Tree." *Corlit* 3 (July 1974): 22–24.

Gilroy, Beryl. *Black Teacher.* London: Cassell Compass Books, 1976.

———. *Boy-Sandwich.* London: Heinemann International, 1989.

———. *Frangipani House.* London: Heinemann International, 1985.

———. *In for a Penny.* London: Cassell Compass Books, 1980; Holt Saunders, 1982.

Gittens, Joyce. "Funeral Interlude," *Bim* 2, no. 7 (1946): 14–15.

———."I Remember Pampalam." *Bim* 2, no. 8 (1947): 20–24.

Giuseppi, Undine, ed. *Writing Is Fun.* San Fernando: Undine Giuseppi, 1972.

Giuseppi, Neville, and Undine Giuseppi, eds. *Backfire*, pp. 52–57. London: Macmillan, 1973.

Gonzales, Maria. "Eternal Scrunters." *New Voices* 4, nos. 7 and 8 (1976): 97–98.

Greig, Dorothy. "The Orspital." *Beacon* 2, no. 3 (July 1932): 17–18.

Grenada Independence 1974: Cultural Potpourri. St. George's, Grenada, 1974.

Guy, Rosa. *Bird at My Window.* London: Souvenir Press, 1966; Philadelphia: Lippincott, 1970.

———. *The Friends.* London: Gollancz; New York: Holt, Rinehart and Winston, 1973.

———. *Edith Jackson.* New York: Viking, 1978.

———. *A Measure of Time.* New York: Holt, Rinehart and Winston, 1983.

———. *My Love, My Love or the Peasant Girl.* New York: Holt, Rinehart and Winston, 1985.

———. *Ruby.* New York: Viking, 1976.

Hamilton, Aileen. "The Trees." *Bim* 6, no. 21 (1934): 2–3.

Hannays, Kitty. *Notebook by Macaw.* Port of Spain, Trinidad: Trinidad Publishing Co., 1962.

Harney, Leonore. "Brandy Ahoy." *Bim* 10, no. 37 (1963): 56–59.

———. "Operation Blue Shell." *Bim* 10, no. 10 (1965): 235–39.

Hodge, Merle. *Crick Crack, Monkey.* London: A. Deutsch, 1970; London: Heinemann, 1981.

———. "How Many Caribbeans?" In Lowell Fiet, ed., *West Indian Literature and Its Political Context*, pp. 15–19. Río Piedras, Puerto Rico: University of Puerto Rico, 1988.

Honeychurch, Beth. "Barter." *Bim* 2, no. 8 (1947): 52–53.

Jack, Yvonne. "Cheers." Tunapuna, Trinidad: Tapia Printing Co., 1972.

Johnson, Amryl. *Long Road to Nowhere.* London: Virago, 1985.

———. *Sequins for a Ragged Hem.* London: Virago, 1988.

Jolly, Dorothy. "A Carnival Sacrifice." *Corlit* 3 (July 1974): 39–43.

———. "The Cocktail Party." *Corlit* 3, nos. 1 and 2 (January–April 1976): 30–33.

———. "A Surprise for Mother." *Corlit* 4 (December 1974): 42–43.

Jones, Marion Patrick. *J'Ouvert Morning.* Port of Spain, Trinidad: Columbus Publishers, 1976.

———. *Pan Beat.* Port of Spain, Trinidad: Columbus Publishers, 1973.

Joseph, Annmarie. "The Country Property." *New Voices* 3, no. 5 (1975): 32–34.

———. "The Excursion People." *Corlit* 2, nos. 1 and 2 (April–July 1975): 15–18.

Joseph, Barbara. "House Full, Kitchen Full." *Corlit* 4 (December 1974): 15–19.

Killikelly, Kathleen. *The Power of the Dog. Book One. The Fig Tree.* Barbados: Privately published, 1974.

Kincaid, Jamaica. *Annie John.* New York: Farrar, Straus, Giroux, 1985; New York: Plume Book/New American Library, 1986.

———. *At the Bottom of the River.* New York: Farrar, Straus, Giroux, 1984; New York: Aventura/Vintage Books, 1985.

———. *A Small Place.* New York: Farrar, Straus, Giroux, 1988.

Kirton, Enid. "The Locho." *New Voices* 3 (1974): 23–30, 50.

———. "Pen Portraits." Trinidad: Privately published,1975.

———. "Sense Make Before Book." *New Voices* 3, no. 5 (1975): 29–31.

———. *Voices of the Earth.* Relevance series no. 1. Gasparillo: Rilloprint, 1972.

Layne, Jeannette. "A Fistful of Rainbows." *Bim* 12, no. 48 (1969): 249–53.

———. "No Place Like Home." *Bim* 14, no. 54 (January–June 1972): 65–68.

———. "Telephone Conversation." *Bim* 12, no. 47 (1968): 151–55.

Love and the Hardware Store and Other Stories. Port of Spain, Trinidad: Imprint, 1977.

Lovell, Dorothy. "Father Beer." *Bim* 13, no. 49 (1969): 25–30.

———. "Grannie's Birthday." *Bim* 12, no. 47 (1968): 167–74.

———. "The Shoe." *Bim* 12, no. 48 (1969): 239–43.

Marshall, Paule. "Barbados." In Langston Hughes, ed., *The Best Short Stories by Negro Writers: An Anthology from 1899 to the Present.* Boston: Little, Brown, 1967.

———. *Brown Girl, Brownstones.* New York: Avon Books, 1970; Old Westbury, N.Y.: Feminist Press, 1983.

———. *The Chosen Place, the Timeless People.* New York: Harcourt, Brace & World, 1969; New York: Vintage, 1984.

———. *Reena and Other Stories.* Old Westbury, N.Y.: Feminist Press, 1981.

———. *Praisesong for the Widow.* New York: G. P. Putnam & Sons; London: Virago, 1983.

———. *Soul Clap Hands and Sing.* New York: Atheneum, 1961; London: W. H. Allen, 1962; Old Westbury, N.Y.: Feminist Press, 1981.

———. "To Da-duh in Memoriam." *New World Quarterly* 3, nos. 1 and 2 (1966–67): 97–101.

Maxwell, Marina Omowak. *Play Mas and Hounsi Kanzo.* Trinidad, 1976. [drama]

McTair, Dionyse. "Soul." *Savacou,* nos. 3 and 4 (December 1970 and March 1971): 89.

Mills, Therese. *The Boy Who Ran Away and Other Stories.* Maracas, Trinidad: Trinidad College Press, 1976.

———. *Christmas Stories.* Port of Spain, Trinidad: College Press, 1973.

———. *The Shell Book of Trinidad Stories,* pp. 99–105. Port of Spain, Trinidad: Privately published, 1973.

Napier, Elma. "Carnival in Martinique." *Bim* 4, no. 15 (1951): 155–57.

———. "No Voyage for a Little Barque." *Bim* 4, no. 14 (1951): 85–87.

Nichols, Grace. *Leslyn in London.* Hodder, 1984. [children's literature]

———. *Trust You Wriggly.* Hodder, 1980. [children's literature]

———. *Whole of a Morning Sky.* London: Virago, 1986.

Payne, Millicent. "The Chink in His Armor." *Bim* 11, no. 41 (1965): 17–23.

———. "A Christmas of Long Ago." *Bim* 11, no. 44 (1967): 253–59.

———. "A Flashback." *Bim* 12, no. 45 (1967): 29–36.

Poems and Stories of St. Christopher, Nevis and Anguilla, pp. 2–4. Basseterre, St. Kitts: Extramural Department, University College of the West Indies, 1960.

Prescod, Marsha. *The Land of Rope and Tory.* London: Akira Press, 1985.

Prescod, Pearl. "The Midnight Order: Tales from Tobago." *Chronicle of the West Indian Committee* 70, no. 1414 (November 1965): 597–98.

———. "Tales from Tobago." *Chronicle of the West Indian Committee* 81, no. 1418 (March 1966): 131–32.

Redhead, Eula. "Czien and the Turtle." *Bim* 5, no. 17 (1952): 53–55.

Rhys, Jean. *After Leaving Mr. Mackenzie.* London: Jonathan Cape. 1931; London: A. Deutsch, 1969; New York: Harper & Row, 1972; New York: Vintage Books, 1974.

———. *Good Morning, Midnight.* London: Constable, 1939; London: A. Deutsch, 1967; Harmondsworth: Penguin, 1969; New York: Harper & Row, 1970.

———. *The Left Bank and Other Stories.* London: Jonathan Cape, 1927; New York: Books for Libraries, 1970.

———. *Quartet*, London: A. Deutsch, 1969; New York: Harper & Row, 1971; New York: Vintage Books, 1974.

———. *Sleep It Off Lady*. London: A. Deutsch, 1976; New York: Harper, 1976.

———. *Smile Please*. New York: Harper & Row, 1979.

———. *Tigers Are Better Looking, with a Selection from the Left Bank Stories*. London: A. Deutsch, 1968; New York: Popular Library, 1976.

———. *Voyage in the Dark*. London: Constable, 1934; Harmondsworth: Penguin, 1969; New York: Popular Library, 1975; New York: Norton, 1982.

Riley, Joan. *The Unbelonging*. London: Women's Press, 1985.

———. *Waiting in the Twilight*. London: Women's Press, 1987.

Rostant, Lorain. "Those I Do Not Know." *Bim* 11, no. 41 (1965): 54–55.

Saint, Margaret. "The Artist Finds Love." *Bim* 1, no. 2 (1943): 45–46.

Seacole, Mary. *The Wonderful Adventures of Mrs. Seacole in Many Lands*. London: Oxford University Press, 1988.

Seaforth, Sybil. *Growing Up with Miss Milly*. Ithaca, N.Y.: Calaloux Publications, 1988.

Senior, Olive. *Summer Lightning*. London: Longman, 1986.

Shinebourne, Janice. *The Last English Plantation*. Leeds, Yorkshire: Peepal Tree Press, 1988.

———. *Timepiece*. Leeds, Yorkshire: Peepal Tree Press, 1986.

Skeete, Monica. "The Black Elephant." *Bim* 14, no. 53 (1971): 31–37.

———. "The Emigrant." *Bim* 12, no. 47 (1968): 196–201.

———. "Joe." *Bim* 9, no. 34 (1962): 107–10.

———. "The Return." *Bim* 8, no. 31 (1960): 142–45.

———. "The Road." *Bim* 13, no. 49 (1969); 2–8.

———. "The Scholarship." *Bim* 8, no. 32 (1961): 229–33.

———. "Spanish Figurine." *Bim* 12, no. 46 (1968): 70–74.

Squires, Flora. "Aunt Suzie's Rooster." *Bim* 12, no. 45 (1967): 11–14.

Sulter, Maud. *As a Black Woman*. London: Akira Press, 1985.

———. "Everywoman's Right, Nobody's Victory." In Pearlie McNeill et al., eds., *Through the Break*. London: Sheba Feminist Publishers, 1987.

———. "Wild Women Don't Get the Blues: Alice Walker in Conversation with Maud Sulter." In Shabnan Grewal et al., eds., *Charting the Journey: Writings by Black and Third World Women*. London: Sheba Feminist Publishers, 1987.

Themes: Verse and Prose from U.W.I. St. Augustine. St. Augustine: University of the West Indies, 1970.

Themes III: Verse and Prose from U.W.I., St. Augustine. St. Augustine: University of the West Indies, 1972.

Themes IV: Verse and Prose from U.W.I., St. Augustine. St. Augustine, University of the West Indies, 1973.

Walcott, Elizabeth. "Pig-money." *Bim* 3, no. 9 (1948): 45–47.

Walcott, Ursula. "The Theatre Tickets." *Bim* 1, no. 3 (1943): 37–40, 97–99.

White, Golde. "How the Poor Live." *Bim* 2, no. 7 (1966): 28–30.

———. "Hypnotics." *Bim* 3, no. 10 (1949): 101–3.

Wilson, Cynthia. "Enter Mable." *Bim* 14, no. 56 (1973): 205–7.

———. "Gran Nan." *Bim* 14, no. 55 (1972): 142–45.

Wynter, Sylvia. *The Hills of Hebron*. New York: Simon & Schuster, 1962; London: Longman, 1984.

———. *Jamaica Is the High of Bolivia*. New York: Vantage Press, 1979.

Yawching, Donna. "The Beggar." *Bim* 14, no. 53 (1971): 31–37.

Conference participants at the First International Conference on the Women Writers of the English-speaking Caribbean, April 1988.

Contributors

Opal Palmer Adisa, born in Jamaica, is a doctoral candidate at the University of California at Berkeley. A storyteller and community organizer, Adisa, the recipient of the 1987 Pushcart Prize for her story "Duppy Get Her," is the author of *Bake-Face and Other Guava Stories* (1986) and *Traveling Women* (1989). Her poems have been widely anthologized in both the United States and Jamaica.

Phyllis Allfrey, born in Dominica, was one of the most distinguished writers of the Caribbena. She is the author of *Orchid House* (1983) and other works.

Valerie Belgrave, born in Trinidad, received her B.A. from Sir George Williams University (Concordia). Belgrave, who uses batik as an art form, working only in the traditional method of wax resist and submerge dying, is the author of *Tia Marie* (1988). Belgrave has exhibited in Trinidad and Canada.

Erna Brodber, born in Jamaica, attended the University College of the West Indies, where she received a B.A. and is the university's first M.Sc. graduate. Brodber was awarded a doctoral fellowship for medical school at the University of Washington to practice psychiatric anthropology. She has taught at the University of the West Indies and the Institute for Social and Economic Research. In 1984 she left the university to establish Blackspace, a company devoted to facilitating research on the Africans of the diaspora. She is the author of *Jane and Louisa Will Soon Come Home* (1980), *Myal* (1988), and numerous monographs.

Afua Cooper, born in Jamaica, received her B.A. from the University of Toronto, where she is currently a graduate student. A professional writer, Cooper conducts many writing workshops in Toronto. She is the author of *Breaking Chains* (1984), and her work has been recorded in *Woman Talk* (1985) and *Poetry Is Not a Luxury* (1987).

LEAH CREQUE-HARRIS, born in the United States, is one of the first women to receive a B.A. in Black Studies at Wellesley College. She also received an M.B.A. from Atlanta University and is presently a doctoral candidate at Emory University. She is director of Government and Foundation Resources at Spelman College. Creque-Harris's work has appeared in *SAGE: A Scholarly Journal on Black Women, American Visions, Tiger Lilly*, and *Minorities and Women in Business*.

SELWYN R. CUDJOE, born in Trinidad, is an associate professor of black studies at Wellesley College. The author of *V. S. Naipaul: A Materialist Reading* (1988), *Movement of the People* (1983), and *Resistance and Caribbean Literature* (1980), Cudjoe has also written for the *New York Times, Boston Globe, Harvard Educational Review, Caribbean Quarterly*, and many other publications.

DARYL CUMBER DANCE, born in the United States, is professor of English at Virginia Commonwealth University and the author of *Shuckin' and Jivin': Folklore from Contempory Black Americans* (1978), *Folklore from Contemporary Jamaicans* (1985), and *Long Gone: The Mecklenburg Six and the Theme of Escape in Black Folklore* (1987). Dance edited *Fifty Caribbean Writers: A Bio-Bilbliographical and Critical Sourcebook* (1986).

JEAN D'COSTA, born in Jamaica, received her undergraduate degree from the University College of the West Indies and her M.Litt. from Oxford University. A professor of English at Hamilton College, New York, D'Costa has served as a consultant for the Jamaica Ministry of Education and the Joint Board of Teacher Education. She is the author of *Sprat Morrison* (1972), *Escape to the Last Man Peak* (1976), *Voice in the Wind* (1978), and *Roger Mais: The Hills Were Joyful Together and Brother Man* (1979).

LAURA NIESEN DE ABRUNA, born in the United States, is an associate professor of English at Ithaca College. She is the author of *The Refining Fire: Herakles and Other Heroes in T. S. Eliot's Work*, and her articles have appeared in *Modern Fiction Studies, World Literature Written in English*, and other publications.

CLARA ROSA DE LIMA, born in Trinidad, is the owner of an art gallery and the chairperson of the working committee of the Music Foundation of the Trinidad and Tobago Youth Orchestra. The author of nine books, short stories, and innumerable articles, de Lima does biweekly commentaries for Radio Trinidad and has traveled widely.

BERYL GILROY, born in Guyana, was trained as a teacher at the Government Training College in Guyana, where she worked on a UNICEF food program after World War II. Gilroy received a B.A. from the University

College in London, an M.A. from Sussex University, and a Ph.D. from Century University. She runs a private clinic as a counseling psychologist working mostly with black women in England and writes about current problems and the black condition in England. Gilroy is the author of *Black Teacher* (1976), *Frangipanni House* (1986), and *Boy-Sandwich* (1989). Her short stories are read on the BBC occasionally.

LORNA GOODISON, born in Jamaica, attended the University of Iowa and was a Bunting Fellow at Radcliffe College. Recipient of the Bronze Musgrave Medal and the Centenary Medal from the Institute of Jamaica for poetry, Goodison is the author of *Tamarind Season* (1980), *I Am Becoming My Mother* (1986), and *Heartease* (1988). Her poems have been translated into French, Hebrew, German, and Spanish.

VERONICA MARIE GREGG, born in Jamaica, is an assistant professor of English at Spelman College, the winner of a United Kingdom Scholarship (1984–87), and has taught at the University of the West Indies and Queen's University and Richmond College in London.

ROSA GUY, born in Trinidad and raised in New York City, is the prize-winning author of ten novels, including *Bird at My Window* (1965), *The Friends* (1973), *A Measure of Time* (1983), and *My Love, My Love* (1985). Guy is co-founder of the Harlem Writers Guild.

CLAIRE HARRIS, born in Trinidad, received a B.A. from the National University of Ireland (Dublin) and diplomas of Education and Mass Media and Communications from the University of the West Indies (Jamaica) and the University of Nigeria (Lagos) respectively. Harris is the author of *Fables from the Women's Quarters*, winner of a Commonwealth award for *Traveling to Find a Remedy* (1986), and winner of the first Alberta Culture Poetry Award.

MERLE HODGE, born in Trinidad, worked and studied in France and Denmark and traveled extensively in Europe, West Africa, and the Caribbean. Hodge worked in Grenada from 1979 to 1983 and is actively involved in the Women's Movement in the Caribbean and a member of the Women and Development Studies Group at the University of the West Indies (St. Augustine), where she teaches part time. Hodge is the author of *Crick Crack Monkey* (1970) and various articles.

GLASCETA HONEYGHAN, born in Jamaica, is an assistant professor of English at Boston Business School. A graduate of Mico Teachers' College in Jamaica, Honeyghan received her B.A. from Boston State College and an M.A. from University of Massachusetts (Boston). She has completed two manuscripts, "Father Sleeps with Mudpies" and "I'll Take a Fallen Star."

MARION PATRICK JONES (O'CALLAGHAN), born in Trinidad, attended the Imperial College of Tropical Agriculture (now the St. Augustine campus of the University of the West Indies) and did graduate work in social anthropology at London School of Economics. While in London, Jones became active in race relations and helped to found CARD (Campaign Against Racial Discrimination) (UK). The author of *Pan Beat* (1973), *J'Ouvert Morning* (1976), and the forthcoming *Parang*, Jones (as O'Callaghan) has also written the introduction and notes to *Sociological Theories, Race and Colonialism* and *Southern Rhodesia: The Effects of a Conquest Society in Education, Science and Culture.*

LUCILLE MATHURIN MAIR, born in Jamaica, received her B.A. from the University of London and her Ph.D. from the University of the West Indies (Jamaica). She serves as regional coordinator of Women Development Studies at the University of the West Indies (Jamaica) and has been the United Nations assistant secretary-general, special adviser to UNICEF on women's development (1981–82), and secretary general of the World Conference of the United Nations Decade for Women (1979–81). She is the author of *The Rebel Woman in the British West Indies during Slavery* (1975), *International Women's Decade: A Balance Sheet* (1985), and *Women and Men: A New Alliance* (1985).

GRACE NICHOLS, born in Guyana, earned a Diploma in Communications from the University of Guyana. Her first collection of poems, *i is a long memoried woman*, won the 1983 Commonwealth Prize. Nichols is also the author of *The Fat Black Woman Poems* (1984), two children's books, *Trust You Wriggley and Baby Fish and Other Stories* and *Whole of a Morning Sky* (1986).

ARTHUR PARIS, a native New Yorker, graduated from City College of New York and received his Ph.D. from Northwestern University. An associate professor in sociology at Rutgers University, Camden, Professor Paris has taught at Cornell, the University of Pennsylvania, and the Free University in Berlin. He is the author of *Black Pentecostalism: Southern Religion in the Urban North* (1981), and has published in the *Journal of Ethnic Studies, Socialist Review,* and *Review of Black Political Economy.*

DONNA PERRY, born in the United States, is associate professor of English at William Paterson College and teaches literature and women's studies courses. Her essays have been included in several collections. The recipient of the New Jersey Governor's Fellowship in the Humanities, Perry spent the 1989–90 academic year researching and writing on the interconnections between race, class, and gender in selected novels by contemporary women writers.

INEKE PHAF, born in the Netherlands, has been educated at the University of Leiden, the Free University in Berlin, and the Gemeine-University of Amsterdam and received her Ph.D. from the Free University in Berlin. As associate professor at the Free University in Berlin, Professor Phaf is the author of many books and articles published in Dutch, French, and Spanish. She is the coeditor (with Gina Lavrpa) of *Literature and Women from Four Continents* (1987).

MARLENE NOURBESE PHILIP, born in Tobago, is a poet, writer, and lawyer who lives in Toronto. She has published two books of poetry, *Thorns* (1980) and *Salmon Courage* (1983), and has received Canada Council awards on two occasions. She is the author of *Harriet's Daughter* (1988), and her manuscript collection of poetry, *She Tries Her Tongue* (1989) was awarded the 1988 Casa de Las Americas prize. Philip's essays, reviews, and articles have appeared in magazines and journals in Canada and the United States, and her poetry and prose have been anthologized extensively.

HELEN PYNE TIMOTHY, born in Jamaica, is the dean of Arts and General Studies, University of the West Indies (Trinidad). Her articles have appeared in *World Literature Written in English* and many other publications.

RHODA E. REDDOCK, born in Trinidad, received her B.A. at the University of the West Indies (Trinidad) and her Ph.D. at the University of Amsterdam. A research fellow at the Institute of Social and Economic Research, University of the West Indies (Trinidad), Reddock is the editor (with Maria Miew) of *Women's Liberation and National Liberation*. She is the author of *Elma Francois* (1988).

IAN ROBERTSON, born in Guyana, is chairman of the Educational Foundations and Teacher Education Department, Faculty of Education, University of the West Indies (Trinidad). He also served as chairman of the English Department at the University of Guyana.

MARIA CRISTINA RODRIGUEZ, born in Puerto Rico, received her B.A. and M.A. degrees from the University of Puerto Rico and her Ph.D. from the City University of New York. An assistant professor of English at the University of Puerto Rico, Rodriguez is the film coordinator for the Cultural Activities Program there and since 1981, a film critic for *Claridad*, a weekly newspaper.

SYBIL SEAFORTH, born in Jamaica, attended Wolmers High School for Girls (Jamaica) and the University College of Swansea, South Wales, where she received a diploma in youth work in 1959. She worked with a Kingston family organization as a caseworker and the Jamaica Youth Clubs Council as a youth club organizer. Seaforth, who is on the staff of the Faculty of Education at the University of the West Indies (Trinidad), has been published in the *School Paper of Trinidad and Tobago, Trinidad Express*, and *Trinidad Guardian*. *Growing Up with Miss Milly* (1988) is her first full-length novel.

OLIVE SENIOR, a former editor of *Jamaica Journal*, is the author of *Summer Lightning and Other Stories* (1986) and *Talking of Trees* (1985). Her work has appeared in *Callaloo* and other publications.

MARIE-DENISE SHELTON, born in Haiti, received her B.A., M.A., and Ph.D. from the University of California, Los Angeles. She is an associate professor of French at the Claremont McKenna College. Professor Shelton's articles have appeared in *French Review, Presence Africaine, Presence Francophone,* and *Contemporary French Civilization.*

JANICE SHINEBOURNE, was born in Guyana and immigrated to Britain in 1974. A full-time community activist in Southall (an area of London with a mixed Afro-Asian population), Shinebourne is the coeditor of the *Southall Review* and author of *Timepiece* (1986) and *The Last English Plantation* (1988).

ENA THOMAS, born in Trinidad, is a lecturer in Spanish Literature at the University of the West Indies (Trinidad). She received her B.A. and M.A. from the University of Toronto and her Ph.D. from Cornell University. Professor Thomas, whose research interest lies in Spanish Caribbean literature, has published several conference papers in this area of study.